Myths and Facts about Football

GW00385209

Myths and Facts about Football: The Economics and Psychology of the World's Greatest Sport

Edited by

Patric Andersson, Peter Ayton and Carsten Schmidt

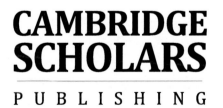

Myths and Facts about Football: The Economics and Psychology of the World's Greatest Sport,
Edited by Patric Andersson, Peter Ayton and Carsten Schmidt

This book first published 2008.

Cambridge Scholars Publishing

12 Back Chapman Street, Newcastle upon Tyne, NE6 2XX, UK

British Library Cataloguing in Publication Data
A catalogue record for this book is available from the British Library

Copyright © 2008 by Patric Andersson, Peter Ayton and Carsten Schmidt and contributors

All rights for this book reserved. No part of this book may be reproduced, stored in a retrieval system,
or transmitted, in any form or by any means, electronic, mechanical, photocopying, recording or
otherwise, without the prior permission of the copyright owner.

ISBN (10): 1-4438-0114-3, ISBN (13): 978-1-4438-0114-0

TABLE OF CONTENTS

Team Behaviour and Performance

Referee Behaviour

Part II: Off-Pitch Phenomena

Fan Behaviour and Demand for Football

Expert and Market Predictions of Match Outcome

Labour Market and Conditions for Footballers

Stock-Market Reactions to Events of Listed Football Clubs

PREFACE

DANIEL FINKELSTEIN[1]

I constantly find myself called a spoilsport. Why? Because I insist on subjecting football clichés to rigorous analysis. I can't just sit there and listen to someone saying that the worst time to concede a goal is just before half time without wondering—is it true? I can't see home advantage change the course of a tournament without wondering—how does it work? I can't see a team sack its manager without wondering—did he really deserve it? And I robustly reject the idea that such analysis spoils the romance of football. I am not rejecting the banter, the punditry, the weird stats. I just want them to be true. Who can argue with that?

I have to admit that I was a football fan for about 35 years before it occurred to me that data told you the story of soccer. Actually, it didn't so much occur to me as to my friend and collaborator Dr Henry Stott, who was at Warwick University when I first met him. Henry was part of a new wave of academics, a number of them represented in this volume, who had begun to model football hand use sophisticated statistical methods to reveal football's secrets.

Quite early on in my conversion to a football data fanatic, I came across the work of Peter Ayton and admired his insights. So when he told me that this volume was appearing I was excited, and remain so. I think you should be too.

I think the sort of material he together with Patric Andersson and Carsten Schmidt have gathered in this book represents the future of sports writing. People are always a bit surprised to find me deadly serious about that, but if I wasn't I wouldn't bother with football stats at all.

I believe data can tell you far more than commentators, experts, former players or casual pundits. I believe that objective measurement is not just a way to rank and value players, but the only way. I believe a statement

---

[1] Daniel Finkelstein OBE is the author of the "Fink Tank"—a regular column appearing in 'The Times' and the only regular sports feature devoted to using scientific methods for predicting and understanding football.

made about football that can't be quantified and tested using data is a non statement.

Over the next ten years, managers are going to twig to this. When there are millions of pounds at stake they aren't going to go on valuing players by reading Shoot magazine and watching a video, are they? So we, the data fiends, we're going to take over the world my friends. Starting here. Starting with this book.

ACKNOWLEDGEMENTS

Football is a simple game; 22 men chase a ball for 90 minutes and at the end, the Germans win.

Those famous words were uttered by the English former footballer Gary Lineker after England had lost the semi-final in the World Cup 1990 against West Germany on penalties. There is, however, much more to say about the game of football, at least from the scientific point of view. As shown by the present book, this sport is imbued with various phenomena that should not only be interesting for researchers in economics, psychology, and other behavioral sciences, but may also stimulate people sharing a professional or recreational interest in football. A variety of those phenomena is thoroughly described and analysed in this volume, which could not have been completed without the support and engagement of many people to whom we are grateful.

First and foremost, we are indebted to all authors who have contributed chapters to the book. They have put down a great deal of efforts to produce papers that empirically investigate fascinating topics. Many authors have also actively taken part in the peer-review process and, thus, helped to improve the quality of this book.

Second, we wish to thank all individuals who have patiently acted as reviewers and, accordingly, given invaluable comments to different versions of the chapters. In alphabetical order, they are: Leif Brandes, Thomas Brenner, Rene Cyranek, Marco Caliendo, Mattias Ekman, Kimmo Eriksson, David Hardman, Peter Högfeldt, Magnus Johannesson, Alexander Klos, Stefan Luckner, Daniel Memmert, Håkan Nilsson, Johan Pütz and Tim Rakow.

Third, we appreciate the professional and helpful assistance from Amanda Millar, Vlatka Kolic and Carol Koulikourdi at Cambridge Scholars Publishing. We thank the student assistants Dominik Matzat, Rudolf Meinholz and Tobias Vogelmann for their support and patience during the tedious formatting procedure.

Fourth, we wish to express our sincere gratitude to the Sonderforschungsbereich 504 of the University of Mannheim and the European Association for Decision Making for financial support that enabled us to organise the University of Mannheim workshop on "Economics and Psychology of Football", which was held in June 2006 (see www.sfb504.uni-mannheim.de/EconPsyFootball06). Most chapters of the present book originated from papers presented at that workshop. In connection, Patric Andersson wants to gratefully acknowledge research grants provided by Handelbankens Forskningsstiftelser. And Carsten Schmidt thanks Deutsche Bahn for upgrading their ICE trains servicing Mannheim - Berlin with power plugs.

Fifth, we would like to thank Raphael Abiry for contributing the cover artwork. The picture displays Johan Neeskens famous penalty, awarded during the 1st minute of the 1974 World Cup final, where he shot straight towards the middle of the goal—with goalkeeper Sepp Maier moving to his right.

Finally, we would like to extend a special thanks to our families and friends for encouragement while this book project was being completed.

Patric Andersson, Center for Media and Economic Psychology, Stockholm School of Economics, Sweden.

Peter Ayton, Department of Psychology, City University, London, United Kingdom.

Carsten Schmidt, Sonderforschungsbereich 504, Mannheim University, Germany.

Chapter One

Introduction and Overview

Patric Andersson, Peter Ayton and Carsten Schmidt

The television show Monty Python Live at the Hollywood Bowl from 1982 features a comic sketch called International Philosophy—Return Match, where a team of famous German philosophers (such as Leibniz, Kant, Hegel, Schopenhauer, Nietzsche and Heidegger) plays against a team of equally famous Greek philosophers (such as Plato, Aristotle, Heraclitus, Sophocles, Socrates and Archimedes) in a football match in a crowded Olympic stadium in Munich. Seemingly, like many occasions in real life, the television commentator views the Germans as the favourites. Once the referee (characterised by Confucius) blows the whistle for kick-off, the philosophers turn away from the ball, hands on chins in deep contemplation and commence ambling aimlessly around on the pitch thinking deeply and occasionally gesticulating rather than kicking the ball. They are apparently absorbed in deep contemplation on, presumably, the subject of football. Nothing much appears to happen until the very last minute of the match, when the striker of the Greek team, Archimedes, has an idea, shrieks "Eureka" and runs towards the ball and kicks it, whereupon the Greeks start to actually play football. Within seconds, they manage to score a goal (a diving header by Socrates from a cross from Archimedes) which turns out be decisive. The German philosophers surround the referee protesting frantically against the goal using their respective school of thoughts; for example, Hegel arguing that "reality is merely an a priori adjunct of non-naturalistic ethics", Kant via the categorical imperative holding that "ontologically it exists only in the imagination" and Marx claiming it was offside. But their protests are in vain and the Greeks win the match.

In a sense, it is not surprising that the philosophers pondered the game of football. The nature of this sport seems to have a rather high degree of complexity. In particular, scientific analyses of league competitions in several popular team-sports (e.g., American football, baseball, basketball, football and ice-hockey) suggest that football is the most competitive sport, in the sense that better teams are occasionally beaten by the underdogs (Ben-Naim, Vazquez & Redner, 2007). On the basis of analyses of matches in prior World Cups, Wagenaar (1988) estimated that the influence of chance on the outcome was about 95%, but stressed that the margin between a game of chance and a game of skill was weak and almost undetectable. Like Wagenaar, one may argue that the presence of uncertainty makes football thrilling and interesting to watch.

Football is also associated with various phenomena that relate to, among other things, strategic choice, decision-making, management of resources, competition, judgmental forecasting, motivation and labour markets. Additionally, this worldwide game is surrounded by different cognitive beliefs, which may shape behaviour and expectations. For example, the conception that players who have scored goals in consecutive matches are thereby more likely to score in their next match has not only implications for coaching and the action on the pitch, but also the evaluation of performance and betting. As a consequence, contemporary economists, psychologists and researchers in various other disciplines are attracted by football to the extent that they conduct scientific investigations. Another reason for their attraction is the abundance of available statistics, permitting rigorous analyses of football-related phenomena. Unlike the philosophers in the aforementioned comic sketch, the scientists have a good understanding of how the game of football is played.

The present book aims to describe economic and psychological analyses of phenomena in and about football. Particular focus is put on evaluating some everyday myths and common conceptions that are associated with this sport. Here are three examples: (1) many sports commentators seem to believe that a team runs a greater risk of letting a goal in just after it has scored, (2) the team that starts in a penalty shoot-out has an advantage over its opponent and (3) many people appear to think that extensive knowledge of football is essential for accurate predictions. Besides establishing the degree of truth in such ideas, this book also presents evidence for phenomena not necessarily related to any widely held beliefs. Some of the issues that will be covered concern strategies in penalty-taking, mental processes underlying referee decisions, the role of fans on the match outcome, the risk of relegation for newcomers in league football, determinants of the duration of footballer careers, the effects of differences in salaries among players and stock-market reactions to events of listed football clubs.

The remainder of this introductory chapter proceeds as follows. In the next section, the rationale for the present book is described. Then comes a brief description of economic and psychological research on football aimed to illuminate its development and differences in perspectives and methods. The penultimate section outlines the contents of the book. Finally, this chapter ends with a discussion of conclusions and suggestions for further research.

Rationale for the Book

In essence, the present book is the upshot of two scientific meetings. Firstly, in 2005 two of the editors took the initiative to convene a symposium at an international conference on behavioural research on judgment and decision-making (i.e., SPUDM-21), which took place in the beautiful city of Stockholm in Sweden. The idea was to illustrate the potentials of using features and data from the game of football to evaluate the extent to which theories of decision-making and empirical findings from laboratory sessions with students apply to real life. After all, football is imbued with a range of decision-making tasks. Besides involving uncertainty and monetary effects, those tasks may, for example, require assessments of probabilities (e.g., the likelihood of match-outcomes) and call for instantaneous responses in a stressful environment stretching the limit of human information-processing capacity (e.g., decisions about whether a player is offside). The three papers, which were discussed at the symposium, concerned three different topics: (1) cognitive fallacies about the nature of the game of football (e.g., the beliefs that players who have scored goals in consecutive matches are more likely to score next times), (2) behavioural tendencies of referees to make biased decisions in favour for the home team and (3) the use of intuitive versus analytical procedures to make accurate forecasts. As hinted by the symposium, studying phenomena in and about football does not only enrich scientific knowledge of how decisions are made in natural settings, but also provides valuable empirical tests of the validity of theories.

Secondly, as a consequence of the symposium, the editors of the present book decided a year later to organise an international workshop with two main goals: (1) taking stock of the interdisciplinary approaches and perspectives used to empirically investigate behaviour, cognitive fallacies, decisions, predictions, strategic choices and other phenomena in and about football and (2) bringing together economists, psychologists and researchers from other behavioural sciences sharing an interest in conducting scientific investigations of those issues. The workshop was opportunely scheduled to take place in Mannheim, Germany—just a week before the start of the 2006 World Cup (see http://www.sfb504.uni-mannheim.de/EconPsyFootball06). In all, the workshop assembled about 45 researchers in economics, psychology and related disciplines who came mainly from the European continent. Some 25 papers were presented and they dealt with two broad topics: (1) beliefs and behavioural tendencies of the actors on the pitch (i.e., players and referees) and (2) off-pitch phenomena like predictions of match outcomes, the labour market for footballers and the role of team performance. Many of those papers are reported in the present book. Besides several interesting findings, the workshop showed that there was little interaction between economists and psychologists in that they seemed to conduct studies related to football with limited awareness of each other—despite the fact that their studies often concerned similar phenomena. One of the participating psychologists remarked vividly that economists often failed to acknowledge psychological findings. Thus, the workshop concluded that there was an urgent need to build bridges between researchers from different disciplines; a need that motivated the present book. The interdisciplinary synergy we attempted and continue with this volume echoes other similar tentative but growing debates between psychology and economics manifested in papers, conferences and edited books (See e.g. Hertwig and Ortmann 2001, Brocas and Carrillo, 2003; 2004).

There have been a few earlier attempts to connect scientists interested in empirical investigations of behavioural phenomena with football. In 2006, two important anthologies were published. One of them is written from the perspective of economics and addresses issues like the determinants of attendance at football matches, the factors underlying transfer values, the effectiveness of clubs in maintaining their competitive edge and the efficiency of betting markets (Gerrard, 2006). The other anthology takes a different angle and looks at the role of marketing for club managers, sports manufacturers and other actors in the football industry to improve revenues, trade marks and values (Desbordes & Chadwick, 2006). At the time of the World Cup 2006 in Germany, the International Journal of Sports Psychology published a timely special issue devoted to various research problems related to football such as what personal characteristics are required for successful refereeing, techniques for developing skills in playing football and mental factors that may impair penalty shoots. Also from 2006 came an intriguing bestseller entitled "How to score: Science and the beautiful game" that gives scientific insights into a broad variety of topics such as the history of tactics, the aerodynamics of ball flights and the physiological and psychological aspects of playing football (Bray, 2006). In 2001, Dobson and Goddard (2001) released an influential book that not only gives a comprehensive account on how economics applies to and explain various topics in professional football at club level, but also presents new empirical findings in regard to English league football. In addition, there are some books that have considered the sociology of football (Giulianotti, 1999) and the managerial aspects of the business of football (Morrow, 1999). Nevertheless, to the best of our knowledge, there appears to be a paucity of scientific work that blends economics and psychology when investigating phenomena in and about football. The present book seeks to fill this gap.

Economic and Psychological Analyses of Phenomena in Football

To shed light upon the degree of attention among economists and psychologists to carry out research in regard to football, we consulted various bibliographic databases (e.g., EconLit, SSCI, Scopus). Using the keywords "football" and "soccer", we conducted a search in Scopus and tracked publications over the past three decades.[1] It was found that the number of articles dealing with football (and soccer) in economics and psychology was 5 and 18 in the 1980s. In the 1990s, the corresponding number had risen to 33 and 143 publications. From 2000 to 2007, it amounted to staggering 100 and 385 articles. In the area of business studies, which arguably relates to economics, during the same periods of time had the following frequencies of football-related papers: 2, 58 and 295. Searches in other bibliographic databases (e.g., EconLit and SSCI) gave similar results. Additionally, a check with the webpage of the Social Science Research Network (see www.ssrn.com) showed that over the last three years (2005-2007) there were some 25 working papers related to (the European definition of) football. Thus, there appears to be a growing interest among economists and psychologists to investigate phenomena in and about football.

Searching for prior publications in the aforementioned databases enabled us also to find out about the early published research on football in the economic and psychological sciences. In the early 1960s, the psychologists Cohen and Dearnaley (1962) conducted a fascinating study aimed at empirically investigating the ability of footballers to assess the

---

[1] For simplicity, we did not exclude publications that concerned American football, as that would have been a tedious task.

chance of making goals from different distances. The study is mainly based on experiments, where players from two professional clubs (Manchester United and West Bromwich Albion) in the English Football League and two amateur teams took part as participants. Each participant was, among other things, instructed to individually mark six positions on the pitch where he felt that he would score with an accuracy of 0.01, 0.20, 0.40, 0.60, 0.80 and 0.99, respectively. From each of those positions, he then made five shots to the goal, which was not guarded by a keeper and his performance was recorded. Before selecting the positions, the participants had been informed that their judgments of skills would be evaluated in such a manner. As expected, the levels of expected and actual accuracy were found to be negatively related to the distance to goal. The correspondence between expected and actual accuracy was somewhat good, although there was a tendency of exaggerating the true performance. Specifically, circa 44% (22%) of the judgements overestimated (underestimated) the true performance, whereas the remainder were accurate. To some extent, those results relate to the notion of overconfidence, which is the propensity to overestimate the correctness of one's predictions (e.g., see Griffin & Brenner, 2004).

Furthermore, Cohen and Dearnaley (1962) observed that the players, on average, managed to score 5 out of 5 shots from a closer distance to the goal (mean 26 feet) than expected distance (mean 21feet), indicating underestimation of skills. No substantial differences could be found between the professionals and the amateurs. In an attempt to verify their findings, Cohen and Dearnaley (1962) analysed three filmed matches (i.e., the FA Cup final in 1956, the European Championships final in 1960 and a league match) and tried to count the number of shots made within and outside the penalty area as well as their success rates. Their analyses showed that the frequency of successful shots was greater within than outside the penalty area (i.e., 13 goals out of a total of 44 attempts vs. 1 goal out of 32 attempts), an observation that agreed with the results from the experiments. Despite the intriguing approach and results, the study of Cohen and Dearnaley (1962) has received only modest attention by scientists. Over the years, this study has only been cited eight times.

Apparently, it took the economists roughly a decade longer than the psychologists to realise the potentials of using football as a vehicle to carry out scientific investigations. In the early 1970s, Sloane (1971) argued that the football club could be viewed as a firm that has the objective to maximise its value, or as it is generally referred to in economics, utility. He theorised that the value function of the club included the following interdependent variables: profit, security, spectator attendance, playing success and health of the league in which the club plays. For example, a club might have to ensure that it is not relegated from a league rather than optimizing success. In light of the fact that some football clubs are governed by people who may have other motives than purely monetary ones (e.g., a quest for power or a wish that the local club survives), Sloane (1971) discussed the possibility that profit maximisation did not apply to football clubs. Over the years, this study has been cited about 29 times, implying that it has had some impact on contemporary economists.

Those seminal papers are instructive in that they illuminate the differences in approaches and perspectives used in economics and psychology when investigating football-related phenomena. On the one hand, economists concentrate on evaluating whether actual actions with real-life incentives deviate from that assumed by theoretical models of rational behaviour as well as to what extent any deviations could impair economic efficiency. An important assumption is that individuals act rationally in terms of specifying their goals and making decisions in accordance to those goals; an assumption that has been heavily disputed over the years (see e.g., Simon, 1979; Hogarth & Reder, 1986; Thaler, 1992; Gigerenzer & Selten, 2002). On the other hand, psychologists tend to look at mental and motivational factors underlying behaviour and reasons for individual differences. Unlike economics, psychology is not typically built around fundamental axiomatic postulations and can, thus, be regarded to be a somewhat fragmented discipline with an amalgam of diverse strands of research that have different perspectives and traditions. One might, therefore, argue that psychologists can be more innovative and less conservative in their choice of research topics than economists. Nevertheless, psychological research is usually based on theory and often motivated by paradoxes in prior findings.

There are also methodological differences between the two disciplines, as suggested by our bibliographic searches and the contents of the present book. Typically, economic research on football-related phenomena relies on available statistics concerning penalties, goals, bookings, odds, attendance, stock-prices and other relevant facts. For example, Bird (1982) collected data on attendance and admission prices from 33 seasons as well as on retail price index to model the demand for English League football. When appropriate, economists try to take advantage of changes of rules and other circumstances in the environment of football to perform field experiments. For instance, in an attempt to investigate the effects of increased incentives, Garicano and Palacios-Huerta (2006) made comparisons between matches played in seasons when wins gave two and three points, respectively. By using available statistics, economists can ensure that behaviour is observed in its natural environment where individuals are sufficiently experienced and motivated.

In contrast, psychologists tend to conduct experiments, surveys, interviews and other procedures in order to acquire reliable empirical materials regarding behaviour and its underlying processes. An instructive example is the aforementioned study of Cohen and Dearnaley (1962). By conducting their own data collections, psychologists are not restricted to consider hypotheses that are easily tested by available statistics—although questions might be raised about reliability and validity. Unlike economists, psychologists seldom bother about the role of incentives when performing experiments (Hertwig & Ortmann, 2001). Nevertheless, psychological studies exist that employ "natural" rather than experimentally contrived data. For instance, Ayton (1997) evaluated odds from British bookmakers and found that the odds for a general match outcome (e.g., a win) were often smaller than the sum of the odds for the same outcome given specific events (e.g., a win after winning, drawing, or losing the first half). Thus, the bookmakers seemed to assess (implicit) probabilities in a somewhat biased manner.

Contents of the Present Book

The remainder of the present book is organised around various aspects of football. Like the game itself, it is divided into two halves. Whereas the first half concentrates on phenomena that are explicitly related to the performers on the pitch, the second half concern issues that are linked to the actions of the agents off the pitch. In all, the book spans 20 separate chapters that are all based on empirical investigations. In what follows, the contents of the two halves are listed and each of their chapters is briefly described.

First half: On-pitch phenomena

In the first half of the book, consideration is given to (erroneous) beliefs and behaviour of footballers and referees. Specifically, there are ten chapters touching on four interacting themes or parts: myths and flawed beliefs, strategic choice, team behaviour and performance and referee behaviour and its underlying factors.

Myths and flawed belief: This section consists of three papers that examine the rationality of some widely held beliefs and conceptions about the nature of the game of football. Firstly, Peter Ayton and Anna Braennberg take a careful look at the validity of some myths about causal relationships regarding the scoring of goals in football matches. Their empirical materials include a survey involving professional footballers from a club in the English Premier League as well as statistical analyses of available data on some seasons of the aforementioned league. Basically, the survey confirms that professional footballers share, to some extent, beliefs about the game that run counter to the results of the analyses. Contrary to the beliefs of the footballers, the authors report the following empirical findings: (1) a player who scored in his last few games does not increase his chances of scoring in his next game, (2) scoring just before half-time does not have any extra impact on the outcome of the game and (3) teams are not more likely to concede a goal immediately after scoring. That, the beliefs of such experts are at variance with statistically measurable aspects of the game raises interesting questions about the validity of our reliance on experience as a basis for judgment and, more parochially, suggests that there may be opportunities for developing and informing strategies based on analysis rather than intuition.

Secondly, Moritz Daum, Jan Rauch and Friedrich Wilkening investigate whether professional footballers have adequate knowledge of the laws of momentum. Their chapter applies the literature on intuitive physics showing that many adults possess naïve ideas about matter, energy and the forces those concepts have on each other. Due to this so-called naïve Aristotelian concept of physics, people tend to underestimate the momentum of a moving object when they try to redirect it to a target and, thus, miss the target. Daum and his colleagues analyse all matches of the 2006 World Cup and identify some 377 situations where a forward player redirected a ball, which came from a cross, by kicking or heading it towards the goal. Those situations are then evaluated with respect to positions and angles. As regards the shots, Daum et al. find that the observed distribution were almost in line with that of the theoretical model, suggesting that the players were aware of the physical laws. In contrast, but consistent with prior research, the observed distribution of the headers deviates from that of the model, indicating systematic errors and reliance on naïve physics among the footballers. The authors speculate that the reason for this tendency originates from cognitive factors.

Thirdly, Martin Kocher, Marc Lentz and Matthias Sutter survey beliefs related to penalty shootouts. Such a breathtaking procedure is now commonly used in cup competitions to settle matches that end with a draw when 90 minutes and 30 minutes overtime has been played. The authors have collected data on the penalty shoot-outs from 20 years of the German Football Association Cup (DFB-Pokal). Contrary to some frequently invoked myths, they do not find any evidence that the home team win more often than the away team or that taking the first penalty would give a decisive advantage. Their analyses also suggest that in the early rounds of the cup, professional footballers are more likely to miss when the penalty is decisive, but this tendency disappears the closer the team is to the final. However, in later rounds, players of the home team are slightly more likely to fail to convert penalties than the players of the away team. The authors discuss their findings in light of literature concerning the influence of social pressure and "choking".

Strategic choice: This section is devoted to the choice behaviour of footballers when taking penalty kicks. Specifically, the behaviour of both actors involved in such a situation is considered. Starting from the perspective of the striker, the game theorists Wolfgang Leininger and Axel Ockenfels note that the scoring probability of penalties taken before 1974 was significantly lower than those taken after 1976. The authors attribute this finding to institutional changes. In particular, they argue that the *institution* of the penalty duel before 1974 could be depicted, in game-theoretical terms, as a so-called 2 * 2 game between the striker and the goalkeeper. Such a game involved two behavioural options: shot (or dive) to the left or the right corner of the goal. After 1976, the institution of the penalty-taking was modified to the form of a so-called 3 * 3 game involving the previously mentioned options as well as the alternative to shoot (or stay) in the middle of the goal. Thus, the choice set of the players had been expanded. Leininger and Ockenfels claim that this change in the perception of penalty-duels (as two different games) was caused by the "shrewd and revolutionary" penalty taken by the Dutch player Johan Neeskens in the final of the 1974 World Cup between West Germany and Holland. In the first minute, Neeskens aimed a penalty straight into the middle of the goalmouth. The introduction of this new innovative strategy is said to have been completed when, in 1976, the Czechoslovak player Panenka followed the example of Neeskens and decisively settled the European Championships final between West Germany and Czechoslovakia. The authors end their chapter by discussing the application of game theory to the game of football.

Focusing on the perspective of the goalkeeper, the psychologists Ofer Azar and Michael Bar-Eli analyse the outcomes of 286 penalties in international matches. Their analyses indicate that given the empirical distribution of kicks, the difficulties in foreseeing the behaviour of the striker as well as the need for immediate action, the best strategy for goalkeepers is to simply remain in the middle of the goal. Despite this alleged rational strategy, the data show that goalkeepers stay put in less than 6.3% of the penalties. The authors argue that the observed behaviour depends on "action bias" triggered by the conventional norm saying that goal keepers must dive when trying to save penalties. A survey of 32 professional goalkeepers gives evidence that confirms the existence of this norm. According the survey, a conceded goal yields worse feelings for goalkeepers when staying in the middle of the goal (= omission of action) than diving to one of the corners. As argued by the authors, this observed tendency of biased decision-making is somewhat remarkable, because goalkeepers have incentives to act in a rational manner and also frequently encounter this type of situation.

Team behaviour and performance: This section includes three chapters that survey phenomena related to the team of footballers on the pitch. To open this part, psychologists Chanan Goldschmidt and Gary Bornstein introduce the interesting idea that the way a footballer celebrates the goal he (or, for that matter, she) has just made reveals his (her) attitudes towards his (her) team and team-mates. Their idea steams from the fact that scoring a goal implies rewards for both the individual player as well as his (her) team. Drawing on literature from economics and psychology, the authors hypothesise that football clubs with team-oriented scorers will perform better than clubs with self-oriented scorers. Post-scoring behaviour of 125 goals were evaluated with respect to three categorical variables: (1) the degree of attention to the spectators or the team-mates, (2) the direction of the running of the scorer after the goal (spectators vs. team-mates) and (3) the number of team-mates embracing the scorer. In the terminology of Goldschmidt and Bornstein, team-oriented (or self-absorbed) players tend to turn to their attention and run to their team-mates (or the spectators) and hug at least seven (or less than two) of their team-mates. The authors find some tentative empirical support for their hypothesis, but acknowledge the need for further research to establish the validity of their intriguing methodology and the robustness of their observations.

Stimulated by evidence showing that the colour of sportswear has an impact on the likelihood of winning in many individual sports (e.g., boxing, tae kwon do, wrestling and judo), Matthias Sutter and Martin Kocher investigate whether such a tendency is present in football. Based on analyses of data from the German Football League (i.e., Bundesliga), they document that this tendency does not appear to exist in the world's greatest sport. This finding is perhaps not so surprising when one considers the nature of football (cf. Ben-Naim et al., 2007). The authors discuss possible reasons for why the colour of sportswear is associated with different effects in individual and team sports.

The section ends with a chapter by Lionel Page and Katie Page investigating the empirical support of the Second Leg Home Advantage.

This notion refers to the effect which occurs when teams are, on average, more likely to win a two-stage knockout competition when they play at home in the second leg. Examining some 5,000 matches from more than 50 years of three different European football cup competitions, the authors show that this effect exists and is still significant after controlling for extra time and team ability. It should be noted that the effect seems to have weakened over the recent years. The authors argue that the Second Leg Home Advantage could be attributed to the differential stakes involved in the two matches. After all, the second match in a two-stage knockout is decisive.

Referee behaviour: This section spans two chapters concerning economic and psychological analyses of referee decision-making. Firstly, Peter Dawson analyses of patterns in the incidence of disciplinary sanction (yellow and red cards) taken against players in the English Premier League over the period 1996-2003. His analyses show an increase in the number of offences subject to disciplinary sanction, but there is no consistent trend in the incidence of disciplinary sanctions. However, individual referee effects make a significant contribution to the explanatory power of the model, suggesting inconsistencies between referees in the interpretation or application of the rules.

Secondly, drawing on psychological principles of perception and psycho-physics, Ralf Brand, Henning Plessner and Christian Unkelbach examine two of the more controversial refereeing tasks: judging offside and awarding yellow cards. As regards the former task, the authors cite evidence suggesting that about a quarter of the judgments are incorrect and discuss possible reasons for this gloomy fact. One explanation concerns psychophysical limitations in perception and the argument is as follows. To judge offside correctly, the lineman has to simultaneously keep at least five objects (i.e., two players of the attacking team, the last two players of the defending team and the ball) in his/her visual field; a task that is impossible for the human eye to resolve. Another explanation is called optical-error hypothesis and stems from the fact that it is very difficult for the linesman to maintain the optimal position where offside can be correctly decided. Once he deviates from this position, he will ultimately make systematic errors. Moreover, Brand and his colleagues assume that the decision to award a yellow card can be characterised as a categorical task where the referee must classify any given contact scene between two or more players into categories like "no foul", "foul" and "severe foul punishable with a yellow card". Following this assumption, the authors describe a theoretical model of the mental processes underlying decisions of such classifications as well as quote recent empirical evidence illustrating how this model applies to refereeing. They conclude that the study of basic psychological processes is highly important for understanding (flawed) referee decision-making and for developing measures that help referees to improve their skills.

Second half: Off-pitch phenomena

The second half of the book focuses on phenomena that concern attitudes and behaviour of actors at the side of the pitch. Specifically, ten chapters deal with four themes: (1) fan behaviour and demand for football, (2) predictions of match outcomes, (3) labour market and conditions for footballers and (4) stock-market reactions to events of listed football clubs.

Fan behaviour and demand for football: This section starts with a chapter by Rob Simmons, where he challenges the conventional economic analysis of demand for football and argues that it rests on flawed assumptions. In particular, it assumes that fans are passive utility-maximizing consumers and that they react positively to uncertainty of the outcome. In contrast, he suggests that fans are indeed active and only interested in the prospect of success for their teams. After all, fans try to help their teams by putting pressure on the players of the opposing team and the referees through various activities. Occasionally, they may also harass the manager of their own team when it does not meet up with their expectations. Simmons surveys recent research on the role of attendance to match outcome. He concludes that fan pressure often gives an edge to the home team, but could also have less desirable consequences in that it could lead its players to underperform. For example, research points out that the players of the home team tend to miss their penalties to a larger extent than those of the away team, as also described by the previously mentioned chapter of Kocher and his colleagues.

The section continues with a chapter concerning how supporters evaluate their favorite clubs. Vyacheslav Jevtushenko, Mathias Landsberg and Magnus Söderlund look into the matter by applying two approaches originating from consumer research. One of them implies that fans give an overall evaluation of their club as well as evaluate it with respect to different attributes (e.g., playing performance and home stadium facilities). The other approach assumes that fans accumulate in their memory salient incidents associated with their club (e.g., a win of cup final and relegation from the first league). Based on a survey involving 1047 avid Swedish football fans, the authors document the following findings: (1) both negative and positive incidents in the life of a supporter influence how their favorite club is perceived, (2) the influence of negative incidents tends to deteriorate over time, whereas the influence of positive incidents remains intact. Thus, the memories of an infamous loss will vanish, but the memories of a successful cup final will live forever.

Finally, José Lejarraga and Guillermo Villa analyse the sporting mortality of professional football teams. They hypothesise that professional sports leagues exhibit a liability of newness, meaning that new teams are the first to go down. Using data from the Spanish Football League for seasons 1992/1993 to 2003/2004, they estimate demotion probabilities and explore the possibility of a liability of newness. Their results show that new teams are more likely to be relegated. Based on the demotion probabilities, a novel measure of competitive balance is introduced and proved to be a significant determinant of attendance. The authors discuss their findings in light of the literature on organisational failure.

Expert and market predictions of match outcome: This section is devoted to illuminating the ability of individual football experts and so-called experimental asset markets to predict the outcome of international football tournaments like the World Cup and the European Championships. The section consists of three chapters. Firstly, Patric Andersson addresses the question: How good are football experts in predicting football? He argues that three main groups of experts exist: tipsters (i.e., those who issue forecasts and betting advice in the newspapers), odds-setters (i.e., those who assess the chances for different sports events) and pundits (i.e., those who make forecasts of football on a non-professional basis). Besides surveying prior economic and psychological research on the area, he conducts an empirical investigation on the ability of professional tipsters and odds-setters to predict the outcomes of previous World Cup matches. This investigation is based on archival data. Prior research suggests that forecasting ability varies between different football experts in that tipsters seem to be poor at predicting, whereas odds-setters are good at producing reasonably accurate probabilistic forecasts. On balance, the empirical investigation gives results that are fairly consistent with prior research. Specifically, it indicates that tipster performance is modest and that odds-setters give pretty realistic probabilistic forecasts of the match outcomes of the World Cup, although they exhibit some tendencies of under- and overestimate the actual frequencies. Such tendencies relate to, what is called in the jargon of economists, the favourite-longshot bias. As claimed by the author, when evaluating the forecasting performance of football experts one must take into account the fact that the sport, which they try to foresee, is associated with high complexity and a limited degree of predictability.

Secondly, Carsten Schmidt and Axel Werwatz tackle the general question: How well do markets predict the outcome of an event? For the Euro 2000, the authors innovatively set up an experimental asset market where subjects bought and sold contracts regarding the winning teams of individual matches. Besides comparing market-generated probabilities with odds of bookmakers, the authors identified the determinants of the quality of the market prognosis. The market performed better than random and was slightly better than the odds (in terms of mean square error). Moreover, the more certain the market predicted the outcome of an event to be the more accurate was the prediction.

Thirdly, Carsten Schmidt, Martin Strobel and Henning Oskar Volkland revisit the analysis of the previous chapter by using data of the World Cup 2002 prediction market. In addition, they propose a new method for testing predictive accuracy by means of a non-parametric test for the similarity of probability distributions and evaluate the incorporation of information in market prices by comparing pre-match and half-time price data. They find a reversed favourite-longshot bias—stating that bettors overestimate the favourites' probability of winning and underestimate the longshots' probability of winning—when analysing market prices before the start of the match and this bias does not disappear with the inflow of new information until half-time. Unlike the markets bookmakers' appear to be perfectly calibrated. Consistent with the study by Schmidt and Werwatz in the previous chapter the markets do assign relatively higher probabilities to their favourite when compared to the odds-setters. Together with a long streak of surprising outcomes this fact appears most likely to be responsible for the predictive inaccuracy of the 2002 World Cup prediction market.

Labour market and conditions for footballers. This section begins with a chapter by Bernd Frick, Gunnar Pietzner and Joachim Prinz that aims to identify the individual characteristics influencing the duration of player careers. To investigate this issue, the authors rely on a unique data set on all footballers that have played in the German Football League (Bundesliga) in any of the seasons from 1963/64 to 2002/03. On average, the career of the players lasted less than four years. The statistical analyses show that the length of the career was affected by player age, position, tenure with the current team, number of games played and number of goals scored per season. For example, goalkeepers tended to have the longest career, whereas forwards had the shortest. Besides individual characteristics, the livelihood of footballers depends on the performance of the club for which a player is active. The closer a team finishes to the bottom of the league, the higher is the probability that its individual players disappear from the league. The authors discuss their findings in light of the changes in employment legislation (e.g., the Bosman-ruling).

Bruno Frey, Sascha Schmidt and Benno Torgler end this section and report on an empirical study examining the effects of relative income difference among football players. Their study is motivated by the paucity of empirical evidence in economics together with the greater availability of statistics in football. Their data set covers eight seasons of the German premier football league (Bundesliga) and includes a salary proxy and several performance variables. The results show that player performance is strongly affected by relative income position. When the salary of a player falls short of the average as this difference increases, his willingness to perform decreases, leading to a reduction of productivity. The larger the income differences within a team, the stronger are the effects of positional concern. Team composition also significantly affects behaviour. Frey and his colleagues conclude their chapter by discussing how those findings, which are based on the behaviour of football players, apply to business life.

Stock-market reactions to events of listed football clubs: In the final section of the second half, which concerns off-pitch phenomena, attention is drawn to the shareholders (and investors) of listed football clubs and how they react to different events related to the clubs. This section includes two chapters. Firstly, José Allouche and Sébastien Soulez consider three types of events and examine their effects on the (adjusted) stock-prices of listed clubs in the English football leagues. The types of events deal with (1) sports performance (i.e., wins or losses in cup competitions), (2) acquisitions and sales of players and (3) the business of the club. The employed data set includes all major events happening to the 14 listed football clubs (e.g., Manchester United, Newcastle and Leeds United) on the London Stock Exchange across three seasons. Adopting the traditional methodology of event studies in finance, the authors document that wins (losses) were associated with increasing (decreasing) stock-prices, but that the stock-market reacted differently depending upon the characteristics of the clubs as well as the nature of the performance. For example, the reactions to wins (losses) were larger (smaller) for clubs in the Premier League than clubs from the first and second divisions. Defeats (victories) in European cup competitions meant that the stock-prices plummeted (increased). Whereas sales of players had no effects, signing new players lead to drops in the stock-prices. As regards business events, news regarding sponsors and construction work on stadium was associated with positive reactions.

Secondly, Jan-Christoph Rülke and Georg Stadtmann take a closer look at how the stock-market responds to match outcomes of a listed football clubs by applying two different approaches of news models. The authors use four seasons of stock-market data for Borussia Dortmund, which is the only German football club that is listed. Besides the commonly employed adjustment of the stock-price changes, the authors control for expectations of match outcomes by considering the odds from bookmakers. Their analyses suggest that there is a link between sporting success and subsequent changes in the stock-market and that alternation in the corporate governance tends to affect the stock price.

Conclusions and Pointers for Further Research

Our firm belief is that future research on behaviour, cognitive fallacies, decisions, predictions and strategic choices in regard to football would benefit from interdisciplinary perspectives and approaches. Parallels can be drawn from behavioural economics, which has been stimulated by findings from psychological studies of decision-making and has incorporated them into formal models of human behaviour (cf. Thaler, 1992; Laibson and Zeckhauser, 1998). The field of behavioural finance also heavily capitalises on psychological concepts and has increased our understanding of investor and stock-market behaviour (Wärneryd, 2001). Psychologists can also profit from an awareness of economic perspectives (cf. Wärneryd, 1988).

The studies presented in this book, while all focused on football, give an indication that they can tell us about far more than just football; on reviewing the chapters in this book it is striking how often general aspects of behaviour not specific to football are revealed. Sometimes indeed issues can be analysed in football contexts *more* clearly and easily than in the broader contexts of life where one can envisage that they also apply. In this regard the famous words of Bill Shankly the legendary Liverpool manager of the 1960s and early 1970s have a certain resonance: "Some people believe football is a matter of life and death. I'm very disappointed with that attitude. I can assure you it is much, much more important than that." The game of Football offers such an ideal opportunity to investigate such general issues as strategic choice, behavioural decision-making, management of resources, competition, judgmental forecasting, motivation and labour markets arguably because, unlike the many contexts in life where we wish to understand these issues, it has a clear-cut structure with well defined rules and objectives and offers some clear criteria for measuring performance.

That discussion and analysis of the game of football could be so effectively and hilariously parodied by Monty Python is also a sobering warning to those who attempt to use formal methods to draw out implications from the game. However, we trust that one contribution of this book is to show that an analytic approach can offer real insights and progress in the understanding of a wide variety of types of behaviour involved in football. Finally, reviewing the evidence it is clear that Karl Marx was, in this one instance at least, correct: Socrates' goal was plainly offside.

References

Ayton, P. (1997). "How to be incoherent and seductive: Bookmakers' odds and support theory." *Organizational Behavior and Human Decision Processes*, 72(1), 99-115.

Ben-Naim, E, F.Vazquez and S. Redner (2007). "What is the most competitive sport?" *Journal of Korean Physics Society*, 50.

Bird, P. J. W. N. (1982). "The demand for league football." *Applied Economics*, 14(6), 637-649.

Bray, K. (2006). *How to score: Science and the beautiful game*. London: Granta Book.

Brocas, I. and Carrillo, J. D. (2003). *The Psychology of Economic Decisions. Vol.1: Rationality and Well-being*. Oxford University Press.

Brocas, I. and Carrillo, J. D. (2004). *The Psychology of Economic Decisions. Vol.2: Reasons and Choices*. Oxford University Press.

Cohen, J. and E. J. Dearnaley (1962). "Skill and judgment of footballers in attempting to score goals. A study of psychological probability." *British Journal of Psychology*, 53(1), 71-88.

Desbordes, M. and S. Chadwick (2006). *Marketing and Football: an international perspective*: Butterworth-Heinemann.

Dobson, S. and J. Goddard (2001). *The economics of football*. Cambridge, UK: Cambridge University Press.

Garicano, L. and I. Palacios-Huerta (2006). "Sabotage in Tournaments: Making the Beautiful Game a Bit Less Beautiful." *CEPR Discussion Paper 5231*.

Gerrard, B. (2006). *The Economics of Association Football*. Cheltenham, UK: Edward Elgar Publishing.

Gigerenzer, G. and R. Selten (2002). *Bounded rationality: The adaptive toolbox*. Cambridge, MA: MIT Press.

Giulianotti, R. (1999). *Football: A Sociology of the Global Game*: Polity Press.

Griffin, D. and L. Brenner (2004). "Perspectives on probability judgment calibration." In *Blackwell handbook of judgment and decision-making*.

D. J. Koehler and N. Harvey eds. Oxford: Blackwell Publishing, 177-199.

Hertwig, R. and A. Ortmann (2001). "Experimental practices in economics: A methodological challenge for psychologists?" *Behavioral and Brain Science*, 24(3), 383-403.

Hogarth, R. M. and M. W. Reder (1986). *Rational choice: The contrast between economics and psychology*. Chicago: The University of Chicago Press.

Laibson, D. and R. Zeckhauser (1998). "Amos Tversky and the Ascent of Behavioral Economics." *Journal of Risk and Uncertainty*, 16(1), 7-47.

Morrow, S. (1999). *The New Business of Football: Accountability and Finance in Football*: Palgrave Macmillan.

Simon, H. A. (1979). "Rational decision making in business organizations." *The American Economic Review*, 69(4), 493-513.

Sloane, P. J. (1971). "The economics of professional football: The football club as utility maximiser." *Scottish Journal of Political Economy*, 18(2), 121-146.

Thaler, R. H. (1992). *The winner's curse: Paradoxes and anomalies of economic life*. Princeton, NJ: Princeton University Press.

Wagenaar, W. A. (1988). *Paradoxes of gambling behavior*. Hove: Lawrence Erlbaum Associates.

Wärneryd, K.-E. (1988). "Economic psychology as a field of study." In *Handbook of economic psychology*. W. F. Van Raaij, G. M. Van Veldhoven, and K. E. Wärneryd. eds. Dordrecht, The Netherlands: Kluwer Academics Publishers, 3-41.

—. (2001). *Stock-market psychology : How people value and trade stock*. Cheltenham, London: Edward Elgar Publishing.

PART I:

ON-PITCH PHENOMENA

CHAPTER TWO

FOOTBALLERS' FALLACIES

PETER AYTON AND ANNA BRAENNBERG[1]

Football enthusiasts sometimes hold strong beliefs about the game that they may often spend considerable time discussing and analysing. However, psychological research has shown that even widespread and firmly held beliefs can be fallacious; a notable example is a classic paper published by Gilovich et al. (1985) which showed that, contrary to popular belief in the "hot hand", basketball players are not more likely to score after a run of successful scoring attempts.

Of course streaks of successful scoring attempts do occur—but not any more than chance. Sometimes a coin will come up heads four or five times in a row, yet it would be a mistake to assume that it was any more or less likely to come up heads next time—coins have no memory. It might be objected that games of skill are not the same as chance events and many players have a better than 50% chance of scoring with their scoring attempts, but it turns out that the *independence* of successive coin tosses from each other is a reasonable approximation to the degree of dependence of successive scoring attempts in basketball. Gilovich et al's paper analysed the scoring attempts for an entire season for a professional team—the Boston Celtics. The analysis showed that, if anything, players are less likely to score next time given that they have been on a streak of success.

[1] Ayton, Braennberg: Department of Psychology, City University, London, United Kingdom. We would like to thank audiences at the European Association for Decision Making SPUDM conference, Stockholm, August, 2005 and the EconPsyFootball06 in Mannheim for comments and Helen David of 'English Eccentrics' for research assistance.

Gilovich et al also analysed series of free throws for college players. The analysis of free throws controlled for a possible quibble that players in open play might be attempting more difficult shots after successful scoring attempts and so be performing in a "hot hand" fashion even if they weren't generating streaks of success beyond those expected by chance. The analysis of free throws showed no dependence between the outcomes of scoring attempts: belief in the hot hand is a fallacy.

Although Gilovich et al's claim that there are no streaks in basketball has been greeted with some academic scepticism (e.g. Hooke, 1989; Wardrop, 1995; 1998) and even disbelief (Larkey et al. 1989) the statistical case has been robustly defended (Tversky and Gilovich, 1989a 1989b). Consequently, despite credible claims that there could be some benefits for players believing in the hot hand (Burns, 2004) and that there really are streaks in some sorts of human skilled performance (Gilden and Wilson, 1995; 1996) including in other sports such as golf (Clark, 2003), bowling (Dorsey-Palmateer and Smith, 2004), horseshoe pitching (Smith, 2003) and even pocket billiards (Adams, 1995) there are no credible proponents of the view that basketball players really do get "hot". For a review and discussion of hot hand studies in sports see Bar-Eli et al. (2006).

It is tempting to take the existence of the hot hand fallacy as an indication of the reliability of basketball observers' powers of induction and, by extension, the reliability of observers of all sports—and perhaps even observer reactions to any situations where they attempt to make sense out of what is essentially randomness. If so then people don't look so clever. However, despite the impressiveness of this spectacular fallacy, it could be that the hot hand fallacy is a peculiar and unrepresentative instance of inductive inference. Bearing in mind the reports referred to above that streaks in human skilled performance *do* occur in various other diverse sports perhaps people might be forgiven for assuming—wrongly as it turns out—that they also occur in basketball players' scoring attempts (see Ayton and Fischer, 2004).

However, that the discovery of the hot hand fallacy is not an isolated or idiosyncratic quirk in sports fans' reasoning is corroborated by other similar discoveries in tennis. Klaassen and Magnus (2007) summarise extensive work (see Magnus and Klaassen 1999,a,b,c) showing that numerous common beliefs about tennis are at variance with empirical analyses of the game. Thus for example, players are not more likely to lose a point immediately after a double fault. Nor are players who have broken an opponent's serve more likely to lose their own serve in the next game.

Taking the new balls or electing to serve first are also found to make no difference to the outcome of a game—despite the frequent assertion of commentators to the contrary.

Given this background the case for investigation of the validity of beliefs about football is fairly clear. Accordingly we investigated a series of common beliefs about football.

The "Hot Foot" Fallacy

The closest thing to the hot hand fallacy in basketball is what we have termed the "hot foot" fallacy in football—that is the idea that footballers show streaks in their scoring performance. Compared to basketball football is a low scoring game. While it was possible for Gilovich et al to analyse successive individual scoring attempts by players we could not easily obtain similar data for footballers. Instead we treat successive games as successive scoring attempts and investigate whether they have scoring streaks across sequences of games. Confirmation that observers of football—including attentive experts—believe that players' scoring in successive games does have some sequential dependency came from a small survey of English Premier league players. We asked two questions addressing this issue of fifteen members of the first team squad of a prominent team—ten of whom were international players. When asked "Do you think players go on and off form even when fully match fit?" 14 replied positively. When asked the more specific question: "Imagine one of your players had scored in each of his last two games. Do you think he would be more or less likely than usual to score in the next game?" 13 replied "more likely". Belief in the "hot foot" may not be universal but a strong majority of our admittedly small sample of professional players do believe in it. Game by game variations in scoring performance are a recurring component of commentary on players; indeed players are picked and dropped from the team as a function of their recent goal scoring record—they are said to be on or off 'form'. But what is the statistical evidence for this selection strategy? Does a player who has scored in his previous game have a better chance of scoring in his next game?

We examined the goal scoring records for the top 12 goal scorers in the English premier league for the 1994-95 & 1995-96 seasons and looked to see if there was any sequential dependency in their runs of scoring or not scoring across successive games. Table 1 depicts the scoring record in 86 games played over two seasons by one player—Alan Shearer. The table shows 36 games where Shearer failed to score and 50 where he scored.

Table 1: Alan Shearer's games 1994-95 & 1995-96 seasons.

	Previous no-score	Previous score	Sum
No score	12	24	36
Score	24	26	50
Sum	36	50	86

With the data collated so we can see if the goals were scored in games where the player had scored in his previous game or not we can test for an association between the outcomes in successive games. Statistical analysis shows no significant association between the player scoring in a game and whether he scored in his previous game (χ^2 (1)=1.85, p=0.174).

One possible problem with this analysis is that the difference in scoring rate between home and away games might obscure a tendency for the player to score in successive games. As players typically score more often at home games than away games, and as home and away games typically alternate during the season, a tendency to score after previously scoring might be concealed in this analysis. To circumnavigate this issue we analysed the scoring record for home and away games separately. Over this period Alan Shearer scored in 34/43=79% of all his home games. If he had failed to score in his previous game (whether that game was at home or away) then his hit-rate was 17/20=85%; if he had scored in his last game then his hit-rate was lower at 17/23=74%. This difference in scoring is not statistically significant (Fisher exact test, p=0.47). Over the same period Shearer scored in 16 away games and failed to score in 27—a rate of 16/43=37%. If he had previously not scored his hit rate was 7/16=44%. But if he had scored last game then his rate was 9/27=33%. Again, this difference in scoring rate as a function of previous success is not significant (χ^2 (1)=0.47, p=0.5). In summary, both in away and home games, contrary to the hot foot hypothesis Shearer has a slightly higher strike rate if he failed to score on his last outing—although this is not a statistically significant effect.

We performed the same analysis for twelve players altogether—see table 2. None of the associations for any player home or away show a pattern of scoring such that players are more likely to score if they scored in their previous game.

One might reasonably object that these analyses at the level of individual players lack statistical power. The last row of table 2 shows the data aggregated across the top twelve scorers; analyses of these data show no statistically significant evidence that players' scoring has runs of success and failure that are any different from chance. For away games the

Table 2: Scoring probabilities for twelve English Premier League players (1994-95 & 1995-96 seasons) as a function of scoring or not in the previous game.

Player	Home $p\left(\dfrac{score}{score}\right)$	$p\left(\dfrac{score}{no\text{-}score}\right)$	Away $p\left(\dfrac{score}{score}\right)$	$p\left(\dfrac{score}{no\text{-}score}\right)$
Peter Beardsley	0/7=0%	12/29=41%	0/11=0%	6/29=21%
Mark Bright	3/9=33%	6/25=24%	1/6=16%	5/22=23%
Eric Cantona	6/12=50%	9/20=45%	6/16=38%	6/14=43%
Andy Cole	4/10=40%	9/26=35%	2/13=15%	8/23=35%
Les Ferdinand	9/17=53%	16/24=67%	9/24=38%	7/17=41%
Robbie Fowler	7/17=41%	16/27=59%	6/18=33%	6/24=25%
Dean Holdsworth	2/6=33%	7/27=26%	2/8=25%	3/25=12%
Matt Le Tissier	6/11=55%	11/34=32%	3/16=19%	8/25=32%
Alan Shearer	17/23=74%	17/20=85%	9/27=33%	7/16=44%
Teddy Sheringham	3/17=18%	11/26=42%	3/13=23%	12/30=40%
Chris Sutton	3/5=60%	3/23=13%	3/8=38%	4/24=16%
Ian Wright	11/19=58%	8/17=47%	7/14=50%	7/22=32%
Total	71/153=46%	125/298=42%	51/174=29%	79/271=29%

chances of these players scoring is the same—29%—whether they scored in their previous game or not; for home games the small difference in scoring rates is not statistically significant (χ^2 (1)=0.82, p=0.37). Any belief in the 'hot foot' also appears to be a fallacy.

Is There a Good Time to Score? Are Goals Just Before Half-Time Worth More?

A common commentator cliché is that a goal scored just before half time has a bigger impact on the game than a goal scored at any other time. As with the "hot hand" fallacy this has some psychological plausibility: it is easy to imagine that the team who just scored will go in to the dressing room team talk cock a hoop at their success while the other team will be engaged in divisive recriminations—tearing themselves apart arguing about who was to blame for the goal. Of course such effects could occur as a result of a goal being scored at any time in the game, but the proximity of a goal to the half-time interval with its opportunity for reflection, judgment, exhortation and recrimination could result in a greater effect on

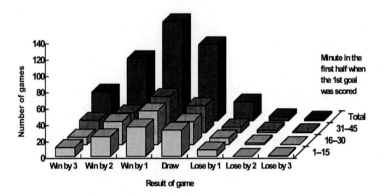

Figure 1: Seven outcomes of games for teams scoring in each period of the first half.

the way players resume the game after the interval. But is this actually the case?

We analysed the results of all 355 English Premier league games between August 1992 and October 1995 that were poised 1-0 at half time. Thus, one team had conceded a goal in the first half. But the time when that goal was scored doesn't have any effect on the game; rates of win, lose or draw hardly vary at all as a function of *when* the 1st goal was scored. Figure one plots seven outcomes for teams scoring in each of the three 15-minute periods of the first half. No clear dependency seems evident here though there is insufficient data to test for this statistically. Table three shows the same data collapsed into three possible outcomes—win, lose or draw and a statistical analysis of these data confirms there is no association between the time of the goal in the first half and these outcomes (χ^2 (4)=0.59, p=0.96).Our survey of Premier League players revealed less endorsement for this belief among the players than was evident for the hot foot hypothesis. We asked: "Imagine you go in at half-time from a game 1-0 ahead. Do you think it is better if the goal was scored just before half-time rather than earlier in the game?" Nine of the fifteen players asked to respond Yes or No responded "Yes". When asked "Do you think it gives you a better chance of winning the game if the goal was scored *just before half-time* rather than earlier in the game?" only five of the fifteen responded "Yes". Thus the belief that a goal just before half time is worth more than one earlier is held by some players, although not a majority.

Table 3: Three outcomes of games for teams scoring in each period of the first half.

Period in first half when goal is scored (minutes)	Outcome of game		
	Win	Draw	Lose
1-15	71	32	9
16-30	78	28	10
31-45	83	33	11

Does Scoring a Goal Make a Team More Vulnerable?

Another commentator cliché is that a team is never more vulnerable than when it has just scored a goal. A gesture frequently exhibited at certain times by coaches on the touchline appears to confirm that the belief is held by professionals. In the immediate aftermath of a goal it is not uncommon for the television cameras to show the coach of the scoring team on the touchline pointing each index finger at the side off his head (see figure 2). His gesture appears to be exhorting the players to concentrate and stay "cool" and to remain vigilant and "focussed". Of course coaches undoubtedly want their players to manifest this attitude throughout the game but the fact that the gesture only appears to occur during the aftermath of a goal suggests that coaches feel that it is at this particular time that the players are in need of a reminder not to let things slip.

Our survey of Premier league players revealed some evidence for this belief among the players. When asked: "Do you think teams are temporarily more vulnerable *just after scoring* a goal?" eleven of the fifteen said "Yes". When asked the rather more specific question: "Do you think teams are more likely to concede a goal *just after scoring* than at other times during a game?" only six of the fifteen responded "Yes". It appears then that some of the players do hold the view that scoring makes them more vulnerable though only a minority believe that this would result in the team being more likely to concede a goal.

How could the validity of this belief be tested? One way of examining this idea is to look at games with a 1-1 score line. All games that end in 1-1 show that each team was capable of scoring against the other—but are the equalising team more likely to score just after they had conceded a goal than at any other time? Across the 1994-95 and 1995-96 premier league seasons there were 127 games that ended 1-1. For each game we divided the time remaining after the 1st goal into four quarters. If teams are more

Figure 2: How a coach gestures to his team after they score a goal.

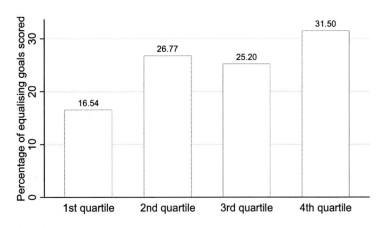

Figure 3: Percentage of teams conceding in each quartile since scoring.

vulnerable after scoring then we would expect more equalising goals in the 1st quarter than the 4th. But actually, as shown in figure 3, equalising goals are more common in the fourth quarter (31%) than the first (17%).

Often in the immediate aftermath of a goal a considerable amount of time is consumed in celebratory behaviour that results in a delay in the start of play. This may well be the reason why the first period of time has a lower scoring rate than the later periods. It is even possible that a greater vulnerability to conceding is masked by the reduced opportunity to score caused by post-goal celebrations and the delay in the commencement of play. However with the present data we have been unable to find any evidence for teams being more vulnerable after scoring.

Concluding Comments

Our analyses suggest that there are misconceptions about the game—some of which are held by top professional players. We should make it clear however that we entirely concede that, with more data, more sensitive analyses could reveal evidence for some of the effects that we have been attempting to find. Indeed, in regard to the evidence for the effects of a goal just before half-time, recent analyses of nearly 20,000 games indicates that there is a discernible effect on the outcomes of games of goals scored just before half-time (Page and Ayton, 2008). Note that an individual watching every single game of a Premier League team—home and away—would take nearly ten years to see the 355 games we analysed here—and of course many of these would not offer opportunities to evaluate the just before half time effect—e.g. goalless draws. To observe the 20,000 games analysed by Page and Ayton would take 30,000 hours. Even someone doing nothing but watch football matches continuously eight hours a day for five days a week (everyone needs some time off) would take almost 14 and a half years to amass the experience needed to detect the effect found in that study—and that of course assumes that they would be able to intuitively apply the appropriate statistical analysis on the enormous data set that they had accumulated. Plainly statistical analysis offers major advantages to anyone attempting to understand the causality of the game.

Nevertheless what is striking when one looks at the way football is discussed is how rarely any statistical analyses are presented to corroborate the pundits' judgments. Why isn't statistical analysis of the game a more prominent part of the popular presentation and discussion of football? In an earlier article discussing some of the analyses presented here it was suggested that dispensing with proper analysis allows the pundits more freedom to air their speculations—untrammelled by the constraints that could be supplied from statistical analysis (Ayton, 1998). After all, one thing that players and coaches and even mere seasoned observers of the game can use to justify their claims to expertise is their often considerable experience of monitoring the game. Another possibility is that people over-rate their ability to analyse the game and spot patterns by observation. For example, in their analysis of people's perception of biased roulette wheels, Keren and Lewis (1994) have shown that people greatly underestimate the number of observations needed for a reliable detection of biased numbers.

A feature of human reasoning—underlying all three of the fallacies observed here—is that people tend to see patterns in randomness. Of course football is not simple randomness, but, like nearly everything that one seeks to explain, there is a random element. Nisbett, Krantz, Jepson and Kunda (1983) have presented evidence that people do tend to neglect the role of randomness when reasoning about causes of events, including sporting events, preferring to attribute outcomes to available causal factors rather than invoke chance.

In all games the outcome is determined by a mixture of skill and chance. The world chess champion could in a single game lose to a lesser player because he is tired, has a headache or is distracted by a woman in a red blouse. The role of random factors is often acknowledged in the way sporting contests are organised. The world chess championship consists of a series of 24 games to exclude the fluctuating elements and let the underlying small but structural differences of skill emerge. Similar arrangements are made for many other sports.

The degree to which games are affected by chance can also be analysed and quantified. Wagenaar (1988) analysed all World Cup tournament matches from 1930-86 to measure the influence of luck in these games. Wagenaar did this by measuring the intransitivities in outcomes of the games. Consider: if there was no luck involved in football matches, and outcomes were determined solely by the stable strength of teams, then if team A beats team B and team B beats team C, transitivity requires that A should always beat C. Over the course of a tournament teams probably wouldn't vary that much in terms of their underlying strength. Of course, key players might drop out or in from one game to the next due to injuries but arguably this would be a small factor overall. Wagenaar found 172 triads of matches where he could test for intransitivities and found 30 intransitivities. Wagenaar's analysis of this degree of inconsistency in game outcomes indicated that, on average, 95% of the outcome of each game is due to non-stable factors—chance if you will. Actually it is possible that intransitivities in the outcomes of games could occur for certain deterministic reasons other than pure chance. If underlying strength of teams was determined by more than one parameter—teams could use variable tactics are used for different types of opposition—then intransitivities could occur for causal reasons. For example, a team (B) with very tall forwards might be able to beat a short team (C) but lose against one with one tall defenders (A); meanwhile the short team (C) might beat team A by using different tactics that their tall defenders could not block. Nonetheless, Wagenaar claims that it is the uncertainty about game outcomes that makes games exciting and that if it was always close to 100% certain which team would win the games would be boring.

The origins of the phrase "back to square one" date from pre-television times when football commentators on radio referred to a numbered grid pattern printed in the "Radio Times"—a weekly magazine published by the British Broadcasting Corporation (BBC) which has, since 1923, provided BBC programme listings. The grid pattern was referred to by early football commentators during radio broadcasts to identify the spatial locations on the pitch where the action was taking place. "Square one"—including the area where goal kicks were taken—was where the game re-started after an attack broke down. Since these early innocent days commentary, analysis and "punditry" on the game have grown enormously such that, for top matches, it is not unusual to see as much or even more broadcast time devoted to the discussion of the game as there is to the coverage of the match itself. BBC television coverage of the 2008 English FA Cup final for example started at 12.30 and finished at 17.30—300 minutes of broadcasting—with no commercial breaks—for a 90 minute match. Before, during and after the game fans, players, coaches, former players and former coaches—experts—are quizzed and offer pronouncements on the possible tactics and outcomes of the game. There are often intense discussions of numerous putatively diagnostic signs of victory and defeat that can be divined in the patterns that are perceived in the complex array of data that comprise football matches and their precursors. The possibility suggested by the kinds of analyses presented here is that the enormous amount of expert discussion that accompanies the game may be largely froth with little to offer by way of valid insight.

Sports psychologists are another group of experts who may be vulnerable to the illusions described here—though, given their claims to scientific status and their, training in and awareness of, scientific methods they really should know better. In the following, we give details of sports psychologists' comments on the idea that teams are vulnerable after scoring. In a football magazine article entitled "The fatal five minutes" a series of three sports psychologists endorse the hypothesis that the effect is real, giving plausible reasons—but no evidence.

> They say you are at your most vulnerable when you've just scored, and it's amazing how often that is proved true. I think it's inevitable that teams relax mentally and lose concentration when they scored an important goal while the other team is still stung by it (Dr George Sik).

> If you celebrate too much you will burn off all the extra energy the boost of the goal has given you. By the time you face the kick-off you might feel completely drained when the other team re-starts (Dr Windy Dryden).

> If done properly, team goal celebrations can be demoralising for the opposition, but if they are too exaggerated they can be a double edged sword. The fact that the scoring team is huddled together gives the opposing team the chance to make eye contact and harden their resolve. And if the celebrations are too over the top it is likely to put fire in their bellies" (Stephen Smith).

Tellingly, none of these sports psychologists offered any evidence for their prognostications but it is noticeable that they do offer a kind of causal reasoning—albeit with a rather *ad hoc* flavour—to corroborate their unsupported intuitions.

It is perhaps revealing that although data exist in abundance to explore the validity of existing beliefs, and perhaps generate entirely new insights about football and other sports, the opportunity is not often pursued. Statistics do appear to be increasingly cited in sports coverage, but these often have a rather "trainspotter" uselessness about them. Thus, though simple tallies of number of free kicks and fouls may be useful, there are also dubiously pertinent historical precedents ("the last time a goalkeeper whose Mother in law's maiden name began with an 'R' saved a penalty was in 1893...")—but why no attempts to statistically model the causality of the game? This needn't require any advanced ability in mathematics to understand and could be done in a fairly straightforward and accessible way. For example, our analysis of the impact of a 1st half goal showed that less than 10% of English premier league teams 1-0 down at half-time end up winning the game. This seems surprisingly low. Why don't we hear such pertinent base-rates discussed at the half-time interval? Is it because football pundits don't think such base rates are relevant to individual games their discussions are usually oriented around—a kind of base rate neglect (Kahneman and Tversky, 1973)? Or perhaps it is important to their self-justification to present the game as a mystery intelligible only to those with inside knowledge such as themselves? It is time the burgeoning industry of sports punditry was subjected to audit and the kind of rigorous analysis the pundits aver to apply to football.

Rather than welcoming scientific analyses of the game there is a distinct possibility that professionals will display resistance to, or even complete rejection of, any discoveries provided by statistical analyses of football. When told about Gilovich et al's (1985) research, one top coach, reportedly responded:

> Who is this guy? So he makes a study. I couldn't care less. (Red Auerbach, coach of the Boston Celtics, see Sagan, 1987).

Another top coach who was sent a copy of the paper argued that:

> I think there are so many variables involved in shooting a basketball that a paper like this really doesn't mean anything. (Bob Knight, basketball coach, letter retrieved from http://thehothand.blogspot.com/2006_07_01_archive.html).

McKean (1987) quotes Amos Tversky one of the authors of the original hot hand study on the resistance he encountered to the findings:

> I've been in an endless number of arguments since then... I've won them all, and yet I didn't convince a soul... I had philosophers at Berkeley jumping up and down on tables, red in the face. USA Today ran an article in which they asked all sorts of basketball greats, Red Auerbach, Jerry West, all the heroes of my childhood, what do they think of this, and it was headlined, high-handed professor's comments called hot air. I couldn't believe the intensity of the reaction (Amos Tversky).

That the experience of experts could, in their own minds, over-rule any analysis was, in Tversky's mind apparently quite clear. McKean (1987) reports Tversky as claiming that the most troubling finding of the basketball study, is that even repeated exposure to the random process doesn't diminish people's belief in the hot hand.

> The more basketball you see, the more you're convinced. Nobody can tell you otherwise. You know it in your bones (Amos Tversky).

The New York Times[2] also reports Tversky as arguing that the more intimately their subjects knew the game, the more firmly they believed in hot hands.

Since the pioneering work on judgment and decision making of Kahneman and Tversky (see Kahneman, Slovic and Tversky, 1982; Kahneman and Tversky 2000) showing that people's judgments and decisions violate normative models of judgment and choice it has been tempting to see the psychology of judgement and decision-making as being concerned with how people fail to make reasonable judgments and decisions. Books oriented around - or even entirely consisting of - discussion of human fallacies and errors have appeared regularly (cf. Ariely, 2008; Brafman and Brafman, 2008; Dawes, 2001; Gilovich, 1991; Pohl, 2004; Sutherland, 1992). Undoubtedly people's judgements and decisions do show systematic biases and errors, though the extent to which one should conclude that people's thinking is fairly characterised as being 'irrational' has been the source of much heated debate over the years. Nonetheless, given the fallibility of judgment, it makes sense to evaluate any hypotheses one has about the game with rigorous analysis. The evidence for the football fallacies identified here suggests that intuition is not a reliable basis for making critical decisions about the game.

References

Adams, R. M. (1995). "Momentum in the performance of professional tournament pocket billiards players." *International Journal Of Sport Psychology, 26*, 580-587.

Ariely, D. (2008). *Predictably irrational: the hidden forces that shape our decisions*. New York: HarperCollins.

Ayton, P. (1998) "Fallacy Football." *New Scientist, 159 (2152)* (19 September 1998), 52.

Ayton, P. and I. Fischer (2004). "The Hot-Hand Fallacy and the Gambler's Fallacy: Two faces of Subjective Randomness?" *Memory & Cognition, 32*, 1369-1378.

Bar-Eli, M., S. Avugos, and M. Raab (2006). "Twenty years of "Hot Hand" research: Review and Critique." *Psychology of Sport & Exercise, 7*, 525-553.

Brafman, O. and R. Brafman (2008). *Sway: The Irresistible Pull of Irrational Behavior*. New York: Doubleday.

---

[2] "Hot Hands' Phenomenon: A Myth?" NewYork Times, April 19th, 1988.

Burns, B. D. (2004). "Heuristics as beliefs and as behaviors: The adaptiveness of the "hot hand." *Cognitive Psychology, 48*, 295-331.

Dawes, R.M. (2001). *Everyday Irrationality: How Pseudo- Scientists, Lunatics, And The Rest Of Us Systematically Fail To Think Rationally.* Boulder, CO: Westview Press.

Dorsey-Palmateer, R. and G. Smith (2004). "Bowlers' Hot Hands." *The American Statistician, 58*, 38-45.

Gilden, D. L. and S. G. Wilson (1995). "On the nature of streaks in signal-detection." *Cognitive Psychology, 28*, 17-64.

Gilden, D. L., and S. G. Wilson (1996). "Streaks in skilled performance." *Psychonomic Bulletin & Review,2*, 260-265.

Gilovich, T (1991). *How We Know What Isn't So: The Fallibility of Human Reason in Everyday Life.* NY: The Free Press.

Gilovich, T., R. Vallone A. and Tversky (1985). "The hot hand in basketball: On the misperception of random sequences." *Cognitive Psychology, 17*, 295-314.

Hooke, R. (1989). "Basketball, baseball, and the null hypothesis." *Chance: New Directions for Statistics and Computing, 2*, 35-37.

Kahneman, D. and A. Tversky (1973). "On the psychology of prediction." *Psychological Review*, 80, 237-251.

Kahneman, D., P. Slovic and A. Tversky (1982). *Judgment under uncertainty: Heuristics and biases.* New York: Cambridge University Press.

Kahneman, D. and A. Tversky eds. (2000). *Choices, values and frames.* New York: Cambridge University Press.

Keren G. and C. Lewis (1994). "The Two Fallacies of Gamblers: Type I and Type II." *Organizational Behavior and Human Decision Processes, 60*, 75-89.

Klaassen, F. J., G. M. and J. R. Magnus (2007). "Myths in tennis." In: *Statistical Thinking in Sports*, (eds. J. Albert and R.H. Koning), Chapman & Hall/CRC Press: Boca Raton, Florida, USA, 217-240.

Larkey, P. D., R. A. Smith and J. B. Kadane. (1989). "It's okay to believe in the "hot hand"." *Chance: New Directions for Statistics and Computing, 2*, 22-30.

Magnus, J. R. and F. J. G . M. Klaassen (1999a). "The effect of new balls in tennis: four years at Wimbledon." *The Statistician (Journal of the Royal Statistical Society, Series D).* 48, 239-246.

Magnus, J. R. and F. J. G. M. Klaassen (1999b). "On the advantage of serving first in a tennis set: four years at Wimbledon." *The Statistician (Journal of the Royal Statistical Society, Series D).* 48, 247-256.

Magnus, J. R. and F. J. G. M. Klaassen (1999c). "The final set in a tennis match: four years at Wimbledon." *Journal of Applied Statistics, 26,* 461-468.

McKean, K. (1987). "The Orderly Pursuit of Pure Disorder." *Discover.* January. 72-81.

Nisbett, R. E., D. H. Krantz, D. Jepson and Z. Kunda (1983). "The use of statistical heuristics in everyday reasoning." *Psychological Review.* 90: 339-363.

Page, L. and P. Ayton (2008). "The half-time effect: Are goals scored just before half-time worth more?" Paper presented at *Economics and Psychology of Football 2008.* Innsbruck, Austria. mimeo.

Pohl, R. (ed.) (2004). *Cognitive Illusions.* Hove: Psychology Press.

Sagan, C. (1997). *The Demon-Haunted World: Science as a Candle in the Dark.* New York: Ballantine Books

Smith, G. (2003). "Horseshoe Pitchers' Hot Hands." *Psychonomic Bulletin & Review.* 10: 753-758.

Sutherland, S. (1992). *Irrationality: The enemy within.* London: Constable and Company.

Tversky, A. and T. Gilovich. (1989a). "The cold facts about the "hot hand" in Basketball." *Chance: New Directions for Statistics and Computing.* 2: 16-21.

Tversky, A. and T. Gilovich. (1989b). "The "hot hand": statistical reality or cognitive illusion?" *Chance: New Directions for Statistics and Computing.* 2: 31-34.

Wagenaar, W-A (1988). *Paradoxes of gambling behavior.* Hove and London: Erlbaum.

Wardrop, R. (1995). "Simpson's paradox and the hot hand in basketball." *The American Statistician, 49,* 24-28.

Wardrop, R. L. (1998). "Basketball." In J. Bennett. (ed) *Statistics in Sport.* London: Arnold: 65-82.

CHAPTER THREE

INTUITIVE PHYSICS:
NAÏVE CONCEPTS ABOUT THE BALL'S
MOMENTUM AMONG PROFESSIONAL
FOOTBALL PLAYERS

MORITZ M. DAUM, JAN RAUCH
AND FRIEDRICH WILKENING[1]

In football matches the following situation can be observed from time to time: a defending player tries by heading to redirect a ball coming from a cross, in order to prevent an attacking player from scoring. In the case where the defender redirects the ball away from his own goal, there is no problem. But if the defender tries to redirect the ball towards his own goal but past the near post in order to clear for a corner, and if he underestimates the momentum of the ball, it can happen that the ball is redirected not past but in his own goal. Situations like this can be seen not only in amateur leagues; they were also seen during the 2006 World Cup held in Germany. In the first knockout round match between Argentina and Mexico, Mexican forward Jared Borgetti headed a corner kick into his own goal as he lunged to beat the Argentinian player Hernán Crespo to the ball.

This was clearly not what Borgetti had intended. What might have happened in this situation is that Borgetti did not take the momentum of the ball into account correctly. As a result, instead of heading the ball beside the goal next to the near post, he headed it straight into his own

[1] Daum: Department of Psychology, Max Planck Institute for Human Cognitive and Brain Sciences, Stephanstrasse 1A, D-04103 Leipzig, Germany, Email: moritz.daum@cbs.mpg.de, Tel.: +49 341 9940 276, Fax: +49 341 9940 204: Rauch: Wilkening: Department of Psychology, University of Zürich, Zürich, Switzerland.

goal. Failure to consider the momentum of a ball correctly can be seen as a misconception about basic laws of classical mechanics. Such misconceptions can be found not only in football but also in various other fields of what is called the domain of *intuitive physics*. Unfortunately (or fortunately for the defending players), own goals of this sort are very rare and are therefore difficult to analyse statistically. But there is another, similar situation that can be observed frequently in almost every football match: An attacking player aiming to score from a cross redirects the ball outside the far post of the goal. This could result from exactly the same misconception about the laws of classical mechanics mentioned above.

Intuitive Physics

Human beings in all cultures experience basic laws of physics (or classical mechanics) from a very early age, generally long before the start of formal physics instruction in school. Studying intuitive physics in children and adults has for a long time been considered as the *via regia* to the investigation of the development of cognitive functions (Piaget, 1929). This idea is based on the fact that the laws of classical mechanics can often be expressed by rather simple rules with a finite (and often small) number of influencing factors, and can be traced back to the seminal work of Piaget (1929). Piaget's goal of genetic epistemology led quite naturally to his predominant interest in the development of children's physical knowledge. His numerous fascinating findings opened up a domain of developmental and cognitive research and continue to motivate researchers up to the present day to study in further detail the questions that he raised. Today the field of intuitive physics is recognised as a foundational domain in the study of general issues of knowledge acquisition (Wellman and Gelman, 1998).

Intuitive physics raises questions to investigate in nearly every branch of psychology (Anderson and Wilkening, 1991), including important basic areas of research like perception, cognition and goal-directed actions. By their biological nature, human perceptual-motor skills are the result of a long evolutionary history, which was always and still is constrained by the laws of classical mechanics. A further aspect of intuitive physics is that whereas the physical world consists of formal laws that can be learned on a theoretical level, we also have naïve concepts about the physical world that influence our behaviour. Sometimes these naïve concepts result in expectations that are consistent with the formal rules, but sometimes they do not. Several studies report astonishing misconceptions about the laws of classical mechanics that can be found even among adults that are reasonably well educated in physics (McCloskey et al., 1980; McCloskey et al., 1983).

Intuitive physics can be studied via explicit tasks (i.e. tasks assessing consciously accessible knowledge that can be verbalised) but also via implicit tasks (i.e. tasks assessing knowledge not consciously accessible or that cannot be verbalised). This is a great advantage for comparison across different ages and cultures (Krist et al., 1993; Schwartz and Black, 1999). It allows the comparative study of nonverbal behaviour and conscious reflection and thus comparisons of the different levels of implicit and explicit knowledge.

From a very early age, infants possess and develop capacities to represent physical objects and reason about object motion. At the age of 2½ months, infants are able to represent the continued existence of a hidden object and understand that the existence of this object continues after it disappears from sight (Baillargeon, 1987; Baillargeon et al. 1985; Spelke et al.,1992). Similarly, infants are able to understand that objects are solid and cannot move through each other (Hespos and Baillargeon, 2001a, 2001b; Spelke et al., 1992). From these and other studies, Spelke (1994) concludes that young infants have systematic knowledge (core knowledge) about three principles in the domain of physics: continuity (objects move on connected, unobstructed paths), cohesion (objects move as connected, bounded units) and contact (objects affect one another's motion if and only if they touch).

These fascinating findings coming from developmental research are at odds with findings from research with adults showing that even well educated adults hold beliefs about simple phenomena of motion that are astonishingly at variance with the physically correct Newtonian theory. Most influential in this context was the work of McCloskey (1983). McCloskey popularised the term "intuitive physics" for a broad scientific community and showed that the naïve concepts about motion that adults have were not just local naïve concepts but formed a coherent theory, in this case similar to the medieval theory of impetus. The theory of impetus assumes that the motion of an object is maintained by a force internal to the object and is acquired when the object is set in motion. Additional assumptions about this theory were that first, the impetus of a moving object progressively dissipates, which causes the object to decelerate and to stop, and second, the curvature of the motion is determined by the impetus; the object can move straight on, sideways and (celestial bodies, for example) on circular paths.

McCloskey and colleagues (Caramazza et al., 1981; McCloskey et al., 1980; McCloskey et al., 1983) showed that many people believe that objects that are constrained to move on curved paths acquire a curvilinear impetus that causes the object to remain moving on this curvilinear path for some time, even after the constraints on the motion are removed. For example, McCloskey et al. (1980) presented adult participants with pictures of a C-shaped tube lying flat on a table. The task was to imagine a ball rolling through the tube and to predict the ball's trajectory after exiting the tube. The correct answer would be a straight line tangential to the curvature at the end of the tube. That is what 67% predicted. The other 33% of the participants, however, predicted a curved path, which fits into the medieval concept of impetus. In a similar task, when asked to judge how an object released from an airplane would fall, only half of the participants correctly considered the object's former motion in the direction of the moving airplane; the other half did not and answered that the object would fall to the ground in a straight and vertical line. This naïve belief became known as the *straight-down belief* (McCloskey et al., 1983).

Knowledge about momentum seems to be a further topic in which naïve concepts compete with Newton's laws of classical mechanics. If a resting object is pushed, then it is obvious that it moves in the direction of the impact. But what happens if this object is already moving in a certain direction before it gets an additional impact in another direction? Does the object (1) continue to move in the same direction as it did before (no effect of the impact on the object's motion direction), (2) continue to move in the direction of the impact (no effect of the object's prior movement on the subsequent motion direction) or (3) move on a trajectory that results from a combination of the object's prior movement and the direction of the impact? Answer (2) would fit into an Aristotelian theory of the integration of forces, according to which, objects, whether already moving or not, simply continue to move only in the direction that you push them.

That theory, however, is completely at odds with Newton's laws of classical mechanics. Newton's *first law* states that every object will remain at rest or in uniform motion in a straight line unless compelled to change its state by the action of an external force. This is the definition of inertia. Newton's *second law* explains how the velocity of an object changes when it is subjected to an external force (see Figure 1). This law defines a *force* to be equal to change in *momentum* (mass times velocity) per change in time. Since in classical mechanics the mass is constant, the change in momentum is a change of the amount or the direction of the velocity.

$$F_{total} = ma \qquad\qquad (1)$$

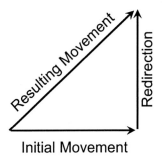

Initial Movement

Figure 1: Discrete version of F = ma, where F is the resulting force, m is the mass of the object, and a is its acceleration, i.e. the velocity change (amount or direction) per time unit induced by the force. An object with an initial movement with the direction of a deflection and the resulting direction of movement.

Here, *m* is the mass of the object, and *a* is its acceleration, i.e. the velocity change (amount or direction) per time unit induced by the force. For an externally applied force, this means that the change in velocity depends on the mass of the object. An external force will cause a change in velocity, and likewise, a change in velocity will generate a force. The *third law* states that forces occur in equal and opposite pairs: Whenever object A exerts a force on object B, then object B also exerts an equal force on object A. The two forces are equal in magnitude and opposite in direction.

People's intuitive knowledge about the integration of forces has been investigated before (diSessa, 1982; Mohr, 2001; White, 1984). In all of these studies, children and adult participants were asked to judge how a moving object has to be pushed (diSessa, 1982; White, 1984) or asked to actively push a moving object (Mohr, 2001) to hit a target. The results showed consistently that children and adults often hold the naïve concept that it is only the final impact of a series of impacts that determines the direction of an object's motion. DiSessa (1982) asked participants working at a computer screen to point and "kick" a moving "dynaturtle" to redirect it towards a defined target. To make a right turn, all of the tested participants spontaneously generated the sideways impact shown in Figure 2b, and they were surprised and even expressed consternation when they perceived the result shown in Figure 2c.

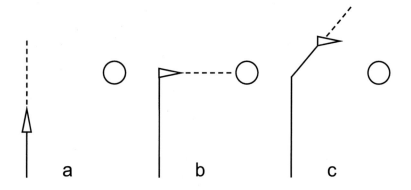

Figure 2: (a) Object is moving upwards; (b) expected motion after a sideward impact; (c) actual movement after the sideward impact (following diSessa, 1982).

The task used by diSessa (1982) explores the problem of impulse integration, impulse being the change in momentum of an object to which a force is applied, on a rather abstract level. Studies that compared performance on an abstract verbal task with performance on a concrete action task, however, showed knowledge dissociations between the two task formats (Huber et al., 2003; Krist et al., 1993; Schwartz and Black, 1999). To test whether this abstract knowledge about the integration of physical forces was improved in an action condition, Mohr (2001) compared an abstract verbal task to a task in which participants had to actively push a moving object in order to hit a target. The results showed that in the first trial, about 25 % of the participants performing the verbal task and about 40% of the participants performing the action task responded according to the naïve Aristotelian concept. Usually children and adults show a quite sophisticated intuitive knowledge in action tasks in which rather intuitive or concrete knowledge is accessed as compared to judgment tasks, where a more abstract and formal knowledge is accessed. But Mohr (2001) showed that there are also situations in which this intuitive knowledge is outperformed by formal knowledge.

The Present Study

Research on impulse integration has revealed three major results: First, even adults follow a naïve Aristotelian concept of physics and underestimate the momentum of a moving object when they try to redirect an object towards a goal. Second, this naïve concept seems to be stronger when people perform action tasks than when they perform abstract verbal tasks. And third, feedback about the consequences of a performed redirection improves performance immediately. The purpose of the present study is to investigate intuitive knowledge about impulse integration in a more natural situation, with people who are highly trained experts in object redirection. Through improvement via feedback, experts should be capable of performing the task perfectly. Professional football players are highly skilled experts in redirecting objects, and situations in which an attacking player tries to redirect a ball coming from a cross in order to score a goal can be found in almost every football match in the world. This reflects exactly the situation of the studies previously reported (diSessa, 1982; Mohr, 2001; White, 1984), where a moving object has to be pushed to hit a target.

Post-Hoc Analysis of the World Cup 2006

To investigate knowledge in professional football players about the integration of forces, we analysed all of the 64 games of the 2006 World Cup. To analyse the direction of the ball coming from a cross after the redirection by the attacking player attempting to score a goal, the following variables were determined.[2] 1) x and y coordinates of the position of the player that shot the cross pass ("*cross origin*"), 2) x and y coordinates of the position of the striking player ("*goal shot*") and 3) the position at which the ball crossed the goal line after redirection, or would have crossed the goal line if it wasn't intercepted by the keeper or a defender ("*baseline crossing*"). We excluded all cases where the attacking player did not hit the ball intentionally, and the ball missed the goal at a distance further than 7.32 m (= width of the goal) from the near post or the far post.[3] This restriction was applied to minimise the possibility that the

---

[2] Coding was done from television screens by two independent observers. As coordinates we used the goal line as x-axis and the centre of the goal being the origin of the y-axis. X- and y variables are reported in meters. Almost all of the situations analysed were highly relevant scoring chances for one of the teams and were therefore repeatedly presented from various different viewing angles. An accurate determination of the above mentioned coordinates was thus possible. In order to check the reliability of scoring, a random sample of 25% of the games was scored by both observers, showing a high level of reliability (Pearson's correlation), which was r = .96.

[3] We define the near post as the goal post near the cross origin position, and the far post as the second goal post, which is further away from the cross origin position.

ball missed the goal only because the attacking player was unable to get into the right position to redirect the ball and did not make proper contact with the ball. Additionally, all cases in which the attacking player was offside were excluded. This was done to avoid any effects of interference by the player's possible awareness of the referee stopping play and a resulting possible change in his intention.

Results

A total of 377 situations were analysed in which an attacking player redirected a ball coming from a cross towards the goal with the intention of scoring. From these 377 analysed cross balls, 238 were redirected by heading (headers, 63.1 %). The other 139 cross balls (36.9 %) were redirected either by foot (n = 134, 35.6 %) or in another way (e.g. bicycle kicks, knee, etc., n = 5, 1.3 %). Due to the very small number of these other shots, they were integrated into the analysis of the other redirections. For exact values of the mean positions, see Table 1. From the 377 crosses, 229 came from the right side (60.7 %) and 148 from the left side (39.3 %).

Position of Baseline Crossing

As a first step, the position we determined where the ball crossed or would have crossed the baseline (see Table 1). Overall, this position was at a distance of 1.1 m behind the centre line of the goal with respect to the position from which the ball came.[4] This was significantly different from the centre of the goal, t(degree of freedom = 376) = 5.11, $p < .01$. This was also true for redirections by headers, t(237) = 5.62, $p < .01$, but not for other redirections, where the baseline crossing position did not differ from the centre of the goal, t(138) = 1.04, $p = .30$. For headers, this position was significantly further beyond the centre of the goal ($M = 1.5$ m) than for other redirections ($M = 0.4$ m, t(375) = 2.65, $p < .01$). In this context it is important to note that the x positions of the goal shot of the headers and the other redirections did not differ from each other, t(375) = .93, $p = .35$. All further analyses were calculated separately for the headers and the other redirections.

---

[4] The centre line of the goal is defined as the imaginary line perpendicular to the goal line proceeding from the centre of the goal, it corresponds to the y-axis displayed in Figure 3.

Table 1: Mean determined x and y coordinates for the positions of cross origin, goal shot and baseline crossing, the mean angle of redirection and the theoretical mean angle was calculated based on an assumed normal distribution of shots.

	Cross Origin		Goal Shot		Baseline Crossing		Mean Angle	Theoretical Angle
Redirections	x	y	x	y	x	y		
All	23.1	11.9	-1.2	9.4	-1.1	0	95.4	88.8
Headed	25.5	11.6	-1.4	8.0	-1.5	0	98.8	88.0
Other	18.7	12.5	-0.8	11.8	-0.4	0	89.6	87.9

Mean Angle of Redirection

In a second step, the mean angle of redirection was calculated from the three positions *cross origin, goal shot* and *baseline crossing* (see Table 1). The mean angle of the redirections by headers was larger than the theoretical mean angle, $t(237) = 4.59$, $p < .01$, whereas the mean angle of the other redirections did not differ significantly from the theoretical mean angle, $t(138) = .65$, $p = .52$. Additionally, the mean angle of the headers was significantly larger than the mean angle of the other redirections, $t(375) = 2.50$, $p < .01$. In line with our expectations from previous work (diSessa, 1982; Mohr, 2001; White, 1984), redirections by headers were deflected in a more obtuse angle than redirections using the foot and than what one would expect if the redirections were normally distributed.

Direction of Goal Shots

In a next step, the direction of the ball after its redirection by the attacking player was analysed. Therefore, the baseline was divided into four areas and the number of shots towards these areas was counted (see Figure 3): (1) The ball missed the goal next to the near post (henceforth called miss, near post side), (2) the ball crossed the baseline between the near post and the centre of the goal (goal, near post side), (3) the ball crossed the baseline between the centre of the goal and the far post (goal, far post side) and (4) the ball missed the goal next to the far post (miss, far post side). The results of the separate analyses of the headers and the other redirections are shown in Figure 4.

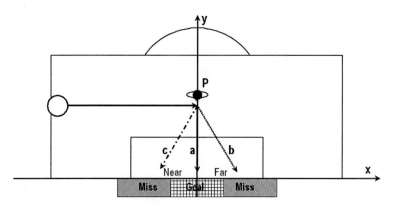

Figure 3: Schematic representation of the situation analysed in the present study, with a ball coming from a cross and being redirected by a player (P): theoretical mean direction of a redirection (a), direction of the ball after an intended redirection towards the centre of the goal (b), direction of redirection to achieve a redirection towards the centre of the goal (c). In addition, the defined goal sections and the coordinate axes are shown; see text for details.

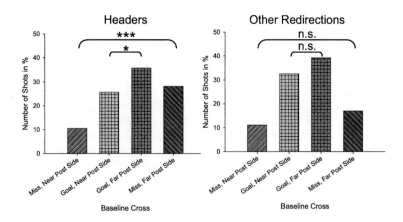

Figure 4: Directions of redirections by heading (left panel) and other redirections (right panel), * significant at the 5% level, *** significant at the 0.1% level.

Headers

A chi-square test with distance (near side post vs. far side post) and goal (goal vs. miss) was conducted and yielded a significant effect, $\chi2(1, N = 238) = 5.22$, $p < .05$. Significantly more headers went in direction of the goal (goal, near post side + goal, far post side = 61.3 %) than missed the goal (miss, near post side + miss, far post side 38.7 %), $\chi2(1, N = 238) = 12.25$, $p < .001$. More headers crossed the baseline on the far side of the centre of the goal (goal, far post side + miss, far post side = 63.9 %) than the near side of the centre of the goal (goal, near post side + miss, near post side = 36.1 %), $\chi2 (1, N = 238) = 18.3$, $p < .001$. For those headers that missed the goal, more missed the goal at the far post side (72.8 %) than at the near post side (27.2 %), $\chi2(1, N = 92) = 19.17$, $p < .001$. For those headers redirected in the direction of the goal (i.e. towards the areas goal, near and far post side), more went towards the far goal area (goal, far post side 58.2 %) than towards the near goal area (goal, near post side 41.8 %), $\chi2(1, N = 146) = 3.95$, $p < .05$.

Other Redirections

Another chi-square test with distance (near side post vs. far side post) and goal (goal vs. miss) was conducted and yielded no significant effect. For the other redirections, significantly more shots were directed towards the goal (goal, near side post + goal, far side post 69.8 %) than missed the goal (miss, near side post + miss, far side post 30.2 %), $\chi2 (1, N = 139) = 21.76$, $p < .001$. However, in contrast to the headers, there was no difference between the number of shots crossing the baseline on the far side of the centre of the goal (goal, far side post + miss, far side post = 56.1 %) and the number of shots crossing the baseline on the nearer side of the centre of the goal (goal, near side post + miss, near side post = 43.9 %). For shots missing the goal, there were not more shots that missed the goal at the far side post (59.5 %) than at the near side post (40.5 %). For shots directed towards the goal, there was no significant difference between the number of shots towards the far goal area (goal, far post side 54.6 %) and towards the near goal area (goal, near post side 45.4 %).

Direction of the Ball depending on the Position of the Attacking Player

For a more precise look at the results, the direction of the ball was analysed with respect to the position of the attacking player at the point of redirection. The position of the attacking player was categorised analogously to the direction of the shots. Specifically, we defined four

Table 2: Number of redirections by heading (upper panel) and other redirections (lower panel) depending on the position of the player.

	Player Position – Headers			
Direction	Near Side	Near Goal	Far Goal	Far Side
Miss, Near Post Side	5	8	8	4
Goal, Near Post Side	12	13	14	22
Goal, Far Post Side	8	17	37	23
Miss, Far Post Side	8	15	19	25
	Player Position – Other Redirections			
Direction	Near Side	Near Goal	Far Goal	Far Side
Miss, Near Post Side	5	3	3	6
Goal, Near Post Side	12	12	10	10
Goal, Far Post Side	12	12	12	17
Miss, Far Post Side	8	5	1	11

Miss, near post side: The ball missed the goal next to the near post; Goal, near post side: The ball crossed the baseline between the near post and the centre of the goal; Goal, far post side: The ball crossed the baseline between the centre of the goal and the far post; Miss, far post side: The ball missed the goal next to the far post (See also Figure 3).

different areas: (1) beside the goal next to the near post (near side), (2) in front of the goal between the near post and the centre of the goal (near goal), (3) in front of the goal but between the centre of the goal and the far post (far goal), and (4) beside the goal next to the far post (far side). The results are shown in Table 2. As it cannot be considered as a result of a naïve concept if a player redirects the ball towards the goal (near goal or far goal), only those redirections were analysed where the redirected ball missed the goal next to either the near or far post.

Headers

It was tested whether the distribution of headers that missed the goal at the far post compared to headers that missed the goal next at the near post depended on the position of the attacking player. A chi-square test revealed no significant result. When a ball was headed towards the goal, the distribution of missing balls did not differ in dependency on the position of the player.

Other Redirections

Due to the small number of misses per player position when the ball was redirected other than by heading, no statistical analysis could be performed. The distribution of the redirections is shown in Table 2. As with the headers, it allows us to assume that the position of the attacking player had no influence on the proportion of misses.

Goals

Finally, the distribution of scored goals was analysed. From the 377 situations analysed, 55 goals were scored. Of these 55 goals, 21 were attempts towards the near goal area and 34 goals were scored from attempts towards the far goal area. The distribution was similar when scored by heading. Of 27 goals scored via redirections by heading, 9 goals were scored from headers towards the near goal area and 18 were scored from headers towards the far goal area. Of the remaining 28 goals scored from other redirections, 12 goals were scored from shots towards the near goal area, and 16 goals were scored from shots towards the far goal area.

Discussion

In the present study, the 64 games of the 2006 World Cup in Germany were analysed post hoc concerning situations in which a ball coming from a cross pass was redirected by an attacking player to score a goal. The theoretical distribution of shots towards the goal should be equal for both the far and the near part of the goal. This assumed equal distribution was only found in redirections by kicking, but not in redirections by heading. When a ball was redirected by heading, the players tended to redirect the ball more often towards the far side of the goal than to the near side. The number of headers that missed the goal next to the far post was greater than the number of headers that missed the goal next to the near post. Similarly, the number of headers towards the area of the goal between the centre and the far post was larger than the number of headers that were redirected towards the area of the goal between the centre and the near post. The angle of redirection was larger in headers than in the other redirections. Further analyses showed that this distribution was independent of the redirecting player's position, the distance of the next defending player and the effective length of the cross pass.

These findings support earlier results by diSessa (1982), White (1984) and Mohr (2001). The simplest interpretation of these findings would be that the football players relied on a naïve Aristotelian concept of impulse integration and did not take into account the ball's impetus prior to the impact by heading. However, Mohr (2001) showed that participants adapted very fast to the correct behaviour. In the present study, all participants were highly trained experts who practice redirecting moving objects every day, and most of them have been doing so from a very early age. Thus, professional football players have a long history of experience coming from the feedback from innumerable attempts to redirect a cross ball into the goal. In general, we found that football experts show a naïve concept about impulse integration when heading a cross ball towards the goal. This tendency of misconception was not found for redirecting cross balls with the foot. One probable reason for this difference between headers and other redirections is that when a player redirects a cross ball by kicking, he has (at least) one more available degree of freedom. When heading a ball, in most cases the heading player uses his forehead. When shooting with the foot, the player can adjust the position of his foot. In doing so, it is possible to use an Aristotelian concept of physics and underestimate the ball's movement. But because of this added degree of freedom, it is possible that the ball will move in the direction of the impact after the redirection (see Figure 5). Theoretically, a player can also choose between different angles when heading a ball, but the point on the head at which you have to hit the ball is incomparably smaller than on the foot, which can be compared to a straight bar that is more or less 30 cm long. Thus the better performance with the foot might not be due to a different cognitive processing of the task but could be based on technical or even physical differences or benefits.

Naïve concepts about laws of classical mechanics in experts have been previously reported in the literature. McCloskey et al. (1980), for example, found erroneous knowledge on abstract tasks about motion trajectories. But in McCloskey's study the students' expertise was rather abstract and had been learned on a theoretical level, whereas the task they used was of a rather natural type. Thus, the transfer of the theoretical knowledge to the natural situation could be responsible for the emergence of the naïve concept found in McCloskey's study. The situation analysed in the present study has no transfer demands from a theoretical level to a natural situation. The expertise of football players', which they acquire over years of training, reflects exactly the situations that were tested in the present study in which the acquired expertise has to be applied. The question arises as to why experts apply a suboptimal strategy in a highly trained task, in view of the fact that previous studies have found that even young children's sensorimotor actions tend to be very close to what is prescribed by the laws of classical mechanics and often reflect the algebraic rules

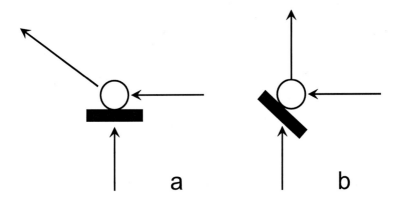

Figure 5: Redirection by foot with the foot held parallel to the ball's initial movement path (left panel) and the position of the foot adapted (right panel).

inherent in them (e.g. Krist et al., 1993). There are two possibilities with different theoretical implications: First, the action errors might be purely sensorimotor errors, thus representing implicit or embodied knowledge. If so, we have discovered one of the very rare cases—and probably the most outstanding example reported so far—of falsely embodied knowledge in extremely skilled experts in their sensorimotor domain. Second, the errors might not be purely sensorimotor but instead include cognitive elements and originate from deliberately planned actions. We favour the latter alternative, and the reasons for this are discussed in the following section.

Cognitive Load

One possible reason for the discussed failure in football matches might be that the competitive characteristics of a football match require a larger amount of cognitive capacity than normal training situations. The demands of a football match are different than the demands of the usual training situation. Missing a shot, for instance, has less crucial implications in training than in a competition. The competitive characteristics of a professional football match might lead to increased mental pressure on the players and therefore lead to neglect knowledge even about well-trained behaviour. Human cognitive capacity has repeatedly been shown to be limited. Neuroimaging research, for example, showed that performing two tasks simultaneously led to a greater increase of activation of the brain regions involved than performance of either task in isolation, but no new area was activated beyond those regions activated by either task (Bungeet al., 2000). This result suggests that there is an availability limit of cognitive resources, because additional resources were not recruited from new, separate neural regions to cope with task demands. Cognitive load can also interfere with performance across domains. For example, research on driving behaviour in combination with an additional cognitive task showed that drivers' ability to detect a car ahead and to decelerate was impaired by about half a second in terms of braking reaction time (Lamble et al., 1999). If the situational constraints lead to an increase in the demands on cognitive capacity (such as in the competitive situation of a football match), this may lead to a reduction of other performance levels.

Pressure-packed situations often cause decrements in performance on cognitive and motor tasks. *Performance pressure* has been defined as an anxious desire to perform at a high level (Hardy et al., 1996). It is thought to vary as a function of the personally felt importance of the situation (Baumeister, 1984). This phenomenon is also known under the term *choking under pressure* and seems to be visible not only in sensorimotor or action-based skills (Baumeister, 1984; Lewis and Lindner, 1997; Masters, 1992, see also the chapter by Kocher, Lenz, and Sutter in the present book) but also in cognitive tasks like mathematical problem solving (Beilock and Carr, 2005) or category-learning tasks (Markman et al., 2006).

Two types of explanations of the choking under pressure phenomenon are being discussed currently. First, theories of *self-focus* or *explicit monitoring* propose that performance under pressure increases both anxiety and self-consciousness about performing correctly. This enhances the attention paid to skilled processes and their step-by-step control (Baumeister, 1984; Lewis and Lindner, 1997). When performing a task under pressure, we try harder to exert conscious control over the steps needed to perform, on the assumption that this will increase the chance of success. This may reflect the phenomenon that was found in the present study. Redirections in football are highly trained skills, and the underlying motor programs might run largely unattended, without the services of working memory. When a football player that is under pressure starts to focus attention on the "how to" redirect the ball to score, sensorimotor control might change from an automated process to step-by-step control and may lead to a disruption of the well-learned redirection process (Beilock and Carr, 2001; Kimble and Perlmutter, 1970; Langer and Imber, 1979; Lewis and Lindner, 1997; Masters, 1992).

The second prominent explanation for choking under pressure is the *distraction hypothesis* (Beilock and Carr, 2005; Markman et al., 2006). In this view, pressure leads to a decrease of available working memory resources, which then has a negative influence on cognitive performance. Working memory is filled with thoughts about the situation and its importance, and these thoughts compete with the attention normally required for performance (Beilock and Carr, 2005; Lewis and Lindner, 1997). Due to the situational constraints of a World Cup football match, attentional focus might shift from task-relevant cues to task-irrelevant cues, such as worries about the situation and its consequences (e.g. loss of a particular match or the elimination from the tournament). This shift of focus changes a single task into a dual-task situation, in which controlling execution of the actual task and worrying about the situation compete for attention.

However, one argument against all of the hypotheses about cognitive load and pressure is that practice and mental simulation of competitive situations with high emotional and cognitive pressure are definitely part of professional athletes' training. This would suggest that the difference between practice and competition should not cause the differences.

Goal-Goal Dissociations

Another explanation of the present findings could be that it is generally difficult to combine differing affordances (perceived action possibilities) to achieve a goal. In the situation where an attacking player has to hit a cross ball towards a goal, he has to solve a problem that we call *goal-goal dissociation*. To redirect the ball towards a certain position, the player has to take into account the momentum of the ball before the impact and must therefore gear the shot not towards the position that the ball should be shot to but towards a virtual position, so as to integrate both the impulse of the ball and the impulse of the shot (see Figure 6). The player has to redirect the ball towards a virtual position that differs from the position to which the ball should be directed. In reaction time tasks it has been shown that a choice reaction can be performed more quickly if the response corresponds spatially to the stimulus – even when stimulus location is irrelevant to the task (Simon and Small, 1969, but see Hommel, 1993). It is easier if a stimulus (i.e. the goal) and the response (the direction of the shot) are spatially congruent than if they differ. It is thus likely that an increase in the incongruency between the goal and the virtual goal leads to an increase in the difficulty of the task in which a ball has to be shot towards a goal. Further support for this hypothesis comes from research on

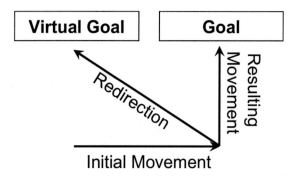

Figure 6: Dissociations between the direction that a player has to aim in (redirection) in order to redirect the ball in a certain direction (resulting movement).

the different pathways of the visual system. Within the visual system, visual information is processed in two different pathways. The ventral visual system (temporal lobe) processes the identification of objects, and the dorsal visual system (parietal lobe) processes visual information for determining action (Milner and Goodale, 1995). Information about the location of the cross ball might thus be processed differently than the motor processes controlling the aiming of one's own head and body to redirect the ball towards the goal.

Decision Making Heuristics

In the situations analysed in the present study, the task that the attacking player has to solve is definitely a physical one. If you consider the multiplicity of influencing factors like distance of the cross, speed, height, spin and so on, it seems to be a rather difficult one. If you also consider that the player has very little time to integrate the perceptual input of an approaching cross ball, you might come to the conclusion that the task is almost impossible to solve. However, many years ago Chapman (1968) showed that a baseball player has to use an astonishingly small amount of information to adapt his behaviour and run to the right position to catch the ball at the right time (see also McLeod and Dienes, 1996; Oudejans et al.,1996). Chapman (1968) assumes that "obviously no ball player ever solves trigonometric equations to catch a ball" (p. 870). Catching a fly ball in baseball is a similarly complex physical problem to redirecting a cross ball towards a goal in football. The evaluation of the situation has to be performed in a very short time and is based more on an extremely simplified version compared to exact solutions of mathematical equations. Similarly, in the game of handball experienced players make decisions during play that are often based on less information than theoretically needed. Strategies producing fewer generated options often result in better and more consistent decisions (Johnson and Raab, 2003).

Decisions based on a simplified set of rules like "less-is-more" or "take-the-first" heuristics seem to result in rather good performance when decisions have to be made rapidly, as it is the case in many areas of sports (Goldstein et al., 2001). Strategies of this kind are called *fast and frugal heuristics* (e.g. Gigerenzer, 2004). They are fast, because they can help solve problems within seconds, and they are frugal, because they require little information (Gigerenzer, 2004). These fast and frugal heuristics show "that simple, psychologically plausible mechanisms of inference and choice are, in certain reasonable environments, capable of surprisingly good performance" (Conolly, 1999, p. 480). A frugal strategy can be used for the interception of a moving object, like catching a ball while running. When the ball is descending, a catcher only needs to fixate on the ball and adjust his running speed so that the angle of gaze remains constant (McLeod and Dienes, 1996). As the situation analysed in the present study requires fast decisions in a complex situation, we can assume that an attacking player acts on the basis of fast and frugal heuristics. A possible heuristic of this kind could be "apply a force in the direction of the position in the goal you want to hit". This heuristic ignores the momentum of the ball for efficiency reasons and therefore leads automatically to the observed larger number of redirected balls moving towards the area further from the centre of the goal. As our results show, about two-thirds of all of the redirections are shots towards the goal. This proportion of "successfully" redirected balls in addition to the goals scored might function as a strong reinforcement of the strategy, making it seem worth continuing the use of the simplified heuristic.

Finally, we would like to close this chapter on naïve concepts about classical mechanics among professional footballer players by adapting the words of Seville Chapman (1968, p. 870):

> [Football] is still a great game, even if the physics in it is unknown to the players.

References

Anderson, N. H. and F. Wilkening (1991). "Adaptive thinking in intuitive physics." In *Contributions to information integration theory. Vol. 3: Developmental.* N. H. Anderson ed. Hillsdale, NJ: Erlbaum, 1-42.

Baillargeon, R. (1987). "Object permanence in 3 1/2- and 4 1/2-month-old infants." *Developmental Psychology*, 23(5), 655-664.

Baillargeon, R., E. S. Spelke and S. Wasserman (1985). "Object permanence in five-month-old infants." *Cognition*, 20(3), 191-208.

Baumeister, R. F. (1984). "Choking under pressure: Self-consciousness and paradoxical effects of incentives on skillful performance." *Journal of Personality and Social Psychology*, 46(3), 610-620.

Beilock, S. L. and T. H. Carr (2001). "On the fragility of skilled performance: What governs choking under pressure?" *Journal of Experimental Psychology: General*, 130(4), 701-725.

Beilock, S. L. and T. H. Carr (2005). "When high-powered people fail: Working memory and choking under pressure in math." *Psychological Science*, 16(2), 101-105.

Bunge, S. A., T. Klingberg, R. B. Jacobsen and J. D. E. Gabrieli (2000). "A resource model of the neural basis of executive working memory." *Proceedings of the National Academy of Sciences of the United States of America*, 97(7), 3573-3578.

Caramazza, A., M. McCloskey and B. Green (1981). "Naive beliefs in sophisticated subjects - misconceptions about trajectories of objects." *Cognition*, 9(2), 117-123.

Chapman, S. (1968). "Catching a baseball." *American Journal of Physics*, 36(10), 868-870.

Conolly, T. (1999). "Action as a fast and frugal heuristic." *Minds and Machines*, 9(4), 479-496.

diSessa, A. A. (1982). "Unlearning Aristotelian physics: A study of knowledge-based learning." *Cognitive Science*, 6(1), 37-75.

Gigerenzer, G. (2004). "Fast and frugal heuristics: The tools of bounded rationality." In *Handbook of judgment and decision making*. D. Koehler and N. Harvey eds. Oxford, UK: Blackwell Publishing, 62-88.

Goldstein, D. G., G. Gigerenzer, R. M. Hogarth, A. Kacelnik Y. Kareev, G. Klein, L. Martignon, J. W. Payne and K. Schlag (2001). "Group report: Why and when do simple heuristics work." In *Bounded Rationality: The Adaptive Toolbox*. G. Gigerenzer and R. Selten eds. Cambridge, MA: MIT Press, 173-190.

Hardy, L., R. Mullen and G. Jones (1996). "Knowledge and conscious control of motor actions under stress." *British Journal of Psychology*, 87(4), 621-636.

Hespos, S. J. and R. Baillargeon (2001a). "Infants' knowledge about occlusion and containment events: A surprising discrepancy." *Psychological Science*, 12(2), 141-147.

Hespos, S. J. and R. Baillargeon (2001b). "Reasoning about containment events in very young infants." *Cognition*, 78(3), 207-245.

Hommel, B. (1993). "Inverting the Simon effect by intention: Determinants of direction and extent of effects of irrelevant spatial information." *Psychological Research*, 55(4), 270-279.

Huber, S., H. Krist and F. Wilkening (2003). "Judgment and action knowledge in speed adjustment tasks: Experiments in a virtual environment." *Developmental Science*, 6(2), 197-210.

Johnson, J. G. and M. Raab (2003). "Take The First: Option-generation and resulting choices." *Organizational Behavior and Human Decision Processes*, 91(2), 215-229.

Kimble, G. A. and L. C. Perlmutter (1970). "The problem of volition." *Psychological Review*, 77(5), 361-384.

Krist, H., E.F. Fieberg and F. Wilkening (1993). "Intuitive physics in action and judgment: The development of knowledge about projectile motion." *Journal of Experimental Psychology: Learning, Memory, and Cognition*, 19(4), 952-966.

Lamble, D., T. Kauranen, M. Laakso and H. Summala (1999). "Cognitive load and detection thresholds in car following situations: Safety implications for using mobile (cellular) telephones while driving." *Accident Analysis and Prevention 31*.

Langer, E. and G. Imber (1979). "When practice makes imperfect: Debilitating effects of overlearning." *Journal of Personality and Social Psychology*, 37(11), 2014-2024.

Lewis, B. and D. Lindner (1997). "Thinking about choking? Attentional processes and paradoxical performance." *Personality and Social Psychology Bulletin*, 23(9), 937-944.

Markman, A. B., W. T. Maddox, D. A. Worthy (2006). "Choking and excelling under pressure." *Psychological Science*, 17(11), 944-948.

Masters, R. S. W. (1992). "Knowledge, knerves, and know-how: The role of explicit versus implicit knowledge in the breakdown of a complex motor skill under pressure." *British Journal of Psychology*, 83(3), 343-358.

McCloskey, M. (1983). "Intuitive physics." *Scientific American*, 248(4), 122-130.

McCloskey, M., A. Caramazza and B. Green (1980). "Curvilinear motion in the absence of external forces: Naive beliefs about the motion of objects." *Science*, 210(4474), 1139-1141.

McCloskey, M., A. Washburn and L. Felch (1983). "Intuitive physics: The straight-down belief and its origin." *Journal of Experimental Psychology: Learning, Memory, and Cognition*, 9(4), 636-649.

McLeod, P. and Z. Dienes (1996). "Do fielders know where to go to catch the ball or only how to get there?" *Journal of Experimental Psychology: Human Perception and Performance*, 22(3), 531-543.

Milner, A. D. and M. A. Goodale (1995). *The visual brain in action.* Oxford: Oxford University Press.

Mohr, S. (2001). *Entwicklung intuitiven Wissens über Bewegungsgesetze [The development of intuitive knowledge about the laws of motion].* Aachen, Germany: Shaker.

Oudejans, R. R. D., C. F. M. Michaels, F. C. Bakker and M. A. Dolné (1996).. "The relevance of action in perceiving affordances: Perception of catchableness of fly balls." *Journal of Experimental Psychology: Human Perception and Performance*, 22(4), 879-891.

Piaget, J. (1929). *The child's conception of the world.* Totowa, NJ: Littlefield, Adams.

Schwartz, D. L. and T. Black (1999). "Inferences through imagined actions: Knowing by simulated doing." *Journal of Experimental Psychology: Learning, Memory, and Cognition*, 25(1), 116-136.

Simon, J. R. and A. M. Small (1969). "Processing auditory information: Interference from an irrelevant cue." *Journal of Applied Psychology*, 53(5), 433-435.

Spelke, E. S. (1994). "Initial knowledge: Six suggestions." *Cognition*, 50(3), 431-445.

Spelke, E. S., K. Breinlinger, J. Macomber and K. Jacobson (1992). "Origins of knowledge." *Psychological Review*, 99(4), 605-632.

Wellman, H. M. and S. A. Gelman (1998). "Knowledge acquisition in foundational domains." In *Handbook of child development: Vol. 2. Cognition, perception and language (Fifth ed.).* D. Kuhn and R. S. Siegler eds. New York: Wiley, 523-573.

White, B. Y. (1984). "Designing computer games to help physics students understand Newton's law of motion." *Cognition and Instruction*, 1(1), 69-108.

CHAPTER FOUR

PERFORMANCE UNDER PRESSURE: THE CASE OF PENALTY SHOOTOUTS IN FOOTBALL

MARTIN G. KOCHER, MARC V. LENZ AND MATTHIAS SUTTER[1]

The World Cup 2006 in Germany was decided in favour of Italy in a penalty shootout, after the match against France had been tied after 120 minutes. Italy had the opportunity to take the first penalty kick, and football fans' folk wisdom has it that moving first is a big advantage. In fact, in this particular instance France's team failed on its second penalty, thus loosing the World Cup to Italy.

Penalty shootouts in football are obviously exciting and can be very dramatic. In fact, it is even reported that male observers have an increased risk of heart attack during penalty shootouts ("Mein Gott, Elfmeter", broadcast on ARTE television on July, 2nd, 2004). Besides its excitement, though, a penalty shootout can have considerable economic consequences. Admittedly, winning or losing the World Cup is an extreme example of the importance of performance in a penalty shootout. However, even on a lower level penalty shootouts have important economic implications in case they determine the losing team to be eliminated from a particular tournament, thus stripping the losing team from potential future revenues.

In this paper we examine the determinants of success or failure in penalty shootouts in the German football cup competition, called the *DFB-Pokal*. This annual cup competition has a tournament structure. The

[1] Kocher: University of Munich, Germany and University of Innsbruck, Austria: Lenz: University of Cologne, Germany: Sutter: University of Innsbruck, Austria and University of Gothenburg, Sweden. We would like to thank an anonymous referee and the editors of this volume for helpful comments. Torben Krueger was of great help in organizing the data.

winner of a match is promoted to the next round, whereas the loser is eliminated from the whole tournament. If a cup match ends with a draw after 120 minutes (i.e., a draw after 90 minutes regular time and also an equal score after 30 minutes overtime), the winner of the match is determined through a penalty shootout. We consider 95 such shootouts in the period 1986 to 2006.

Penalty shootouts provide a natural environment to study the performance of professionals under social pressure and under high incentives. Both aspects are important in many labour market situations. Generally, higher incentives are supposed to lead to better performance (see Prendergast, 1999 for a survey). Yet, increasing the size of the stakes might have counterproductive effects at some stage. A decrease in performance when stakes are too high and when, thus, the burden on the professional is too heavy has been observed (Ariely et al., 2005). Likewise, social pressure may inhibit performance, somewhat surprisingly not only when performing in front of a hostile audience, but partly even more so in midst a supporting and friendly audience (Butler and Baumeister, 1998). Such a decrease of performance due to social pressure is called *choking under pressure* (Baumeister, 1985), and there is a literature in psychology that studies possible reasons for it, ranging from public expectations (Strauss, 1997), the importance of achieving success (Kleine et al., 1988) to simple distraction (Beilock and Carr, 2005 and Markman et al., 2006).

The influence of social pressure and incentives on performance have long been examined in social psychology, but only recently so in economics. Whereas most of the studies have used an experimental framework, there are only a few papers on choking under pressure in naturally occurring environments. One paper that is closely related to ours is Dohmen (2007), who has examined the incidence of choking under pressure in penalty kick situations in the German premier football league (*Deutsche Bundesliga*). He shows that penalty kickers more often fail (by missing the goal without the keeper's interference) in front of the *home* audience than in front of the (more hostile) *away* audience. This provides sound evidence for the importance of choking under social pressure.[2] Furthermore, Dohmen (2007) finds that incentives increase performance

---

[2] Note that this effect is different from what is known as the "home bias" in team sports (Courneya and Carron, 1992), which refers to the fact that home teams win significantly more often than visiting teams. Much of this home bias (in professional football) can be explained by a subconscious desire of referees to please the crowd (see Dohmen, 2005, Garicano et al., 2005 and Sutter and Kocher, 2004).

by showing that the likelihood of choking is lower if the current score of a game is a tie. It is these situations where scoring a goal is most important.

In his paper, Dohmen (2007) mentions two possible limitations of his results. First of all, assessing penalty kicks during regular time or overtime might be subject to an endogeneity problem as subjects typically self-select into the task of kicking it. Second, Dohmen (2007, p.652) notes that "ideally, one would like to be able to observe football players in situations in which successful kicking determines, for example, the championship", because a large fraction of penalty kicks in the *Bundesliga* that his study takes into account are not relevant for finally winning or losing the match.

Our paper on penalty shootouts is able to overcome both limitations, at least to the greatest possible extent. First, in a penalty shootout each team has to determine at least five players to shoot, and in many cases those involve also less trained penalty kickers. Second, in the *DFB-Pokal* the winner of the shootout is promoted to the next round (or, in case the shootout takes place in the final, is the winner of the entire tournament), whereas the loser is eliminated from the cup. Although *DFB-Pokal* shootouts are usually less important than determining the championship (as ideally desired by Dohmen, 2007, see above), they are much more important than the typical penalty in a regular *Bundesliga*-match (where a penalty at a score of 3-0, for instance, is very unlikely to have any particular importance). Hence, our results should be viewed as complementing Dohmen's (2007) evidence by considering an environment where incentives are even higher and where the endogeneity problem is less severe.

The rest of the paper is organised as follows. In section 1 we describe our data and provide some aggregate statistics. In section 2 we estimate the determinants of a player succeeding or failing in the shootout. Section 3 concludes the paper.

Data and Basic Statistics

We consider penalty shootouts in the *DFB-Pokal* from 1986 to 2006. The *DFB-Pokal* is the second most important competition in German professional football after the championship in the *Bundesliga*. The clubs from the First and Second *Bundesliga* are automatically qualified for the cup competition. In addition to these professional clubs several amateur (and partly semi-professional) clubs from lower leagues (typically the third and the fourth leagues) can qualify for the cup competition. In case a professional club (from the first or the second league) plays against a club from the third or a lower league, the match always takes place at the stadium of the lower-ranked club. This rule applies to all rounds (except for the final which is played at a pre-determined stadium), and it contributes considerably to the attractiveness of the cup competition because the "underdogs" challenge the "favourites" on their home turf.

The data of the shootouts have been retrieved by resorting to the print edition of *Kicker Sportmagazin*, the most important magazine for German football (see www.kicker.de). Prior to the season 1991/92 the rules of the *DFB-Pokal* stipulated to play a second match (in the other team's stadium) if a match ended with a draw after 120 minutes. Only if there was again a draw after 120 minutes in the second leg, a penalty shootout had to determine the winner. Only from 1991/92 onwards the rule was changed such that a penalty shootout was imminent after a draw in regular time and overtime in order to avoid a second match (which often caused problems due to difficulties in finding a convenient date for both clubs). Accordingly, the number of shootouts has increased significantly since 1991/92.

The rules of a penalty shootout (officially referred to as *kicks from the penalty mark* in the FIFA laws of the game 2006, retrievable at www.fifa.com) determine that each team selects at first five players (out of the eleven players who have been playing on the field in the 120th minute). Then, it is randomly determined by the toss of a coin which team places the first penalty kick. During the whole shootout teams alternate in kicking. The shootout is terminated as soon as the number of penalty conversions of one team cannot be matched by the other team. For the first 10 kicks (five from each team) this means that the shootout is over whenever one team has scored more goals than the other could score, even if it were to complete its five kicks. The earliest possibility to terminate the shootout is after the sixth kick, if at that time the score is 3-0 for one team (which cannot be equalised any more through the remaining two attempts of the other team). If, after both teams have taken five kicks, both have scored the same number of goals, or have not scored any goals, kicks continue to be taken in the same order until one team has scored a goal more than the other from the same number of kicks. Each penalty kick during the shootout is taken by a different player and all eligible players must take a kick before any player can take a second kick. In principle, this sequence can go on indefinitely.[3] However, the longest shootout in our data set includes 24 kicks.

---

[3] Several less important rules not mentioned here can be found in the FIFA Laws of the Game 2006 (www.fifa.com).

Table 1: Summary statistics of main data.

Variable (N=95)	Mean (Standard deviation)
Number of penalties in shootout	10.62
	(3.48)
	[Min=6; Max=24]
Home team begins in shootout	0.51
	(0.50)
Home team wins shootout	0.53
	(0.50)
Beginning team wins shootout	0.48
	(0.50)
Relative frequency of scoring	0.75
	(0.43)
Audience	15,169
	(15,591)
	[Min=962; Max=76,200]

In total we have gathered complete data for 95 shootouts in the period 1986 to 2006.[4] We have recorded the identity of both clubs, the identity of the home team, the score after 90 and after 120 minutes, and the number of spectators. Furthermore, our data set identifies the round of the cup competition (changing between a total of six and seven over the time frame of our study), which team strikes first, the result of each penalty kick (goal or no goal), and the total number of penalty kicks. Table 1 summarises the most important variables.

Results

Home Advantage and First-mover Advantage in Penalty Shootouts

We start our results section by noting from Table 1 that two of the most widespread myths concerning penalty shootouts cannot be corroborated. These myths claim 1) that beginning the shootout yields a significant advantage, and 2) that home teams win more often due to the

---

[4] Unfortunately, we could not use 36 penalty shootouts from the late 1970ies and early 1980ies, because the order of kicks was ambiguous from the reports. Note that the relative frequency of home teams winning in these 36 matches was also 53% (i.e. 19 out of 36 matches), which coincides with the relative frequency of the 95 matches examined in this paper (see Table 1).

support of the fans. In fact, neither myth contains a grain of truth. Home teams win in 53% of all shootouts, and the team that happens to kick first in 48%. Neither of the two relative frequencies is significantly different from 50%. It is particularly noteworthy that the relative frequency of the home team winning in a shootout is, in fact, considerably smaller than the frequency of home teams winning in a match during the regular *Bundesliga* season. Excluding games that end with a draw, home teams win 68% of matches in the *Bundesliga* (in the season 2000/01, which is rather typical in this respect; see Sutter and Kocher, 2004), whereas in penalty shootouts in the *DFB-Pokal* it is only 53%. There are two intuitive explanations for this difference: First, choking could influence penalty conversion of home team players negatively. Second, the often-reported home bias of referees can hardly materialise during shootouts.

The Determinants of Scoring in a Penalty Shootout

A total of 1009 penalties were kicked in the 95 shootouts. 74.6% of all penalty kicks were converted.[5] This figure is remarkably close to the overall conversion rate of 74.2% in the *Bundesliga* in the years 1963 to 2004 (Dohmen, 2007), which implies that the overall performance of penalty kickers is not significantly different between the *DFB-Pokal* shootouts and the *Bundesliga*. This finding implies that the increased tension and the–at least on average–higher incentives in the *DFB-Pokal* do neither increase nor decrease performance of kickers.[6] In fact, it might be the case that two opposing effects cancel out each other. The higher stakes (of either being promoted to the next round or eliminated) might increase performance *ceteris paribus*, but the larger pressure (not to fail) might decrease performance (much in the spirit of choking under pressure).

---

[5] Unlike Dohmen (2007) we are not able to distinguish for all of our 95 penalty shootouts (only for the more recent ones) whether a failed penalty was saved by the goalkeeper or due to the kicker missing the goal or hitting the bar. Although these types of failure differ with respect to their causes, the ultimate consequence for the shooting team is identical, meaning that our binary measurement of penalties (converted or failed) captures everything that is important for the outcome of a shootout. Note further that, if one started to distinguish, one would also have to take into account whether a penalty was saved because of a brilliant save of the goalkeeper or a poor shot of the player (the latter also being a possible sign for choking under pressure).

[6] We assume that there is no difference in performance of goalkeepers in the two competitions. This does not necessarily have to be the case, but proving a difference would be difficult, to say the least.

Next we report a panel probit regression of the likelihood of converting a penalty kick in a shootout, where each shootout is treated as a panel in order to take into account the sequential nature of a shootout. In Table 2 we show four different models, where in each of them the outcome of a penalty kick (goal or no goal) is the dependent variable and where we consider the following independent variables: "Home player" indicates whether the penalty is kicked by a player of the home team (=1). This variable examines whether home team players are more or less likely to convert a penalty. "Goal difference" denotes the goal difference between the team of the current penalty kicker and the opposing team before the current kicker attempts to convert. This variable can range from +2 to –3 (the latter occurs when team A converts its first three penalties, whereas team B fails on its first two attempts). In general, this variable is intended to capture the path dependence in a shootout, because it might be the case that players are less likely to score a goal when their team is already in a disadvantageous situation. Furthermore, this variable captures the degree of pressure on the kicking player.[7] "Decisive penalty" denotes penalties that *can* decide the match in either way. For instance, if the score of the shootout is 5-4 against team A, and a player of team A has to kick the fifth penalty of his team, then this is coded as a decisive penalty, because failing on this kick would decide the shootout against team A. Hence, even if the fifth player of team A scores and, thus, equalises to 5-5, the penalty is classified as decisive, because it had the potential to terminate the shootout. The variable "Home * decisive" captures decisive penalties that are kicked by the home team. Hence, this variable specifies how the likelihood of scoring a decisive penalty differs between home team and visiting team.

Model (1) in Table 2 includes all 95 shootouts. Figures in Table 2 indicate the marginal effects of the various variables. Note that none of the variables in model (1) is significantly different from zero. Hence, overall there is neither a home advantage (for good or for bad), nor any effect of particularly large incentives when a penalty is decisive. The same results

---

[7] Note that our measure of goal difference implies that the second-moving team may (and typically does) start with a goal difference of –1 in case the beginning team has converted its penalty. Using this measure–instead of using alternatively the difference in the number of failed penalties of each team (which would imply a score difference of zero before the second-moving team's turn even if the beginning team has scored)–seems more appropriate when examining the effects of the psychological pressure to convert a penalty.

Table 2: Panel probit regression of the determinants of scoring a goal in the shootout.

Included shootouts	Model (1)[a] 95 (all shootouts)	Model (2)[a] 91 (all with known attendance)	Model (3)[a] 60 (all in 1st and 2nd round)	Model (4)[a] 35 (all after 2nd round)
Home player	-0.059	-0.063	-0.029	-0.114
	(0.096)	(0.099)	(0.120)	(0.161)
Goal difference	0.025	0.034	0.023	0.001
	(0.056)	(0.057)	(0.073)	(0.089)
Decisive penalty	-0.128	-0.121	-0.447	0.533
	(0.153)	(0.161)	(0.189)*	(0.296)[+]
Home * Decisive	0.143	0.077	0.603	-0.707
	(0.213)	(0.220)	(0.273)*	(0.376)[+]
Attendance (in 1000s)		0.0002 (0.001)		
Observations	1009	956	642	367
Log likelihood	-570.9	-5368	-352.3	-202.0

[+] Significant at the 10% level, * significant at the 5% level. Standard errors in parentheses.
[a] Dependent variable: outcome of a penalty kick (goal or no goal).

persist if we add the attendance in model (2). Larger crowds do not have a significant impact on the likelihood of scoring, either.[8]

A closer inspection of the data reveals that in the first two rounds of the *DFB-Pokal* it is very often the case that professional clubs have to play against amateur (or at best semi-professional) clubs at the amateur club's turf. In later rounds of the cup competition (covering rounds 3 to 6 or 7) there are typically at best one or two amateur clubs left, and thus professional clubs are typically competing against each other. Hence, the character of the matches changes quite a bit over the course of the *DFB-Pokal*, because in early rounds we have the classical "David against Goliath"-scenario where the Goliath (the professional club) is often in a situation where a clear win is publicly expected and where a defeat

---

[8] The number of observations is reduced to 91 in model (2) since we have four matches with unknown attendance in our data set. We have also run models with a number of additional variables (like including dummies for the number of the penalty kick, dummies for the kicker being a professional or for which league the respective team is playing in). None of these additional variables ever turned out to have a significant effect on the likelihood of scoring.

would be regarded a disaster (losing against an underdog and thereby being stripped from potentially large future revenues). The amateur teams (the "David" in this case) cannot lose much, though, because it would be considered normal to be defeated by a professional team.

Recall that a penalty shootout is only necessary when the game is tied after 120 minutes. In matches of "David against Goliath" this means that the underdog has already succeeded in neither being defeated at the end of the regular time nor at the end of the overtime. Hence, reaching the shootout can already be considered a success for these teams, and it might potentially entail a boost of motivation for the underdog's players.

Model (3) shows that two variables from model (1) become significant when we consider only shootouts in the first two rounds of the *DFB-Pokal*. Decisive penalties are significantly more often not converted than non-decisive ones. This indicates that the increased incentives in case a penalty is possibly decisive have a negative effect on performance. However, the interaction effect of "Home player" and "Decisive penalty" ("Home * decisive") is significantly positive and counterbalances the negative coefficient of "Decisive penalty" for the home teams. This finding implies that in the first two rounds the visiting team's players are those who actually fail on the decisive penalties. As indicated above, the respective players of the penalty kicks are typically from professional clubs who would have been expected to win easily already before the shootout.[9]

Somewhat surprisingly, the significant effects in rounds 1 and 2 of the *DFB-Pokal* are reversed if one considers only the later rounds (see model (4)). In these later rounds the decisive penalties are more likely to be converted successfully. This effect resembles Dohmen's (2007) finding of penalties being more often successful if they are particularly important. Like Dohmen (2007) we also find that home teams are more likely to fail in the later rounds (see "Home * decisive"), which can again be explained by choking under (friendly) social pressure.[10]

---

[9] The results from model (3) in Table 2 remain fully robust when considering only matches where the home team is from a lower league than the visiting team. The latter (smaller) data set unambiguously confirms that kickers from the favorite team are more likely to miss on decisive penalties. The marginal effect of "decisive penalty" is -0.63 ($p < 0.01$), whereas the marginal effect of the interaction term "Home * Decisive" is 0.57 ($p = 0.07$).

[10] Since the distinction between the first two and the later rounds may seem arbitrary, we have also estimated a model which uses all data from all rounds, but interacts the four independent variables included in models (3) and (4) with dummies for the particular rounds. Decisive penalties are significantly less often converted in rounds 1 and 2, and home teams convert their decisive penalties

In sum, our findings for rounds 3 onwards (until the final) seem to be largely in line with Dohmen's (2007) results. However, our findings for rounds 1 and 2 clearly tell a different story. In these early rounds the home crowd seems to encourage the performance of the home team player when a penalty is decisive. Put differently, the visiting teams fail in the decisive moments significantly more often in these early rounds. We think that the visiting teams, typically being the favourites in these earlier rounds, might suffer from the disappointment of having to go through the burden of performing a penalty shootout and not winning the match in regular time or overtime. Such a disappointment could decrease motivation and, consequently, performance in the penalty shootout. In contrast, the lower-ranked home teams could not be motivated more.

Besides this presumed psychological effect it might also be the case that professional teams spare some of their best players in the early rounds in the expectation of winning without the best formation. Casual evidence proves that this is sometimes the case. However, it is not straightforward what it would imply for the performance in the shootout, because even players who are not in a club's regular team could be high performers in penalty kicks.

Conclusion

We have studied penalty shootouts in the *DFB-Pokal*, the German football cup competition. Contrary to some often invoked myths we have neither found a first-mover advantage nor any systematic advantage of home teams. In fact, home teams win as likely as visiting teams, and teams that start the penalty shootout win as likely as the other team. Though, a striking finding has been that in the early rounds home teams are more likely to convert their penalties if they are decisive, whereas visiting teams (typically the professional teams in these early rounds) are more likely to fail on decisive penalties. In later rounds, however, decisive penalties are, in general, more often converted, and home teams fail more often on these occasions. The latter results seem to be a confirmation of earlier findings by Dohmen (2007). Our setting, however, satisfies more closely what Dohmen (2007) had considered desirable, namely studying penalty kicks when they are actually important for the team.

---

significantly more often in round 2, but significantly less often in round 3 (all *p*-values at least smaller than 0.1). All other variables (interacted with the round-dummies) are not significantly different from zero, which–for the later rounds–is particularly due to the relatively small number of observations.

Our former results on the early rounds of the competition where visiting teams fail on the decisive penalties more often can also be taken as an indication of a performance-decreasing effect of high pressure. In fact, it seems reasonable that the pressure for the players of the visiting teams (typically the favourite teams in these rounds) is much higher than for the local (often amateur) team. Seen from this angle, we think it is justified to conclude that professionals actually do choke under pressure.

References

Ariely, D., U. Gneezy, G. Loewenstein, and N. Mazar (2005). "Large stakes and big mistakes." *Federal Reserve Bank of Boston Working Paper 05-11.*

Baumeister, R. F. (1985). "Choking under pressure: Self-consciousness and paradoxical effects of incentives on skillful performance." *Journal of Personality and Social Psychology,* 46(3), 610-620.

Beilock, S. L. and T. H. Carr (2005). "When high-powered people fail: Working memory and "choking under pressure" in math." *Psychological Science,* 16(2), 101-105.

Butler, J. L. and R. F. Baumeister (1998). "The trouble with friendly faces: Skilled performance with a supportive audience." *Journal of Personality and Social Psychology,* 75(5), 1213-1230.

Courneya, K. S. and A. V. Carron (1992). "The home advantage in sport competitions: A literature review." *Journal of Sport and Exercise Psychology,* 14(1), 13-27.

Dohmen, T. (2005). "Social pressure influences decisions of individuals: Evidence from the behavior of football referees." *IZA Discussion Paper 1595.*

Dohmen, T. (2007). "Do professionals choke under pressure?" *Journal of Economic Behavior and Organization,* 65(3-4), 636-653.

Garicano, L., I. Palacios-Huerta and C. Prendergast (2005). "Favoritism under social pressure." *Review of Economics and Statistics,* 87(2), 208-216.

Kleine, D., R. M. Sampedro and S. Lopes Melo (1988). "Anxiety and performance in runners." *Anxiety Research,* 1, 235-246.

Markman, A. B., W. T. Maddox and D. A. Worthy (2006). "Choking and excelling under pressure." *Psychological Science,* 17(11), 944-948.

Prendergast, C. (1999). "The provision of incentives in firms." *Journal of Economic Literature,* 37(1), 7-63.

Strauss, B. (1997). "Choking under pressure: Positive öffentliche Erwartungen und Leistungen in einer motorischen Aufgabe." *Zeitschrift für Experimentelle Psychologie,* 46, 636-655.
Sutter, M. and M. G. Kocher (2004). "Favoritism of agents - The case of referees' home bias." *Journal of Economic Psychology,* 25(4), 461-469.

CHAPTER FIVE

THE PENALTY-DUEL AND INSTITUTIONAL DESIGN: IS THERE A NEESKENS-EFFECT?

WOLFGANG LEININGER
AND AXEL OCKENFELS[1]

Angsthasen! (Wimps!)—Harald 'Toni' Schumacher in a conversation with us about penalty kickers, who shoot to the middle of the goal.

In soccer, penalty kicks and shootouts are taken from twelve yards (= 10.9728 meters) out from goal, with only the goalkeeper between the penalty taker and the goal. Penalty kicks were first introduced in Ireland in the 1891-92 season in order to punish a foul within the penalty area. Penalty shootouts were introduced in 1970 to determine who progresses after a tied match. Since then, penalty taking determined the outcome of numerous soccer games and tournaments, including, for instance, the FIFA World Cup finals 1994 between Brazil and Italy, and 2006 between Italy and France. In this paper, we ask what strategies in penalty-taking can be considered 'clever' or 'rational.' We focus in particular on strategies that involve shooting to the middle of the goal.

Game theory analyzes and predicts behaviour when people interact with each other. Taking the framework of the interaction—the game—as given, game theory offers solutions. A *game* includes the rules of interaction, the strategies available to the 'players,' and the payoffs (or 'utilities') each player assigns to all possible outcomes of the game. A solution (equilibrium) is a prediction or recommendation which strategy to

[1] Leininger: Department of Economics, University of Dortmund (TU), 44221 Dortmund, Germany: Ockenfels: Department of Economics, University of Cologne, Albertus Magnus Platz, 50923 Cologne, Germany. We thank René Cyranek for his various efforts to trace data on penalties, and Toni Schumacher and Hans-Jörg Butt for sharing their opinions and expertise on penalties with us. Ockenfels gratefully acknowledges the support of the Deutsche Forschungsgemeinschaft.

choose, assuming that all players wish to maximize their given payoffs. A *game form* is the description of an interactive decision situation without the specification of particular payoffs for the players involved. The idea of the game form is to describe, analyse and evaluate (e.g. in terms of efficiency) equilibrium behaviour for any kind of preferences players of this game may reasonably have. A game form can be identified with an *institution* within which players have to act. From this perspective, game theory focuses on behaviour arising from a given set of institutional rules and asks how institutions affect behaviour. The answer, as we will argue, may depend on the *shared* perceptions of the interactive decision situation by the players. Regarding penalty taking, the institutional rules are pretty clear, even though they may change over time. According to the official FIFA laws

> a penalty kick is awarded against a team that commits one of the ten offences for which a direct free kick is awarded, inside its own penalty area and while the ball is in play. A goal may be scored directly from a penalty kick. [...] The ball is placed on the penalty mark. The player taking the penalty kick is properly identified. The defending goalkeeper remains on his goal line, facing the kicker, between the goalposts until the ball has been kicked. (see http://www.fifa.com/en/laws/Laws14_01.htm).

The strategies available to the players are, however, less obvious, and in fact we will discuss the impact of different possible sets of strategies— and hence different game forms—on *behaviour* in this paper. We will also argue that the payoffs assigned to the outcomes of penalty taking, goal or no goal, are more subtle than has previously been assumed. Players may not only want to maximize respectively minimize the probability of a goal, but there are also indications that players have preferences over the strategies that can be chosen.

A (too) Simple Game Theoretic Model

Let us begin with the simplest possible game theoretic modelling of what might be called the 'penalty-duel.' A penalty-duel involves two players, the kicker and the goalkeeper. The interests of the players are perfectly opposing; success of the kicker implies failure of the goalkeeper, and the other way round. More precisely, the conflict structure is such that the goalkeeper wants to coordinate his action with the one of the kicker, while the kicker aims at discoordination of actions. We also assume that the two players must move simultaneously, implying that players are not able to react to the movements of the opponent (i.e. no rebounds are considered). Indeed, many observers argue that neither does the speed of the ball allow goalkeepers to react to the ball's course (e.g., Palacios-Huerta 2003) nor does a goalkeeper wish to move early in order to avoid signalling to the kicker about his intentions. Furthermore, Chiappori et al. (2002), among others, provide empirical evidence suggesting that moves of the players in penalty taking are simultaneous ones. Summing up, from a simple game theoretic perspective, a penalty-duel can be seen as a simultaneous, two-person game with strictly opposing preferences.

A simple model assumes that the kicker (K) has only two strategies; he can either choose to kick to the left side (**L**) or to the right side (**R**); the option of shooting to the middle is ignored here for the moment. Accordingly, the goalkeeper (G) can either jump to the left or to the right side. (Here and in the following, left and right is defined from the kicker's perspective.) If both players choose the same side (the top left or the bottom right corner of Figure 1), the goalkeeper succeeded in coordination and manages to save the penalty. In this case, the kicker's payoff is zero and the goalkeeper's payoff is normalized to one. In the cases, when the goalkeeper fails to jump to the side chosen by the kicker, who succeeded in discoordinating actions, there is a goal and the goalkeeper's payoff is zero while the kicker's payoff is normalized to one. For simplicity, we abstract away from the possibility that the kicker misses the goal. The following table then shows the 'payoffs' from the four potential pairs of actions (in the following analyses the variables x and y denote the choice probabilities of the corresponding actions):

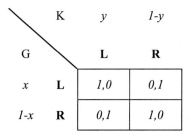

Figure 1: Game I—A simple penalty game.

Payoffs always sum up to the same amount, regardless of the strategies being chosen. Normalizing this amount to one gives the payoffs a probability interpretation; kickers aim to maximize the probability of scoring, while goalkeepers aim to minimize this probability.

What is rational behaviour in the penalty-duel as described in Game I? A good strategy should be a best response to the opponent's strategy. When all players choose a best response to the other players' strategies, these strategies constitute what is called a (Nash) *equilibrium* in game theory. In equilibrium, nobody has a unilateral incentive to deviate from his own strategy. Out of equilibrium, however, there is at least one player who can improve upon his outcome by switching the strategy. From another perspective, any prediction that is not equilibrium would be problematic, because such prediction would be based on the assumption that at least one player does not play in line with his interests. Summing up, equilibrium strategies are not only rational strategies but also good candidates for predictions of behaviour.

Games like the penalty-duel, in which payoffs always sum up to the same constant, are called *constant-sum games* and are well-understood from the very beginning of game theory. A constant-sum game is equivalent to a zero-sum game, because the value of the constant is arbitrary; it measures utility, which can be freely normalized. A unique feature of this class of games is, that any Nash equilibrium consists of strategies, which react optimally to the 'worst case' possible. Indeed, in games with strictly opposing interests, this is a reasonable belief. Not all games considered in this paper are constant-sum, but all are strictly competitive. *Strictly competitive games* have the property that an advantageous change in behaviour for one player is automatically disadvantageous to the other one. Such games are the ordinal equivalents of zero-sum games.

It can easily be seen that the penalty-duel has no equilibrium in so-called *pure strategies*. If the goalkeeper chooses **L**, the kicker's best response is **R**. But if the kicker chooses **R**, the goalkeeper's best response is **R** etc. No pair of pure strategies constitutes an equilibrium. However, the general notion of a mixed strategy, which refers to *probability distributions* over actions such as **R** and **L**, always admits an equilibrium. When mixing, players choose their actions randomly. In our Game I, there is a unique equilibrium in mixed strategies, which gives an equal chance of winning to each player. The probabilities of choosing **L** respectively **R** for the kicker and the goalkeeper, respectively, in Game I are:

$$(x, 1 - x) = (0.5, 0.5) \text{ and}$$

$$(y, 1 - y) = (0.5, 0.5). \tag{1}$$

Clearly, when following these strategies, each player chooses a best response against the opponent's strategy. The resulting equilibrium payoffs for the goalkeeper and the kicker, respectively, are calculated as the expected payoffs given the equilibrium strategies and can be interpreted as probabilities of success. For Game I, these payoffs are given by

$$\Pi_G = \Pi_K = 0.5 \qquad (2)$$

for the goalkeeper and the kicker, respectively.

Randomization is a strategic device to make sure that there is no recognizable pattern in the behaviour of a player that could be exploited by the opponent to his detriment. The *Fundamental Lemma* (see e.g. Osborne 2004, Chapter 4) characterizes mixed strategy equilibria of finite games as follows:

> A mixed strategy profile is a (mixed strategy) Nash equilibrium, if and only if, for each player, the expected payoff to every action to which a player's strategy assigns positive probability is the same (and at least the expected payoff to any action which is assigned zero probability).

So, any player's expected payoff in equilibrium is his expected payoff to any of his actions that he chooses with positive probability. A player is thus indifferent between these actions; more precisely, he is *made* indifferent by the opponent's behaviour, to which all these pure strategies are best replies. And this aim in turn determines the choice of probabilities by the opponent. Randomization does not imply, however, that a player actually flips a coin, he may still choose a pure strategy. But his mixed strategy represents a consistent way to reason about the opponent's behaviour (who may have several best replies against this strategy). There are empirical studies of mixed equilibrium play in soccer by Chiappori et al. (2002), Palacios-Huerta (2003), Moschini (2004), and Sonnabend (2006), and in tennis by Walker and Wooders (2001). A survey of empirical and experimental studies on mixed-equilibrium play related to penalty taking in soccer is provided by Sonnabend (2006). The interpretation of behaviour as game-theoretic *equilibrium* behaviour separates these studies (as well as ours) from Azar and Bar-Eli (Chapter 6), who study actions of goal-keepers exclusively by treating them as *individual* decisions under uncertainty.

We finally note that, mainly because of this random element in the strategies, penalty shootouts have been criticized as an unsatisfactory way to decide a soccer game. However, later in this paper, we will develop a more realistic model, in which the players' skills affect the probability of success, so that the outcome is still influenced but not entirely determined by randomness.

Stability and Institutional Design

The institutional context is critical to game-theoretic analysis. Optimal strategies depend on the rules of the game, on the assumed payoff structure, and on the set of strategies available to the players. Game theoretic equilibrium identifies mutually stable strategies within a given institution, but equilibrium analysis typically does not address the stability of the institutions themselves. The mutual stability of institutions and behavioural patterns can be addressed in evolutionary models, where institutions and behaviour are allowed to affect each other through co-evolution; see e.g. Güth and Ockenfels (2003, 2005). Here we want to emphasize evolution of institutions through *behavioural innovation*, which affects the set of strategies available to the players *within* the rules of soccer as specified by the governing bodies. In particular, we emphasize that the simple game studied above, is not stable against the introduction of a new behaviour of the kicker, namely, opting for the middle of the goal. If the goalkeeper insists on opting for corners exclusively, this would guarantee success for the kicker choosing middle, **M**. Consequently, the goalkeeper is forced to consider strategy **M** as well and a new game, Game II, results:

G \ K		y_1	y_2	y_3
		L	M	R
x_1	L	1,0	0,1	0,1
x_2	M	0,1	1,0	0,1
x_3	R	0,1	0,1	1,0

Figure 2: Game II—A penalty game which includes the middle strategy.

The analysis of this 3x3-game confirms that the kicker *gains* from the introduction of **M** *in equilibrium* as equilibrium strategies are now given by $(x_1, x_2, x_3) = (y_1, y_2, y_3) = (1/3, 1/3, 1/3)$.

Note that the kicker, who succeeds in six of the nine possible instances in discoordinating actions, now has a probability of success, which is twice the one of the goalkeeper, who (as before) only succeeds on the diagonal in coordinating actions. The reason is that equilibrium strategies make the realization of all nine instances equally likely. This *reduces* the expected payoff of the goalkeeper from 1/2 in the previous game to 1/3 and *increases* the payoff of the kicker from 1/2 to 2/3: $\Pi_G = 1/3$ and $\Pi_K = 2/3$. The point is that this advantage for the kicker survives the *best* response of the goalkeeper (to the *best* behaviour of the kicker).

We credit Johan Neeskens, a Dutch midfielder playing for Ajax Amsterdam and FC Barcelona in the 1970s, with this clever innovation, which gradually changed the *perception* of the essence of the penalty game by kicker *and* goalkeeper from a 2x2 to a 3x3 game. E.g., the German site of "Wikipedia" mentions that ever since the 1974 World Cup Final, Neeskens is credited by soccer commentaries as the inventor of the *Neeskens-variant* ('Neeskens-Variante') of taking a penalty: shooting straight to the middle, while the goalkeeper dives for a corner (http://de.wikipedia.org/wiki/Johan_Neeskens). In this game the referee awarded a penalty to the Netherlands against Germany in the second minute of the game, which Neeskens had the nerve to take in precisely this way – while Sepp Maier, the German goal-keeper, opted for his right corner. As mentioned by "Wikipedia" the double prominence of the occasion, a penalty in the second minute of a World Cup Final, propelled the *Neeskens-variant* to international prominence and recognition as a valid and serious option for taking a penalty. It is not known to us, whether there ever was a penalty at a similarly important or internationally prominent occasion, which was (intentionally?) taken this way before.

However, there was another—and now in Germany equally historical—penalty taken this way at an almost equally important and prominent occasion two years later: the last penalty of the penalty shoot-out that decided the final of the European Championships in 1976 between Germany and Tchechoslovakia. It was taken by Antonin Panenka, who delicately chipped the ball right into the middle of the goal mouth—while Sepp Maier opted for his left corner. Panenka undoubtedly did so intentionally. He later said: "I knew long before that I would take the penalty this way." His own goalkeeper warned him the night before the final that—if the occasion should arise—doing so would be "too arrogant." Panenka himself was aware of the risk: "If Maier would have stayed put, they would have sent me to the factories for the next 25 years. The communists would have accused me of ridiculing their system" (Martens, 2003). Alas, it went well to the fame of Panenka (and the Neeskens-variant).

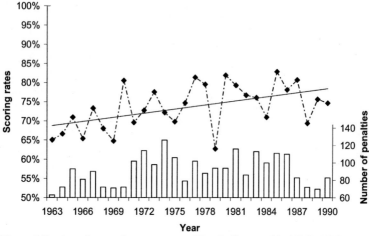

Figure 3:Total numbers and success rates of Bundesliga penalties 1963-1990.

These observations lead us to the following claim: *before* 1974 (and the Neeskens-penalty) the 'institution' penalty-duel was a standard of behaviour, according to which kickers chose **L** or **R** and goalkeepers did likewise. That is, a 2x2-game form gives an adequate description of the penalty situation. *After* 1976 (and the Panenka-penalty) the 'institution' penalty-duel was perceived as a 3x3 game form constrained by certain behavioural rules.

In order to check for the empirical validity of our claim, we tried to get adequate data from penalty kicks and shootouts before Neeskens' and after Panenka's goal. However, although we spoke to Bundesliga and national goalkeepers, journalists, TV stations, professional sports data providers, many scientists, and others, we could not trace detailed data that include information about the players' strategies and sufficient data from penalties before 1974. What we have, however, are the following summary statistics of Bundesliga penalties from 1963-1990 (Resource: Bundesliga Datenbank, Ismaning).

Figure 3 shows scoring rates (points, left y-axis) and total number of penalties (bars, right y-axis) per season in the German Bundesliga between 1963 and 1990. The overall success rate of penalty kicks is 74%, ranging from 62% (1963) to 82% (1985). The average success rate from 1963 to 1973 is 69%, and the average success rate 1977-1987 is 77%. (Hence we interpret the first period of ten years as pre-Neeskens and the second (after Panenka's penalty) as past-Neeskens). Applying an exact Mann Whitney

U test, this difference is significant at the 1% level (two-sided). The same test yields a two-sided $p = 0.013$ if we compare the 1963-1974 with 1975-1990.

The graph in Figure 3 suggests, however, that the difference is at least partly due a general trend (the straight line shows the result of a simple linear regression), which might be due to the evolution of the equipment, or abilities and training methods; in fact, statistics cannot reveal a structural break in the mid seventies, which would be an indicator that Neeskens' innovation caused a significant advantage for the kicker. However, it might also be that Neeskens' innovation diffused only slowly over time, so that our data would be too rough to detect supportive evidence for our claim. An ultimate test must be left to further research based on more detailed data about shot and jump directions before and after 1974.

Opting for Alternative M: Why is the Middle Relatively Unattractive to Players?

While there is anecdotic evidence, there is no statistically unambiguous evidence in our data that Neeskens' innovation significantly changed the way penalty kicks were executed.

Several statistical tests applied to our limited data from the Bundesliga could not reveal a structural break in the mid-seventies. Part of the reason might be that the middle is a less attractive strategy than the corners to both, kicker and goalkeeper: Based on data from 459 penalties from French and Italian League 1997-2000, Chiappori et al. (2002) found that

- the kicker chooses middle less often than either corner,
- the goalkeeper chooses middle less often than either corner, and
- the goalkeeper chooses middle less often than the kicker (in fact, goalkeepers almost never stay in the middle).

As a consequence, kicking to the middle on average has the highest probability of scoring (81.0% as compared to 70.1% for the right corner and 76.7% for the left corner; see Table 4 in Chiappori et al. 2002). Obviously, these observations are not in line with our simple model of Game II, which suggests that the middle should be as attractive as each of the corners. They also appear inconsistent with the Fundamental Lemma described above: in equilibrium, the expected payoff to every action to which a player's strategy assigns positive probability should be the same.

Chiappori et al. (2002) explain some of these effects with heterogeneity with respect to the players' capabilities to score when choosing one of the three strategies, left, right and middle. For instance, it is typically easier for a kicker to score when kicking to the converse side of his strong foot. This heterogeneity can explain why certain strategies are more often chosen than others by certain kickers. But it cannot explain the superior average scoring rate for the middle strategy. So we suspect that heterogeneity is only part of the explanation.

In order to find out more about why the middle seems a rather unattractive strategy despite the strategic advantage of using it, we asked Harald 'Toni' Schumacher and Hans-Jörg Butt about their strategies in penalties. Toni Schumacher is considered one of the world's best goalkeepers during the 1980s and was capped 76 times for Germany. We interviewed Schumacher on 21 August 2006 in Cologne. Hans-Jörg Butt is an active goalkeeper, who was playing in the Bundesliga for Bayer Leverkusen. He is most remarkable—and unique—among German goal keepers, because he is not only considered a 'penalty killer'—"Wikipedia" notes that he on average saves 7 out of 10 penalties—, but at the same time one of the most successful penalty *takers*. He had 26 Bundesliga goals from the penalty spot to his credit, when he moved to the Portuguese club of Benfica Lisbon in 2007. So, if anyone knows how to put himself into the opponent's shoes, it is him. Our meeting with Hans-Jörg Butt took place on 31 August 2006 in Leverkusen.

Both goalkeepers confirm that there is heterogeneity among kickers, though the classifications they use are quite different. Toni Schumacher mentioned that there are four types of kickers distinguishable according to whether they shoot with the left or right foot, and whether the shot is powerful or more technically demanding. A powerful shot from a right-footer, for instance, would most likely go to the left corner. Hans-Jörg Butt, on the other hand, classifies kickers according to whether they try to react to goalkeepers, or whether they choose the corner independent of the movements of the goalkeeper. So, there is heterogeneity—implying that we should not observe equal probabilities for choosing the actions right, middle and left. At the same time, however, both goalkeepers suggested that the unattractiveness of the middle-strategy is also driven by an asymmetric *payoff* structure, which has not been considered in earlier work. Toni Schumacher, for instance, noted that he *never* just stayed in the middle. Asked why, he responded that this would be "against my honour." When we remarked that, knowing this, a kicker's best response would be to shoot in the middle, he answered that a kicker, who shoots in the middle, "does not deserve to kick a penalty against me," and that this would be "a different game" (sic!). While Hans-Jörg Butt also pointed out that there are technical difficulties with shooting to the middle ("schippen"), he reasoned that it is a larger "disaster" for the kicker when a shot to the middle is saved (recall Panenka's statement!), than it is a disaster for the goalkeeper when he does not save a shot to the middle. A kicker, who gets caught with middle, is a "fool" ("Depp"). Both views indicate that the payoffs associated with corner and middle actions need to be treated differently.

The following variation of Game II incorporates Butt's argument, the new game has an asymmetric, but still constant-sum payoff structure; i.e. the goalie gains from making the kicker look like a fool:

G \ K		y_1 L	y_2 M	y_3 R
x_1	L	1,0	0,1	0,1
x_2	M	0,1	$1+b,-b$	0,1
x_3	R	0,1	0,1	1,0

Figure 4: Game III—A penalty game with modified payoffs.

The following table gives equilibrium strategies for different values of the parameter $b > 0$:

Table 1: Equilibrium strategies for Game III.

	$b=0$	$b=\dfrac{1}{2}$	$b = 1$	$b = \infty$
x^*	$\left(\dfrac{1}{3},\dfrac{1}{3},\dfrac{1}{3}\right)$	$\left(\dfrac{3}{8},\dfrac{1}{4},\dfrac{3}{8}\right)$	$\left(\dfrac{2}{5},\dfrac{1}{5},\dfrac{2}{5}\right)$	$\left(\dfrac{1}{2},0,\dfrac{1}{2}\right)$
y^*	$\left(\dfrac{1}{3},\dfrac{1}{3},\dfrac{1}{3}\right)$	$\left(\dfrac{3}{8},\dfrac{1}{4},\dfrac{3}{8}\right)$	$\left(\dfrac{2}{5},\dfrac{1}{5},\dfrac{2}{5}\right)$	$\left(\dfrac{1}{2},0,\dfrac{1}{2}\right)$

The general formulae for the unique mixed strategy equilibrium of Game III and the equilibrium payoffs are given by

$$x^* = (x_1, x_2, x_3) = ((1 + b)/(3 + 2b), 1/(3 + 2b), (1 + b)/(3 + 2b)) \quad (3)$$

$$y^* = (y_1, y_2, y_3) = ((1 + b)/(3 + 2b), 1/(3 + 2b),(1 + b)/(3 + 2b)),$$

and the equilibrium payoffs are :

$$\Pi_G = (1 + b)/(3 + 2b) \text{ and}$$

$$\Pi_K = (2 + b)/(3 + 2b). \quad (4)$$

The equilibrium is symmetric, **M** is used less and less often with increasing b in favour of **L** and **R**, and the kicker gets a higher payoff than the goalkeeper for all b. The extreme values for b yield our Games I and II: $b = 0$ obviously results in Game II, while, interestingly, b going to infinity yields *equilibrium play* of Game I (which is a 2x2-game) in this 3x3-game. The unique mixed strategy equilibrium in this limiting case is no more completely mixed. It only mixes over the corner strategies **L** and **R**, which are the only strategies in Game I. Butt's argument therefore accounts for the different treatment of corner and middle options by the two players. Azar and Bar-Eli (Chapter 6), who only look at goalkeepers' behaviour, explain the lower choice frequency of **M** as an "action bias", which distorts preferences towards "action" (jump) and against "inaction" (stay in the middle).

Alternatively, consider yet another variation, Game IV. Suppose that there is some uncertainty as to whether a penalty is actually saved when both, kicker and goalkeeper choose the same corner. This uncertainty is represented by t in [0,1], where t represents the capability of the kicker; i.e. $t = 1$ implies that the kicker always scores when kicking to one of the corners, even when the goalkeeper jumps to the same side. Kicking to the middle will not score when the goalkeeper chooses to remain in the middle, however. Accordingly, $t = 0$ implies that the kicker never scores when the goalkeeper jumps to the same side, because, say, the kicker cannot shoot sufficiently powerful and accurate (as was implicitly assumed in the Games I-III). In this sense, t represents the quality of the kicker.

G \ K		y_1	y_2	y_3
		L	M	R
x_1	L	$1-t,t$	0,1	0,1
x_2	M	0,1	1,0	0,1
x_3	R	$0,1$	$0,1$	$1-t,t$

Figure 5: Game IV—An equivalent penalty game with modified payoffs.

Dependent on t equilibrium strategies are given by

$$x^* = (x_1, x_2, x_3) = (1/(3-t), (1-t)/(3-t), 1/(3-t)) \qquad (5)$$

$$y^* = (y_1, y_2, y_3) = (1/(3-t), (1-t)/(3-t), 1/(3-t))$$

and payoffs by

$$\Pi_G = (1-t)/(3-t) \text{ and}$$

$$\Pi_K = 2/(3-t). \qquad (6)$$

By inspection of (5) and (6), and perhaps somewhat surprisingly, this story yields the *same* prediction for equilibrium behaviour as (3) and (4) did for Game III before: Game II now corresponds to the extreme value $t = 0$, and *equilibrium play* of Game I follows for $t = 1$. But note that the equilibrium payoffs in the latter case are now 0 (for the goalkeeper) and 1 (for the kicker). Perfect kickers ($t = 1$) never miss, if they aim for a corner (irrespective of the goalkeepers action). So Game IV, too, may account for the relative unattractiveness of the strategy **M**. An outside observer could not say, whether observed behaviour (frequency of actions by each player) results from equilibrium play of Game III according to (3) with parameter b or of Game IV according to (5) with parameter $t = b/(1 + b)$ as both games determine equilibrium identically (!) under this condition. In fact, both games (and hence interpretations) are strategically equivalent: the payoffs in Game IV can be obtained by an affine transformation of the payoffs in Game III, which means they must have the same (mixed strategy) equilibria.

Once realized, this should not be too surprising to the reader. The more reliably a kicker can score by shooting to one of the corners, the greater the *relative* disaster from being unsuccessful when shooting to the middle and the larger the payoff to the goalkeeper to have succeeded against a high-quality kicker. In the end, both payoff presentations tell the same story from two different angles. In equilibrium then the *same* behaviour is required to level *relative* advantages of pure strategies in a mixed strategy equilibrium according to the Fundamental Lemma (see above). Game IV, too, may be regarded as an institutionally changed version of a 2x2 game:

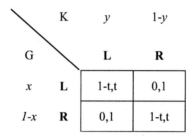

Figure 6: Game V—Another penalty game with modified payoffs.

Comparing the 3x3 Game IV with the 2x2 Game V yields a slightly different, but related story for the unattractiveness of the middle strategy. Game V is identical to Game IV with the exception that the middle strategy is not present. That is, by comparing the equilibrium outcomes of Game V with the outcomes of Game IV, we can again measure the effect of having the middle strategy available.

In equilibrium of Game V, the probability of choosing **L** or **R** is $x^* = y^* = \frac{1}{2}$ for both players (and all t from [0,1]). The scoring probabilities (equilibrium payoffs) for goalkeeper and kicker, respectively, are $\Pi_G = (1 - t)/2$ and $\Pi_K = (1 + t)/2$. Observe that the kicker's payoff ranges from $1/2$ for $t = 0$ to 1 for $t = 1$.

Comparison of equilibrium payoffs in Games IV and V yields that $2/(3 - t) - (1 + t)/2 = (1 - t)^2/(6 - 2t) > 0$ for all t in [0,1). Hence, the introduction of **M** to the strategy sets of the penalty game works in favour of the kicker. Yet, a high quality kicker (t large) only stands to profit marginally from the availability of the middle strategy and hence uses it rarely when indeed it is available. For instance, comparing scoring probabilities to the kicker in both games, we obtain:

- For $t = 0$ the scoring probability increases from 1/2 to 2/3.
- For $t = \frac{1}{2}$ the scoring probability increases from 0.80 to 0.87.
- For $t = 0.80$ the scoring probability increases from 0.90 to below 0.91.
- For $t = 1$ the scoring probability in both cases is 1.

Assume now that kickers have private information about their quality t. Then, each shot reveals information about the payoffs involved, and thus about the kicker's quality. In particular, a shot to the middle decreases the estimation of a kicker's t (This might mirror Toni Schumacher's statement that considering shots to the middle would involve a "different game."). A testable hypothesis from this might be that amateur soccer players, with smaller skill values t, shoot to the middle more often than professionals. For this reason, kickers may hesitate to choose the middle.

Explaining the Players' different uses of M

So far, in all equilibria of all games kickers and goalkeepers opted for **M** with the *same* probability. However, Chiappori et al. (2002) remarked that goalkeepers very rarely chose **M** compared to kickers. In their data, only 11 out of 459 goalkeepers remained in the middle, while 79 out of 459 kickers chose to kick to the middle. This is in line with the statements of both, Toni Schumacher and Hans-Jörg Butt, who stressed that staying in the middle is a very unlikely strategy for goalkeepers. Schumacher's further elaboration, that a shot to the middle, whether successful or not, discredits a kicker with dishonourable or "un(sports)manly" behaviour, takes the argument further: the following model captures this new aspect without increasing the number of parameters compared to our Games III and IV. The new Game VI reflects the idea that not only missing in the middle is bad for the kicker, but also *scoring* to the middle yields smaller payoffs to the kicker than scoring by shooting to one of the corners. This yields the following *non*-constant-sum game, which nevertheless is strictly competitive:

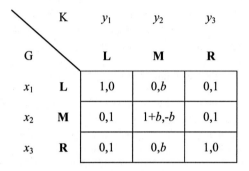

Figure 7: Game VI—A non-constant-sum penalty game.

Table 2 gives equilibrium strategies for some values of the parameter b:

Table 2: Equilibrium strategies for Game VI.

	b = 1	b = 0.8	b = 0.6	b = 0.5
x^*	$\left(\dfrac{2}{5},\dfrac{1}{5},\dfrac{2}{5}\right)$	$(0.43, 0.14, 0.43)$	$(0.47, 0.06, 0.47)$	$\left(\dfrac{1}{2},0,\dfrac{1}{2}\right)$
y^*	$\left(\dfrac{2}{5},\dfrac{1}{5},\dfrac{2}{5}\right)$	$(0.39, 0.22, 0.39)$	$(0.38, 0.24, 0.38)$	$\left(\dfrac{3}{8},\dfrac{1}{4},\dfrac{3}{8}\right)$

The formula for equilibrium strategies reads:

$$(x_1, x_2, x_3) = \left(\frac{1+b}{4b+1}, \frac{2b-1}{4b+1}, \frac{1+b}{4b+1}\right)$$
$$(y_1, y_2, y_3) = \left(\frac{1+b}{3+2b}, \frac{1}{3+2b}, \frac{1+b}{3+2b}\right) \tag{7}$$

For the relevant parameter range $0.5 < b < 1$ (4) tells us, that both players use **M** less often than **L** or **R**, and the goalkeeper less often than the kicker. At the extreme value $b = 1$ (scoring to the middle is as good as scoring to a corner) both players use middle with the same probability. A decrease in b, i.e. making scoring to the middle less attractive than scoring to a corner, leads to *less* frequent use of **M** by the goalkeeper and *more* frequent use by the kicker. These – at first sight counterintuitive consequences – are once more easily understood by the content of the Fundamental Lemma about the strategic interaction in mixed strategy equilibrium: the decreased attractiveness of **M** to the kicker has to be offset by the goalkeeper with a balancing decrease in attractiveness of **L** and **R** in order to restore indifference for the kicker between all options. The goalkeeper does so by choosing **L** and **R** *more* often at the expense of choosing **M**. This more than offsets the lost attractiveness of **M** to the kicker, who now opts for **M** *more* often. At the other extreme ($b = \frac{1}{2}$) this argument drives the goalkeeper to *always* choosing **L** or **R** (and hence *never* going for **M**). Because of the relative unattractiveness of scoring to the middle, the kicker uses **M** nevertheless only with probability $\frac{1}{4}$.

Still, for all b in (0.5, 1) it is true, that the kicker's payoff in equilibrium exceeds the goalkeeper's payoff:

$$\Pi_G = (4b^2+5b+1)/[(4b+1)(3+2b)] < \Pi_K = (4b^2+8b+1)/[(4b+1)(3+2b)]$$

More importantly, the scoring probability is larger than $\frac{1}{2}$, and varies between $15/24 = 0.625$ for $b = \frac{1}{2}$ and $16/25 = 0.64$ for $b = 1$.

This simple one-parameter model captures the essential features of the data, in particular with respect to the strategy **M**, and confirms Neeskens' intuition that establishing the middle alternative as a valid option for the kicker results in an *advantage* for the kicker. It increases the probability of scoring *in equilibrium*, when both players behave optimally according to the recommendations of game theory.

Conclusions

Game theory is shown to be a powerful tool to analyze and describe strategic behaviour in the penalty-duel. We, in particular, emphasize that game theoretic advice and predictions depend critically on the exact characterization of not only the underlying game pattern but also the perceptions of this by the players. In more sociological terms, a penalty-duel interlocks the *roles* of kicker and goalkeeper in an interactive decision situation. Analysis of the institution penalty-duel as a game does not only require to model the objective rules of the game as determined by the FIFA, but also the players' expectations about how the different roles are supposed to perform. Identifying such games can be difficult. Players may change their behaviour and hence the way the institution is perceived over time, they may even differ in their perceptions of the game being played at a given time; and the perceptions may differ between insiders, who are actually playing the game, and outsiders, who are trying to understand behaviour.

In game theory players reason to find an optimal strategy by taking the game as given. However, understanding the (equilibrium) interaction is only part of the art of playing games. Neeskens and Panenka demonstrated that going beyond shared perceptions of how to play the game (i.e. fulfil the roles of the institution), and devising new, innovative strategies may yield a competitive edge. They possibly changed the way penalty-kicks are perceived in a permanent way. Their innovation accounts for and answers to the growing competitiveness of professional sports—and in particular soccer—due to increased commercialization. While game theory may capture the consequences of institutional change created by innovators such as Neeskens and Panenka, it cannot as easily portray creativity in institutional design, because that would have to start with a description of all conceivably available strategies.

Breaking out of conventions and (re)shaping the way institutions are perceived can, of course, also be a clever strategy with long-lasting effects in economic and social environments. There is a growing literature on such economic design challenges; see, e.g., Roth (2002) or Kittsteiner and Ockenfels (2006) for selective reviews. Also, there appears to be more room for institutional design in penalty taking. Toni Schumacher and Hans-Jörg Butt mentioned many other strategies that add to the institutional complexity and that are neither considered by the game models in this paper, nor by any other game theoretic approaches to penalty taking that we are aware of. Toni Schumacher, for instance, mentioned that a couple of 'signals' from the kicker helped him to save penalties, such as the line of sight after the kicker has put the ball on the penalty spot, or the position of the foot of the supporting leg. Both goalkeepers also noted that they tried to make the kicker insecure. Toni Schumacher (Hans Jörg Butt) mentioned, for instance, that he would lean towards the corner which he did (not) choose, or that he sometimes offered the kicker a bet. Moreover, Hans Jörg Butt gave an intriguing account of his strategies as a penalty taker and goalkeeper, which suggests that a penalty duel could be modelled as a waiting game. It is exactly these kinds of subtleties that seem to make the duel interesting.

Another conclusion from our study is that even if players perceive institutions differently, they might in fact play the same game, with perfectly equivalent incentive structures. So, different perceptions do not necessarily exclude standard game theoretic analyses. However, game theoretic analysis must take the perceptions of the players seriously. We demonstrate how a number of empirical observations and statements by goalkeepers (and a kicker) about the attractiveness of the middle option in penalty taking can be accounted for by an equilibrium analysis of the penalty duel with modified payoffs. Kickers and goalkeepers do not only have preferences on the outcome of the game, goal or not goal, but also on the way the kick is taken or saved, which has to do with the perception of their roles. Although new behaviour in a role may become legitimate, it need not be perceived as acceptable as the traditional one. More specifically, our study strongly suggests that a shot or even goal to the middle is evaluated differently than a shot or goal to a corner by both, goalkeepers and kickers. We show for the first time, that this observation has great explanatory power for actual behaviour.

References

Azar, O. and M. Bar-Eli (2008). "Biased Decisions of Professional Football Players: Do Goalkeepers Dive too Often for Penalty Kicks?" In *Myths and facts about football: The economics and psychology of the world's greatest sport*. P. Andersson, P. Ayton and C. Schmidt. eds. Cambridge: Cambridge Scholars Press.

Chiappori P.-A., S. Levitt and T. Groseclose (2002). "Testing Mixed Strategy Equilibrium when Players are Heterogeneous: The Case of Penalty Kicks in Soccer." *American Economic Review*, 92(4), 1138-1151.

Güth, W. and A. Ockenfels (2003). "The Coevolution of Trust and Institutions in Anonymous and Non-anonymous Communities." In *Jahrbuch für Neue Politische Ökonomie 20*. M. J. Holler et al. eds. Tübingen: Mohr Siebeck, 157-174.

Güth, W. and A. Ockenfels (2005). "The Coevolution of Morality and Legal Institutions: An Indirect Evolutionary Approach." *Journal of Institutional Economics*, 1(2), 155-174.

Kittsteiner, T. and A. Ockenfels (2006). "Market Design: A Selective Review." *Zeitschrift für Betriebswirtschaft*, Special Issue 5, 121-143.

Martens, R. (2003). *Elfmeter! Kleine Geschichte einer Standardsituation*. Frankfurt a. M.: Eichborn Verlag.

Moschini, G. (2004). "Nash Equilibrium in Strictly Competitive Games: Live Play in Soccer." *Economics Letters*, 85(3), 365-371.

Osborne, M. (2004). *An Introduction to Game Theory*. New York: Oxford University Press.

Palacios-Huerta, I. (2003). "Professionals Play Minimax." *Review of Economic Studies*, 70(2), 395-415.

Roth, A. E. (2002). "The Economist as Engineer: Game Theory, Experimental Economics and Computation as Tools of Design Economics." *Econometrica*, 70(4), 1341-1378.

Sonnabend, H. (2006). *Testing the Empirical Validity of Mixed-Strategy Equilibria: Penalty Kicks in German Professional Soccer*. Diploma Thesis: University of Bonn.

Walker, M. and J. Wooders (2001). "Minimax Play at Wimbledon." *American Economic Review*, 91(5), 1521-1538.

CHAPTER SIX

BIASED DECISIONS OF PROFESSIONAL FOOTBALL PLAYERS: DO GOALKEEPERS DIVE TOO OFTEN FOR PENALTY KICKS?

OFER H. AZAR AND MICHAEL BAR-ELI[1]

Penalty kicks in football occur either after certain offences or at the end of the game, to untie a game or a match, in certain tournaments (including the World Cup, the European Championships and many other leading tournaments). A kick is shot from the penalty mark which is located eleven meters from the goal and no player other than the goalkeeper is allowed to stand between the goal and the penalty mark, thus giving the kicker a very high probability of success in scoring a goal. Because of the short distance between the ball and the goal and because of the high speed of the ball during penalty kicks, the goalkeeper generally cannot afford to wait until he sees clearly to which direction the ball is kicked (according to Palacios-Huerta (2003), the time it takes the ball to get from the penalty mark to the goal is about 0.3 seconds). Consequently, the goalkeeper has to make a decision whether to dive to one of the sides

[1] Azar: Department of Business Administration, Guilford Glazer School of Business and Management, Ben-Gurion University of the Negev, P.O.B. 653, Beer-Sheva 84105, Israel. Bar-Eli: Department of Business Administration, Guilford Glazer School of Business and Management, Ben-Gurion University of the Negev, P.O.B. 653, Beer-Sheva 84105, Israel. This chapter is part of a bigger project on penalty kicks, and is partially based on data and analysis reported in Bar-Eli et al. (2007a). We are very grateful to our collaborators in the project, Ilana Ritov, Yael Keidar-Levin, and Galit Schein, for their help and contribution. We also thank two anonymous reviewers and the editors of this volume, Patric Andersson, Peter Ayton and Carsten Schmidt, for helpful comments and suggestions. Finally, we are grateful to Galit Dori for excellent research assistance and to the goalkeepers who agreed to dedicate their valuable time and participate in our study.

or to stay in the centre at about the same time that the kicker chooses where to direct the kick. This creates a simple but interesting real-life example of decision making under uncertainty: the goalkeeper has to choose whether to dive to the right, the left or to stay in the centre, in order to minimise the risk of a goal being scored, under uncertainty regarding the direction of the ball.

Because a goal achieved in a penalty kick counts as any other goal and because the number of goals scored in an average football game is small[2], the importance of the goalkeeper's (as well as the kicker's) performance during the penalty kick is tremendous. World Cup and European Championships matches have been won on more than one occasion by the results of penalty kicks (either during the game or following a tied game), for example.

Not only the outcome of the game might depend on the goalkeeper's and kicker's performance during a penalty kick, but also huge amounts of money can be affected by the outcome of penalty kicks. Players receive bonuses for winning games, teams can make large amounts of money by winning and climbing to the next stage of a tournament and the goalkeeper's reputation and thus future earnings also depend on his performance, to give a few examples.[3] Since players in top leagues earn hundreds of thousands and often millions of dollars annually, it is clear that the goalkeeper's performance and reputation have a very significant monetary effect and the goalkeeper has huge incentives to do his best throughout the game and in penalty kicks in particular.

---

[2] For example, in the Korea/Japan 2002 World Cup, an average of 2.52 goals per match were scored, see http://www.fifa.com/images/pdf/IP-301_12A_comparative.pdf. In the 2006/7 season, the average number of goals in the European top leagues was as follows: England–2.45, France–2.25, Germany–2.74, Holland–2.99, Italy–2.55 and Spain–2.48 (see www.footballstats.com).
[3] Because football is a very prominent sport in many countries, the monetary amounts involved are also huge. For example, Manchester United had in 2004 revenues of 169.1 million British Pounds, and staff costs of 76.9 million Pounds (Manchester United Annual Report, 2004, accessed online at www.manutd.com). A couple of years ago, Malcolm Glazer, an American Businessman, paid 790 million GBP to purchase more than 75% of the group's shares (Rachlevsky, 2005). To get an idea about how Manchester United's numbers compare with more aggregate football revenues, we note that Manchester United sold 1.29 million seats in home games in the UK first league during the 2004 season, whereas in total 54.7 million seats were sold during the 2004 season in the first leagues of France, Denmark, Germany, Holland, Italy, Spain and the UK (the attendance data were taken from www.footballstats.com and include only regular league matches in the first league in these countries).

Consequently, penalty kicks exhibit a decision problem with huge incentives, making it very intriguing to find whether expert goalkeepers exhibit any deviation from rational decision making. In particular, we conjectured that goalkeepers choose to dive to one of the sides (rather than to stay in the centre) during a penalty kick more than is optimal.[4] We wanted to examine systematically whether this conjecture is correct and if it is, to provide possible explanations for it. The decisions of the kicker and the goalkeeper—where to shoot and dive, respectively—are also associated with time pressure and instant responses and therefore share many characteristics of "naturalistic decision making" (see Klein, 1999).

Despite the fact that goalkeeping involves decision making (see for example the football goalkeeping coaching guidelines in Welsh (1990), the area of goalkeepers' decision making is still under-researched. One aspect of goalkeepers' behaviour that did receive some attention is their behaviour during penalty kicks. For example, Chiappori et al. (2002), Palacios-Huerta (2003) and Azar and Bar-Eli (2005) studied the behaviour of goalkeepers and kickers during penalty kicks and examined whether they match the predictions of game theory and in particular the mixed-strategy Nash equilibrium. Leininger and Ockenfels (Chapter 5) also analyse penalty kicks using game theory. They discuss, among other things, how the game is modified when instead of just two options–left and right–the kicker and the goalkeeper have three options: left, right and centre. Leininger and Ockenfels (Chapter 5) claim that adding the option to kick to the centre improves the average scoring rate of the kicker. Others studied cognitive processes such as anticipation, cue utilisation and response time (see for example McMorris and Colenso, 1996, Morris and Burwitz, 1989 and Savelsbergh et al., 2002).

A great number of studies involving subjective judgment of decision outcomes found that the evaluation of an outcome depends not only on the outcome itself, but also on the way in which this outcome came about. Thus, in a series of studies, Kahneman and Tversky (1982) found that

---

[4] It is often possible to rationalise various behaviours by adding to the utility function of the decision maker non-traditional elements (from the perspective of economics) such as psychological motivations (see Bar-Eli et al., 2007b). Then it becomes tricky to define whether certain behaviour is optimal or biased. We follow here the idea that the team's objective is to maximise its chances to win the game. This requires that the goalkeeper will maximise the chances to stop penalty kicks. We therefore treat any behaviour of the goalkeeper that deviates from maximizing the stopping chances as non-optimal or biased, even though such biased behaviour can be rationalised if we assume that the goalkeeper is not interested only in the question whether a goal was scored.

people feel a more poignant emotional reaction to bad outcomes that result from actions relative to otherwise identical outcomes that did not involve actions.

Kahneman and Miller (1986) proposed the norm theory to explain the above phenomena. According to this theory, outcomes are perceived as worse when people can easily imagine that a better outcome could have occurred. They further assume that in general it is easier to mentally "undo" an action that had occurred than to imagine having taken an action when none had occurred. Consequently, the reaction to outcomes of action is stronger than the reactions to outcomes of inaction (omissions). Consistent with this proposal, Ritov and Baron (1990, 1992, 1995) showed, in a series of investigations, that people tend to judge acts that are harmful (relative to the alternative option) as worse than omissions that are equally harmful (relative to the alternative) or even more harmful (for a review, see Baron, 1994). This effect was labelled the "omission bias" (see also Kordes-de Vaal, 1996).

While the explanation of Kahneman and Miller (1986) is based on the idea that people can more easily imagine the alternative to action than to inaction, in some situations actions (rather than inaction) are the norm. We might expect, according to the rationale behind the norm theory, that in those cases it would be harder to think of an alternative to the action than to inaction. Consequently, norm theory would predict that in such circumstances an "action" rather than an "omission" bias would occur: people would prefer to choose an act that leads to a negative outcome than to choose inaction that leads to the same outcome. Confirming this prediction–and in line with some previous research (Ritov and Baron, 1990 and Spranca et al., 1991) Ritov and Baron (1994) demonstrated that when actions were more expected than inaction, adverse outcomes of failure to act were judged worse than identical outcomes of action (see also Miller and Taylor, 1995).

We hypothesised that the goalkeeper's behaviour during penalty kicks in football may be affected, at least partly, by preference for action (an "action bias"). The grave consequences of the action bias in this context can be demonstrated by the 1974 World Cup final game, when Neeskens of The Netherlands kicked to the goal's centre, but West Germany's goalkeeper Maier dived left and missed the ball. The French past national goalkeeper Bernard Lama often claimed that in many occasions where he managed to save a penalty, he simply did not dive. Ironically, his team, Paris Saint-Germain, lost the European Cup final game in 1997 to Barcelona, as a result of a penalty kick shot by Ronaldo to the centre–and missed by the diving Lama.

The norm, as the data we collected reveals (and as we confirmed also in an additional study reported below), is to dive to either side (rather than to stay in the centre). Consequently, according to the norm theory, goalkeepers would experience a bad outcome (not stopping a penalty kick) more strongly when it results from not obeying the norm (staying in the centre) rather than from obeying the norm (diving). That is, goalkeepers would feel more regret when they do not stop a penalty kick if they did not dive than if they dived. Therefore we hypothesised that goalkeepers would choose to dive more than is optimal, exhibiting an "action bias". The analysis in the following sections shows that this conjecture was supported by data we collected on penalty kicks. Thus, our study supports the predictions of the norm theory where the norm is to act rather than to prefer inaction. Moreover, the study does so in a natural setting (as opposed to a lab setting) and in a context where incentives for making correct decision are huge, supporting the claim that biases in behaviour often persist even when incentives for optimal decision making exist.

To reinforce the results of the penalty kicks study, we conducted another study in which the attitudes and opinions of top professional goalkeepers were elicited. The results in that study support the idea that the norm during penalty kicks is that the goalkeeper dives to one of the sides. The results also support our explanation for the tendency of goalkeepers to dive too much, because goalkeepers report feeling worse about a goal being scored when it follows from inaction (staying in the centre) than from action (diving). Another finding is that goalkeepers are more satisfied from stopping a penalty kick when it was shot to one of the sides than when it was shot to the centre.

Study 1: Analysis of Penalty Kicks

The Data

To determine whether football goalkeepers exhibit the action bias and dive during penalty kicks more than is optimal, we searched in the archives of various television channels, found different football matches and watched the games to see whether the games involved penalty kicks.[5] For those penalty kicks that we found, we asked three independent judges to determine to which part of the goal the ball was kicked, to which

---

[5] Israeli TV channels mostly cover football matches in various top European leagues, in important championships worldwide (e.g., the European Championships and the World Cup) and in the Israeli premier league.

direction the goalkeeper dived (if at all) and whether he stopped the ball, using a diagram of the goal's area.[6] A total of 311 kicks were analysed.

After the three judges evaluated the kicks, we excluded kicks they decided were shot to the goalposts and the crossbar or outside the goal (18 such kicks existed in the data). The reason is that we later use the sample to estimate the probability of stopping a penalty kick by diving to the side or by staying in the centre. Balls that did not reach a point inside the goal frame are not scored goals, on one hand, but are not successes of the goalkeeper in stopping the ball, on the other hand. Therefore they do not belong in the sample. We also eliminated seven cases in which there was a significant disagreement between the judges. Thus the sample size in the rest of the analysis consists of 286 observations.

Results and Analysis

Table 1 presents the data, divided according to the direction of dives and kicks. There is a potential confusion about directions in this context. If the goalkeeper dives to his left and the kicker kicks towards his left, those are two opposite directions even though both are "left". To avoid this confusion, in what follows, when we mention right or left, it is from the goalkeeper's perspective. The top numbers present the raw frequencies and the bottom ones present the distribution in percentages.

Table 1 shows that the decisions taken by the kicker and the goalkeeper are usually simultaneous. If the goalkeeper could observe to which direction the ball is headed and only then choose to which direction to dive, he would always dive to the direction of the kick. If, on the other hand, the kicker had time to observe to which direction the goalkeeper dived and only then kick the ball, he would always kick to a different direction from what the goalkeeper chose. The fact that the directions of the kick and the dive match in 43% of kicks rather than in 0% or 100% of the kicks suggests that neither the kicker nor the goalkeeper can always figure out what the other chose when choosing their action, but rather their decision is usually simultaneous. The data, however, also suggests that the goalkeeper might have some noisy signals about the kick's direction, because he does better than the 33.3% rate he would obtain if he chose

---

[6] The diagram divided the goal area to thirds both horizontally and vertically, thus creating a 3X3 grid with nine cells inside the goal area, in addition to other areas that represent the goalposts, the crossbar, and areas outside the goal frame. To get a feeling for the task the goalkeeper performs, the size of a football goal is 8 yards (7.32 meters) wide and 8 feet (2.44 meters) high.

Table 1: Joint distribution of dives and kicks.

		Dive direction			
		Left	Centre	Right	Total
Kick direction	Left	54 (18.9%)	1 (0.3%)	37 (12.9%)	92 (32.2%)
	Centre	41 (14.3%)	10 (3.5%)	31 (10.8%)	82 (28.7%)
	Right	46 (16.1%)	7 (2.4%)	59 (20.6%)	112 (39.2%)
	Total	141 (49.3%)	18 (6.3%)	127 (44.4%)	286 (100.0%)

randomly or the 39.2% he would if he always chose to dive right. The data can be consistent with a small percentage of cases where the goalkeeper waits to see to which direction the ball heads before choosing his action and a large percentage of cases in which the kicker and goalkeeper choose their actions simultaneously (see Bar-Eli et al., 2007a).

Additional essential information is which kicks the goalkeepers succeeded to stop. Table 2 presents information about the number and characteristics of penalty kicks that were stopped by the goalkeepers.

Not surprisingly, most of the kicks stopped occur when the goalkeeper chooses the same direction in which the ball was kicked. We can see, however, that in a few cases a goalkeeper who dived to one of the sides was still able to stop a ball directed towards the centre. It is clear why this is possible if we remember that a kick that is classified as "Centre" need not be at the exact centre, but rather at any point in the middle third of the goal, so diving to the left allows the goalkeeper to potentially stop a ball directed a bit to the left of the centre. In addition, the goalkeeper might stop the ball with his legs when he dives to the side and the kick is to the centre.

Table 3 presents the average stopping chances, computed as the number of kicks stopped divided by the number of kicks (for each combination of kick direction and dive direction).

One can employ two different methods for estimating the probability that a goalkeeper has to stop a kick. One is to take the total number of balls stopped when choosing a certain direction and divide it by the total number of dives to that direction. Goalkeepers in the sample, for example, dived left 141 times and stopped 20 balls, yielding a 14.2% stopping rate. This computation takes into account the correlations in the data between

Table 2: The number of stopped penalty kicks.

		Dive direction			
		Left	Centre	Right	Total
Kick direction	Left	16	0	0	16
	Centre	4	6	1	11
	Right	0	0	15	15
	Total	20	6	16	42

Table 3: Chances of stopping a kick.

		Dive direction			
		Left	Centre	Right	Overall
Kick Direction	Left	29.6%	0.0%	0.0%	17.4%
	Centre	9.8%	60.0%	3.2%	13.4%
	Right	0.0%	0.0%	25.4%	13.4%
	Probability of Stopping (PS)	14.2%	33.3%	12.6%	14.7%
	Alternative Probability of Stopping (APS)	12.3%	17.2%	10.9%	

the direction of the kick and the dive and thus assumes that the goalkeeper in question has roughly the same amount of cues about the kick direction that others had. The results of this approach are presented under "Probability of Stopping (PS)". Combining the choices of right and left to an action that we can denote "dive" and comparing the payoff from this action (36 stopped kicks vs. 232 scored goals) to the payoff of "stay in the centre" (six stopped kicks vs. twelve scored goals) allows us to reject the null hypothesis that the two actions give the same payoff (stopping probability), $\chi^2 (1, N = 286) = 5.33$, $p=0.02$.

A second approach is to use the marginal distribution of kicks and to assume complete independence between kick and dive direction. In this case, the probability of stopping the kick by diving left, for example, is the probability that the kick goes to the left (32.2%) times the probability of stopping a left kick when diving left (29.6%), plus the probability of a kick towards the centre (28.7%) times the probability of stopping a kick to the centre when diving left (9.8%), plus the probability of a kick heading right (39.2%) times the probability of stopping a right kick when diving left (0%). The probabilities are based on the data presented in Tables 1 and 3, assuming that the probability of a kick towards a certain direction is the same as its relative frequency in the data and the chances to stop a certain kick by a certain dive are given by the corresponding cells in Table 3. The result in this case gives a stopping probability of 12.3% and the corresponding probabilities for choosing to dive to the right or to stay in the centre are given in the line labelled "Alternative Probability of Stopping (APS)".

Because goalkeepers in the sample were choosing the correct direction a bit more often than if they were choosing in random, the APS is lower than the PS. For example, the PS method implicitly assumes that when the goalkeeper chooses to dive to the left, the chances that the kick also heads left are higher than 32.2% (overall frequency of kicks to the left), while the APS method does not.[7]

Using a Probit regression (as shown in Table 4), we further examine how the goalkeeper's behaviour affects the chances to stop penalties. STOPPED, the dependent variable is a dummy variable that equals 1 if the kick was stopped. DIVE-RIGHT and DIVE-LEFT are dummy variables that are equal to 1 if the goalkeeper dived right or left, respectively. Similarly, KICK-RIGHT and KICK-LEFT are dummy variables that are equal to 1 if the kick was aimed right or left, respectively.

Table 4 suggests that compared to the benchmark case of staying in the centre, the goalkeepers' strategies to dive right and to dive left have a statistically significant negative effect on the chances to stop the kick. That is, given the distribution of kicks, the goalkeeper is better off staying in the centre of the goal than diving either right or left. We can also see that from the kicker's perspective, given goalkeepers' behaviour, kicking to one of the sides rather than to the centre has no statistically significant effect on the chances of the goalkeeper to stop the kick. This is the result of two opposite effects: on one hand, as Table 3 shows, when the goalkeeper chooses the same direction as the kick, he has the highest chances to stop it when it is directed to the centre (60% vs. 25.4% and

---

[7] Notice that the PS method can be thought of as identical to the APS method, except that instead of taking the overall distribution of kicks, it takes the distribution of kicks conditional on the goalkeeper choosing a certain direction. For example, when the goalkeeper chooses to dive to the left, the conditional probability (conditioning on dive to the left) for a left kick becomes 54/141=38.3%, for a centre kick 41/141=29.1%, and for a right kick 46/141=32.6%. Multiplying these probabilities by the stopping probabilities of 29.6%, 9.8%, and 0%, respectively, and adding up, gives us (not surprisingly) 14.2%, as the direct computation of the PS also showed.

Table 4: Probit regression results.

	Coefficient[a]	Marginal effect[b]
DIVE-RIGHT	-0.80	-0.17
	(0.35)*	
DIVE-LEFT	-0.76	-0.17
	(0.34)*	
KICK-RIGHT	0.11	0.03
	(0.24)	
KICK-LEFT	0.31	0.07
	(0.25)	
Constant	-0.49	
	(0.32)	
Observations	286	
Log likelihood	-116.3	

* Significant at the 5% level. Standard errors in parentheses.
[a] Dependent variable: STOPPED.
[b] The marginal effect is the discrete change in the probability when the dummy variable changes from 0 to 1.

29.6%). This makes the choice of centre less attractive for the kicker. On the other hand, as Table 1 shows, the goalkeeper stays in the centre in only about 6% of the kicks. This makes it more attractive to kick to the centre. The coefficients of KICK-RIGHT and KICK-LEFT being not statistically significant suggest that these two effects roughly cancel out each other.

Assuming that goalkeepers try to maximise the chances of their team to win, their optimal action is to choose the direction where the probability of stopping the ball is maximal. We can see in Table 3 that both the PS and APS methods suggest that the goalkeeper should choose to stay in the centre; the difference between stopping chances in the centre and either left or right are large. This can also be seen in the regression results reported in Table 4.

Do we observe goalkeepers who always choose to stay in the centre, as the optimal behaviour dictates? The answer is no. In fact, goalkeepers almost always choose to dive to one of the sides! Only in 6.3% of the kicks analysed they stayed in the centre. This suggests some kind of a bias. We want to emphasise that we do not argue that the equilibrium of this game involves goalkeepers who always stay in the centre, because once goalkeepers will always stay in the centre, kickers will change their behaviour and will no longer aim to the centre. But when we ask whether goalkeepers behave optimally given the current distribution of kicks, the answer seems to be no.

We propose that the reason for goalkeepers not staying in the centre is action bias. Because the norm (as can be seen in the data and in the following section) is that goalkeepers choose action (diving to one of the sides) rather than inaction (staying in the centre), norm theory (Kahneman and Miller, 1986) predicts that a negative outcome would be amplified following inaction. That is, an identical negative outcome (a goal being scored) is perceived to be worse when it follows inaction rather than action. The intuition why is that if the goalkeeper dives and a goal is scored, he might feel "I did my best to stop the ball, by diving, as almost everyone does; I was simply unlucky that the ball headed to another direction (or could not be stopped for another reason)." On the other hand, if the goalkeeper stays in the centre and a goal is scored, it looks as if he did not do anything to stop the ball; he remained at his original location (centre) without diving to any side. Because the negative feeling of the goalkeeper following a goal being scored (which happens in most penalty kicks) is amplified when staying in the centre, the goalkeeper prefers to dive to one of the sides, even though this is not optimal, exhibiting an "action bias".

We can obtain an approximate quantitative measure of the action bias if we adopt a simple principle (that also underlies the concept of mixed-strategy Nash equilibrium). This principle says that if several actions are chosen by a player with a positive probability, the player must be indifferent between them. The rationale behind this principle is that if a player is not indifferent between the actions, this means that one action has a lower expected payoff; but a rational player has no reason to play an action that yields an expected payoff that is lower than that of other actions. To use this principle to quantify the action bias, we have to treat diving right and diving left together as one action "to dive", otherwise there are too many free parameters and they cannot be solved for. We therefore replicate in Table 5 the computation of Table 3 but with only two actions, "centre" and "dive". For example, the data include 196 kicks in which the kicker chose either left or right and also the goalkeeper chose to dive to one of the sides. Of these, 31 were stopped, so the stopping probability in the top left cell in Table 5 is 31/196=15.8%.

Even with this simplified version of the penalty kick interaction, if the utility level of the goalkeeper depends on his action, on the kicker's action and on the outcome (whether or not a goal was scored), we potentially have to define $2^3=8$ utility levels. However, we only have one equation that can be used to solve for these utility levels–the equation that states that the expected utility from diving and from staying in the centre should

Table 5: Chances of stopping a kick with two possible actions.

		Goalkeeper		
		Side	Centre	Overall
Kicker	Side	15.8%	0.0%	15.2%
	Centre	6.9%	60.0%	13.4%
	Probability of Stopping (PS)	13.4%	33.3%	
	Alternative Probability of Stopping (APS)	13.3%	17.2%	

be equal. So in order to simplify the decision problem and make it possible to quantify the action bias, we assume that the goalkeeper's utility does not depend on the kicker's choice of side or centre. In addition, we assume that when the ball is stopped, the goalkeeper's utility is the same regardless of whether he dived or not. We normalise this utility level to 0. Finally, we normalise the goalkeeper's utility level when he dives to the side and a goal is scored to -1. Now, the only free parameter is the goalkeeper's utility level when he stays in the centre and a goal is scored. We denote it by Z and we find its value using the required equality in the expected utility between diving and staying in the centre. We can compute Z using either the probability of stopping (PS) or the alternative probability of stopping (APS). Table 6 presents both alternatives. Z is the value that equates the value in the column "E(U) of Side" to the value in the column "E(U) of Centre". In other words, if the goalkeeper perceives the disutility from getting a goal when staying in the centre to be Z, then he is indifferent between diving and staying in the centre and then the goalkeepers' decisions sometimes to dive and sometimes to stay in the centre can be justified.

We can see that the value of Z is sensitive to whether we adopt the PS method or the APS method. Using the PS method, Table 6 suggests that goalkeepers' behaviour can be rationalised if goalkeepers suffer 30% (5% using the APS method) more disutility from a goal when they stayed in the centre than when they dived.

Table 6: Quantifying the action bias.

	E(U) of Side	E(U) of Centre	Z
PS	$0.134 * 0 + 0.866 * (-1)$	$0.333 * 0 + 0.667 * Z$	-1.30
APS	$0.133 * 0 + 0.867 * (-1)$	$0.172 * 0 + 0.828 * Z$	-1.05

Study 2: Goalkeepers' Attitudes and Satisfaction when Stopping a Penalty Kick

Our explanation discussed above for the seemingly non-optimal decision making by goalkeepers is based on the argument that the norm is to dive to one of the sides rather than to stay in the centre. While it is evident from the data that goalkeepers almost always dive to one of the sides and therefore this can be considered the norm, we wanted to make the assertion that diving is the norm even stronger by asking the top professional goalkeepers for their opinion. Since getting such top goalkeepers to participate in a survey provides a rare and not easily-obtained opportunity to look into the attitudes of top goalkeepers, we decided also to examine whether their attitudes about penalty kicks support our conjecture that goalkeepers feel worse when they do not stop a penalty kick following inaction (staying in the centre) than following action (diving to one of the sides).

To collect data from the top goalkeepers available to us, we used the following procedure: we compiled a list of the two goalkeepers in each of the teams in the premier league (the highest league in Israel) and of the opening (and therefore better) goalkeeper in each of the teams in the National League (the second highest league). Since each league has 12 teams, this resulted in a list of 36 goalkeepers, who are the top professional goalkeepers in Israel. We succeeded in recruiting 32 out of these 36 goalkeepers to participate in the study.

The first question we presented to the goalkeepers was "When goalkeepers try to stop a penalty kick, what is the most normal thing they will do? Dive right / dive left / stay in the centre of the goal." In accordance with our conjecture, the vast majority of goalkeepers (25 of the 32) thought that the most normal thing is to dive to one of the sides, while only seven thought that staying in the centre is the most normal action. This indicates that diving is the norm (as our data from study 1 also suggested), $\chi^2 (1, N = 32) = 10.13, p=0.001$.

The next question asked "When goalkeepers try to stop a penalty kick, what is the least probable thing they will do? Dive right / dive left / stay in the centre of the goal." Twenty-five respondents said the least probable thing is that the goalkeeper will stay in the centre, while seven said it is to dive to one of the sides, once again supporting the argument that diving is considered to be the norm, $\chi^2 (1, N = 32) = 10.13, p=0.001$.

The third question tries to measure the regret from the same outcome–a goal being scored–but following different possible actions, either diving to one of the sides or staying in the centre. The exact question was:

How bad will you feel, on a 1-10 scale (1=won't feel bad at all, 10=feel very bad), in each of the following situations, which present the outcome of a penalty kick in an important game?

You dived right and a goal was scored _____

You dived left and a goal was scored _____

You stayed in the centre of the goal and a goal was scored _____

Let us denote the answers of the goalkeepers to the three scenarios as R (right), L (left) and C (centre). Each of these is a number between one and ten, representing how bad the goalkeeper feels after a goal being scored, when he chose to dive right, left or to stay in the centre. The responses of each goalkeeper were converted to two data points: one was obtained by taking the difference C–R and the other by the difference C–L. Since we are only interested in differences between the centre and the sides (and not the differences between right and left), we analyse these two differences jointly. We thus have a dataset of 64 such differences (two for each goalkeeper times 32 goalkeepers).

Our hypothesis suggests that goalkeepers feel worse about a bad outcome (a goal being scored) after inaction (staying in the centre), because the norm is to take an action (to dive). That is, we hypothesised that the differences mentioned above will be positive on average. The average difference was indeed positive, 0.61. A one-tailed t-test reveals that we can reject the hypothesis that the mean difference in the population is zero with a p-value of 0.018.[8]

Another approach to analyse the data can be to ignore the magnitude of the difference and only to consider its sign. If goalkeepers feel the same when a goal is scored regardless of whether they dived or stayed in the centre, the number of positive and negative differences should be similar. In the data, however, there are 22 positive differences and only eight negative differences, suggesting that goalkeepers feel worse when a goal is being scored after they stayed in the centre (compared to when they dived to one of the sides), $\chi^2(1, N = 30) = 6.53, p=0.011$.

---

[8] We also examined the dissatisfaction from a goal after diving right vs. diving left. The difference is small in magnitude (the average response is 8.34 for diving right and 8.13 for diving left) and is not statistically significant (the p-value of the two-tailed t-test for difference in means is 0.18 for a paired sample and 0.70 for an unpaired sample).

Another interesting question we wanted to explore is whether goalkeepers feel more satisfied when they stop a penalty kick that is shot to the sides (compared to stopping one in the centre). Nineteen of the best Israeli goalkeepers were shown a picture of an actual goal taken from the penalty point. On a diagram of the goal area that divides it to nine equal-size cells (dividing the goal area to thirds both horizontally and vertically), nine balls were drawn in places corresponding to the centre of each of the nine cells. The goalkeepers were told: "Look carefully at the picture in front of you; as you can see, this is a football goal, to which the nine balls appearing in the diagram correspond. The different balls represent different locations of penalty kicks that you stopped. Please mark the kick that stopping it caused you the most satisfaction."[9] The results indicate that goalkeepers are more satisfied when they stop a penalty kick shot to one of the sides: 16 of the goalkeepers indicated one of the cells in the right or left (or more than one such cell) as the location that causes them the most satisfaction when they stop a penalty kick; only three indicated one of the cells in the centre, $\chi^2 (1, N = 19) = 8.89$, $p=0.003$. This suggests another potential reason why goalkeepers almost always dive: they derive more satisfaction from stopping a kick by diving than by staying in the centre. In other words, not only they prefer to dive conditional on missing the ball (as we saw before), but also they prefer to dive conditional on stopping the ball.[10]

Conclusion

The analysis of 286 football penalty kicks in top leagues and championships worldwide shows that while the utility-maximizing behaviour for goalkeepers is to stay in the goal's centre during the kick, in 93.7% of the kicks the goalkeepers chose to dive to one of the sides. This non-optimal behaviour suggests that goalkeepers might exhibit biased decision making, despite their vast experience and the huge incentives they face. According to our hypothesis, the reason for this non-optimal behaviour is "action bias"–the opposite of the more famous "omission

---

[9] This is a translation of the original text, which was in Hebrew; words in bold letters also appeared in bold in the original survey.
[10] It should be noted that these preferences do not necessarily mean that goalkeepers should always dive; if in a certain kick the goalkeeper thinks that by staying in the centre his chances to stop the ball are much higher than by diving, he should stay in the centre, because the outcome (goal or no goal) is not independent of his choice.

bias". The reason that the usual bias is reversed here is that usually the norm is to choose inaction, while in the penalty kicks case, the norm is to act (to dive to the side rather than to stay in the centre).

According to norm theory (Kahneman and Miller, 1986), people have stronger feelings associated with outcomes when they come from abnormal causes. Consequently, because the norm is that goalkeepers dive to one of the sides, the disutility associated with missing a ball might be greater following a non-common behaviour (staying in the centre) than following normal behaviour (diving to the side). The action bias might explain the intriguing difference between goalkeepers' optimal behaviour and actual behaviour.

To reinforce the findings in the first study, we conducted another study in which the attitudes and opinions of top professional goalkeepers were elicited. The results in that study support the claim (based on the first study data) that the norm during penalty kicks is that the goalkeeper dives to one of the sides. The results also support our explanation for the tendency of goalkeepers to dive too much, because goalkeepers report feeling worse about a goal being scored when it follows from inaction (staying in the centre) than from action (diving).

The survey of professional goalkeepers reveals also that they are more satisfied stopping a penalty kick by diving than by staying in the centre. This might be an additional reason why they almost always dive. We can think of a few additional potential reasons why goalkeepers dive so often. One is that they want to appear as trying hard to stop the kick and diving requires more effort than staying at the centre. Another reason could be that they just do not want to deviate from what others are doing; other goalkeepers dive, consequently they are expected to dive and therefore they dive, without thinking too much whether this really maximises their chances to stop the kick. The explanation of the action bias also uses the observation that diving is the norm, but it is a different explanation. In the action bias story, because diving is the norm, goalkeepers feel more regret following a goal if they did not dive than if they dived. Here we do not consider any particular outcome (of stopping the ball or not), but rather suggest that goalkeepers prefer to "follow the herd" in their behaviour.

Another possible reason may be that goalkeepers believe that diving makes the game more interesting and enjoyable for their team's fans. Finally, it is possible that in their trainings goalkeepers are instructed to dive during penalty kicks and therefore they follow these directions. The question then becomes why are they instructed to dive?

Throughout this chapter we claimed that based on the penalty kicks data, maximizing the chances to stop a penalty kick requires to stay in the centre of the goal instead of diving, assuming that at the point at which the decision has to be made the goalkeeper cannot observe in which direction the ball is heading. We want to emphasise that this argument is based on the current distribution of kicks. If goalkeepers will always choose to stay in the centre, however, kickers will start aiming all balls to the sides and it will no longer be optimal for the goalkeeper to stay in the centre. The distribution of dives and kicks that will constitute an equilibrium (in which both the kicker and the goalkeeper will be happy with their choices given what the other player does) therefore involves randomised actions by the players (i.e., a mixed-strategy equilibrium). That is, kickers will kick left, right or to the centre with some probabilities (not necessarily equal probabilities) and similarly goalkeepers will choose to dive left, right or stay in the centre with certain probabilities. Here, however, we consider the question what is optimal for goalkeepers given the current behaviour of kickers; analyzing the mixed-strategy equilibrium of the game is a different topic and is beyond the scope of this chapter (for game-theoretic analysis of penalty kicks, see Chiappori et al., 2002, Palacios-Huerta, 2003, Azar and Bar-Eli, 2005 and Leininger and Ockenfels, Chapter 5).

References

Azar, O. H. and M. Bar-Eli (2005). "Do soccer players play the mixed-strategy Nash equilibrium?" *Working Paper*. Ben-Gurion University of the Negev.

Bar-Eli, M., O. H. Azar, I. Ritov, Y. Keidar-Levin and G. Schein (2007a). "Action bias among elite soccer goalkeepers: The case of penalty kicks." *Journal of Economic Psychology*, 28(5), 606-621.

Bar-Eli, M., O. H. Azar and Y. Lurie (2007b). "(Ir)rationality in action: Do soccer players and goalkeepers fail to learn how to best perform during a penalty kick?" *Working Paper*. Ben-Gurion University of the Negev.

Baron, J. (1994). *Thinking and deciding*. New York: Cambridge University Press.

Chiappori P.-A., S. Levitt S. and T. Groseclose (2002). "Testing mixed-strategy equilibria when players are heterogeneous: The case of penalty kicks in soccer." *American Economic Review*, 92(4), 1138-1151.

Kahneman, D. and D. T. Miller (1986). "Norm theory: Comparing reality to its alternatives." *Psychological Review*, 93(2), 136-153.

Kahneman, D. and A. Tversky (1982). "The psychology of preferences."
    Scientific American, 246(1), 160-173.
Klein, G. (1999). *Sources of power: How people make decisions.*
    Cambridge, MA: MIT Press.
Kordes-de Vaal, J. H. (1996). "Intention and omission bias: Omission
    perceived as nondecisions." *Acta Psychologica*, 93(1-3), 161-172.
Leininger, W. and A. Ockenfels (2008). "The penalty-duel and
    institutional design: Is there a Neeskens-effect?" In *Myths and facts
    about football: The economics and psychology of the world's greatest
    sport.* P. Andersson, P. Ayton and C. Schmidt, eds. Cambridge:
    Cambridge Scholars Press.
McMorris, T. and S. Colenso (1996). "Anticipation of professional
    goalkeepers when facing right- and left-footed penalty kicks."
    Perceptual and Motor Skills, 82(3), 931-934.
Miller, D. T. and B. R. Taylor (1995). "Counterfactual thought, regret, and
    superstition: How to avoid kicking yourself." In *What might have
    been: The social psychology of counterfactual thinking.* N. J. Roese
    and J. M. Olson eds. Hillsdale, NJ: Erlbaum, 305-331.
Morris, A. and L. Burwitz (1989). "Anticipation and movement strategies
    in elite soccer goalkeepers at penalty kicks." *Journal of Sports
    Sciences*, 7(1), 79-80.
Palacios-Huerta, I. (2003). "Professionals play minimax." *Review of
    Economics Studies*, 70(2), 395-415.
Rachlevsky, O. (2005). "A Jew sends away fans." *Maariv (Weekend
    Supplement)*, 27(May), 62-67.
Ritov, I. and J. Baron (1990). "Reluctance to vaccinate: Commission bias
    and ambiguity." *Journal of Behavioural Decision Making*, 3, 263-277.
Ritov, I. and J. Baron (1992). "Status-quo and omission biases." *Journal
    of Risk and Uncertainty*, 5(1), 49-61.
Ritov, I. and J. Baron (1994). "Biases in decisions about compensation for
    misfortune: The role of expectation." *European Journal of Social
    Psychology*, 24(5), 525-539.
Ritov, I. and J. Baron (1995). "Outcome knowledge, regret, and omission
    bias." *Organizational Behaviour and Human Decision Processes*,
    64(2), 119-127.
Savelsbergh, G. J. P., A. M. Williams, J. van der Kamp and P. Ward
    (2002). "Visual search, anticipation and expertise in soccer
    goalkeepers." *Journal of Sports Sciences*, 20(3), 279-287.
Spranca, M., E. Minsk and J. Baron (1991). "Omission and commission in
    judgment and choice." *Journal of Experimental Social Psychology*,
    27(1), 76-105.

Welsh, A. (1990). *Goalkeeping*. London: A. & C. Black.

CHAPTER SEVEN

POST-SCORING BEHAVIOUR
AND TEAM SUCCESS IN FOOTBALL

GARY BORNSTEIN
AND CHANAN GOLDSCHMIDT[1]

> It was Young's first goal from outside the penalty area. Young then ran round the Riverside like a manic computer character. He admitted: "As you can see, I don't know how to celebrate goals. I'd still be going if the lads hadn't caught me." (Daily Mail, Monday, November 5, 2007)

The benefits of winning a team-sport competition (e. g., the league's championship, gold medals, bonuses, pride) are by and large public goods for the members of the winning team. That is, these benefits are jointly provided to the members of the team and are shared by all of them equally, regardless of how much they contributed to the team's success (Bornstein, 1992; 2003). This payoff structure gives rise to free-riding. Knowing that they cannot be excluded from enjoying the public goods once they are provided, individual players may be tempted to reduce their contribution to the collective team effort. As a result, the team may lose the competition and the public goods will not be provided. That free-riding, or social loafing, reduces group performance has been demonstrated in various social contexts (Kerr, 1986; Kerr and Bruun, 1983; Latane et al., 1979; Steiner, 1972; Kerr and Tindale, 2004), including sporting activities (Huddleston et al., 1985; Williams et al., 1989).

Another potential source of free-riding in team sports has to do with the fact that some individual actions are evaluated separately and rewarded differentially. Players often face a decision between acting in a way that enhances their private good (trying to score a goal) and contributing to the

[1] Bornstein: Goldschmidt: Department of Psychology, The Hebrew University, Jerusalem, Israel.

public good (passing the ball to another player who is in a better position to score). Again, selfish behaviour on the part of individual players may reduce the team's overall efficiency and its chances of winning the competition.

The game of football is a particularly good example of the payoff structure described above. Winning in this game demands continuous effort by the individual players at a considerable personal cost (e.g., physical exertion, risk of injury). Much of this effort (e.g., moving away from the ball, helping the defense players) is not rewarded at the individual level. When the collective team effort results in scoring a goal, however, the lion's share of the reward (e.g., fan adulation, media attention and higher "market" value) accrues to the individual scorer.[2]

The present study investigates the straightforward hypothesis that, other things being equal, more cohesive football teams whose players are more team-oriented will perform better than less cohesive teams with more self-oriented players. Team-oriented players are more likely to "take the group interest into account when making their own decisions" (Messick and Brewer, 1983, p. 23), and, consequently, are more likely to invest the necessary effort even when this is personally costly and make the choices that promote the team's collective success rather than their own.

A recent definition in the sport context conceptualised cohesion as

> a dynamic process that is reflected in the tendency for a group to stick together and remain united in the pursuit of its instrumental objectives and/or for the satisfaction of member affective needs (Carron et al., 1998, p. 213).

The innovation of our study is the way team cohesion was measured. We analysed the behaviour of football players immediately after scoring a goal and rated it on a scale ranging from individualistic to team-oriented, depending on the direction of scorer's attention, his location , and the number of other team members whom he made contact with. Our assumption is that the players' post-scoring behaviour reveals naturally, in an uncensored way, the subjective importance they attach to the private and public benefits associated with this event. Whereas the behaviour of team-oriented players indicates that they put a higher value on the

---

[2] Indeed, a study by Friedman et al. (1986) shows that 86% of the passes leading to scoring a goal (i.e., assists) were made from within the penalty area—sixteen meters from the goal. This indicates that scoring a goal is in most cases only the final act in a succession of co-operative team moves.

collective team's benefit, selfish players are visibly more interested in their private benefit.

The mean post-scoring behaviour of the scoring players on a particular team constitutes the team's level of cohesion. Team cohesion, in turn, is predicted to be positively correlated with the team's success, as indicated by its position in the league at the end of the season. The rest of the paper is organised as follows: Section 2 briefly reviews the literature on team cohesion and performance, section 3 describes our study in more detail, and section 4 concludes the paper.

Team Cohesion

The relationship between team cohesion and team performance is argued to depend on the type of interdependence within the team. Carron and his colleagues (Carron, 1988; Carron and Brawley, 2000; Cox, 1990) divided team sports into four categories based on the type of intragroup dependence. The first category is that of "non-dependence," which characterises sports like bowling or rifle-shooting where there is no need for co-ordination between team members in order for the team to compete successfully. The second category is "coactive dependence," which applies to competitions like rowing or tug-of-war where all the members of the team perform similar activities at the same time, and their collective performance determine the team's success. The third category of "reactive-proactive dependence" applies to sports like American football and baseball, where a team member can instigate a move but needs the co-operation of the rest of the team to complete it successfully (proactive dependence), or where a player has to wait for the others to make various moves in order to make his own (reactive dependence). Finally, the fourth category, that of "interactive dependence," characterises team sports such as football and basketball, where all the members of a team rely on each other's actions during the entire competition. Carron and his colleagues hypothesise that the relations between team cohesion and team success should become stronger as one moves up the list from the category of "non-dependence" to that of "interactive dependence"—a hypothesis that has received considerable empirical support (for a review of the relationship between cohesion and performance, see Carron, et al., 2002).

Team cohesion has been almost invariably measured by questionnaires, and most notably by the Group Environment Questionnaire (GEQ) developed by Widmeyer et al. (1985) specifically for team sports. This measurement procedure, and the conceptual model underlying it, is based on the assumption that cohesion is a team property that can be assessed through group members' beliefs and perceptions about their team—perceptions that reflect their personal (individual) and collective concerns. The GEQ was used, for example, by Hardy et al. (2003) to study team cohesion and the use of imagery in sport among varsity athletes and national-level synchronised skaters. Another study used this questionnaire to investigate the relationships between pre-competition group cohesion, mood, and performance in a football team over the course of a season (Lowther and Lane, 2006). Kozub and McDonnell (2000) studied rugby union teams, using the GEQ, and found positive relationship between cohesion and performance.

Most research has operationalised group success as the position of the team in a competitive tournament or at the end of the season (Spink, 1990; Watson et al., 2001). Others define success as the percentage of victories at end or mid-season (in volleyball teams, Paskevich et al., 1999). Nevertheless, Bray and Whaley (2001) questioned the use of a team's win/loss record and its derivatives as the primary measure of team performance.

The present study assessed team cohesion by analyzing the post-scoring behaviour of the team's scorers and in this respect is different from other questionnaire-type studies. Team success was operationalised, rather traditionally, as the team's position in the league at the end of the season.

Method

Measuring Post-Scoring Behaviour (PSB)

We videotaped 125 goals scored in the Israeli premier league games of 1992 and filmed by the IBA (Israel Broadcasting Authority)3. Each scorer's behaviour immediately after scoring a goal was rated on three variables: the direction of his attention, the location he ran to, and the number of other players he made physical contact with. Each variable ranged from 1 to 3 (with 3 as the most team-oriented), and the final PSB—"Post-scoring-behaviour" score was the sum of the scores on the 3 variables, ranging from 1 to 9—from a score of 1 which means a very selfish behaviour to 9 which means very "team" behaviour (see Table 1).

---

3 The dataset is from 1992 because of technical reasons only: as a part of a project done during the second author's doctoral studies in one of the first author's courses, a whole year of T.V. coverage of the Israeli premier league matches was taped on video. Years after both authors decided to work on that dataset in a unique and new way—thus this article was born.

Table 1: Post-scoring behaviour (PSB) as a combination of the three variables.

Score	Direction of attention	Physical spot to which the player runs after scoring	Number of other players making physical contact with the scorer
1	The player's attention—his look or any other behavioural indication—is turned towards the crowd	The player runs towards the crowd, beyond the lines of the field	Two or fewer players touch the scorer
2	The player's attention is turned towards the coach or a particular member of the team	The player runs towards the crowd and/or the coach, without passing the boundaries (within 10m of the line)	3 to 6 players touch the scorer
3	The player's attention is focused on two or more of his teammates	The player runs towards the center of the field (or the area where most of the other players happen to be)	7 or more players touch the scorer

The inclusion of the third index as a measure of team-oriented behaviour is based on the observation that the other players almost invariably try to make contact with the scorer. However, whether or not they succeed depends mainly on the behaviour of the scoring player himself. A scene where the scorer is being chased by his team mates while trying to avoid them, often with amazing agility, is a universal phenomenon well-known to football fans throughout the world.

Measuring Team Success

Team success was operationalised as the rank of the team in the premier league at the end of the regular season. By this time, each of the twelve teams in the league has played 22 games, twice against every other team (once at home and once on the road).

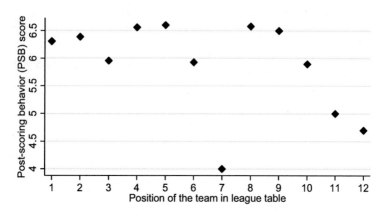

Figure 1: Scatter plot position of the team vs. average post-scoring behaviour (PSB) score of each team.

Results

To assess the reliability of the PSB index two independent judges, other than the one who rated them in the first place, analysed 36 randomly selected goals. The correlation between the PSB scores given by the two judges was r =.85 (p < .0001). The PSB scores of all the scoring players on a particular team were averaged to determine the PSB score of the team. Figure 1 displays a scatter plot of the position of each team at the end of the regular season by the mean PSB score of the team.

Since our analysis was based on IBA recordings, teams that were more attractive to the viewers—those that were more successful during the season—were filmed more frequently than others. Table 2 displays the relative position of the teams at the end of the football season and the distribution of the 125 recorded goals among the 12 teams, and also the PSB score for each team. As can be seen, the two teams at the top of the league were filmed much more often than the other teams (obviously, these two teams also scored more goals). The two top teams were responsible for 42.4% of the goals analysed, as compared with only 6.4% of the goals for the two bottom teams. This fact obviously affects the reliability of the PSB score at the team level, since the reliability of this score is directly proportional to the number of goals analysed for each team. There are also differences in the importance or criticality of the goals. A winning goal in an important match is more likely to be

Table 2: Position, post-scoring behaviour (PSB index & position) and number of goals analysed.

Position	Team	Goals analysed (no. of players who scored at least one goal)	Position according to PSB	PSB score for each team
1.	Maccabi Tel-Aviv (T.A.)	26(9)	6	6.31
2.	Bnei Yehuda	27(7)	5	6.39
3.	Maccabi Haifa	11(5)	7	5.96
4.	Hapoel Petah-Tikva (P.T.)	8(5)	3	6.56
5.	Beitar Tel-Aviv	9(6)	1	6.6
6.	Maccabi Netanya	12(6)	8	5.93
7.	Maccabi Petah-Tikva (P.T.)	5(3)	12	4.0
8.	Zafririm Holon	10(6)	2	6.58
9.	Hapoel Beer-Sheba (B.S.)	5(3)	4	6.5
10.	Hapoel Tel-Aviv (T.A.)	4(3)	9	5.9
11.	Maccabi Yavneh	3(3)	10	5.0
12.	Hapoel Jerusalem	5(4)	11	4.7

celebrated than inconsequential goal in an unimportant match. Nevertheless, we did not distinguish between goals based on their importance, and analysed the PSB score of all goals in exactly the same way. This renders the average PSB score of the team more meaningful than a personal PSB for each individual goal. Unfortunately, we were unable to analyse all goals in that season, because all matches in the Israeli premier league were not filmed by IBA.

We computed the rank-order correlation (Spearman correlation coefficient – in all correlations here) between the team's mean PSB score and the team's position at the end of the season. The correlation between the PSB ranking and team success was positive but non-significant $r(12)=.44$ (p <.15).

After an additional check of the original data it appears quite clear that each player has his own particular PSB pattern. The most obvious fact is that foreign players behave rather differently from local ones: The foreign players show a clear pattern of cooperative team behaviour regardless of the team they played for, mainly running towards their team mates, rather than towards the crowds. We can think of two explanations for this difference. First, the foreign players, being a minority (and typically newcomers) on the team, make an extra effort to join in and be liked by the majority of the local team members. Second, the foreign players are less dependent on the crowd for "rewards" than the local ones and consequently tend to turn less towards the stands. Indeed, the PSB score of the ten foreign players in the league (M = 7.13, SD =1.62) with the PSB score of the 50 local players (M = 5.83, SD =1.44) indicates a significant difference between the two groups (p < .05). Given that the behaviour of the foreign players was quite uniform and significantly different from that of the local players, we computed the correlation between the teams' PSB scores and their success once again, this time excluding the foreign players from the analysis. (In this analysis one team dropped out for lack of almost any material to analyse.) The rank-order correlation between the PSB index and team success increased to r (1 1) =.65 *(pay attention that this correlation is after omitting one team)*. This correlation is significantly different from zero (p <.05).

As a complement to the measurement of team success, and another way of substantiating the PSB score as a measure of team cohesion, we computed the rank-order correlation between the PSB ranking and team success separately for the home matches and the matches away from home (for this purpose we created separate position tables for home and away matches). The correlation between the PSB ranking and team success at home was positive and significant, r(12)=.59 (p <.05), whereas the correlation between the PSB ranking and team success away from home, while positive, was statistically insignificant, r(12)=.37. Again, it seems that post-scoring behaviour is affected by the presence of the home crowd.

Conclusions

We observed the spontaneous behaviour of football players after they scored a goal, and rated it on a scale ranging from individualistic to team-oriented. We assumed that team-oriented players are more likely to contribute to the team's collective effort even at personal cost. Consequently, we hypothesised that a more cohesive team whose players are more team-oriented would be more successful. The fact that post-scoring behaviour was found to be a fairly good predictor of team success supports this reasoning. Of course, more research is needed to establish the validity of our behavioural index as an indicator of team cohesion and we could speculate that the results might be different if data from another league was used. In addition, the present study, being correlational in nature, cannot provide conclusive evidence as to the direction of causality. It is quite possible that players become more team-oriented as the team becomes more successful rather than the other way around (Grieve et al., 2000). Regardless of the direction of causality, it seems advisable for coaches to pay attention to their players' post-scoring behaviour, as it can provide them with useful information about the players' attitudes towards the team. Moreover, coaches may want to consider structuring their players post-scoring behaviour. It is possible that by disallowing "private" celebrations and requiring the players to participate in collective post-scoring rituals, coaches can promote team cohesion and reduce the "production loss" resulting from selfish behaviour.

References

Bornstein, G. (1992). "The Free rider problem in intergroup conflicts over step-level and continuous public goods." *Journal of Personality and Social Psychology*, 62(4), 597-606.

Bornstein, G. (2003). "Intergroup conflict: Individual, group, and collective interests." *Personality and Social Psychology Review*, 7(2), 129-145.

Bray, C. D. and D. E. Whaley (2001). "Team cohesion, effort, and objective individual performance of high school basketball players." *The Sport Psychologist*, 15(3), 260-275.

Carron, A. V. (1988). *Group Dynamics in Sport*. London, ON: Spondyin.

Carron, A. V., L.R. Brawley and W.N. Widmeyer (1998). "Measurement of cohesion in sport and exercise." In *Advances in sport and exercise psychology measurement*. J. L. Duda ed. Morgantown, WV: Fitness Information Technology, 213-226.

Carron, A. V. and L. R. Brawley (2000). "Cohesion: Conceptual and measurement issues." *Small Group Research*, 31(1), 89-106.

Carron, A.V., M. M. Colman, J. Wheeler and D. Stevens (2002). "Cohesion and performance in sport: A meta-analysis." *Journal of Sport and Exercise Psychology*, 24(2), 168-188.

Carron, A. V., N. W. Widmeyer and L. R. Brawley (1985). "The development of an instrument to assess cohesion in sport teams: The group environment questionnaire." *Journal of Sport and Exercise Psychology*, 7(3), 244-266.

Cox, R. H. (1990). *Sport Psychology: Concepts and Applications (Second ed.)*. Dubuque, Iowa: C. Brown publishers.

Friedman, Z. (1986). "Analyzing the ball passes before scoring a goal in soccer." *Physical Training*, 3, 6-8.

Grieve, F. G., J. P. Whelan and A. W. Meyes (2000)."An experimental examination of the cohesion-performance relationship in an interactive team sport." *Journal of Applied Sport Psychology*, 12(2), 219-235.

Hardy, J., C. R. Hall and A. V. Carron (2003)."Perceptions of team cohesion and athletes' use of imagery." *International Journal of Sport Psychology*, 34(2), 151-167.

Huddleston, S., S. G. Doody and M. K. Ruder (1985). "The effect of prior knowledge of the social loafing phenomenon on performance in a group." *International Journal of Sport Psychology*, 26, 176-182.

Kerr, N. L. (1986). "Motivational choices in task groups: A paradigm for social dilemma research." In *Experimental Social Dilemmas*. H. Wilke et al. eds. Frankfurt a. M.: Verlag Peter Lang, 1-27.

Kerr, N. L. and S. Bruun (1983). "The dispensability of member effort and group motivation losses: Free rider effects." *Journal of Personality and Social Psychology*, 44(1), 78-94.

Kerr, N. L. and R. S. Tindale (2004). "Group performance and decision making." *Annual Review Psychology*, 55(1), 623-655.

Kozub, S. A. and J. F. McDonnell (2000). "Exploring the relationship between cohesion and collective efficacy in rugby teams." *Journal of Sport Behaviour*, 23(2), 120-130.

Latane, B., K. Williams and S. Harkins (1979). "Many hands make light the work: The causes and consequences of social loafing." *Journal of Personality and Social Psychology*, 37(6), 823-832.

Lowther, J. and A. Lane (2006). "Relationships between mood, cohesion and satisfaction with performance among soccer players." *Athletic Insight: The Online Journal of Sport Psychology*, http://www.athleticinsight.com/Vol4Iss3/MoodandPerformance.htm, last visited 14/11/2007.

Messick, D. M. and M. B. Brewer (1983). "Solving social dilemmas as a review." In *Review of Personality and Social Psychology (Vol. 4)*. L. Wheeler and P. Shaver eds. Beverly Hills: Sage, 11-44.

Paskevich, D. M., L.R. Brawley, K.D. Dorsch and W.N. Widmeyer (1999). "Relationship between collective efficacy and cohesion: Conceptual and measurement issues." *Group Dynamics: Theory, Research, and Practice*, 3(3), 210-222.

Spink, K. S. (1990). "Group cohesion and collective efficacy of volleyball teams." *Journal of Sport and Exercise Psychology*, 12(3), 301-311.

Steiner, I. D. (1972). *Group processes and productivity*. New York: Academic Press.

Watson, C. B., M. N. Chemers. and N. Preiser (2001). "Collective efficacy: A multilevel analysis." *Personality and Social Psychology*

Bulletin, 27(8), 1057-1068.

Williams, K. D., S. A. Nida, L. D. Baca and B. Latané (1989). "Social loafing and swimming: Effects of identifiability on individual and relay performance of intercollegiate swimmers." *Basic and Applied Social Psychology*, 10(1), 73-81.

CHAPTER EIGHT

SHIRT COLOUR AND TEAM PERFORMANCE IN FOOTBALL

MARTIN G. KOCHER AND MATTHIAS SUTTER[1]

The colour of sportswear has a significant impact on the outcome of many contests among individuals. Red or blue shirts, for instance, have been shown to increase the likelihood of winning in boxing, tae kwon do, wrestling or judo. The findings of Hill and Barton (2005a) as well as Rowe et al. (2005) that are based on data from the 2004 Olympic Games in Athens are particularly remarkable because the shirt colour was randomly assigned to contestants, which means that the colour could not have been systematically correlated to a contestant's ability.

Wearing a red shirt was found to increase the probability of winning especially in tight contests in which there was hardly any asymmetry in a priori abilities. Put in a broader context, the results of Hill and Barton (2005a) for physical contests among humans are very much in line with research on the influence of red colouration in animals, which shows that the intensity of red colouration correlates significantly with male dominance and testosterone levels (Andersson et al., 2002; Pryke et al., 2002; Setchell and Wickings, 2005).

Rowe et al. (2005), however, concluded that there is nothing special about red in terms of colour-associated winning biases. Rather, they attributed the effects of different colours to the different visibility of shirts, arguing that red and blue shirts should lead to superior performance than paler colours or white.[2]

---

[1] Kocher: University of Innsbruck and University of Munich. Sutter: University of Innsbruck and University of Göteborg. We would like to thank Hakan Fink and Daniel Matt for excellent research assistance as well as Patric Andersson, Peter Kappeler and Stephan Kroll for very helpful comments on the paper.
[2] Hill and Barton (2005b) challenge this explanation in a reply by referring to light and visibility arguments as well as by providing evidence for a gender effect—

Frank and Gilovich (1988) have shown that the shirt colour has also an influence in team sports by influencing the decisions of referees. In a controlled experiment, they demonstrated that referees were more likely to penalize teams wearing black shirts than those wearing white shirts. Yet, whether this kind of influence on referee decisions is decisive for real competitions still needs some clarifications, as the paper by Plessner (2005) demonstrates.

In this paper we show that the colour of the teams' shirts does not have any significant influence on the outcome of matches in the *German Bundesliga*. Therefore, we provide evidence that the findings regarding the influence of shirt colour in individual sports (as established by Hill and Barton, 2005a, or Rowe et al., 2005) do not carry over to the game of football and, most likely, to other kinds of team sports.

One explanation for the discrepancy between individual combat sports and team sports with regard to the effects of colour on performance is that the effects of colour are supposed to be much less salient in a team because other factors like team cohesion or the support by team-mates are more dominant.

Data and Methodology

We consider all 306 matches in the season 2000/01 of the *German Bundesliga*. The shirt colour of the teams has been determined by consulting the relevant issues of the German football magazine *Der Kicker*. We distinguish in our data analysis between home and away teams because the shirt colour might interact with the well-established home team advantage in football (Courneya and Carron, 1992; Nevill and Holder, 1999; Sutter and Kocher, 2004). Home teams won 161 out of 306 matches (i.e. 53%). There were 69 drawn matches and 76 won of away teams (25%).

The season 2000/01 actually provides a favourable environment for detecting a possible effect of the shirt colour because Bayern München, which became champion, played in red shirts in all home matches and in those away matches in which the home team did not wear red. Note also that Schalke 04, ranked second at the end of the season, wore blue shirts in almost all matches.

---

significant effects of the red shirts are only obtained for men and not for women— that corroborates their sexual-selection hypothesis.

Results

The most prominent shirt colours in the season 2000/01 were white (29% of cases), red (23%) and blue (21%). Shirts with a combination of red and black were worn in 9% of cases, green shirts and yellow-black shirts in 6% of cases each. It seems noteworthy that teams used black shirts in less than 1% of cases.

Panel A of Figure 1 displays the influence of red shirts. Home teams won slightly more often in case they wore red (55% of matches) than when they did *not* wear red (52%), irrespective of the opponent's colour in the latter case. Yet, the difference in winning probabilities is far from being significant for each of the three conditions ($\chi^2 = 0.19$, d.f. $= 2$, $P > 0.5$). The same pattern arises for away teams, which won 23% of all matches when they wore red, 24% when neither the home team nor the away team wore red and 29% when the home team had red shirts ($\chi^2 = 0.83$, d.f. $= 2$, $P > 0.5$).

Since Hill and Barton (2005a) have shown that the colour red is particularly important in tight contests we have also considered tight matches separately. Since a tight game cannot be classified by the final score of that match—because it might already have been influenced by the shirt colour—we classify matches as *tight* if the two teams are separated by not more than three positions in the league's ranking before the match. The median difference is five positions, hence matches with a difference of at most three positions can be considered as tight matches. Our definition yields 98 tight games. Home teams win 14 out of 25 matches (56%) when wearing red and 34 out of 73 matches (47%) when wearing another colour ($\chi^2 = 0.66$, d.f. $= 1$, $P > 0.5$). Away teams also cannot take advantage from wearing red shirts since they win equally likely when wearing red (4 out of 18 matches) as when wearing non-red shirts (18 out of 80 matches) ($\chi^2 = 0.01$, d.f. $= 1$, $P > 0.5$). Obviously, red shirts do not even influence the final outcome of a tight football match.

We can corroborate these aggregate results by considering single teams. Given that only three out of 18 clubs both used red and non-red shirts in home matches, data are too scarce to assess the impact of red shirts on a home team's likelihood of winning statistically. Yet, for away teams we are able to perform such a test because ten out of 18 clubs both used red and non-red shirts for away matches. While five out of the ten teams performed relatively better with red shirts than with non-red ones, the other five teams performed worse with red shirts (binomial test, $P = 1.0$).

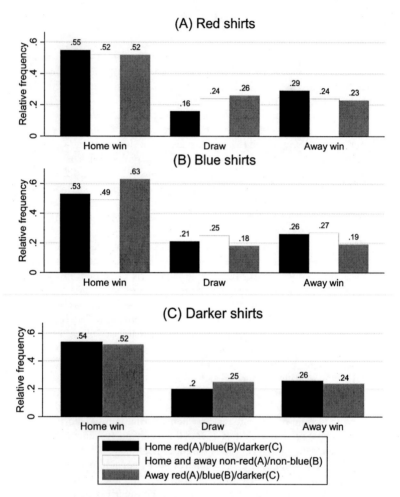

Figure 1: Influence of shirt colour. Relative frequency of outcomes (home win / draw / away win). (A) Red shirts. Home teams wore red in 73 of 306 matches and away teams in 66 matches. (B) Blue shirts. Home teams wore blue in 57 matches, and away teams in 72 matches. (C) Darker shirts. Home teams wore the darker shirt in 149 matches, and away teams in 157 matches. The relative frequency of winning does not depend significantly on any of the colours (χ^2-tests), both for home and away teams.

On average, teams won 23% of their away matches in red shirts and 21% when their shirts were of a different colour (predominantly white, blue, or green).

Panel B of Figure 1 shows the impact of blue shirts, which is the second most frequent colour among football teams. Similar to our results for red shirts, wearing blue shirts does not have a significant impact on winning, either. None of the statistical tests comes close to being significant. The same result is obtained for white shirts. Wearing white vs. wearing non-white shirts has no influence on the likelihood of winning, neither for home teams nor away teams. Finally, we have also checked whether the darkness of shirts has an impact. Assessing the darkness and brightness of shirts was achieved by comparing the relative darkness of both teams' shirts on black-and-white photographs. Panel C of Figure 1 shows that also wearing the darker shirt does not affect winning probabilities.

Conclusion

Whereas the colour of sporting attire has a significant impact on performance in individual combat sports, a similar effect could not be established for team sports. One reason for this apparent difference between combat sports and team sports might be that competition is perceived differently in individual sports and football. Perhaps the signal of a shirt's colour is much less salient in team competitions, or team members feel much less intimidated subconsciously by an aggressive colour like red when comforted at the same time by the presence and support of team-mates. It could also be that the shirt colour has a measurable impact in individual sports, because individual mistakes are much more costly in individual sports than in team sports. If colours influence individuals' performance subconsciously, this should be more important then in individual sports than in team sports.

Of course, one may wonder whether our findings for a national league carry over to international matches as well. In fact, Hill and Barton (2005a) mention preliminary evidence of the results of the Euro 2004 international football tournament, indicating that red shirts seem to have enhanced the performance of football teams. Given the very low number of observations for just a single international football tournament, a more thorough analysis—covering much more international games—seems to be warranted.

References

Andersson, S., S. R. Pryke, J. Ornborg, M. J. Lawes and M. Andersson (2002). "Multiple receivers, multiple ornaments and a trade-off between agonistic and epigamic signalling in a widowbird." *American Naturalist*, 160(5), 683-691.

Courneya, K. S. and A. V. Carron (1992). "The home advantage in sport competitions: A literature review." *Journal of Sport and Exercise Psychology*, 14(1), 13-27.

Frank, M. G. and T. Gilovich (1988). "The dark side of self- and social perception: Black uniforms and aggression in professional sports." *Journal of Personality and Social Psychology*, 54(1), 74-85.

Hill, R. A. and R. A. Barton (2005a). "Red enhances human performance in contests." *Nature*, 435(7040), 293.

Hill, R. A. and R. A. Barton (2005b). "Hill & Barton reply." *Nature*, 437, E10-E11.

Nevill, M. and R. L. Holder (1999). "Home advantage in sport: An overview of studies on the advantage of playing at home." *Sports Medicine*, 28(4), 221-236.

Plessner, H. (2005). "Positive and negative effects of prior knowledge on referee decisions in sports." In *The Routines of Decision Making*. T. Betsch and S. Haberstroh eds. Hillsdale: Lawrence Erlbaum, 311-324.

Pryke, S. R., S. Andersson, M. J. Lawes and S. E. Piper (2002)."Carotenoid status signaling in captive and wild red-collared widowbirds: Independent effects of badge size and color." *Behavioral Ecology*, 13(5), 622-631.

Rowe, C., J. M. Harris and C. Roberts (2005). "Seeing red? Putting sportswear in context." *Nature*, 437(7063), E10.

Setchell, J. M. and E. J. Wickings (2005). "Dominance, status signals and coloration in male mandrills (mandrillus sphinx)." *Ethology*, 111(1), 25-50.

Sutter, M. and M. G. Kocher (2004). "Favoritism of agents - The case of referees' home bias." *Journal of Economic Psychology*, 25(4), 461-469.

CHAPTER NINE

THE SECOND LEG HOME ADVANTAGE: EVIDENCE FROM EUROPEAN FOOTBALL CUP COMPETITIONS

LIONEL PAGE AND KATIE PAGE[1]

If we could play at home in the second leg, it would be a big plus for us, I once played for Palace when we beat Charlton in the second leg of a play-off semi-final and the atmosphere was unforgettable. We have done it the other way round before, but I know the value of playing the second match at home (Dougie Freedman, Crystal Palace Striker).

The second leg at home is normally a slight advantage (Arsene Wenger, Coach of Arsenal).

I think it will be a big advantage for us to play the second leg at home in Holland. Sometimes people make mistakes and it is better to make your mistakes in the first leg away from home because there is still time to put things right in the second match (Patrick Kluivert, Player for the Netherlands).

Maybe we have a slight advantage because we are playing the return match at home (Carlo Ancelotti, Coach of AC Milan).

Is this second leg extra home advantage (hereafter SLHA) effect fact or fiction? This is the topic of this chapter. The SLHA effect occurs when, on average, teams are more likely to win a two-stage knock-out competition when they play at home in the second leg. That is, both teams

[1] Lionel Page: Westminster Business School, University of Westminster, London, UK. Katie Page: Heythrop College, University of London ,UK. We thank both the reviewers for their helpful comments and suggestions. An earlier version of this paper was originally published as Page, L & Page, K (2007). The second leg home advantage: Evidence from European football cup competitions. *Journal of Sports Sciences*, 25(14), 1547-1556. (www.informaworld.com).

have a home advantage but this advantage is significantly greater for the team who plays at home second.

The home advantage in sport is an effect that has been widely studied and is well documented (Pollard, 1986; Courneya and Carron, 1992; Nevill and Holder, 1999; Pollard 2002; Pollard and Pollard, 2005; Pollard, 2006a), however, to date, this extra SLHA effect has not been empirically investigated. Home advantage exists in a variety of different team sports including football (Barnett and Hilditch, 1993; Clarke and Norman, 1995), baseball (Thorn and Palmer, 1985), hockey (McGuire *et al.*, 1992) and basketball (Varca, 1980; Greer, 1983; Snyder and Purdy, 1985). The home advantage effect has been most widely studied in football, especially in the English premier league (Barnett and Hilditch, 1993; Clarke and Norman, 1995; Nevill *et al.*, 1996; Nevill and Holder, 1999; Pollard, 2006b) but also in the World Cup (Brown *et al.*, 2002).

There are four reviews of the home advantage effect in sport: Courneya and Carron (1992), Nevill and Holder (1999), Carron *et al.* (2005) and Pollard (2006a). All of these reviews provide an overview of the prior research and help conceptualise the inter-relationships between the empirical findings in order to focus future research. The home advantage has been the subject of many empirical studies; however, the causes of this effect are still unclear.

Several factors have been suggested to explain the home advantage effect. Among the most discussed causes of home advantage are the effects of the crowd (Agnew and Carron, 1994; Nevill *et al.*, 1999), the familiarity with the pitch (Moore and Brylinsky, 1995, Barnett and Hilditch, 1993) and travel related factors (Clarke and Norman, 1995; Pace and Carron, 1992; Recht, 1995).

Other factors that have been proposed as explanatory variables of the home advantage effect include referee bias (Nevill *et al.*, 1996; Nevill *et al.*, 1999; Nevill *et al.*, 2002) and territoriality (Pollard, 2006). In addition, some researchers have proposed other predominantly psychological factors as important in explaining the home advantage including mood and confidence (Terry *et al.*, 1998; Waters and Lovell, 2002).

It is clear that the home advantage effect exists and is a robust effect that it is likely due to a combination and interaction of several factors (crowd, travel, referee decision-making, mood and confidence). However, an area of the home advantage literature that has received much less attention (we know of no academic study) but which is discussed by players, commentators and coaches alike is the perceived extra advantage a team gains by playing at home in the second leg of two-stage knock-out competitions (the SLHA).

The SLHA is a concept that is relevant in all two-stage knock-out competitions, in particular the European Cup competitions and the World Cup qualification rounds. The other main competitions which include knock-out rounds in a two-stage home and away format are: continental club competitions like the CONMEBOL (Confederación Sudamericana de Fútbol) Copa Libertadores and Copa Sudamericana, the CAF (Confederation of African Football) Champions League, the CONCACAF (Confederation of North, Central American and Caribbean Association Football) Champions Cup, and the AFC (Asian Football Confederation) Champions League; and some national competitions like the Carling Cup in England, the Copa del Rei in Spain and the MLS play-off in the United States.

The media, coaches, players and fans all talk of this SLHA effect but very little is known about whether it actually exists and, if it does, what are its likely causes. Therefore, a scientific study is interesting simply in order to establish the existence or non-existence of such an effect. Beyond this mere knowledge, information about the SLHA may also be important in other areas. If it exists, such an effect should be included in forecasting models like those of Dixon and Coles (1997), Dixon and Robinson (1997), and Forrest and Simmons (2000) when applied to European Cup matches. The existence and magnitude of such an effect is also of interest for bookmakers and gamblers. In addition, coaches and managers could use information about the effect in their match preparation.

Analysing data from three major European Cup competitions, the existence of a SLHA effect over the 1955-2006 period is examined. The changes in the effect over time are also investigated. While many possible explanations have been proposed for the existence of a home advantage, as far as we know, no researchers have proposed possible explanations for a systematic difference in the home advantage between two legs, and more specifically, for the existence of a higher home advantage in the second leg, resulting in a SLHA.

No previous research has addressed the existence of SLHA; therefore no specific hypotheses are presented in this chapter. Rather we propose a research question which is to determine whether the SLHA exists. Specifically, in a knock out round with teams of equal ability does the team which plays at home in the second leg have a higher probability to win the round?

Method

Data

The data constitute a total number of 6,182 knock-out rounds, each one consisting of two legs (12,364 individual matches). These data are from three different European competitions, the Champions League (named Champions Cup until 1998), the UEFA Cup and the Inter-Cities Fairs Cup (the earlier form of the UEFA Cup) and the Cup Winners Cup (CWC). For analysis, only knock-out round matches are taken into account, group matches and one leg finals are not considered. The data from the Champions League are from the start of the competition in 1955 to 2006 and contains information from 1,555 matches. The UEFA Cup data are from 1971 to 2006 representing 2,907 matches, and the Inter-Cities Fairs Cup is from 1955 to 1971 and represents 491 matches. Finally, the data from the CWC spans from 1960 to 1999 (last year of this competition) and contains 1,229 matches. For parsimony, the data from the Inter-Cities Fairs Cup and the UEFA Cup are considered together as one competition for all data analysis. For simplicity each season is hereafter designated by the year in which the season finishes (i.e., the season 1955-1956 is represented by the year 1956).

Data Collection and Procedures

Data were taken from the following websites: (1) http://www.uefa.com (all match scores), (2) http://www.xs4all.nl/~kassiesa/bert/uefa/data and (3) http://www.rsssf.com/ec/ecomp.html. UEFA ranking coefficients were taken from website (2) and these data provide an index of team ability at the time of the competition. Information regarding extra time for the relevant matches was taken from website (3).

The team playing at home second is defined as the second leg home team and the other team as the first leg home team. A binary variable *vic* was created to represent the overall result of the second leg home team over the two legs (0 for a defeat, 1 for a victory). For the majority of the matches (N = 5,327, 86%), this result is determined by the total number of goals scored by each team over the two legs, with the team scoring the highest number of goals being defined as the winning team. When the teams are equal on goals at the end of the second leg, several solutions have been used to determine the winner. Before 1971, a third play-off match was most often used (N = 86), or the result was determined by the toss of a coin (N = 20). On several occasions, the result has been determined by the toss of a coin at the end of a play-off (N = 8, included in the previous numbers).

Subsequently, UEFA launched three new measures to eliminate the need for an extra match and the coin toss. First, the rule of away goals was invented to reduce the number of situations where teams are equal at the end of the two legs. The FIFA regulations (FIFA, 2006) describe the away goals rule as follows: "If both teams score the same number of goals in both matches, the goals scored away will be counted as double". This rule implies that in the case where both teams are equal on goals after the two legs, the team that has scored the greatest number of goals away from home will be declared the winner. The away goals rule was first used in 1966 in the CWC, in 1967 in the Inter Cities Fairs and in 1968 in the Champions Cup. Second, the addition of a period of extra time was introduced in 1965. This period, which consists of two 15 minutes halves, is added to the end of the normal duration of the match when the teams are still equal at the end of full time. Third, a penalty shoot-out was introduced at the end of the extra time in 1971 in all competitions. The most effective of these solutions to determine a winner has been the away goals rule (N = 423), then extra time (N = 186), and finally penalty shoot-outs (N = 148).

For all analysis of the SLHA, the observations with play-off matches and/or coin tosses were eliminated. First, a play-off match means that the round no longer can be defined as a two leg knock-out round. Second, coin tosses make the result of the knock-out round purely random, and hence they do not present any interest in regard to the SLHA. Therefore, the final data set consists of 6,084 observations of two leg knock-out rounds.

Analyses

Assuming the draw is random, if there is no SLHA, on average both teams should have the same level of ability, and the probability for each team to win the knock-out round should be 50%. On the contrary, the SLHA implies that the probability of victory for the second leg home team is higher than 50%.

In some cases the UEFA seeding system allocates the "better" teams as the second leg home team. Therefore, the draw is not completely random and a higher percentage of victory for the second leg home team over the two legs could be a result of differences in teams' ability. In order to accurately assess the real effect of the SLHA it is, therefore, necessary to control for the differences in teams' ability. Since 1979, at the end of each year, UEFA calculates coefficients $coef_{it}$ for each team i which represent the team's success during the competition in the current year t. The sum of the last five years of coefficients gives an index of team i ability:

$$ability_{it} = \sum_{k-1}^{5} coef_{it-k}.$$ (1)

This index is then used by the UEFA in **its** seeding and drawing procedures. The method used to calculate the coefficients has changed twice. Before 1999, a correction for the number of matches played per team was made by dividing the sum of the coefficients by the number of matches. Since 1999, the coefficients are not divided by the number of matches played. Hence, the current coefficients are much higher than the previous ones. From 1999 to 2003, the coefficients were calculated with the addition of 50% of the corresponding country coefficient, and since 2004, this figure changed to 30%.

The seeding and drawing procedures of the cups are complex and have changed several times over the years. Before 1990, the UEFA index was only used to determine the number of berths in the UEFA Cup. They are now used by UEFA in its seeding and drawing procedures. Using this index of team ability it is possible to check if the seeding and drawing procedures tend to designate the better teams as the second leg home team. Table 1 presents the descriptive statistics for the index *ability* for each time period. While the UEFA coefficients did not exist before 1979, the index shown for this period is calculated with the same rules which were used from 1979 to 1999. For each period, the table includes the descriptive statistics of the index and the average difference in coefficients between the second leg home team and the first leg home team

$$\Delta ability = ability_{SLHT} - ability_{FLHT}$$ (2)

divided by the number of knock-out rounds in the corresponding period. If there is no bias in the seeding system, the difference score should not be significantly different from zero. As shown in Table 1 this difference score is positive and significant for each period, indicating a bias in the seeding system which tends to allocate the better teams as the second leg home team.

Therefore, to accurately assess the SLHA, it is necessary to control for differences in team ability. Because the main variable of interest in this study is the victories over two legs, the probability of winning for the second leg home team while controlling for differences in team ability must be estimated. A logistic regression model is used for this purpose. Calling p the probability of an overall victory for the second leg home team, the following logistic regression model may be estimated:

Table 1: Descriptive statistics of the UEFA coefficients.

Period	Variable[a]	Mean[b]	SD	Min	Max	N
1956-1979	ability	2.170	1.709	.5	9.856	3504
	Δability	0.157*	2.994	−8.609	8.609	2064
1980-1989	ability	2.302	1.775	.5	9.054	2602
	Δability	0.227*	3.249	−7.915	8.665	1361
1990-1999	ability	2.263	1.824	.333	9.124	2044
	Δability	0.221**	3.122	−8.608	8.18	1351
2000-2004	ability	25.106	22.506	0	147.233	1112
	Δability	2.723*	34.538	−106.035	132.937	948
2005-2006	ability	23.660	24.978	0	146.35	580
	Δability	2.850	28.902	−121.469	115.174	360

* Significant at the 5% level, ** significant at the 1% level.
[b] Significant difference from 0 calculated with a one sample mean test.
[a] The *ability* is the sum of the team's UEFA coefficients over the last five years. The *ability* is the difference in *ability* between the second leg home team and the first leg home team. Differences in the magnitude for Δability are a result of the different calculation methods used for the UEFA coefficients in the different time periods.

$$\log\left(\frac{p}{1-p}\right) = \alpha + \beta \Delta ability \tag{3}$$

The coefficient α is a constant and β represents the effect of the difference in team ability on the probability of the second leg home team to win. For two teams with an identical level of ability, the estimated probability $\hat{p}_0$ is a function of the estimated constant $\hat{\alpha}$ in model (3):

$$\hat{p}_0 = \left(e^{\hat{\alpha}}/1 + e^{\hat{\alpha}}\right). \tag{4}$$

A test of the hypothesis $\hat{p}_0 = .50$ is evaluated from the z statistic of the constant in the logit model, where $H_0 : \alpha = 0$. Unless stated otherwise, all the tests are two tailed.

Concerning the UEFA index, because of the changes which occurred in 1999 and 2004, the coefficient β in the logistic regression model will have different values over the three time periods. In order to address this problem, three dummy variables were created: $I_{(61-99)}$, $I_{(00-04)}$, $I_{(05-06)}$ where:

$$I_{(t_1-t_2)} = \begin{cases} 1 : t_1 \leq year \leq t_2 \\ 0 : otherwise \end{cases} \tag{5}$$

In order to account for the changes in the UEFA index, the logistic regression model estimated is the following:

$$\log\left(\frac{p}{p-1}\right) = \alpha + \beta_1 I_{(61-99)} \Delta ability + \beta_2 I_{(00-04)} \Delta ability + \beta_3 I_{(05-06)} \Delta ability \tag{6}$$

The model (6) is a version of (3) allowing the coefficients of Δ *ability* to change between sub-periods. As the main aim of this paper is to study the SLHA, and therefore the probability to win for the second leg home team, the paper does not report tables with all of the output from the regression models, but instead, and more importantly, it reports the adjusted value of the variables of interest with its degree of significance relative to the null hypothesis. Last, it should be noted that all analyses, unless otherwise specified, are conducted on the data pooled over the three competitions.

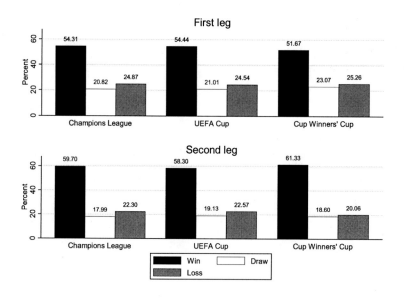

Figure 1: Home advantage by competition and leg.

Results

General Overview

In line with the results from the main national football competitions, there is a significant home advantage effect in all three European football competitions. Figure 1 shows this effect and decomposes it between the first and second legs. These figures are similar to those found previously in the English Premier League (Clarke and Norman, 1995; Nevill *et al.*, 1996) and those of other football competitions such as the World Cup (Brown *et al.*, 2002) and various European national competitions including Finland, Sweden, Belgium and Ireland (Pollard, 2006b). The difference between the percentages of home wins and home losses is a logical extension of Bray (1999) measure of home advantage for teams (home wins minus away wins) to measure the home advantage *in a competition*. Using this measure, the home advantage in the current study is approximately 33 percentage points, averaged over the two legs and the three competitions. It is greater in the second leg (36.8) than in the first leg (28.5).

Table 2: Second-leg home advantage statistics by competition and overall.

	Percentage of global wins for the second leg home team[a]	Corrected for ability[b]	N
Champions League	54.44***	53.49***	1521
UEFA Cup	53.95***	53.29***	1208
Cup Winners' Cup	58.53***	58.65***	3355
Overall	54.98***	54.33***	6084

[a] Significant difference from 50 calculated with a mean test.
[b] Significant difference from 50 calculated with the z statistic of the constant.
*** Significant at the 0.1% level.

Table 2 shows the percentages of global victories over the two legs for the second leg home team both overall and by competition. On average, the probability of winning at the end of two legs for the second leg home team is 55% which is significantly different from 50% at $p<0.001$ using a one-sample two tailed proportion test.

After controlling for differences in team ability, the estimated probability for an overall victory, using the logit model of equation (2), is only slightly lower (54.3%) and still significantly different from 50%. This result indicates that there is a SLHA and that the higher percentage of victories for the second leg home team is not just due to the bias in the UEFA seeding system.

What Happens After Full-Time?

A possible explanation of the SLHA is that the second leg home team wins significantly more often because they have the advantage of benefiting more from the home advantage effect. That is, in the case of equality after two full matches the second leg home team has the additional advantage of extra time being played on their home ground. This is what Nevill and Holder (1999) call a
"rule factor". When looking only at the matches that involved extra time (without penalties, N = 186) there is a significant advantage for the second leg home team. The probability of the second leg home team winning, adjusted for differences in team ability, is 66.42%. This proportion is significantly different from 50% at $p<0.001$. In the case of equality at the end of extra time (N = 148), there also seems to be an advantage to take penalties on the home ground with home teams winning 57.3% ($p<0.10$) of the time. Therefore, at least some of the SLHA effect can be explained by the advantage of extra time and penalties at home.

Table 3: Probability of a victory for the second-leg home team depending on the outcome of the second leg match ended.

	Adj. probability	N
Full time matches		
Champions League	53.15*	1452
UEFA Cup	52.55**	3155
Cup Winners' Cup	58.36***	1143
Overall	53.77***	5750
Matches with extra time		
Overall	66.42***	186
Matches with penalties		
Overall	57.33	148

* Significant at the 5% level, ** significant at the 1% level, *** significant at the 0.1% level.

However, the SLHA cannot entirely be explained by these two extra time situations. There is a clear advantage for the second-leg home team in extra time, however the number of matches are too few (only 3% and 5.5% including penalties) to fully account for the entire SLHA effect. The matches with extra time and penalties were removed from the data set and the analysis re-run. Table 3 shows the adjusted probabilities for the sample restricted to full time matches (N=5,750). There is still a 53.8% chance of the second leg home team winning. Therefore, the SLHA still exists even in matches where there is no extra time or penalties.

Time Trends

The data used for this research span 51 years of European competitions; therefore this allows the study of the SLHA over time. The adjusted probabilities for the second leg home team to win were calculated for each year of the competition by estimating model (1) for each year. Figure 2 shows the changes in the magnitude of the SLHA over time for full-time matches only. A SLHA seems to be present in all the periods with a decreasing trend over time.

To test the statistical significance of changes in the SLHA over time, one dummy per decade was introduced into the logistic regression model (2). In this way, we performed the logistic equivalent of an ANCOVA in order to estimate an adjusted winning probability for the second leg home

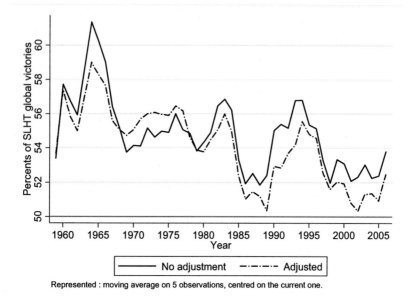

Represented : moving average on 5 observations, centred on the current one.

Figure 2: Probability of an overall victory for the second leg home team.

team per decade, while controlling for differences in ability with UEFA coefficients as covariates. Table 4 presents the estimated probabilities of a second leg home team victory per decade.

The SLHA decreases over time and is no longer significant for a two tailed test in the last decade. The winning probability for the second leg home team in this last decade is, however, still positive. There are no significant differences between the coefficients per decade. However, when a variable *year* is introduced in the logistic regression instead of the decade dummy variables, its coefficient is negative and significant ($p<0.05$), indicating a significant downward trend of the SLHA over time. The corresponding adjusted probability of global victory for the second leg home team decreases approximately 5.4 percentage points from 1956 (57%) to 2006 (51.6%).

Discussion

The aim of this research was to study the existence of the SLHA in two leg knock out encounters. The statistical analysis of 51 years of European

Table 4: Adjusted winning probabilities of the second leg home team per decade.

Period	Adj. probability	L: CI (95%)	H: CI (95%)	N
1956-65[a]	56.14[***]	51.25	60.91	444
1966-75	55.38[**]	52.18	58.54	1078
1976-85	55.14[*]	52.07	58.17	1161
1986-95	53.07	49.98	56.13	1169
1996-06	51.79	49.85	54.22	1898
Overall	53.77	52.38	55.15	5750

* Significant at the 5% level, ** significant at the 1% level, *** significant at the 0.1% level.
[a] The difference in ability is set to zero by default for the years 1956-60 where no ability index is available. The absence of adjustment for this period is however not the reason for the high value of the probability as the non adjusted percentage of victory for this period is actually only 51.9% on 106 matches.

Cup football competitions showed that second leg home teams do have a significant advantage in knock out rounds. This advantage has decreased significantly over time.

Many possible explanations for the home advantage effect have been proposed. However, the SLHA introduces new questions because it is associated with a difference in two home advantages, the one of the first leg home team and the one of the second leg home team. It is, a priori, not clear how the current explanations for the home advantage effect can account for this asymmetry in home advantage.

One possible explanation for the asymmetry in home advantage could relate to the differential stakes involved in the two matches. Specifically, home advantage could be higher for matches which have higher stakes or are more important with respect to their immediate outcomes. The second leg match has a higher stake because it is more decisive. While the stake of the first match is to get an advantage over the other team, the stake of the second match is the qualification. As a consequence of this difference in stakes or perceived importance, several factors already discussed in relation to the home advantage could be influential.

A factor that has been linked to the home advantage effect and studied relatively widely is that of referee bias and its interaction with crowd factors (Nevill and Holder, 1999). It is, therefore, possible that referee bias might be greater in the second-leg match. Specifically, the crowd could perhaps have more influence on the officials in matches of greater importance. For example, it is possible that in matches where there are higher stakes, the crowd is more hostile/aggressive. This could have an impact on the decision making of the referees to further favour the home team. Research could be conducted to examine this possible explanation.

Another explanation suggested for the home advantage involves the tactics of the players and the managers. Specifically, Pollard (2006a) notes that teams playing away from home often adopt a more defensive and cautious approach which may contribute to the home advantage effect. It is possible that there may be an interaction between the types of tactics employed by teams in the second leg as a result of the first leg match. Future research could investigate the tactics of managers, both in terms of their proposed game plan and their behavioural play on the field.

A number of psychological factors may have implications in this asymmetry in perceived stakes /importance. For example motivation and or anxiety levels of the players may be significantly greater in the second leg which may result in increased effort and better performance. Waters and Lovell (2002) identified both individual player confidence and positivity as important factors in explaining the home advantage, but whether these dimensions are different over two legs has not been studied. There is currently very little research on these topics but in future researchers could assess in more detail the psychological states of the players prior to home and away two leg matches to gauge if there are any significant differences in these respects.

It is well established that the home advantage effect has decreased significantly over time (Nevill and Holder, 1999; Pollard, 2006a,b). In this study we found that the SLHA also decreases significantly over time and is now just marginally significant. As the SLHA results from a difference between the home advantages of two teams, factors that explain the decline in the home advantage may be relevant for an explanation of the decline in the SLHA. For example, Smith (2003) has suggested that increased professionalism and the development of a market culture in the game could be factors accounting for the decline in home advantage.

Explanations for the home advantage are far from comprehensive and complete, especially in relation to the interactions between important factors. Therefore, explanations for an asymmetry in home advantage are also difficult to specify given the current state of understanding. Nevertheless, it is an interesting and important phenomenon that certainly warrants further investigation.

In conclusion, in this chapter we have demonstrated that the SLHA exists in three European Cup football competitions. This effect means that the second leg home team has a significantly higher probability to win a two-stage knock-out tie (54.3%). Potentially, the SLHA could in part be explained by the differing abilities of the two teams which arise because of a bias in the drawing procedures. However, the SLHA effect is still significant even after controlling for any differences in team ability. In addition, a small part of the SLHA can be explained by extra time and penalties being played on the home ground of the second leg home team. However, these two factors alone cannot explain the major part of the SLHA. The SLHA has decreased significantly over time and is now much lower than it was at the beginning of the European cup competitions. Future research is needed to further understand the cause of the SLHA effect and the factors that have contributed to its decline.

References

Agnew, G. A. and A. V. Carron (1994). "Crowd effects and the home advantage." *International Journal of Sport Psychology*, 25(1), 53-62.

Barnett, V. and S. Hilditch (1993). "The effect of an artificial pitch surface on home team performance in football (soccer)." *Journal of the Royal Statistical Society*, 156(1), 39-50.

Bray, S. R. (1999). "The home advantage from an individual team perspective." *Journal of Applied Sport Psychology*, 11(1), 116-125.

Brown, T. D., J. L. Van Raalte, B. W. Brewer, C. R. Winter and A. A. Cornelius (2002). "World cup soccer home advantage." *Journal of Sport Behavior*, 25(2), 134-144.

Carron, A.V., T. M. Loughhead and S. R. Bray (2005). "The home advantage in sport competitions: Courneya and Carron's (1992) conceptual framework a decade later." *Journal of Sports Sciences*, 23(4), 395-407.

Clarke, S. R. and J. M. Norman (1995). "Home advantage of individual clubs in English soccer." *The Statistician*, 44(4), 509-521.

Courneya, K. S. and A. V. Carron (1992). "The home advantage in sport competitions: A literature review." *Journal of Sport and Exercise Psychology*, 14(1), 13-27.

Dixon, M. J. and S. G. Coles (1997). "Modelling Association Football Score and Inefficiencies in the Football Betting Market." *Applied Statistics*, 46(2), 265-280.

Dixon, M. J. and M. E. Robinson (1997). "A birth process model for association football matches." *The Statistician*, 47(3), 523-538.

FIFA (2006). *Regulations. 2006 FIFA World Cup.*

Forrest, D. and R. Simmons (2000). "Forecasting sport: the behaviour and performance of football tipsters." *International Journal of Forecasting*, 16(3), 317-331.

Greer, D. L. (1983). "Spectator booing and the home advantage: A study of social influence in the basketball arena." *Social Psychology Quarterly*, 46(3), 252-261.

McGuire, E.J, K. S. Courneya, N. W. Widmeyer and A. V. Carron (1992). "Aggression as a potential mediator of the home advantage in professional ice hockey." *Journal of Sport and Exercise Psychology*, 14(2), 148-158.

Moore, J. C. and J. Brylinsky (1995). "Facility familiarity and the home advantage." *Journal of Sport Behavior*, 18(4), 302-311.

Nevill, A. M. and R. L. Holder (1999). "Home advantage in sport: an overview of studies on the advantage of playing at home." *Sports Medicine*, 28(4), 221-236.

Nevill, A. M., N. J. Balmer and A. M. Williams (1999)."Crowd influence on decisions in association football." *Lancet*, 353(9162), 1416.

Nevill, A .M., S. M. Newell and S. Gale (1996). "Factors associated with home advantage in English and Scottish soccer matches." *Journal of Sports Sciences*, 14(2), 181-186.

Nevill, A. M., N .J. Balmer and A .M. Williams (2002). "The influence of crowd noise and experience upon refereeing decisions in football." *Psychology of Sport and Exercise*, 3(4), 261-272.

Pace, A. and A. Carron (1992). "Travel and the home advantage." *Canadian Journal of Sport Science*, 17(1), 60-64.

Pollard, R. (1986). "Home advantage in soccer: a retrospective analysis." *Journal of Sports Sciences*, 4(3), 237-248.

Pollard, R. (2002). "Evidence of a reduced home advantage when a team moves to a new stadium." *Journal of Sports Sciences*, 20(12), 969-973.

—. (2006a). "Home advantage in soccer: Variations in its magnitude and a literature review of the inter-related factors associated with its existence." *Journal of Sport Behavior*, 29(2), 169-189.

—. (2006b). "Worldwide regional variations in home advantage in association football." *Journal of Sports Sciences*, 24(3), 231-240.

Pollard, R. and G. Pollard (2005). "Long-term trends in home advantage in professional team sports in North America and England (1876 - 2003)." *Journal of Sports Sciences*, 23(4), 337-350.

Recht, L. D., R. A. Lew and W. J. Schwartz (1995). "Baseball teams beaten by jet-lag." *Nature*, 377(6550), 583.

Smith, R. D. (2003). "The home advantage revisited: Winning and crowd support in an era of national publics." *Journal of Sport and Social Issues*, 27(4), 346-371.

—. (2005). "Disconnects between popular discourse and home advantage research: What can fans and media tell us about the home advantage phenomenon?" *Journal of Sports Sciences*, 23(4), 351-364.

Snyder, E. E. and D. A. Purdy (1985). "The home advantage in collegiate basketball." *Sociology of Sport Journal*, 2(1), 352-356.

Terry, P. C., N. Wahond and A. V. Carron (1998). "The influence of game location on athletes' psychological states." *Journal of Science and Medicine in Sport*, 1(1), 29-37.

Thorn, J. and P. Palmer (1985). *The hidden game of baseball*. New York: Doubleday.

Varca, P. E. (1980). "An analysis of home and away game performance of male college basketball teams." *Journal of Sport and Exercise Psychology*, 2(3), 245-257.

Waters, A. and G. Lovell (2002). "An examination of the homefield advantage in a professional English soccer team from a psychological standpoint." *Football Studies*, 5(1), 46-59.

CHAPTER TEN

CRIME AND PUNISHMENT IN PROFESSIONAL FOOTBALL: EVIDENCE FROM THE ENGLISH PREMIER LEAGUE

PETER DAWSON[1]

Disciplinary transgressions by players and sanctions taken by referees play a key role in sporting contests. This is especially true of professional football (soccer), where the performance of players and referees in particular are closely scrutinised. A commonly aired grievance by football pundits, players, managers and fans is the apparent inconsistency in decision-making.

> Evidence of both verbal and physical abuse directed at the referee is commonplace and attitudes towards the 'men in black' are indifferent depending on their refereeing decisions from week to week and game to game (Mason and Lovell, 2000).

One week a manager might applaud a refereeing decision not to award a penalty to the opposition but several weeks later vilify the same referee for sending-off one of his players. This has led to one UK national newspaper describing the modern referee requiring

> the wisdom of Solomon, the patience of Job, the vision of Superman and the thick skin of Del Boy (Daily Telegraph, 19 January 1998; quoted in Elleray, 2004).

In contrast to players, few referees obtain celebrity-like status. The over-whelming majority of referees who make it into the spotlight generally do so as a result of high-profile errors.[2]

---

[1] Dawson: Department of Economics and International Development, University of Bath, Claverton Down, Bath, BA2 7AY, UK.

In some sense this is understandable as few would dispute the potential impact the referee has on a game of football, or even on the outcome of a season. In sporting terms, the margins separating success from failure can be slender, and often depend ultimately on split-second decisions taken by referees and players in the heat of battle. Consider the 2002/03 season in the English Premier League as an example (the final season under observation in the empirical analysis which follows). At the end of the season only five points separated the team that finished in 8th position (Southampton) from the team that finished 15th (Leeds United), who themselves were only 5 points clear of relegation. Yet the financial implications of success or failure for individual football clubs and their players can be huge. At the time of writing (2007) it has been reported that the financial cost of relegation from the Premier League is in the region of £50m.

The purpose of this chapter is to examine more closely the actions of agents on the field of play. In particular we examine whether players do act as rational economic agents and investigate the old adage that referees are biased and inconsistent. This is undertaken by analysing the incidence of disciplinary sanction in the English Premier League. The first task is to present an overview of the economics of crime and punishment, drawing upon previous literature relating to professional team sports.

Economics of Crime and Punishment

The seminal work on modelling the economics of crime and punishment was presented by Becker (1968). The economic approach to crime is based on the concept that there is a market for criminal activity. The supply of crime is determined by the costs and benefits of illegal activities as well as the individual's risk preferences.

We assume from the outset that individuals (professional football players in the present context) are rational utility-maximisers. The decision to whether or not to commit a crime (disciplinary offence on the field of play) depends on the utility they would (expect) to gain from acting illegally versus the gain they would (expect) to gain from acting legally. Formally, the expected utility from committing an offence is given by:

$$EU \;=\; p(Y - f) + (1 - p)U(Y) \tag{1}$$

---

[2] A recent high profile example was the actions of the English referee Graham Poll who booked the Croatian player Josip Simunic three times before dismissing him during a group stage match against Australia in the World Cup finals of 2006.

EU is the expected utility for the individual; p is the *subjective* probability of being caught and convicted, which implies that it is the judgement of the player as to whether he might be caught or not; f is the monetary equivalent of the punishment if convicted; Y is the gain from committing the offence (monetary and psychic income); and U(.) is the individual's von-Neumann-Morgenstern utility index.

Whereas Becker considers the income and punishment equivalents of an offense separated from other income, Brown and Reynolds (1973) take the individual's initial income position as a point of reference. In this case, expected utility becomes:

$$EU = p(\overline{W} - L) + (1 - p)U(\overline{W} + G) \qquad (2)$$

Where $\overline{W}$ represents the present wealth of the individual; the potential gain to committing a crime is G and the loss if caught is L. If no crime is committed, p = 0 (and therefore L = G = 0) and $EU = U(\overline{W})$. If a crime is committed but not detected p = 0, as before, but this time $EU = U(\overline{W} + G)$. Furthermore, it is also possible that the offender who is convicted may retain some gain from the offence (that is, G > L). This implies that even if the probability of detection is high there are still instances where there are benefits to committing the offence.

Ultimately an individual will commit a crime if $EU > U(\overline{W})$. But will the individual accept the "gamble" and commit the offence? This will depend on: (i) Expected gains (G) and losses (L); (ii) the individual's perception of the probability of being caught; and (iii) the individual's attitude to risk.

The standard comparative statics of (1) and (2) demonstrate that an increase in either L or p will reduce the expected utility from committing offences, reducing the number of crimes committed by the individual (regardless of attitude to risk).[3] It provides support for the deterrence theory of crime: increases in the certainty and severity of punishment deter crimes. Becker suggested that fines should be used as the principal form of punishment (because in terms of resource costs they are minimal when compared to, say, imprisonment). A further advantage is the revenue raised could be used to compensate victims.

---

[3] In other modelling approaches, such as the time allocation models of Ehrlich (1973) and Heineke (1978), an increase in the severity of punishment will lead to a reduction in crime if the individual is risk-averse. But if the individual is a risk-taker (or risk-lover) the result is ambiguous.

How does this model relate to professional team sports? Principally this relies on the assumption that disciplinary transgressions in sport are analogous to criminal behaviour. In some cases there is a direct link: player behaviour on the field has occasionally led to criminal prosecutions. The first professional footballer in England to be fined in a criminal court for an assault on an opponent in a game was the Swindon Town midfielder Chris Kamara. In 1988 Kamara was fined £1,200 for grievous bodily harm after he broke the jaw of Shrewsbury Town's Jim Melrose. Other high profile examples include Duncan Ferguson sentenced to three months imprisonment in 1995 for head-butting an opposition player whilst playing for Rangers and Eric Cantona who in January of the same year incurred an eight month suspension and 120 hours of community service for a kung fu style kick at a spectator whilst playing for Manchester United. Perhaps not surprisingly, litigation by recipients of violent tackles against their transgressors has also increased. For example, Paul Elliott filed a lawsuit seeking damages against the Liverpool forward Dean Saunders following a career ending injury in 1992.

Referees have also been recipients of violent behaviour. A BBC regional television programme, Inside Out North West, investigated assaults on football referees discovered 125 football referees were assaulted in England in 2006. In December 2004, a footballer was given a 30 year ban for head-butting an official during a Northern Ireland amateur match. Swedish referee Anders Frisk was forced to retire from refereeing following threats directed to him and his family following controversy in Barcelona's 2-1 win against Chelsea in a Champions League game in February 2005. And in one incident at a Promozione (amateur match) in Puglia (Italy) a referee was threatened with a gun in the changing rooms.

The model also assumes that professional footballers act rationally. Heckelman and Yates (2003) argue that such decision-making is not planned in advanced and based more on 'crimes of passion' rather than on a rational response to cost-benefit analysis.[4] Whilst it is true that some incidents are retaliatory in nature, it is also true that part of the strategic behaviour available to teams is to nullify the impact of the opposition. This is quite likely in situations where a (relatively) weak team faces a strong (high quality) opponent. In an investigation on the impact of transgressions by players in the National Hockey League (NHL), Allen (2005) finds that illegal activity of the opponent does induce a retaliatory response but individual-specific incentives (e.g. success associated with

---

[4] In the case of 'crimes of passion' the net reward from crime is negative (i.e. $G = 0$ in equation 2). This will not however affect the general proposition that an increase in the price of crime will lower the aggregate quantity supplied.

playing aggressively) are quantitatively more important. Important differences also arise with respect to whether the offence was considered violent or non-violent.

The rationality on the part of players is also provided by anecdotal evidence which suggests that disciplinary transgressions increase as the returns to winning increase. For example, the average number of yellow (red) cards at the 2002 World Cup was 4.25 (0.27) whereas in the corresponding (English Premier League) season (2001-2002) values were 3.05 (0.19), respectively.[5] Rationality also appears to be prevalent in other areas of player decision-making, such as penalty-kicks (Palacios-Huerta, 2003).

Previous Literature on Crime and Punishment in Professional Team Sports

In the previous section it was noted that increases in the certainty (i.e. probability of being caught) and severity of punishment deter crimes. One obvious, if perhaps costly, mechanism for increasing the probability of being caught is to increase the level of monitoring. In the context of professional team sports McCormick and Tollison (1984) provide possibly the earliest investigation in their consideration of North American college basketball. They found that an increase in referees from two to three per match led to sharp fall in the number of fouls called. Similar impacts have also been found by Heckelman and Yates (2003) and Allen (2002) with respect to the North American National Hockey League.

Alternatively one could analyse whether transgressions are reduced when the severity of the punishment increases. For example, following a rule change implemented by the English Football Association at the start of the 1998-99 season requiring an automatic red card punishment for the tackle from behind, Witt (2005) finds evidence of an increase in the incidence of yellow cards (awarded for lesser offences), but no increase in the incidence of red cards.

As well as the behaviour of transgressors, research has also focused on the behaviour of the enforcers. In the present context, alleged refereeing bias in favour of the home team is a frequently-aired grievance on the part of managers, players and spectators.

---

[5] It might also reflect a higher detection rate brought about through greater efforts of referees who are influenced by the greater financial rewards associated with such contests.

Garicano et al. (2005), using Spanish league football as a case study, find a tendency for referees to add more time at the end of matches when the home team is trailing by one goal compared to when the home team is leading. Similar findings have been demonstrated in the German premier league (Bundesliga) by Sutter and Kocher (2004) and Dohmen (2005). The latter study also finds evidence of home team bias in the awarding of penalties.

A seemingly important determinant of home team bias which has been investigated by a number of authors is the influence of the crowd. In a laboratory style setting, Nevill et al. (2002) played videotapes of tackles to referees who, having been told the identities of the home and away teams, were asked to classify the tackles as legal or illegal. One group of referees viewed the tape with the soundtrack (including crowd's reaction) switched on, while a second group viewed silently. The first group were more likely to rule in favour of the home team, and the first group's rulings were more in line with those of the original match referee.

This idea of the crowd exerting social pressures on the referee has been developed by Dohmen (2005). He finds that architectural conditions of the match play an important role in the refereeing biased observed, identifying three factors: the size of the crowd, the attendance-to-capacity ratio and the proximity of supporters to the field. In particular, he finds that the allocation of injury time in close matches is longer in stadiums where the crowd is physically closer to the field of play. Home teams are significantly more likely to be awarded a disputable penalty but the physical distance between the crowd and the field is again important. Pettersson-Lidbom and Priks (2007) find similar results in their consideration of Italian football following the Italian government's decision to enforce clubs with sub-standard stadiums to play their home games without spectators.

Recent evidence indicates that enforcers also respond to incentives. Rickman and Witt (2008) apply a natural experiment to assess the introduction of professional referees in English Premier League and find that the degree of favouritism present in the adding of time at the end of matches essentially disappears following the introduction of professionalism. The argument they make to account for this is the higher remuneration associated with the professional status of referees, which, together with increased monitoring, acts as a disincentive effect on (implicit) favouritism.

Players' assessment of the probability of detection may therefore be influenced by the expected behaviour of the referee in charge of the contest. This will be generated by prior knowledge by the treatment of the player by the same official in different contests, or through observations of the treatment of other players with a similar style of play. It will, given the discussions above, also be formed by the context of the game – either by the significance of the contest and / or the size and composition of the crowd. Therefore the same offence may be viewed differently by different referees in different contexts. In forming expectations about certain referees, players, together with managers and coaches, could (potentially) use this to provide a competitive advantage for their team.

Given the same offence may be viewed differently by different officials is itself indicative of the view that officials also use prior information in forming decisions they make. Previous research has found this to be important both prior to contests taking place and as contests unfold. For example, Plessner and Betsch (2001) observe that officials were less likely to award a penalty to a team if they had previously awarded the same team a penalty but more likely to award a penalty to a team if they awarded a penalty to the opposing team. Buraimo et al. (2007), in their consideration of the German Bundesliga and the English Premier League, find that a yellow card previously awarded to the home (away) team increases the probability of the away (home) team receiving a similar sanction. As the authors suggest, this could reflect retaliation effects on behalf of players or the tendency for referees to "even-up" decisions.

Finally Jones et al. (2002) provide evidence which suggests that teams with aggressive reputations affect the number of red and yellow cards awarded. For example on observing a bad challenge by a player with an aggressive reputation the referee may be more inclined to send that player off, because he interprets the challenge as a deliberate attempt to injure an opponent. In contrast, a similar challenge made by a player with little or no aggressive reputation may only lead to a caution because the referee believes in this instance, and based on prior knowledge of the player, the tackle was mis-timed rather than intentional.

In summary, previous literature in this field can be categorised according to the unit of observation (player transgressions, time-added on, penalty-decisions) and on the impact of rule changes on player and referee behaviour. Some studies have investigated the impact of prior knowledge and beliefs and more recently attention has begun to turn to within-game dynamics; the empirical analysis which follows attempts to capture some of these dimensions. The emphasis throughout is on the incidence of disciplinary sanction and centres on two testable hypotheses: whether the incidence of sanctions is stable over time (i.e. whether rule changes deter criminal activity in the long-run) and whether there is variation in referee behaviour in the issuing of such sanctions.

Disciplinary Sanctions in Premier League Football[6]

Referee Decision-Making and Sanctionable Offences

In a sporting contest, referees are assigned the task of implementing the rules of the game and ensuring that players abide by its regulations. With specific reference to professional football, Helsen and Bultynck (2004) in analysis based on the 31 matches of the Euro 2000 estimate that a top referee makes 137 observable decisions in an average match these include inter alia: offside, awarding of free-kicks (direct and indirect), penalties, corners, goal-kicks, throw-ins, substitutions, halting play for serious injury. In the case of free-kicks and penalties, for example, the referee has the discretion to determine whether the foul merits a sanctionable offence, by issuing either a yellow or red card.

Based on the FIFA disciplinary code, a player is shown a yellow card, also known as a booking or caution, if he commits one of the following infringements:

- unsporting behaviour such as foul play, dangerous play or holding on to an opponent's shirt or any part of his body;
- showing disapproval of match officials by word or action (criticising decisions, protesting);
- violation of the Laws of the Game;
- delaying the restart of play;
- failing to comply with the required distance during corner kicks or free kicks;
- entering or re-entering the field of play without prior permission from the referee;
- leaving the field of play without prior permission from the referee;
- play acting (diving, feigning injury, etc.).

There is no further punishment within the match, unless the player commits a second cautionable offence, in which case a red card is awarded and the player is expelled for the rest of the match (with no replacement permitted, so the team completes the match one player short). A red card, also known as a sending-off or dismissal, is awarded for more serious offences, and results in immediate expulsion (again, with no replacement permitted). Again, drawing upon the FIFA disciplinary code, a player is sent off if he commits one of the following infringements:

- serious foul play such as excessive or brute force;

---

[6] This section draws heavily on Dawson et al. (2007).

- brutal action such as violent or aggressive conduct;
- spitting at an opponent or anyone else;
- denying the opposing team a goal or an obvious goal-scoring opportunity by deliberately handling the ball;
- denying an obvious goal-scoring opportunity to an opponent moving towards the opposing goal by committing an infringement punishable by a free kick or a penalty kick;
- making offensive, insulting or abusive remarks;
- second caution during the same match

After the match, a red card results in a suspension, preventing the player from appearing in one, two or three of his team's next scheduled matches. A player who accumulates five yellow cards in different matches within the same season also receives a suspension. On the assumption that players act rationally implies that by committing a red card offence the transgressor will assess the likely cost this will incur on the team during the present game (short-term effect) and the cost incurred on the team by his absence in subsequent matches (long-term effect).

Preliminary Data Analysis

In the statistical analysis which follows the incidence of disciplinary sanction taken against players in the English Premier League is observed over seven seasons (1996-97 to 2002-03). Tables 1 and 2 display frequency distributions for the number of yellow and red cards incurred by the home and away teams in 2,660 Premier League matches played during this period. The disparity in the frequency of yellow and red cards is clear: no red cards were generated in eight-five percent of matches, whereas only seven percent of matches involved no yellow cards. Furthermore in only twenty-four percent of matches did the home team collect more yellow cards than the away team.

Over the period of analysis a number of changes have been made in the content and interpretation of the rules relating to the award of yellow and red cards. The key changes are detailed in Table 3. Most of the changes have increased the range of offences that are subject to disciplinary sanction, although there has occasionally been movement in the opposite direction. Perhaps the most significant change was the directive at the start of the 1998-99 season making the tackle from behind punishable by automatic dismissal. This provides us with the first of our two testable hypotheses: whether the incidence of disciplinary sanction is stable over time. Essentially this provides a test of whether players and/or referees have modified their behaviour over time.

Table 1: Observed numbers (percentages) of yellow cards incurred by the home and away teams, English Premier League, seasons 1996-7 to 2002-3.

		Away team								
		0	1	2	3	4	5	6	7	Total
	0	189	254	158	86	35	9	1	0	732
		(7.1)	(9.5)	(5.9)	(3.2)	(1.3)	(0.3)	(<0.1)	(0)	(27.5)
	1	110	260	264	147	66	23	6	1	877
		(4.1)	(9.8)	(9.9)	(5.5)	(2.5)	(0.9)	(0.2)	(<0.1)	(33)
	2	64	162	158	126	47	25	6	1	589
		(2.4)	(6.1)	(5.9)	(4.7)	(1.8)	(0.9)	(0.2)	(<0.1)	(22.1)
Home	3	18	77	96	72	39	14	3	4	323
team		(0.7)	(2.9)	(3.6)	(2.7)	(1.5)	(0.5)	(0.1)	(0.2)	(12.1)
	4	3	13	29	32	16	8	2	0	103
		(0.1)	(0.5)	(1.1)	(1.5)	(0.6)	(0.3)	(0.1)	(0)	(3.9)
	5	1	3	12	11	2	1	0	1	31
		(<0.1)	(0.1)	(0.5)	(0.4)	(0.1)	(<0.1)	(0)	(<0.1)	(1.2)
	6	0	0	1	2	1	1	0	0	5
		(0)	(0)	(<0.1)	(0.1)	(<0.1)	(<0.1)	(0)	(0)	(0.2)
	Total	385	769	718	476	206	81	18	7	2660
		(14.5)	(28.9)	(27)	(17.9)	(7.7)	(3)	(0.7)	(0.3)	(100)

Source: The Football Association.

Table 2: Observed numbers (percentages) of red cards incurred by the home and away teams, English Premier League, seasons 1996-7 to 2002-3.

		Away team			
		0	1	2	Total
	0	2258 (84.9)	231 (8.7)	8 (0.3)	2497 (93.9)
	1	119 (4.5)	34 (1.3)	3 (0.1)	156 (5.9)
Home team	2	2 (0.1)	3 (0.1)	0 (0)	5 (0.2)
	3	2 (0.1)	0 (0)	0 (0)	2 (0.1)
	Total	2381 (89.5)	268 (10.1)	11 (0.4)	2660 (100)

Source: The Football Association.

Initial consideration of this hypothesis is provided in Table 4, which presents the variation in the average numbers of yellow and red cards awarded against the home and away teams per match by season. The directive issued at the start of the 1998-99 season making the tackle from behind punishable by automatic dismissal is the only rule change that appears to have had a discernible impact on the data. The mean incidence of disciplinary sanction is higher for 1998-99 than for any of the other six

Table 3: Rule changes and changes of interpretation, by season.

Season	Rule changes/changes of interpretation
1996-1997	Referees are reminded to severely punish the tackle from behind.
1997-1998	Failure to retreat the required distance at free kicks and delaying the restart of play are to be interpreted as yellow card offences.
1998-1999	The tackle from behind which endangers the safety of an opponent is to be interpreted as a red card offence. The red card offence of denying an opponent a goal scoring opportunity is changed to denying an opposing team a goal scoring opportunity (widening the scope of this offence).
1999-2000	Simulation (diving, feigning injury or pretending that an offence has been committed) is to be punishable with a yellow card. Referees are reminded to punish racist remarks with a red card. Swearing is also an offence warranting a red card.
2000-2001	Offensive gestures are to be punishable with a red card.
2001-2002	Some relaxation of the rule requiring referees to issue a yellow card if a player celebrates a goal by removing his shirt. However, celebrations that are provocative, inciting, ridiculing of opponents or spectators or time wasting remain punishable by a yellow card. Referees are reminded to punish intentional holding or pulling offences with a yellow card.
2002-2003	Referees are reminded to be strict in punishing simulation and the delaying of restarts, especially if players remove shirts for any length of time celebrating a goal.

seasons in the observation period. Within the 1998-99 season as well, the process of adjustment to the new disciplinary regime is visible in the data: during the first three months of this season the average disciplinary points incurred by both teams per match was 4.34, while the average for the rest of the season was 3.88 (see also Witt, 2005). In subsequent seasons, although this directive remained in force, the incidence of disciplinary sanction returned to levels similar to those experienced before the directive came into effect.

Table 4: Average yellow and red cards and total disciplinary points awarded per match, by season.

Season	Home team			Away team			Both teams		
	Yell.	Red	Total	Yell.	Red	Total	Yell.	Red	Total
1996-7	1.31	0.03	1.35	1.81	0.08	1.93	3.11	0.11	3.28
1997-8	1.30	0.06	1.41	2.02	0.12	2.19	3.32	0.18	3.60
1998-9	1.58	0.07	1.70	2.15	0.12	2.32	3.73	0.19	4.01
1999-0	1.41	0.06	1.50	1.93	0.13	2.12	3.34	0.18	3.62
2000-1	1.36	0.08	1.49	1.80	0.08	1.92	3.16	0.17	3.41
2001-2	1.25	0.08	1.39	1.80	0.10	1.96	3.05	0.19	3.35
2002-3	1.33	0.07	1.43	1.70	0.12	1.88	3.03	0.20	3.31

Two possible explanations are as follows. First, whenever there is an addition to the list of sanctionable offences, players may modify their behaviour so that the numbers of cautions and dismissals remain approximately constant (Witt, 2005). Second, referees may tend to modify their interpretation of the boundaries separating non-sanctionable from sanctionable offences, and those separating cautionable from dismissable offences, so as to maintain an approximately constant rate of disciplinary sanction.

The second testable hypothesis focuses on the variation in the incidence of disciplinary sanction across referees. As previously discussed, inconsistency in the standards applied by different referees is among the most frequent causes of complaint from football managers, players, supporters and media pundits. Table 5 summarises the average numbers of disciplinary points per match awarded against the home and away teams and against both teams combined, by each of the 28 referees who officiated at least 30 Premier League matches during the observation period. There appears to be considerable variation between the propensities for individual referees to take disciplinary action. For example, the most lenient referee (Keith Burge) averaged 2.526 disciplinary points per match over 57 matches, and the most prolific (Mike Reed) averaged 4.541 points over 85 matches.

There also appears to be significant differences in the distribution of disciplinary points awarded by the same referee over time. Figure 1 presents boxplots of four high-profile referees with contrasting distributions. In two cases (Poll and Gallagher) the median number of disciplinary points awarded is highest during the 1998-99 season.

Table 5: Average total disciplinary points awarded per match, by referee.

	Referee	Matches	Disciplinary points awarded		
			Home team	Away team	Total
1	Reed	85	1.79	2.75	4.54
2	Willard	60	1.90	2.35	4.25
3	Barber	147	1.73	2.46	4.19
4	Riley	131	1.63	2.51	4.14
5	Harris	52	1.75	2.33	4.08
6	Knight	41	1.83	2.17	4.00
7	Styles	56	1.93	2.02	3.95
8	Rennie	94	1.82	2.10	3.92
9	Dean	54	1.69	2.11	3.80
10	Wilkes	30	1.40	2.33	3.73
11	D'urso	85	1.62	2.09	3.72
12	Poll	160	1.62	2.07	3.69
13	Bodenham	44	1.46	2.05	3.50
14	Lodge	102	1.39	2.11	3.50
15	Bennett	68	1.60	1.85	3.46
16	Barry	117	1.39	2.06	3.44
17	Jones	112	1.41	1.99	3.40
18	Ashby	33	1.21	2.15	3.36
19	Wilkie	81	1.36	1.98	3.33
20	Dunn	136	1.37	1.96	3.32
21	Elleray	129	1.30	1.98	3.28
22	Winter	143	1.23	1.98	3.21
23	Gallagher	122	1.26	1.92	3.18
24	Halsey	74	1.34	1.73	3.07
25	Alcock	78	1.00	2.03	3.03
26	Wiley	90	1.43	1.58	3.01
27	Durkin	145	1.25	1.47	2.72
28	Burge	57	0.88	1.65	2.53

Note: Referees who officiated at fewer than 30 Premier League matches between the 1996-7 and 2002-3 seasons (inclusive) are not shown in Table 5.

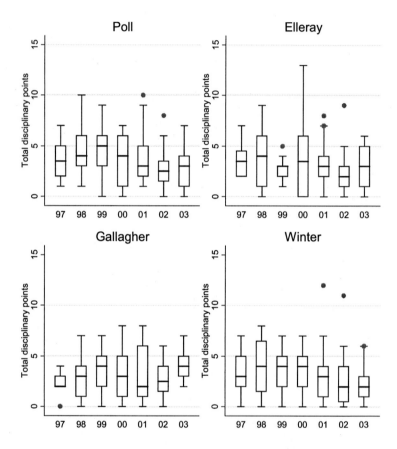

Figure 1: Boxplots of disciplinary sanctions by (selected) referee by season. Note: Each box shows the median, quartiles, and extreme values (outliers).

Thereafter it tends to revert back to the observed trend. For Elleray and Winter, the distributions exhibit much less variation and the median values are broadly comparable across the seven seasons sampled. These findings provide qualified support for our earlier contention that referees tend to modify their behaviour over time in order to maintain an approximately constant rate of disciplinary sanction.

Econometric Analysis

What we have presented thus far could be considered merely circumstantial evidence. One could argue, perhaps with some justification, that some of the variation in disciplinary sanctions between referees reflects the propensity for some referees to officiate a disproportionate number of high profile matches compared to others. In such cases the (possible) higher number of disciplinary sanctions is a corollary of the competitiveness and/or aggressiveness of the two teams involved. Therefore in order to isolate the contribution of referees to the variation in the incidence of disciplinary sanction, a regression model is constructed which includes a number of (control) variables that could influence the match-to-match variation in disciplinary sanctions.

It seems reasonable to expect that the incidence of disciplinary sanction against each team depends on the teams' relative quality (q_j), where q_j = prob(home win in match j) + 0.5 * prob(draw). In general one can think of q_j depending on three principal factors: (i) the talent differential between the two teams; (ii) a home advantage effect; (iii) a tactical decision variable representing the level of 'aggression' contributed by each team. This variable is also included in quadratic form.

A numerical value for q_j for each of the 2,660 matches is generated from an ordered probit match results forecast model developed by Goddard (2005). The model generates probabilities for home win, draw and away win outcomes, based solely on historical data that is available prior to the match in question (e.g. historical and recent performances, significance of the contest etc).[8] A priori, the empirical model allows for two forms of relationship between q_j and the incidence of disciplinary sanction. First, a weaker team that is forced to defend for long periods can be expected to commit more fouls than a stronger team that spends more time attacking. This suggests a negative (positive) linear relationship between q_j and the disciplinary points incurred by the home (away) team. Second, by including the quadratic term ($q_j (1-q_j)$) we are able to capture the possibility that a match between two evenly balanced teams will be keenly contested (perhaps in terms of bit more aggressive behaviour) in order to create a competitive advantage. A positive relationship is expected between this variable and the incidence of disciplinary sanction against both teams.

The incidence of disciplinary sanction for either team might also be affected by the importance of the match for end-of-season championship,

---

[8] Approaches adopted in other studies include the use of bookmaker's odds (e.g. Buraimo et al., 2007) and ranking coefficients (e.g. Papahristodoulou, 2007).

European qualification or relegation outcomes. A team that still has end-of-season issues at stake might be expected to be more determined or aggressive than a team with nothing at stake. In the definitions of the dummy variables $sig_{i,j}$, the algorithm that determines whether a match is significant for either team assesses whether it is arithmetically possible (before the match is played) for the team to win the championship, qualify for European competition or be relegated, if all other teams currently in contention for the same outcome take one point on average from each of their remaining fixtures.

Differences between football teams in playing personnel, styles of play and tactics represent a further possible source of variation in the incidence of disciplinary sanction. There is evidence to suggest that players with bad reputations are more likely to incur the wroth of the official. For example, based on the 2002-03 season (the last season in the sample considered here) the twenty players with the worst disciplinary record accounted for 15% of all yellow cards and 26% of all red cards.

Nonetheless with 22 players (plus substitutes) participating in every match, in an empirical analysis at match level it is impossible to control for every change of playing personnel. Here use is made of managerial spells which act as a proxy for football team-related factors that might produce differences in the incidence of disciplinary sanction and can be justified on the grounds that managers are primarily responsible for tactics and playing styles. Casual observation suggests managerial change is a good proxy for turnover of playing personnel: the removal of a manager is often followed by high player turnover, as the new incumbent seeks to reshape his squad in accordance with his own preferences.

Finally, in order to test the two principle hypotheses identified earlier, dummy variables for each of the seasons under analysis and for the 28 referees who officiated in at least 30 games over this period are also included. Each match yields two discrete dependent variables, relating to the total disciplinary points amassed by the home team and the away team. Table 6 presents results using a zero-inflated bivariate Poisson approach.[9]

The negative sign attached to the parameter φ implies a positive relationship between the two equations: that is the incidence of disciplinary sanction for the home team increases as the incidence of

---

[9] Technical details of the modelling approach adopted and alternatives which were considered are provided in Dawson et al. (2007). Typically a negative binomial probability model is used because of the problem of overdispersion. Specification tests indicate that there was no significant problem with overdispersion in this model, thus justifying the use of the Poisson approach.

Table 6: Bivariate Poisson Estimation Results.

| | Home Team Disciplinary Points | | Away Team Disciplinary Points | |
	Coefficient	z-statistic	Coefficient	z-statistic
q_j	-0.61	-3.16	0.86	3.40
$q_j(1-q_j)$	5.02	5.37	3.02	3.75
sig_j	-0.01	-0.23	0.13	2.71
att_j	13.55	3.14	1.95	1.11
sky_j	0.024	0.54	0.01	0.13

	Joint Tests of Significance
Season	$\chi^2(12) = 34.34$ (p = 0.00)
Dummies	$\chi^2(10) = 12.56$ (p = 0.25)
Referee	$\chi^2(56) = 171.3$ (p = 0.00)
Dummies	$\chi^2(28) = 52.21$ (p = 0.003)
Managerial Spell Dummies	$\chi^2(112) = 264.0$ (p = 0.00)

	Ancillary Parameters
φ	-1.68
π	0.01
ln(L)	-8439.6
LR: $\pi = 0$	$\chi^2 = 3.6$ (p-value = 0.01[a])

Definitions:

q_j = prob (home win in match j) + 0.5*prob (draw).

$q_j (1-q_j)$ represents the product of q_j and the equivalent weighted sum for the away team.

sig_j represents a 0-1 dummy variable, coded 1 if match j is significant for end-of-season championship, European qualification or relegation outcomes, for the home (i=1) or away (i=2) team.

att_j represents the reported attendance at match j.

sky_j equals 1 if match j was televised live by BSkyB; 0 otherwise.

Season dummy: equals 1 if match j is played in season s; 0 otherwise (s represents seasons 1997-8 to 2002-3 inclusive; 1996-7 is the reference category).

Referee dummy: equal 1 if match j is officiated by referee r; 0 otherwise (r=1...28 represents referees who officiated at least 30 Premier League matches within the observation period.

Managerial spell dummy: equal 1 if match j falls within managerial spell m for the home (i=1) or away (i=2) team; 0 otherwise (m=1...56 represents managerial spells that contained at least 30 Premier League matches within the observation period.

φ represents the nature of the correlation between the two equations. The negative sign implies a positive relationship between the incidence disciplinary sanction committed by the home and away teams.

ln(L) is the maximised value of the log-likelihood function.

LR: $\pi = 0$ is the likelihood ratio statistic for a test to compare the zero-inflated Poisson model with the non-inflated Poisson model.

[a] Simulated p-value.

disciplinary sanction increases for the away team, and vice versa. Such a correlation might reflect a tendency for teams to retaliate in kind if the opposing team is guilty of a particularly high level of foul play. Alternatively, a common opinion among pundits and supporters is that some referees, having penalised a player from one team, often look for an opportunity to penalise an opposing player soon afterwards, in an effort to pre-empt the formation on the part of managers, players or spectators of any perception of refereeing bias. Preliminary investigations, based on the 2002-03 season, found that in 26.1% of the 241 matches where the home and away team received at least one yellow card, the first yellow card awarded to the home (away) team was followed by the award of a yellow card to the away (home) team within 10 minutes. Furthermore, as can be observed in Table 1 in approximately 26% of matches both teams received the same number of yellow cards.

This finding is consistent with work carried out by Buraimo et al. (2007), who specifically model the timing of yellow and red cards using minute-by-minute bivariate probit analysis. They find that a yellow card previously awarded to the home (away) team increases the probability of the away (home) team receiving a similar sanction. Interestingly they also find that when one team scores a goal this has a tendency to the increase the probability of a player of the opposing team receiving a yellow card the minutes following the goal.

As previously mentioned, the model defines a quadratic functional form for the relationship between relative quality and the incidence of disciplinary sanction. This relationship is parameterised so that the coefficient reported for q_j, a weighted sum of the home team's win and draw probabilities after allowing for home advantage, and $q_j(1 - q_j)$, a measure of competitive balance. In the case of the former, the sign is negative and statistically significant at the 1% level. This implies that the incidence of disciplinary sanction tends to be higher for (relatively) weak home teams. The positive sign in the away team equation—also statistically significant at the 1% level—suggests a tendency for the away team to endure a higher incidence of disciplinary sanction, which in part can be explained by the home advantage effect.

The incidence of disciplinary sanction also depends on the closeness of the contest: both coefficients are positively signed and statistically significant at the 1% level. This provides support for the hypothesis that the incidence of disciplinary sanction tends to be even greater (for both teams) in matches between evenly balanced teams.

The significance of the match, in contrast, appears to exert no influence on the incidence of disciplinary sanction for the home team. It is however significant for the away team, exerting a positive effect. A possible interpretation is that away teams feel able to 'ease off' in unimportant end-of-season matches; but home teams, perhaps conscious of their own crowd's critical scrutiny, feel obliged to demonstrate maximum commitment at all times, even when no end-of-season issues are at stake.

The findings here indicate that a larger crowd size *increases* the tendency for the *home* team to incur the wroth of the referee – and no effect on the away team. The presence of a large crowd appears to increase the number of disciplinary sanctions issued to the home team. It is quite possible though that a large crowd, which tends to add to the intensity and excitement of the occasion, results in more determined or aggressive play by either or both teams.[10] Although the sign is positive in both equations, there appears to be no evidence to support the view that the behaviour of players or referees is affected by whether the match is televised or not.

Finally we test our two principle hypotheses with respect to disciplinary sanctions over time and the variation in the distribution of sanctions across referees. In the case of testing the stability of disciplinary sanction over time we include dummy variables corresponding to the six seasons from 1997-98 to 2002-03 inclusive (with the 1996-97 season as the reference category). the null hypothesis is $H_0:\beta_{i,s}=0$ for i=1,2 and s=1997-98 to 2002-2003 (inclusive). A Wald test yields $\chi^2(12)=34.34$ (p-value < 0.001), suggesting there was significant season-to-season variation in the incidence of disciplinary sanction. However, if the zero restrictions on the coefficients for 1998-9 are excluded from the null ($H_0:\beta_{i,s}=0$ for i=1,2 and s=1997-98 and 1999-2000 to 2002-03 inclusive), the Wald test yields $\chi^2(10)=12.56$ (p-value=.25). This suggests that with the (temporary) exception of the 1998-99 season there was no significant season-to-season variation in the incidence of disciplinary sanction. This presents qualified support for the view that players modify their behaviour towards and / or referees modify their interpretation of sanctionable offences. In this respect both types of decision-making can be described as rational and is consistent with the findings of Witt (2005) and the economics of crime model as presented in equations (1) and (2).

Recall earlier we identified a significant variation in the average number of disciplinary sanctions across referees. Does this degree of variation in the incidence of disciplinary sanction per referee constitute statistical evidence of inconsistency in refereeing standards? For the

---

[10] This is in contrast with other studies, such as Dohmen (2005), who find that crowd effects, particularly the proximity of the crowd to the field of play, is important. In the English Premier League, stadiums seldom have running tracks separating the crowd from the pitch.

individual referee effects, we include dummy variables corresponding to the 28 referees listed in Table 5 (with the matches officiated by the other nine referees used as the reference category). A Wald test of $H_0:\gamma_{i,r}=0$ for $i=1,2$ and $r=1...28$ yields $\chi^2(56)=171.3$ (p-value < 0.0001). Therefore the null hypothesis is rejected, suggesting there was significant variation in standards between referees.

Given that we have also controlled for team quality and other potential influences on the incidence of disciplinary sanction, the result cannot be attributable to any non-randomness in the assignment of referees to matches: for example, the tendency for referees with a reputation for toughness to be assigned to matches at which disciplinary issues are anticipated by the authorities. On the basis of a Wald test on the 56 managerial spell dummies we also find that there was significant variation between managerial spells: choices made by managers of playing personnel, styles of play and tactics affect the incidence of disciplinary sanction.

Since we have estimated disciplinary sanction by the home team and the away team separately allows one to determine whether there are differences between referees in the degree of home team bias. In other words, do variations in the degree of home team bias on the part of different officials contribute to the observed pattern of refereeing inconsistency? To test this we impose the restriction that the corresponding coefficients on the individual referee dummy variables in the home and away team equations are the same. The null hypothesis would imply that the rate at which away teams tend to incur more disciplinary points than home teams does not vary between referees. A Wald test of $H_0:\gamma_{1,r}=\gamma_{2,r}$ for $r=1...28$ yields $\chi^2(28)=52.21$ (p-value < 0.01).

The implication of this is that not only does there appear to be inconsistencies between referees, but there is variation between referees in the degree of home team bias. This interpretation is consistent with evidence of home team bias in other approaches, which find that the home team is favoured in the calling of fouls and penalty decisions (Sutter and Kocher, 2004, Dohmen 2005), or in the addition of stoppage time at the end of matches (Garicano et al., 2005, Sutter and Kocher, 2004, and Dohmen, 2005).

Conclusions

This chapter has presented an account of the economics of crime and punishment and provided a statistical analysis of patterns in the award of yellow and red cards over a seven-year period in the English Premier League.

Despite an increase over time in the number of offences subject to disciplinary sanction, there was no consistent time-trend in the yellow and red cards data: players and officials appear to have adjusted to changes in the rules so that in the long run the rate of disciplinary sanction remained approximately constant. In this sense, players and referees alike appear to act as rational economic agents.

However the analysis does suggest that there are inconsistencies between referees in the interpretation or application of the rules. Moreover the tendency for away teams to incur more disciplinary points than home teams cannot be explained solely by the home advantage effect on match results. Even after controlling for team quality, a (relatively strong) away team can expect to collect more disciplinary points than a (relatively weak) home team with the same win probability. Therefore the evidence seems to point in the direction of a home team bias in the incidence of disciplinary sanction. This interpretation is consistent with evidence of home team bias in several other studies, which find that the home team is favoured in the calling of fouls and penalty decisions (Sutter and Kocher, 2004, Dohmen, 2005), or in the addition of stoppage time at the end of matches (Garicano et al., 2005., Sutter and Kocher, 2004 and Dohmen, 2005).

Perhaps most significantly of all however, evidence is found of variation between referees in the degree of home team bias; and this variation contributes to the overall pattern of refereeing inconsistency.

It should be stressed that we are not saying that referees are intentionally biased. Human error, not just referees but also players and managers, is inevitable and in many ways add to the spectacle of contests. However, players and managers alike have, given the evidence presented here, been right to question the consistency of such decision-making. At the same time managers and players should be careful about becoming too vitriolic in their opinions of referees since this might influence decision-making made by the referee when he encounters that manager / player in future contests.

References

Allen, W. D. (2002). "Crime, punishment and recidivism: lessons from the National Hockey League." *Journal of Sports Economics*, 3(1), 39-60.

—. (2005). "Cultures of Illegality in the National Hockey League." *Southern Economic Journal*, 71(3), 494-513.

Becker, G. S. (1968). "Crime and punishment: An economic approach." *Journal of Political Economy*, 76(2), 169-217.

Brown, W. and M. Reynolds (1973). "Crime and Punishment: Risk Implications." *Journal of Economic Theory*, 6(5), 508-514.

Buraimo, B., D. Forrest and R. Simmons (2007). "The twelfth man? Refereeing bias in England and German soccer." *International Association of Sports Economists Working Paper 0707.*

Dawson, P., S. Dobson, J. Goddard and J. Wilson (2007). "Are football referees really biased and inconsistent? Evidence on the incidence of disciplinary sanction in the English Premier League." *Journal of the Royal Statistical Society Series A: Statistics in Society*, 170(1), 231-250.

Dohmen, T. J. (2005). "Social Pressure Influences Decisions of Individuals: Evidence from the Behaviour of Referees." *IZA Discussion Paper 1595.*

Ehrlich, I. (1973). "Participation in Illegitimate Activities: A Theoretical and Empirical Investigation." *Journal of Political Economy*, 81(3), 521-565.

Elleray, D. (2004). *The Man in the Middle.* London: Time Warner Books. *FIFA Disciplinary Code.* http://www.fifa.com/aboutfifa/federation/ administration/disciplinarycode.html.

Garicano, L., I. Palacios-Huerta, and C. Prendergast (2005). "Favoritism Under Social Pressure." *Review of Economics and Statistics*, 87(2), 208-216.

Goddard, J. (2005). "Regression models for forecasting goals and match results in association football." *International Journal of Forecasting*, 21(2), 331-340.

Heckelman, J. C. and A. J. Yates (2003). "And a hockey game broke out: crime and punishment in the NHL." *Economic Inquiry*, 41(4), 705-712.

Heineke, J. M. (1978). *Economic Models of Criminal Behaviour.* Amsterdam: North-Holland.

Helsen, W. and J. B. Bultynck (2004). "Physical and perceptual cognitive demands of top-class refereeing in association football." *Journal of Sports Sciences*, 22(2), 179-189.

Jones, M.V., G. C. Paull and J. Erskine (2002). "The impact of a team's aggressive reputation on the decisions of association football referees." *Journal of Sports Sciences*, 20(12), 991-1000.

McCormick, R. E. and R. D. Tollison (1984). "Crime on the court." *Journal of Political Economy*, 92(3), 223-235.

Mason, C. and G. Lovell (2000). "Attitudes, Expectations and Demands of English Premier League Football Association Referees." *Football Studies*, 3(2), 88-102.

Nevill, A. M., N. J. Balmer and A. M. Williams (2002) "The influence of crowd noise and experience upon refereeing decisions in football." *Psychology of Sport and Exercise*, 3(4), 261-272.

Palacios-Huerta, I. (2003). "Professionals Play Minimax." *Review of Economic Studies*, 70(2), 395-415.

Papahristodoulou, C. (2007). "An analysis of Champions League match statistics." *MPRA Working Paper 3605*.

Pettersson-Lidbom, P. and M. Priks (2007). "Behavior under social pressure: empty Italian stadiums and referee bias." *CESifo Working Paper 1960*.

Plessner, H. and T. Betsch (2001). "Sequential effects in important referee decisions: the case of penalties in soccer." *Journal of Sport and Exercise Psychology*, 23(3), 254-259.

Rickman, N. and R. Witt (2008). "Favouritism and financial incentives: A natural experiment." *Economica*, 75, 296-309.

Sutter, M. and M. G. Kocher (2004). "Favoritism of agents - the case of referees' home bias." *Journal of Economic Psychology*, 25(4), 461-469.

Witt, R. (2005). "Do players react to anticipated sanction changes? Evidence from the English Premier League." *Scottish Journal of Political Economy*, 52(4), 623-640.

CHAPTER ELEVEN

BASIC PSYCHOLOGICAL PROCESSES UNDERLYING REFEREES' DECISION MAKING

RALF BRAND, HENNING PLESSNER AND CHRISTIAN UNKELBACH[1]

The use of referees is a necessity in order to ensure the correct conduct of a football match in accordance with the Laws of the Game as prescribed by the International Football Association (FIFA). They rule the match and some of their decisions have a direct impact on its outcome. Accordingly, their performances receive at least sometimes the same attention as the players' in the general public and the media, as well as—although just recently—in scientific research (for an overview, see e.g. Mascarenhas et al., 2006). However, while the interest in players is mostly driven by the fascination of their extraordinary skills and achievements, referees are rather looked at with the suspicion of finding them inevitably error prone. For example, in the scientific literature football referees have been blamed for being systematically influenced by the home crowd (Dawson et al., 2007, Nevill et al., 2002, Sutter and Kocher, 2004), the players' reputation (Jones et al., 2002), the teams' origin (Messner and Schmid, 2007), their own prior decisions (Plessner and Betsch, 2001) and for being inconsistent in general (Dawson et al., 2007). So far, comparably little research has been conducted with the aim of studying football referees' specific assets (e.g., MacMahon et al., 2007). Nevertheless, most authors would agree that the frequently observed imperfection of referees' decision making is at least partly due to the nature of their physically and psychologically extremely demanding task (Helsen et al., 2006, Mascarenhas et al., 2006).

[1] Brand: Department of Sport Science, University of Posdam, Am Neuen Palais 10, 14469 Potsdam, Germany; Plessner: Department of Psychology, University of Leipzig, Seeburgstr. 14-20, 04103 Leipzig, Germany; Unkelbach: Institute of Psychology, University of Heidelberg, 69117 Heidelberg, Germany.

At least sometimes, this task surpasses the limited human capacity to process information. However, decisions have to be made even when situations are ambiguous or unclear, or when important information is missing due to personal or situational factors. In addition, there is always some interaction between referees and the players involved. Because of these factors, it has been argued that many decision situations of referees resemble a typical *social* judgment situation and, thus, can be analysed on the basis of a *social cognition* framework (Plessner, 2005, Plessner and Haar, 2006). Among others, this means that it is useful, at least for pragmatic reasons, to differentiate between several subtasks or steps of information processing (i.e., perception, categorisation, memory processes and information integration). These processes lead from the actual performance (e.g., a player's tackling) to a referee's decision (e.g., sending a player off the field). In principle, an erroneous decision can stem from different processing steps-for example, from the misperception that a player hit his opponent's leg instead of the ball or from the false memory that the player has persistently infringed upon the rules of the game before this situation and is now due for a severe sanction. However, most explanations for erroneous referee decisions in the corresponding literature deal with the later steps of information processing rather than the earlier. For example, Nevill et al. (2002) assume that the influence of the home crowd on referee decisions is partly due to heuristic judgment processes in which the salient, yet potentially biased, response of the crowd is used more or less deliberately as an additional decision cue.

Together, not only the public but also the majority of the scientific literature form a picture of football referees in which they are influenced by all kinds of non-performance factors. These effects are assumed to occur at later stages of information processing, for example, when all the observed and remembered information is integrated into a judgment. In addition, most corresponding explanations refer to intentional concepts such as deliberation, strategic thinking, volition and motivated reasoning. In contrast to this common perspective, the present chapter will focus on some basic psychological principles of *perception* and *psycho-physics* which are active at earlier steps of information processing and which underlie referees' decision behaviour. These comprise rather automatic and "innocent" processes. However, they turn out to provide sufficient explanations for some biases and decision patterns that otherwise could be interpreted as being due to erroneous inference processes at later steps. In the following, we will apply these principles to the understanding of referee decisions in two of their most controversial tasks, i.e. judging offside and awarding yellow cards.

Judging Offside

According to FIFA Law 11, a player is in an offside position if he or she is nearer to the opponents' goal line than both the ball and the second last defender at the moment the ball is played by a team member (see Figure 1 for an illustration of the rule). Due to their suitable sideline positioning, it is mainly the task of assistant referees to judge whether or not a player is in an offside position. The work reported by Helsen et al. (2006) estimates expert assistant referees' error rates in judging offside. Using videotaped data taken from the 64 matches of World Cup 2002 the authors identify a total of 256 observable offside incidents. After having rated this material Helsen et al. (2006) conclude that these World Cup assistant referees have judged 26.2% situations incorrectly (from 222 situations, when offside has been signalled, 58 were wrong; offside has been overlooked by the assistants in 9 out of 25 critical situations). Due to these errors at least five disallowed goals should have been allowed.

Spanish sports medicine specialists Sanabria et al. (1998) and Belda Maruenda (2004) proposed that errors in judging offside should be attributed to the incapability of the human eye and brain of processing all the necessary visual information to apply the rule correctly. This tentative explanation is called the *physiological hypothesis*. Its representatives argue that to judge offside positions correctly, assistant referees have to keep in their visual field at least five objects at the same time (i.e. two players of the attacking team, the last two players of the defending team, and the ball)–and that it is impossible for the human eye to resolve this task.

Consider the accommodation process, the time required for the eye to focus on an object. It takes about 360 milliseconds to focus on the ball at the time it is released by a midfield attacking player. For the purpose of illustration, let's suppose that an offender to whom the ball is passed *moves* toward the attacked goal. The second last defender is *standing motionless* somewhere close to the assistant referee's position. The accommodation time needed to change from far (the release of the ball) to close vision (for detecting the exact position of the motionless defender) is about 640 milliseconds. If the receiving offender runs at a speed of 7.69 m/s (which equals running the 100 meters in 13 seconds), then, in 100 milliseconds, he will have altered his position by 76 cm. It is obvious that the assistant referee cannot actually "see" the relative position of all three objects (ball, receiving offender and defender) *at the same time*!

Generally, it is reasonable to believe that there are comparable situations in which the human eye will actually not be capable of resolving

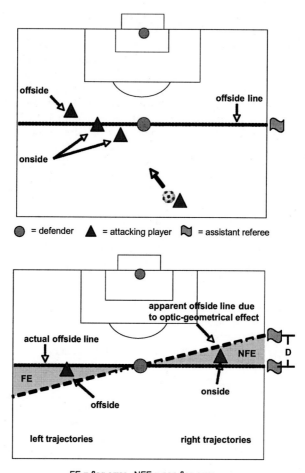

Figure 1: The offside-rule (top) and the optical error hypothesis (bottom).

critical offside situations. Therefore, one cannot deny that the physiological hypothesis helps to explain why it may be not as easy to judge offside situations in football as TV commentators make us sometimes believe. On the other hand, there are a lot of situations in which incidents are "slower" and errors still occur.

One of the most persuasive hypotheses to explain another source of origin of systematic error in offside judgements is the *optical-error hypothesis* proposed by Oudejans et al. (2000). The authors' starting point is the idea that it might be a difficult task for an assistant referee to maintain his optimal position, so as to be best able to make the correct judgement. As soon as an assistant referee is not standing exactly on the offside line (i.e., in line with the second last defender and facing towards the pitch; see Figure 1, picture at the top), this has important implications for his judgements (as shown in the bottom picture in Figure 1): When the assistant's position is only one step ahead of the "actual offside line" and an offender is crossing this offside line between the second last defender and the assistant referee (right trajectory), *non-flag errors* become probable.

This sort of error refers to situation in which assistant referees fail to flag for an actual offside position. With offenders moving on left trajectories more *flag errors* (flagging for a player not being offside) should result respectively. According to Oudejans et al. (2000, p. 33) the geometry of the positions of the players and the assistant referee make such errors "optically inevitable".

Oudejans et al. (2000) have tested their hypotheses using videotaped material from 25 matches of the World Cup 1998. For this subset of data they report 15 flag-errors compared to only 2 non-flag errors with offenders using left trajectories (far from the assistant referee). Using a much larger dataset obtained from video recordings of 200 high-level matches in five European leagues, they count 21 flag-errors compared to 43 non-flag errors for offenders using right trajectories. In fact, most of their empirical data turned out to be in agreement with the optical hypothesis' predictions: The proportion of flag-errors (82%) was much greater when the players used left trajectories than when the players used right trajectories (25%).

In a follow-up study Oudejans et al. (2005) replicated their findings by analyzing special video recordings with 215 potential offside situations from four matches of one team in the Dutch Eredivisie. Comparable to the results of their previous study, assistant referees were exactly in line with the second last defender in only 13.5% of the potential offside situations. Typically, they were positioned about 1 m away from this ideal position. Furthermore, there was a relationship between the speed that the assistant referees were moving and the numbers of errors: There were more errors when the assistant referees were running or sprinting than when they were walking or jogging. This corresponds well to the authors' essential idea: One of the most challenging tasks of assistant referees in football is that they have to "fight for" an exact position on the actual offside line in order to judge offside situations correctly.

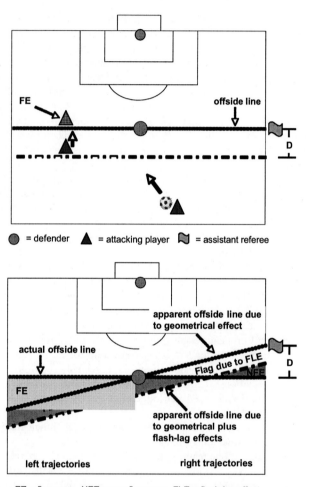

Figure 2: The flash-lag effect (top) and its predictions combining with the optical error hypothesis (bottom).

Another tentative explanation that has been proposed is the *flash-lag effect*, contributed by Baldo et al. (2002). The authors introduce their approach as an attempt to apply to a real life situation a perceptual phenomenon that has been studied in laboratory setups for many years. The flash-lag effect is where "a moving object [i.e. the offender receiving the ball] is perceived as spatially leading its real position at an instant defined by a time marker [i.e. the moment, in which the releasing offender passes the ball]" (Baldo et al., 2002, p. 1205; explanations in square brackets are not in the original text). A football-specific illustration[2] of this effect is given in the top picture in Figure 2. Based on laboratory research, the perceptual advancement caused by the flash-lag effect is estimated as being 0.02 and 0.64 meters. This means that assistant referees perceive the receiving player as being this distance ahead of his actual position.

Baldo et al. (2002) propose the flash-lag effect to be responsible for an overall bias they discovered in Oudejans et al.'s (2000) data, namely that assistant referees generally seem to commit more flag errors (57%) than non-flag errors (43%). Baldo et al.'s (2002) idea is that an assistant referee's positioning ahead of the actual offside line (in Oudejans et al.'s (2000) data, assistants were 1.2 m ahead on average) in combination with the predictions of the flash-lag effect leads to an enlarged area susceptible to flag errors on left trajectories, and a much smaller area susceptible for non-flag errors on right trajectories (bottom picture in Figure 2 for an illustration of this idea).

The introduction of the flash-lag hypothesis to this topic has triggered an interesting debate about which theory comes off best. Helsen et al. (2006, p. 527) contend that their data "clearly support" the flash-lag hypothesis. In contrast Oudejans et al. (2007) state that this conclusion is based on misinterpretations and that Helsen et al.'s (2006) data set is not suited to test the optical error hypothesis.

Further research is necessary to disentangle the two hypotheses (relevant proposals have been described by Mascarenhas et al., 2006). Hopefully, it will show which one of the two hypotheses–or the combination of both, as proposed by Baldo et al. (2002)—will prove to be more successful in explaining erroneous offside judgements in football assistant referees.

As different as the physiological hypothesis, the optical error and the flash-lag hypothesis may appear at first glance, there is one important aspect they all have in common: All of the three hypotheses refer back to our basic concern that it is sensible and necessary to consider *pre-rational* psychological causes for referee's misjudgements—in our offside example: perceptual phenomena—before strategic deliberation or dishonest intentions are alleged.

---

[2] Animated general illustrations of the flash-lag effect can be found in the Internet, for example on a website by Moore and Enns (2007).

Awarding Yellow Cards

As has been said before, the premise of this chapter is that before any wilful or intentional psychological processes in referees are considered, it is necessary to clarify the psychological demands and intricacies of the situation on the football field. One such problem has now been discussed with the flag- and non-flag errors in offside decisions. Another way in which referees heavily impact the outcome of a game is the awarding of personal warnings by showing yellow cards (see FIFA Law 12). The yellow card is relatively new in football's long history. During the World Cup 1966 in England, Argentina played against England in the quarterfinals and the game was officiated by the German referee Rudolf Kreitlein. It was a rough game, and at some point the referee lost control over the situation: an Argentinean player did not leave the field after being sent-off, supposedly because he did not understand the warnings and commands issued by the German referee. To solve this communication problem and avoid such unsportsmanlike scenes in the future, the English referee Ken Aston proposed a system of yellow and red cards for personal warnings and commands, following the internationally known system of traffic lights. The yellow card was first implemented in the World Cup 1970 and has been widely used ever since. Today, the yellow card has become a referee's prime instrument of regulating a game, of demonstrating authority, and of regaining respect among the players. As such, yellow cards represent a prime example of the wilful influence a referee can exert on a game. Or do they?

To show that basic psychological processes operate even in these seemingly clear instances of wilful control (i.e., awarding a yellow card) before any conscious processes and decisions come into play, let us analyse the psychological demands of a referee's judgment situation. We can construe the decision to award a yellow card or not as a categorisation task: a referee must classify any given contact scene between two or more players into the categories of "no foul", "foul", "severe foul punishable with a yellow card", etc. Categorisation tasks of this kind have received much attention in psychology, because to simplify the complexities of the environment, each organism must be able to classify and categorise the events and stimuli surrounding it (Fiedler and Plessner, in press). This basic skill is a necessity, starting from toddlers who must learn to tell "cats" and "dogs" apart, although they share many features, up to world-class referees, who must tell "fouls" and "fouls punishable with a yellow card" apart, although these events also share many of the same features. For simplicity, let us assume that the only dimension on which this decision is based is the severity of the foul–although there are many more dimensions and yellow cards are awarded for many other reasons than just for fouls, of course (e.g., arguing with the referee, pulling another player's jersey, leaving the field without permission, etc.).

A famous theory that explains how people make categorical decisions on one dimension is Parducci's range-frequency theory (Parducci, 1965, Parducci and Wedell, 1986). Drawing on these elaborate models, Haubensak (1992) presented his consistency-model to explain people's categorisation responses. This model rests on two premises: first, to make category judgments, judges develop and calibrate an internal judgment scale, and second, they apply this scale consistently. To illustrate this model, a short excursion into the setup of a classic psycho-physical experiment is in order. Imagine that you are given the task to classify a series of triangles presented to you on a computer screen into three categories: small, medium, and large. Now the first rectangle is presented; how do you know in which category it should be sorted? You cannot apply the category system in a meaningful way, because you do not know anything about the size of the following rectangles: your scale is not calibrated. An immediate implication is that the first judgment should not involve categories at the extremes (i.e. a small or large rectangle in our example). If you place the triangle in the "large" category, all following triangles of the same or larger size are "large" as well. The same goes for the small category. Hence, to preserve the degrees of freedom of the scale until the scale is calibrated, you should (and people do) use the medium category. It is important to note that this is not a prescriptive model of what you "should" do; it does not describe deliberate acts to preserve one's degrees of freedom, but rather what follows necessarily from the proposed scale calibration process.

This model is now directly applicable to the referees' situation when awarding a yellow card (Memmert et al., 2008, Unkelbach and Memmert, 2008). If we substitute the size dimension of the triangles with the severity dimension of an observed foul, and the categories with "light foul", "medium foul", and "severe foul punishable with a yellow card", the same psycho-physical restriction applies. In the beginning of a stimulus series, that is, in the beginning of a game, the referee's scale for that game is not calibrated yet. Hence, she or he must avoid the extreme category of "yellow card", because if this category is used too early, any foul of the same or greater severity must be punished with a yellow card as well. If the game is harsh, this may lead to a flood of yellow cards. In the beginning, referees must preserve their degrees of freedom. In this described situation, an asymmetry of commission and omission is present as well (Spranca et al., 1991), because the light and medium category are of no consequence in terms of degrees of freedom, they are both just fouls. However, to award a yellow card early in the game places strong constraints on a referee's decisional freedom. A direct implication of the consistency model is then that in the beginning of the game less yellow cards are awarded, because in the beginning referees categorise many fouls as medium, although normatively, they should be categorised as extreme and be punished with a yellow card. This simple implication was tested by Memmert et al. (2008) in an analysis of six seasons of the Bundesliga (i.e., the German first-league in football). These six seasons (from 1997/98 to 2002/03) included 1836 games and across all these games, 7555 yellow cards were awarded, yielding an average of 4.11 yellow cards per game. But how are these cards distributed across the 90 minutes playing time? Figure 3 gives a clear-cut answer to this question. For simplicity, the 90 minutes are divided into six categories of 15 min. each plus the stoppage time at the end of the game. As can be seen, the frequency of yellow cards almost doubles from the first fifteen minutes to the second fifteen minutes. Naturally, this could be the case because players need to get into the game, because they are not as "pumped-up" as in the middle of the game, and because yellow cards are also awarded due to repeated fouls (accumulation) and not only on severity of the foul. Notwithstanding all these reasons, the pattern fits perfectly with the predictions from the consistency model. All of the other explanations can be found in the pattern as well; for example, there is a noticeable drop after the halftime break–a time to cool down for the players. Similarly, there is a linear increase in each halftime, which fits with an accumulation account. However, the steep increase in the beginning is well-explained with a finished calibration phase on the side of the referee, especially when we consider a standard recommendation by coaches to players to be aggressive in the first tackle. From this point of view, one would expect more yellow cards in the first fifteen minutes compared to the second fifteen minutes. Yet, because a mere post-hoc analysis of a database is open to many interpretations, we shortly report here an experiment from Memmert et al. (2008) which further corroborates the applicability of the consistency model. They selected 60 scenes from a large pool of foul scenes; in half of these scenes, the actual referees had awarded a yellow card on the field; in the other half they had not done so. In addition, half of each of the "card" and "no-card" scenes were from the beginning of a game ("early scenes"), half were from the end ("late scenes"). Then, 17 DFB (the German Football Association) referees watched these scenes in a

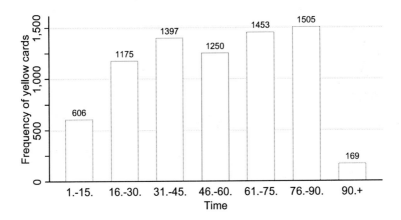

Figure 3: Frequency of yellow cards across six Bundesliga seasons by playing time.

random order and judged whether they would award a yellow card in this scene or not.

The predictions from the consistency model are clear: Because the actual referees in the beginning of the game were not calibrated yet, the referees in the experiment should deviate more from the decision on the field, because they do not have the context of the game and are not constrained by the loss of decisional degrees of freedom. The results confirmed this prediction. Although the referees in the experiment did not know whether a scene was early or late in the game, their judgments varied systematically with this variable. For late scenes, they deviated from the actual referees decisions in 26.9% of the scenes. This deviation significantly increased for early scenes to 32.8%; for example, in the early scenes, they awarded a yellow card in 39.4% of the scenes where no actual yellow card was awarded, compared to 34.8% of the late scenes. Among other things, these results speak against an alternative (motivational) hypothesis concerning the lower frequency of yellow cards in the opening stages of the matches. That is, that the referee is just as rational at the start of each half of the game as during other periods. But he anticipates that the crowd might be less calibrated and/or tolerant of early yellow cards and, thus, does his best to avoid awarding yellow cards at the start in order to prevent an atmosphere of hostility.

It is important that the model is not as rigid as might be implied here. For example, an excessively large triangle, one that almost fills the entire computer screen in the described hypothetical experiment, can be placed in the extreme category with great confidence, just because there is not much more room for larger triangles. Likewise, for an extremely brutal foul in the first minute of the game, a referee can directly award a red card. Because so far, we have tacitly assumed that there is no absolute or memory-based calibration. In the case of triangles, people indeed lack such a scale. A good referee, however, should have such an internal scale ready for the severity of a given foul situation. Nevertheless, the claim is that this existing scale needs to be adjusted to the game at hand; the viability of this claim is reflected in many referees' notion that they need to develop "a feeling for the game" (Brand et al., 2006, Memmert et al., 2008).

And again, the yellow card is indeed an instrument that a referee can use deliberately and wilfully; for example, many referees report that they award a yellow card especially early in the game to show authority and to demonstrate that they will not tolerate any unfair play. Nevertheless, the research we have reported here underscores the point that even at the extreme end of free choices, judgments and decisions adhere to psycho-physical necessities (here: the calibration of an internal scale), and before we discuss the motivational, volitional, or goal-driven aspects of referees in football, it is important to analyse and fully understand the psychological demands and forces that guide behaviour on the football field.

Conclusions

We used the two examples of judging offside and awarding yellow cards in order to demonstrate how error rates and distribution patterns over time can be explained by basic psychological principles, i.e. models of perception and psycho-physics. That does not mean, however, that we completely discharge the idea that referees' decision errors can emerge during later steps of information processing and from motivated or strategic thinking. Of course it is plausible to assume that these later processes will sometimes add to the size of the reported errors and frequently produce errors of their own. What we argue is that basic psychological processes should be studied in order to understand the baseline on which higher inference processes may operate. For example, if a referee's perceived information is already sufficiently biased it is hardly surprising to find his or her final decision to be false. In this case one needs not to assume additional bias during later steps of information processing.

The study of basic psychological processes that underlie referee decisions is in our opinion not only necessary in order to understand referees' at least sometimes erroneous decision making but also in order to develop useful measures that help referees to improve their decision skills (e.g. MacMahon and Plessner, 2007). If these measures are not based on the sound scientific analysis of psychological processes there is a high probability that they turn out to be useless or even counter-productive.

References

Baldo, M. V. C., R. D. Ranvaud and E. Morya (2002). "Flag errors in soccer games: The flash-lag effect brought to real life." *Perception*, 31(10), 1205-1210.

Belda Maruenda, F. (2004). "Can the human eye detect an offside position during a football match?" *British Medical Journal*, 329(7480), 1470-1472.

Brand, R., G. Schmidt and Y. Schneeloch (2006). "Sequential effects in elite basketball referees' foul decisions: An experimental study on the concept of game management." *Journal of Sport and Exercise Psychology*, 28(1), 93-99.

Dawson, P., S. Dobson, J. Goddard, and J. Wilson (2007). "Are football referees really biased and inconsistent? Evidence on the incidence of disciplinary sanction in the English Premier League." *Journal of the Royal Statistical Society Series A: Statistics in Society*, 170(1), 231-250.

Fiedler, K. and H. Plessner (in press). "Induction: From simple categorization to higher-order inference problems." In *Frontiers of social psychology: Social cognition - the basis of social interaction*. F. Strack and J. Förster eds. Philadelphia: Psychology Press.

Haubensak, G. (1992). "The Consistency Model: A process model for absolute judgments." *Journal of Experimental Psychology: Human Perception and Performance*, 18(11), 303-309.

Helsen, W., B. Gilis and M. Weston (2006). "Errors in judging "offside" in football: Test of the optical error versus the perceptual flash-lag hypothesis." *Journal of Sports Sciences*, 24(5), 521-528.

Jones, M. V., G. C. Paull and J. Erskine (2002). "The impact of a team's aggressive reputation on the decisions of association football referees." *Journal of Sports Sciences*, 20(12), 991-1000.

MacMahon, C., W. F. Helsen, J. L. Starkes, and M. Weston (2007). "Decision-making skills and deliberate practice in elite association football referees." *Journal of Sports Sciences*, 25(1), 65-78.

MacMahon, C. and H. Plessner (2007). "The sports official in research and practice." In *Developing elite sports performers: Lessons from theory and practice*. D. Farrow et al. eds. London: Routledge.

Mascarenhas, D. R. D., D. O'Hare and H. Plessner (2006). "The psychological and performance demands of association football refereeing." *International Journal of Sport Psychology*, 37(2-3), 99-120.

Memmert, D., C. Unkelbach, J. Ertmer and M. Rechner (2008). "Gelb oder kein Gelb? Persönliche Verwarnungen im Fußball als Kalibrierungsproblem. [To award or not to award a yellow cad: Personal warnings in soccer as calibration problem]." *Zeitschrift für Sportpsychologie*, 15(1), 1-11.

Messner, C. and B. Schmid (2007). "Über die Schwierigkeit, unparteiische Entscheidungen zu fällen: Schiedsrichter bevorzugen Fußballteams ihrer Kultur [About the difficutly to make impartial decisions: Referess favor culturally familiar football teams]." *Zeitschrift für Sozialpsychologie*, 38(2), 105-110.

Moore, C. M. and J. T. Enns (2007). *Vol. 2007*. http://www.psych.ubc.ca/~ennslab/research/objectupdating/obj_index. html.

Nevill, A., N .J. Balmer and M. A. Williams (2002). "The influence of crowd noise and experience upon refereeing decisions in football." *Psychology of Sport and Exercise*, 3(4), 261-272.

Oudejans, R. R. D., F. C. Bakker and P. J. Beek (2007) "Helsen, Gilis and Weston (2006) err in testing the optical error hypothesis." *Journal of Sports Sciences*, 25(9), 987-990.

Oudejans, R. R. D., R. Verheijen, F. C. Bakker, J. C. Gerrits, M. Steinbrückner and P. J. Beek (2000) "Errors in judging 'offside' in football." *Nature*, 404(6773), 33.

Oudejans, R. R. D., R. Verheijen, F. C. Bakker, J. C. Gerrits, M. Steinbrückner and P. J. Beek, (2005). "How position and motion of expert assistant referees in soccer relate to the quality of their offside judgements during actual match play." *International Journal of Sport Psychology*, 36(1), 3-21.

Parducci, A. (1965). "Category judgment: A range-frequency model." *Psychological Review*, 72(6), 407-418.

Parducci, A. and D. H. Wedell (1986). "The category effect with rating scales: Number of categories, number of stimuli, and method of presentation." *Journal of Experimental Psychology: Human Perception and Performance*, 12(4), 496-516.

Plessner, H. (2005). "Positive and negative effects of prior knowledge on referee decisions in sports." In *The routines of decision making*. T. Betsch and S. Haberstroh eds. Hillsdale: Lawrence Erlbaum, 311-324.

Plessner, H. and T. Betsch (2001). "Sequential effects in important referee decisions: The case of penalties in soccer." *Journal of Sport and Exercise Psychology*, 23(3), 254-259.

Plessner, H. and T. Haar (2006). "Sports performance judgments from a social cognitive perspective." *Psychology of Sport and Exercise*, 7(6), 555-575.

Sanabria, J., C. Cenjor, F. Marquez, R. Guitierrez, D. Martinez and J. L. Prados-Garcia (1998) "Oculomotor movements and football's Law 11." *The Lancet*, 351(9098), 268.

Spranca, M., E. Minsk and J. Baron (1991) "Omission and commission in judgment and choice." *Journal of Experimental Social Psychology*, 27(1), 76-105.

Sutter, M. and M. G. Kocher (2004). "Favoritism of agents - The case of referees' home bias." *Journal of Economic Psychology*, 25(4), 461-469.

Unkelbach, C. and D. Memmert (2008). "Game-Management, context-effects, and calibration: The case of yellow cards in soccer." *Journal of Sport and Exercise Psychology*, 30(1), 95-109.

PART II:

OFF-PITCH PHENOMENA

CHAPTER TWELVE

FAN PRESSURE AND FOOTBALL OUTCOMES

ROB SIMMONS[1]

Conventional economic analysis of demand for football delivers empirical models that are based on two key assumptions. First, fans are treated as passive utility-maximising consumers and second, they are assumed to respond positively to the degree of match uncertainty of outcome. In this chapter, I argue that both tenets are false. A significant impact of match outcome uncertainty on attendance demand has yet to be demonstrated by the empirical literature. Fans are interested in the winning potential of their teams above all and are prepared to make efforts to influence the ability of their teams to win through a number of mechanisms. These include pressure on opposing team players, on referees and on head coaches who are held responsible for failing teams. This chapter will survey some recent attempts to analyse forms of social pressure exerted by fans and suggest that this, rather than further work on outcome uncertainty, will deliver payoffs from research by economists and psychologists.

Early empirical work on attendance demand for football took the conventional neoclassical model of consumer behaviour and applied this to a setting where 'demand' became the number of paying spectators at football matches. In this approach attendance demand is a function of ticket prices, real income and (sometimes) a measure of predicted closeness of contest (outcome uncertainty). The pioneering analysis of Bird (1982) focussed on prices and incomes as determinants of seasonal attendance in English football in the post-war period, Bird regressed numbers of spectators in English league football (as a whole and by

[1] Simmons: The Management School, Lancaster University, Lancaster LA1 4YX, United Kingdom, Phone: +44 1524 594234, Fax: +44 1524 594244, Email: r.simmons@lancaster.ac.uk.
I am grateful to Leif Brandes, David Forrest, Leo Kahane and Joachim Prinz for insightful comments on several of the issues covered here. I also appreciate the constructive comments of an anonymous reviewer.

division) on variables such as real ticket price, a simple measure of travel cost, real disposable income and regional unemployment rate. Demand elasticity with respect to combined ticket price and travel cost was estimated at -0.2 while elasticity with respect to real income was estimated at -0.6. Bird's aggregate seasonal analysis was later extended to a club-by-club treatment by Dobson and Goddard (1995), Simmons (1996) and Forrest, Simmons and Feehan (2002).

The empirical studies following Bird transferred the orthodox theory of individual utility-maximising consumers in to football. Some recognition was given to the role of habit persistence since it was recognised that attendances at clubs in a given season did depend to a large extent on attendances in the previous season (Borland, 1987, Simmons, 1996). However, the sources and explanations for this habit persistence, and indeed how this varies across clubs and leagues, were not vigorously pursued.

Moreover, economic analysis of attendance demand in football (and other team sports) tended to become fixated with the twin problems of outcome uncertainty and competitive balance.. Following the first rigorous theoretical model of a sports league by El Hodiri and Quirk (1971), which in turn drew upon the pioneering contribution of Rottenberg (1956), sports economists devoted considerable efforts to understanding which redistribution policies would deliver greater equality of outcomes and improved competitive balance in different institutional settings. For some (most?) sports economists, e.g. Fort and Quirk (1995), this analysis started from the fundamental proposition of the Coase theorem that the distribution of playing talent is independent of the allocation of property rights of that talent.

This effort to understand the effectiveness of league policies to redistribute resources in sports falls foul of some serious objections. Crucially, the basic premise that fans 'like' more uncertain outcomes does not receive a great deal of empirical support. Borland and Macdonald (2003) offer a comprehensive review of attendance demand studies that consider uncertainty of outcome (see also Szymanski, 2003). They define different levels of outcome uncertainty as match-level, season-level and long-run or championship dominance. Across each level of analysis their review suggests conflicting empirical results. At the match level, a plethora of outcome uncertainty measures have been used. Taking these as appropriate to the problem, Borland and Macdonald find that only three out of 30 cited studies across a wide range of sports support the contention that greater match uncertainty of outcome raises game-day attendance.

Buraimo and Simmons (forthcoming) investigated the match attendance levels in the English Premier League using a large panel data set of 2,553 games over the period 1997/98 to 2003/04. Since many games sell to capacity in this league (1,394 to be precise), they use a tobit censored regression model for estimation.[2] Most of the variables used by Buraimo and Simmons are standard in the literature although the authors did go further than most studies in identifying market size and competition between clubs as important covariates. Their chosen measure of outcome uncertainty, OU, is:

$$OU = PPG_H - PPG_A + HA \qquad (1)$$

HA denotes home advantage and is the absolute value of total number of points divided by maximum gained at home by all teams in the Premier League in the previous season minus total number of points divided by maximum gained away by all teams. PPG_H and $PPGA$ denote home and away team points per game to date, respectively. This measure of outcome uncertainty corrects for home field advantage prevalent in all sports leagues and was first employed by Forrest, Simmons and Buraimo (2005).

Match outcome uncertainty was found to have no statistically significant impact on Premier League attendances. Moreover, Forrest and Simmons (2006) use the same measure of outcome uncertainty in a study of 4,320 English Football League games over the period 1999/2000 to 2001/02 and also found an insignificant role for match outcome uncertainty.

Although this work shows no role for match outcome uncertainty for gate attendances in English football, some role can be found in TV audiences where the spectators are less likely to have strong attachments to participating teams. Forrest, Simmons and Buraimo (2005) find that TV audience demand for the English Premier League *is* affected by the same measure of outcome uncertainty as noted above, controlling for quality and performances of the teams being broadcast. This seems an intuitively plausible result and is one that raises some delicate concerns for football authorities as broadcast revenue has overtaken ticket sales revenues over the last decade in England and elsewhere (Buraimo, Simmons and Szymanski, 2006). Basically, the decision of fans to attend at the stadium is affected by team performance and team quality and not by match outcome uncertainty. In contrast, the decision to watch a game on

---

[2] Modelling attendance demand for the divisions below the Premier League, which comprise the Football League, does not require tobit estimation as few games are capacity constrained.

television is affected by match outcome uncertainty, albeit to a modest degree and over and above indicators of team and match quality.

But fans do much more than just turn up to football matches to 'consume' a product. Watching football is not like consuming food or drink; it has features of an *experience good*, where the experience includes talking about the game to people afterwards and the abiding memory of seeing a superb goal or a brilliant player. Further, fans are part of the product; in Becker's terms football attendance represents a *consumption activity* for which purchase of a ticket is just an input to production of the activity. Fans generate 'atmosphere'—sometimes in a socially undesirable fashion—and can help their team raise the level of performance through crowd noise. In the next section I explore the sources of home advantage in football. I then proceed in section 2 to look at how fan pressure affects players. Sections 3 and 4 consider impacts of fan pressure on referees and head coaches respectively. Section 5 concludes with a plea for further research on the impacts of social pressure exerted by fans.

Fans as a Source of Home Advantage

Home advantage represents the propensity for home teams to win more games than away teams in a given league structure. More precisely, Stefani (2007, p.204) defines home advantage as occurring when a team 'performs better at home against an opponent than playing away against the same opponent'. Two measures of home advantage are commonly adopted: differences in scoring and differences in fractions of games (or points) won. The choice of metric will be dictated by league structure. European football leagues are organised around the principle of teams playing each other home and away, once each. In smaller leagues, such as Scotland, teams may play each other twice home and away. In contrast, in North American leagues, with several divisions and two conferences, teams play only teams from their own division home and away.

Home advantage is prevalent across a wide variety of team sports. Table 1 shows measures of home advantage in a variety of leagues from European football and North American sports. The definition of home advantage derives from Pollard (2002) and for North American sports is the number of home wins expressed as a proportion of total number of wins in a given season. In the rare cases (in American football) where ties occur, the measure is computed with a tie worth one half of a win. European football has a high frequency of draws (around 25 to 30 percent of games) and the home advantage measure is computed as number of

Table 1: Measures of home advantage in sports leagues.

League	Home Advantage	
	(1)	(2)
English Premier League	0.605	
Italy Serie A	0.613	
Spain Liga de Fútbol Profesional	0.631	
European football		0.217
Major League Baseball	0.537	0.075
National Basketball Association	0.607	0.210
National Football League	0.572	0.175

Note: Data in column (1) were compiled by the author: for European football, home advantage is share of points earned at home to total league points achieved in any season, where a win is worth three points and a draw one point. For North American leagues, home advantage is share of home wins in total wins in a given season. All measures are averages over five seasons, 2000-2004. Column (2) shows the home advantage figures computed by Stefani (2007) as sum of home wins minus away wins divided by number of home games.

points gained at home as a proportion of total number of points awarded in a season, where a win is worth three points. Hence, the North American and European measures are not directly comparable.

The widespread appearance of home advantage is readily apparent in Table 1. In European football, home wins easily dominate draws and away wins as the modal outcome. Intriguingly, Spanish *Liga de Fútbol Profesional* has highest probability of home wins in four out of five seasons surveyed here and has highest degree of home advantage across the three European leagues considered here. This might reflect greater local affinity to football teams as these are more integrated into regional cultures and/or greater travel distances for teams playing away in Spain. The English Premier League has slightly greater home advantage than Italy Serie A.

In North America, Table 1 shows that home advantage occurs in American Football, baseball and basketball with the latter showing greatest tendency for home teams to win, according to the results in column (1). Stefani (2007) uses sum of home wins minus way wins divided by number of home games as a measure of home advantage. He finds that amongst the four major North American sports, basketball has the greatest degree of home advantage (see column (2) of Table 1) followed by American football. This result is particularly striking as basketball courts should be more homogeneous in physical characteristics than baseball parks and NFL stadia (which vary greatly in climate conditions, type of turf and whether the roof is open or closed). Compared to other North American sports, fans are closer to the field of play in basketball and crowd intensity may be more of a factor affecting game outcomes.

In the National Football League, 12 teams out of 32 qualify for end-of-season playoffs culminating in the Superbowl. The playoffs are seeded and the top seeds, with the best regular season records, have home field advantage through the playoff rounds. This is a highly prized outcome and it is clear that teams make extra effort to achieve top seed status even after they have won their divisions to qualify for the playoffs. Since the playoffs are in January it is sometimes alleged that teams hosting playoff games in locations with adverse wintry conditions (e.g. Chicago or Green Bay) have a particular home field advantage over teams from the southern States.

Following Courneya and Carron (1992) and Carron *et al.* (2005) the sources of home advantage are:

- Surface and dimensions of the playing area, in which home teams can more readily adapt their playing style to stadium characteristics
- Disruption to away teams through travel
- Partisan fans who may influence critical refereeing decisions
- Partisan fans who give strong vocal encouragement to home team players.

More recent research has evaluated the relative importance of these factors generating home advantage. Each of the four sources of home advantage noted above has some support from empirical evidence. A study of perceptions of American intercollegiate basketball players by Bray and Widmeyer (2000) found that familiarity with home court, home crowd intensity and distance travelled were all factors influencing home team performance. Clarke and Norman (1995) obtained a significant negative correlation between distance travelled and home advantage in English football. Forrest et al. (2005) found that probability of home win is related positively to geographical distance between competing teams in a match. In contrast, a literature review by Nevill and Holder (1999) played down the importance of distance travelled as high levels of home advantage were observed in leagues where distances between teams were small.

Pollard (1986) measured home advantage as the proportion of total wins in a season obtained in home fixtures. Using this measure, Pollard (2002) analysed movements of North American teams to new stadia and found that home advantage during the first season at a new stadium after a move was significantly less than home advantage in the final season in the old stadium. This suggests that physical stadium characteristics and/or fan intensity contribute to home advantage.[3] The study claimed a loss of home advantage of the order of 24% in the first season after relocation to a new stadium. In recent years, several British football teams have moved stadium and the scope for testing 'new stadium' effects on home advantage in football are now more promising than before. Such testing should attempt to go further than Pollard's analysis in separating temporary effects of disruption from permanent changes in stadium architecture and the longer-term effects resulting on home advantage.

In a pair of papers, Pollard and Pollard (2005a) and Pollard (2006) emphasised the importance of travel and familiarity with stadia as key determinants of home advantage. Pollard and Pollard (2005a) offer a long-run study of home advantage in the four major North American sports and English football, with data going back to the 19th century. They note the relative lack of importance of crowd effects on home advantage. Pollard (2006) examined home advantage in football with data from 72 countries in Europe and South America. His study found higher levels of home advantage in leagues where distances between teams and associated topography make travel more demanding. A regression model of home advantage in 51 European countries shows the importance of geographical location, travel and crowd effects as explanatory factors.

The studies by Pollard and Pollard downplay the importance of crowd effects for home advantage. Nevill and Holder (1999) pointed to the importance of fans' intensity of support for the home team but gave greater weight to the importance of crowd influence upon critical refereeing decisions such as penalty kicks, allowed and disallowed goals and cautions and dismissals. They consider that match officials 'subconsciously' favour the home team. This aspect of fan pressure is considered in more detail below.

Hence, studies of home advantage in sports in general, and football in particular, give inconclusive findings. Each of the four sources mentioned above has been found to be important in some studies and natural experiments to differentiate between the competing explanations are lacking. But there is one further aspect which has been underplayed in discussion of home advantage, namely the impact of playing at home on players. A physiological study by Neave and Wolfson (2003) found that the same football players had significantly higher salivary testosterone levels before a home game than an away game. This may be due to increased motivation and expectation of winning home games rather than

---

[3] It is hard to differentiate here between changes in physical characteristics (new pitch with new surface and different playing dimensions) and changes in fan intensity (dispersal of noisier groups of fans, different acoustics and atmosphere).

away games. The increased motivation comes from knowledge that home fans are 'behind the team'. Most pertinently, the bulk of a team's revenues will come from home games (gate revenues, sponsorship and merchandise sales). Players will be well aware that these revenue sources from home games contribute to team budgets and, ultimately, player salaries.[4] Of course, higher testosterone levels might simply reflect increased stress, as opposed to higher motivation, felt from playing at home in front of a crowd with high expectations of winning, itself a function of home advantage.

The dynamics of interactions between familiarity of players with stadia and playing surface, player and fan travel characteristics and the encouragement and intimidation offered by partisan home fans merit further research. The studies by Pollard and Pollard emphasise geographical and travel fatigue effects while Nevill and Holder (1999) emphasise the importance of fan pressure. This lack of consensus in the literature needs to be resolved by further empirical work. Pollard and Pollard (2005b) offer some useful pointers in this regard.

The Influence of Fans on Players

As active stakeholders in the fortunes of their clubs, fans can use chanting and shouting to encourage their players. As noted in the previous section this can contribute to home advantage of teams. Although it is difficult to isolate this particular influence, it would appear that home fans are an important source of home advantage. However, fans' inputs to games can be negative such as when particular players, or even whole teams, are jeered for incompetence and/or perceived lack of effort. Detailed game analysis is needed to investigate positive and negative effects of crowd pressure on players and teams.

One source of negative fan pressure can be the high expectations placed on players who perform critical actions during a game. A clear example of this is the taking of penalty kicks. A well-crafted and pioneering study by Dohmen (2008) reveals the impact of crowd pressure on penalty-takers. Dohmen examines all penalty kicks taken in the top division of the Bundesliga from 1963 through to 2003/04, 3,606 in all. He distinguishes penalties that are missed, i.e. miss the target completely from those, that are successfully scored and those that are saved by

---

[4] I am indebted to David Forrest for impressing this point upon me.

goalkeepers.[5] Dohmen finds that Bundesliga 1 players are more likely to miss penalty kicks when the match is on their home ground. Specifically, penalty misses represent 7.5% of total kicks for home players and 5.6% for away players, a difference that is statistically significant at 5% level. It appears that home teams are awarded more penalties than away teams. This is consistent with either or both home advantage and the conventional expectation in football matches that the home team will apply most of the attacking pressure, although referee bias may also be a factor. One consequence of this, although difficult to test, is that home players might not put as much concentration and effort into their penalty kicks compared to away players, simply because they subconsciously expect another goal scoring opportunity is likely to occur later in the match. Conversely, away team players may be more focussed and concentrated on their penalty kicks knowing that another goal scoring opportunity has a low probability of occurrence. Dohmen finds that the differential between home and away team penalty misses is greater in the first half of the game while gate attendance and capacity utilisation have insignificant impacts on probability of missing. These findings are consistent with an explanation based on effort differentials and cast doubt on the 'fan pressure' explanation (since impact of fan pressure ought to depend on crowd size). One way of resolving the observational equivalence of differential effort and crowd pressure would be to analyse penalty shoot-out competitions in tied Cup games where the state of game and time left are controlled for by construction.

Dohmen does not control directly for the existence of penalty kick specialists. Some players are noted for their penalty-taking expertise and rarely miss. Kicker characteristics could be controlled for in a random effects probit model rather than the standard probit estimated by Dohmen. However, Dohmen does control for the experience of penalty-takers and finds, not surprisingly, that the probability of missing is negatively related to the experience of the kicker. There is a straightforward selection effect here; players who miss penalties will tend to be replaced.[6] Overall, though, Dohmen's finding that home players are more likely than away players to miss penalty kicks seems to be a robust result, at least for the Bundesliga, and worthy of further investigation elsewhere.

---

[5] A penalty can be successful in terms of the ball entering the goal but may be ruled out for an infraction such as encroachment in the penalty area by a team-mate before the kick is taken.

[6] Indeed it is quite common for a penalty taker who misses a kick to be replaced when his team is awarded a second penalty in a match. The incidence of this replacement would be worth investigating.

The Influence of Fans on Referees

Crowd pressure can influence refereeing decisions in several ways, each analysed in the sports economics literature to some extent:[7]

- The award of penalty kicks, free kicks and goals in favour of the home team
- The application of disciplinary sanctions against the opposing team
- The adding or shortening of time added on beyond the full 90 minutes

A literature has grown which seeks to identify refereeing bias under these headings. Of these potential forms of crowd pressure I shall confine attention to the first two. This is because penalty kicks and player dismissals are pivotal events in football matches while extra discretionary seconds added on at the end of a game are less likely to generate changes in game outcomes. This is not to deny the technical rigour of papers on time added on by referees (Garicano *et al.,* 2005, Dohmen, forthcoming).[8]

It is worth stressing that referees are (usually) conscious of concerns of bias. Referees are trained to 'filter out' the intimidatory pressure from players, coaches and fans during a match. Referee performances are assessed by teams and by peer review. Most importantly, career progress depends critically on good performance reviews. Currently, referees at the top level receive either a salary (as in England) or a substantial match fee (as in Germany) so that the monetary incentive to perform well is sustained.[9] The monitoring and performance evaluation of referees is therefore substantial but as we shall now show, some studies find substantive evidence of bias in referees' decisions.[10]

---

[7] Pressure exerted on referees is regularly experienced by the author in his capacity as a qualified English Football Association referee. Even at the lower levels of amateur and junior football, this pressure can be quite intense.

[8] These papers are intended to show an extension to the classic principal-agent problem in incentive design where agents (here, referees) exert favouritism.

[9] At present the annual salary for an English Premier League referee, before expenses such as travel and accommodation, is £38,000 or 53,000 Euros. England is unusual in offering an annual salary to referees; in other European Leagues, including the Bundesliga, referees are paid a match fee appropriate to the division. The introduction of an annual salary in England was a move to encourage referees to become full-time officials and it was thought that this would improve their performance at the top level. To my knowledge, there is no published evidence on whether or not this claim can be substantiated.

[10] All the authors cited in this section make clear that any bias is unintentional and is unlikely to aid career progression.

Critical Refereeing Decisions in a Match

Fans routinely bay for free kicks and penalty kicks when their team is attacking and when they perceive an offence by an opposing player. Although referees are trained to ignore these claims, and also appeals by players, there remains a view that referees are susceptible to pressure. This was illustrated in an experimental study by Nevill et al. (2002). They showed video clips of incidents from an English Premier League game involving 47 tackles by players separately to 40 English referees and asked if the referees would award a foul or not. One set of referees watched the tape with crowd noise played while the other set viewed the incidents in silence. The latter group called 15.5 percent more fouls against the home team. This is indicative rather than demonstrable proof that referees favour home teams; the sample sizes of referees and incidents are rather small. One allegation in the football world is that referees systematically favour large teams and this represents a different type of bias that needs to be separated from bias towards the home team.

Dohmen (forthcoming) again offers an empirical investigation using a large set of Bundesliga games (3,519 in total). He offers evidence that German referees award a disproportionate number of disputable and incorrect goals and penalties in favour of the home team. The data used for testing are independent reports of disputable and incorrect decisions by a specialist firm, IMP AG, hired by the German football league. This firm sends observers to each match to collect a plethora of statistics. Disputable goals and penalty kicks are subjected to post-match assessment using video replays, which of course referees do not benefit from. Goals were correctly awarded at least 95 percent of the time, an appealing result for a statistician. But 1.43 percent of all goals awarded to the home team were incorrect while 0.92 percent of all goals awarded to the away team should have been ruled out. Similarly, 3.52 percent of all goals awarded to the home team were disputable in that the assessors could not agree on the correct decision. 2.29 percent of all goals awarded to the away team were classed as disputable.

In a probit model of likelihood of award of a goal, a disputable decision was more probable if the away team was behind by one goal and if the home team was behind by one or two goals (at 10 percent significance or better). Hence, *both* home and away teams are more likely to be awarded disputable goals if they are one goal behind. The point estimates on marginal effects of being one goal behind are 0.994 for the away team and 1.398 for the home team and it is not clear that these are significantly different. Of course, when a team is a goal behind it has extra incentive to search for a goal to equalise the contest and extra attacking effort may lead to a goal being awarded. But it remains unclear why this should result in more disputable goals. Probably the most common source of dispute is whether or not an attacking player is offside and interfering with play and further analysis would usefully search out this particular sub-category. Referees and their assistants are trained to give benefit of doubt to attackers where offside decisions are debatable. Perhaps more debatable (lack of) offside calls occur when a team is behind and makes extra attacking effort.

Dohmen also finds that home teams are awarded significantly more illegitimate goals than away teams. Further, home teams are most likely to be awarded (*ex post*) illegitimate goals when they are behind in score.

A further interesting result is that referees' decisions to award goals are less likely to be correct when the match takes place in stadia without a track separating fans from the field of play (and officials). This adds to the evidence in support of a fan pressure effect as fans exert less pressure on match officials if they are some way back from the pitch. Moreover, larger teams (such as Bayern Munich) tend to play in bigger stadia with running tracks so the analysis partially controls for any 'big team bias'.

Away teams are found by Dohmen to be more likely to be denied a penalty kick under the 'legitimate' or 'disputable' verdicts of the assessors. 34.8% of penalties awarded to home teams are wrong or disputable whereas 27.4% of away team penalties fall into these categories. Probit estimation reveals that the propensity to offer wrong or disputable penalties is greater when either home or away team is one goal behind. Again, it seems that being behind is associated with more controversial calls by referees rather than 'home team' *per se*.

Overall, Dohmen presents some very interesting empirical results on controversial decisions by referees and these seem to be consistent with impacts of fan pressure. But further work is needed to eliminate competing explanations such as a tendency for officials to try to give benefit of doubt to attacking players. Dohmen's analysis essentially investigates Type I errors. If the null hypothesis that a goal or penalty should not be awarded, then there needs to be evidence in favour of rejection of the null. The null appears to be falsely rejected some of the time. But Type II errors are also important in football. These concern the goals and penalty kicks that ought to be awarded but are not. These are the debatable decisions that occur in fans' conversations after the match and deserve serious scrutiny by econometric analysis using the methods and models adopted by Dohmen.

Disciplinary Sanctions

As well as calling for penalties and free kicks, fans (and players) call for opposing players to be cautioned (yellow card) or dismissed (red card). The pressure for a caution has a large strategic element; fans and players know that two cautions mean automatic dismissal and also that a team of 11 players usually beats a team of 10. Moreover, a player who is cautioned will worry about the prospect of a dismissal and will not compete as aggressively. To the extent that fan pressure is successful in alerting referees to infractions committed by away team players, this then favours the home team. Hence, players and fans may express outrage at tackles that are actually innocent in order to pressure the referee into awarding a caution.[11]

Decisions to award yellow and red cards have been analysed for the English Premier League by Dawson *et al.* (2007). Their sample period is 1996/97 through to 2003/04 and they combine yellow cards (worth one point) and red cards (worth two points) into a single measure of disciplinary points. Using a bivariate conditional negative binomial regression model for disciplinary points incurred by home and away team Dawson *et al.* (2007) reject all of the following hypotheses:

- The propensity for away teams to incur more disciplinary points than home teams is purely a consequence of the tendency for home teams to win more often than away teams (home advantage)
- The number of disciplinary points does not vary across referees
- Conditional on home advantage, the propensity of away teams to incur more disciplinary points than home teams is independent of identity of referee.

However, there are some problems with the analysis in this paper. First, red cards should be treated differently from yellow cards. The former are issued for severe foul play (e.g. a violent tackle), for denying a goal scoring opportunity (the so-called 'professional foul') but also for two yellow cards. The authors do not treat cumulative yellow cards and red cards issued as distinct and separate categories. Second, although the authors control for *ex ante* probability of a home team win (using an elaborate statistical forecasting model) they do not control for state of game when the caution or dismissal occurs. Third, the authors do not distinguish 'home team bias' from 'big team bias'. It is sometimes alleged by football pundits and fans that referees might favour large teams in their

---

[11] Plessner and Betsch (2001) offer evidence to show that referees tend to 'even up' disciplinary sanctions. When a caution or dismissal is delivered to one team it is then followed by a similar sanction to the opposing team.

critical decisions. Fourth, the rejection of the hypothesis of no bias towards home team is derived from inspection of referee fixed effects rather than by examination of coefficients on predictors of referees' decisions.

Using data on English Premier League and Bundesliga Division 1 matches over 2000/01 to 2006/07, Buraimo *et al.* (2007) model probability of caution or dismissal in a given minute of a game. The use of minute-by-minute data enables the authors to control for the state of game at the time of caution or dismissal. *A priori* a team that is behind in score acts more aggressively as they make greater effort to score the goal(s) that will equalise the contest and this tends to lead to higher probability of a yellow or red card being awarded. With additional control variables in place, inferences on bias and favouritism are more robust and more compelling than those derived from analyses that use the match as unit of observation.

Buraimo *et al.* offer two pieces of evidence of referee bias in favour of home teams in the award of yellow and red cards:

- From the Bundesliga they find evidence of favouritism against away teams in that home teams playing in stadia without running tracks have lower probabilities of yellow and red card than home teams playing in grounds without running tracks. This is indicative of a successful impact of fans' 'social pressure' as proposed by Dohmen (forthcoming). The fact that three teams switched stadium design with track removal in the sample period suggests that this is more than just a specific team effect.

- When matches in English Premier League and Bundesliga are re-specified as favourite versus underdog, rather than home versus away, Buraimo *et al.* obtain evidence, via significant coefficients on a *home underdog* dummy variable, of biased treatment of teams in both the Premier League and the Bundesliga, in the award of both yellow and red cards.

The Influence of Fans on Head Coaches

Several researchers have investigated the impact of changing a head coach on subsequent team performance. Audas *et al.* (2002), Bruinshoofd and ter Weel (2003), Dobson and Goddard (1995) and Koning (2003) are notable examples of this sub-genre in sports economics. The consensus of these studies is that the impact of managerial change on team results is at best short-term, lasting a few matches, and further that the rate of head coach dismissals in European football leagues is excessive.[12]

As an example of research examining team performance and managerial change, consider the study of Bruinshoofd and ter Weel (2003) on Dutch football over the period 1988-2000. They point out that teams typically fire the head coach after a run of poor results. For teams facing the threat of relegation, firing a head coach perceived as responsible and replacing with a new coach seems to offer a better prospect of retention of divisional status. In the English Premier League the gap in seasonal revenue streams between Premier League and the tier below is currently estimated at around 40 million Euros. Hence, the financial penalty from relegation is very large.[13] Since teams sack the head coach when results are poor it is necessary to control for team performances where head coaches were not fired even though they were vulnerable to dismissal. The teams who fire head coaches represent a 'treatment' group while the teams whose head coaches were retained are a 'control' group. A difference-in-difference modelling strategy reveals the impact of changing head coach on team performance relative to the control group. Out of 125 instances of head coach change in Dutch football between 1998 and 2000, 35 were attributable to poor performance. The main conclusions of the empirical analysis are:

- If sackings are successful in raising performance, the rate of improvement in results is no greater than what would have been achieved under the previous head coach;
- If sacking are not successful in raising performance, the rate of deterioration in performance is greater than would have occurred under the previous head coach;
- Sacking has equal *ex ante* probabilities of success and failure in team performance.

One comment that is in order here is that some sackings are opportunistic in that teams may see that a head coach with perceived greater talent suddenly becomes available on the managerial job market, perhaps because he was sacked elsewhere. A remarkable feature of the managerial labour market is the regularity with which head coaches fired

---

[12] A conversation with an odds-setter for a leading English bookmaker revealed that odds for match outcomes were only adjusted to account for changes in head coach for short periods of two to three weeks following a new appointment.

[13] Although teams threatened with relegation are more likely to fire head coaches, promoted teams tend to stick with their head coach even though they spend large sums of money on transfer fees and new contracts in order to upgrade their playing squad to compete at the higher level.

at one club are then hired elsewhere.[14] Once a club decides to sack a head
coach it must then consider whether to hire an experienced head coach or a
new head coach without experience. Clubs tend to be risk averse in the
hiring decision, even though they may be regarded as premature in their
firing decision.

Some studies of the managerial labour market in football have
examined the levels of efficiency of teams using stochastic frontier models.
This approach examines the extent to which teams depart from their
production frontiers. The question that is posed is the extent to which
player and managerial inputs can generate good performances, measured
by League points per game or League rankings, given available budgets.
For example, Frick and Simmons (forthcoming) find for the Bundesliga
that smaller teams tend to have greater technical inefficiency than larger
teams. Teams that were recently promoted and teams that recently
changed head coach also generated larger scores of technical inefficiency.

An interesting new study by de Dios Tena and Forrest (2007) sheds
light on the decision to terminate a head coach's contract. De Dios Tena
and Forrest examine 20 within-season managerial dismissals in the
Spanish *Liga de Fútbol Profesional* over seasons 2002/03 to 2004/05. A
probit model of managerial dismissal shows that the probability of
dismissal rises if a team is in the bottom three places in the League,
designated as the 'relegation zone' since three teams are demoted at the
end of season. A dismissal is more likely if the team lost its last match.
The authors construct a measure of team efficiency as actual position
relative to predicted position given team budget. Teams that have lower
league positions relative to that predicted from budgets are more likely to
fire their head coach. There is also a propensity to fire head coaches later
in the season, as shown by a significant impact of a variable denoting
number of match round. The relationship between probability of dismissal
and match round number is modelled as quadratic with a turning point at
round 26. Beyond this match number clubs are less likely to fire their head
coach as presumably there are insufficient games left for a sufficiently
qualified new hire to be installed and to make sufficient difference to

---

[14] Borland and Lye (1996) show that the managerial labour market in Australian
Rules football is characterised by sorting and matching effects. The best coaches
gravitate towards the better-performing teams (who also tend to have the greatest
revenues and the best players). Sorting and matching would appear to be important
features of the managerial labour market in European football.

league position.[15] These results do appear to show that threat of relegation is an important predictor of head coach dismissal.

De Dios Tena and Forrest next offer an ordered probit model of 1050 match results in the Spanish *Liga de Fútbol Profesional*. They generate seven interaction variables between a dummy variable for new head coach and a dummy variable for home team playing its nth home game under new management (where n is between one and seven). Similar interaction terms are created for away teams under new management. Strikingly all the away team interactions are statistically insignificant while the home team change-of-manager terms are significant for first and second (but no more) home games with a new head coach in charge. That is, teams are more likely to win the first and second home games under a new managerial regime, *ceteris paribus*, but away results are unaffected. These results are consistent with the intuition of bookmakers reported in footnote 13. The new finding here is the difference in impact of a new head coach between home and away performances.[16] The significant impacts on home performances, as opposed to away, are consistent with the conjecture offered by Tena and Forrest, a new head coach will generate enhanced fan support as the home crowd gives greater vocal encouragement to the team under the new regime. These two propositions are not easily separated.

Conclusions

I have suggested that football fans are not passive consumers and that they play an active part in football matches. Empirical evidence on audience demand suggests that fans care less about uncertainty of match outcome and more about the prospect of a win for their team. Fans appear to be part of the process that generates home advantage for teams, although assessing the precise mechanism and extent of this fan-based home advantage proves difficult.

Although fan pressure is broadly a positive force affecting team performance- and it is widely acknowledged as such by players, coaches and boards of directors- there are occasions where fan pressure can have

---

[15] The recent introduction of the 'transfer window' in January means that head coaches hired after this time are constrained in their ability to recruit new players. The expectation of a new hire in the second half of the season is then that the new coach makes better use of existing playing talent than the departing coach.

[16] Future research on impacts of head coach turnover would usefully test for the alleged differential in home and away performances following change of coach using a difference-in-difference method applied by Bruinshoofd and ter Weel (2003).

unintended negative effects. One such adverse effect is on players taking penalty kicks. Dohmen's research shows the greater tendency for home team, rather than away team, players to miss penalty kicks.

The evidence on impacts of home fans on critical refereeing decisions turns out to be mixed and inconclusive. This is because studies have not controlled sufficiently both for variations in team effort and aggression as the match unfolds and for 'big team' versus home team effects on refereeing decisions. My own preliminary results on determinants of cautions and dismissals in the English Premier League suggests that state of the game at time of incident and differentials in fan support between competing teams should be considered carefully before home team bias on the part of referees can be demonstrated.

Finally, fan pressure appears to be an important determinant of head coach dismissal and can, at least in the short term, contribute towards improved match results in home games.

Overall, the pressure exerted by fans is an important and under-researched input to football match outcomes. In particular, outcome uncertainty of contests is not an exogenous or static concept and is capable of being affected by fan pressure. Further work is needed across various European Leagues to identify more precisely the sources and magnitudes of impacts of fan pressure on both particular game outcomes and the extent of home advantage. This research should cover not just match results but key incidents within games such as player dismissals and penalty kicks. As improved within-game data becomes more widely available so research on these important issues will develop, building on the pioneering contributions that I have surveyed here.

References

Audas, R., S. Dobson and J. Goddard (2002). "The impact of managerial change on team performance in professional sports." *Journal of Economics and Business*, 54(6), 633-651.

Bird, P. J. W. N. (1982). "The demand for league football." *Applied Economics*, 14(6), 637-649.

Borland, J. (1987). "The demand for Australian Rules football." *Economic Record*, 63(182), 220-230.

Borland, J. and J. Lye (1996). "Matching and mobility in the market for Australian Rules football coaches." *Industrial and Labor Relations Review*, 50(1), 143-158.

Borland, J. and R. Macdonald (2003). "Demand for sport." *Oxford Review of Economic Policy*, 19(4), 478-502.

Bray, S. R. and W. N. Widmeyer (2000). "Athletes' perceptions of the home advantage: an investigation of perceived causal factors." *Journal of Sport Behavior*, 23(1), 1-10.

Bruinshoofd, A. and B. ter Weel (2003). "Manager to go? Performance dips reconsidered with evidence from Dutch football." *European Journal of Operational Research*, 148(2), 233-246.

Buraimo, B. A., D. K. Forrest and R. Simmons (2007). "The twelfth man?: Refereeing bias in English and German soccer." *Lancaster University Management School Working Paper*.

Buraimo, B. A. and R. Simmons (forthcoming). "Market size and attendance in English Premier League football." *International Journal of Sport Management and Marketing*.

Buraimo, B. A., R. Simmons and S. Szymanski (2006). "English football." *Journal of Sports Economics*, 6(1), 29-46.

Carron, A. V., T. Loughhead and S. Bray (2005). "The home advantage in sport competitions: Courneya and Carron's (1992) conceptual framework a decade later." *Journal of Sports Sciences*, 23(4), 395-407.

Clarke, S. R. and J. M. Norman (1995). "Home ground advantage of individual clubs in English soccer." *The Statistician*, 44(4), 509-521.

Courneya, K. S. and A. V. Carron (1992). "The home advantage in sports competitions: A literature review." *Journal of Sport and Exercise Psychology*, 14(1), 13-27.

Dawson, P. M., S. Dobson, J. A. Goddard and J. Wilson (2007). "Are football referees really biased and inconsistent? Evidence from the English Premier League." *Journal of the Royal Statistical Society Series A: Statistics in Society*, 170(1), 231-250.

De Dios Tena, J. and D. K. Forrest (2007). "Within-season dismissal of football coaches: Statistical analysis of causes and consequences." *European Journal of Operational Research*, 181(1), 362-373.

Dobson, S. M. and J. A. Goddard (1995). "The demand for professional League football in England and Wales." *The Statistican*, 44(2), 259-277.

Dohmen, T. J. (2008). "Do professionals choke under pressure?" *Journal of Economic Behavior and Organization*, 65 (3/4), 636-653.

Dohmen, T. J. (forthcoming). "Social pressure influences decisions of individuals: Evidence from the behavior of football referees." *Economic Inquiry*.

El Hodiri, M. and J. Quirk (1971). "An economic model of a professional sports league." *Journal of Political Economy*, 79(6), 1302-1319.

Forrest, D. K., J. Beaumont, J. A. Goddard and R. Simmons (2005). "Home advantage and the debate about competitive balance in professional sports leagues." *Journal of Sports Sciences*, 23(4), 439-445.

Forrest, D. K. and R. Simmons (2006). "New issues in attendance demand: The case of the English Football League." *Journal of Sports Economics*, 7(3), 247-266.

Forrest, D. K., R. Simmons and B. A. Buraimo (2005). "Outcome uncertainty and the couch potato audience." *Scottish Journal of Political Economy*, 52(4), 641-661.

Forrest, D. K., R. Simmons and P. Feehan (2002). "A spatial cross-sectional analysis of the elasticity of demand for soccer." *Scottish Journal of Political Economy*, 49(3), 336-355.

Fort, R. D. and J. Quirk (1995). "Cross-subsidisation, incentives and outcomes in professional team sports." *Journal of Economic Literature*, 33(3), 1265-1299.

Frick, B. and R. Simmons (forthcoming). "The impact of managerial quality on organizational performance: Evidence from German soccer." *Managerial and Decision Economics*.

Garicano, L., I. Palacios-Huerta and C. Prendergast (2005). "Favoritism under social pressure." *Review of Economics and Statistics*, 87(2), 208-216.

Koning, R. (2003). "An econometric evaluation of the effect of firing a coach on team performance." *Applied Economics*, 35(5), 555-564.

Neave, N. and S. Wolfson (2003), "Testosterone, territoriality and home advantage." *Physiology and Behavior*, 78(2), 269-275.

Nevill, A. M., N. J. Balmer and A. M. Williams (2002). "The influence of crowd noise and experience upon refereeing decisions in Association Football." *Psychology of Sport and Exercise*, 3(4), 261-272.

Nevill, A. M. and R. L. Holder (1999). "Home advantage in sport: an overview of studies on the advantage of playing at home." *Sports Medicine*, 28(4), 221-236.

Plessner, H. and T. Betsch (2001). "Sequential effects in important referee decisions: The case of penalties in soccer." *Joirnal of Sport Exercise and Psychology*, 23, 200-205.

Pollard, R. (1986). "Home advantage in soccer: A retrospective analysis." *Journal of Sports Sciences*, 4(3), 237-248.

—. (2002). "Evidence of a reduced home advantage when a team moves to a new stadium." *Journal of Sports Sciences*, 20(12), 969-973.

—. (2006). "Worldwide regional variations in home advantage in Association Football." *Journal of Sports Sciences*, 24(3), 231-240.

Pollard, R. and G. Pollard (2005a). "Long-term trends in home advantage in professional team sports in North America and England (1876-2003)." *Journal of Sports Sciences*, 23(4), 337-350.

Pollard, R. and G. Pollard (2005b). "Home advantage in soccer: A review of its existence and causes." *International Journal of Soccer and Science*, 3, 28-38.

Rottenberg, S. (1956). "The baseball player's labor market." *Journal of Political Economy*, 64(3), 242-258.

Simmons, R. (1996). "The demand for English League football: A club-level analysis." *Applied Economics*, 28(2), 139-155.

Stefani, R. (2007). "Measurement and interpretation of home advantage." In *Statistical Thinking in Sports*. J. Albert and R. Koning eds. Boca Raton, FL: Chapman & Hall/CRC, 203-216.

Szymanski, S. A. (2003). "The economic design of sporting contests." *Journal of Economic Literature*, 41(4), 1137-1187.

CHAPTER THIRTEEN

THE FOOTBALL FAN AND THE CRITICAL INCIDENT: HOW IMPORTANT ARE SPECIFIC INCIDENTS FOR OVERALL EVALUATIONS OF THE FAVOURITE CLUB?

VYACHESLAV JEVTUSHENKO, MATHIAS LANDSBERG AND MAGNUS SÖDERLUND[1]

One important task for research on football supporters is to come to terms with the causal antecedents of the supporter's overall evaluation of his or her favourite club. Given the great influence of supporting one particular team on the lives of many people in contemporary society, such antecedents are likely to uncover *why* so much passion exists with regard to the favourite football club. Moreover, from a club management point of view, and in the light of the increasing use of descriptions of football fans as "customers" and football clubs as "brands" (cf. Tapp, 2004), the identification of the causal antecedents of the overall evaluation serves as a diagnostic tool. That is to say, given that some antecedents are controllable from a management point of view, they can be manipulated by the club to improve the overall evaluation—which in turn is assumed to influence supporter behaviour vis-à-vis the club, such as sporting event attendance and purchases of club souvenirs (Madrigal, 1995; Trail et al., 2005; Wakefield and Blodgett, 1996).

The perhaps most common methodological alternative for identifying causal antecedents to an overall evaluation is to (a) decompose the club's "offer" in terms of a set of attributes (e.g., the extent to which it plays well,

---

[1] Jevtushenko, Landsberg, Söderlund (author for correspondence): Center for Consumer Marketing, Stockholm School of Economics, P.O. Box 6501, SE-113 83 Stockholm, Sweden, Email: Magnus.Soderlund@hhs.se, Tel. 46-8-736 9541.

its home stadium facilities, its supporters etc), (b) ask supporters to evaluate the performance of each attribute for a specific period (e.g., for one particular season) and (c) ask supporters to provide also an overall evaluation of the club. Then, (d) the researcher uses multivariate analysis to assess the relative impact of the attributes' performance on the overall evaluation. Several studies following this design have been undertaken on sport spectators (cf. Trail et al., 2005; Wakefield and Sloan, 1995; Wakefield and Blodgett, 1996). It has also been used at the sport category level rather than the specific club level (e.g., to assess why people like basketball and hockey; cf. Ferreira and Armstrong, 2004). The same approach has been used extensively in many marketing-related studies of customer-supplier relationships, particularly in national customer satisfaction barometers (Johnson et al., 2001). In addition to typical marketing research assumptions of this multi-attribute model (i.e., consumers make evaluations at the attribute level and managers find this level useful from a diagnostic point of view; cf. Mittal et al., 1998), it is implicitly assumed that the customer is able to aggregate his/her performance perceptions collected from many specific occasions in response to questions regarding attribute performance.

A very different approach to assess causal antecedents to overall evaluations, however, does also exist, particularly in service research. This approach, the critical incident technique (CIT), consists of (a) asking the participant to describe one particular critical incident (a highly negative or a highly positive incident related to the customer's interaction with the service firm), and then (b) the researcher classifies the resulting incidents in categories reflecting different causes to an overall evaluation of the supplier (e.g., Bitner et al., 1990; Chung and Hoffman, 1998; Gilbert and Morris, 1995; Meuter et al., 2000). An implicit assumption in this approach is thus that one single incident is so important that it will affect the overall evaluation.

Many football fans are avid collectors of club memorabilia, such as match programmes and souvenirs (Tapp, 2004). Yet, as we see it, football fans are also "collecting" club-related incidents. Such incidents are time-space delimited events related to a team (e.g., "Maradona used his hand when he scored in the 1986 World Cup match between England and Argentina" and "Solskjear banged in 4 goals in 10 minutes when he came in as a substitute against Nottingham Forrest") and we expect that they become stockpiled in the fan's mind in the process of following one particular team. Given the passionate character of being a football fan, we also expect that many such incidents have a highly valenced charge; the fan experiences both agony and ecstasy (Richardson, 2004), and it has been argued that the fan is particularly responsive to specific events perceived as out-of-the-ordinary (Holt, 1995). In other words, we expect that being a football fan involves the accumulation in memory of critical incidents. It is therefore tempting to suggest that the CIT may be useful in a football supporter context—in which we hitherto have not seen any applications of this method. It has, however, been used to examine American football and baseball spectators (Greenwell et al. 2007).

The notion of critical incidents, and the typical way in which service marketing researchers have dealt with them in their studies, however, raise questions. One fundamental question is the extent to which such incidents really contribute to the variation in the overall evaluation. Surprisingly, this question has hardly been addressed in empirical terms (Gremler, 2004). Thus, most CIT researchers *assume* that a negative incident has a negative impact on the overall evaluation—and that a positive incident has a positive impact on the overall evaluation. A problematic aspect of this assumption, however, is that one particular incident (which the respondent thus selects on the request of the researcher) represents a small sample ($N = 1$) from a larger population of incidents that may have occurred in the interaction between the respondent and a supplier. This suggests that the respondent-selected incident competes with *other* incidents in its effects on the overall evaluation. These other incidents, however, are not captured by the standard CIT approach—because the standard approach focuses on *one* single incident which the customer perceives as unusually positive or negative (Edvardsson and Roos, 2001; Gremler, 2004; Sommerfeld and Paulssen, 2007; Stauss and Weinlich, 1997).

Given this sampling-based view of critical incidents, one may question the extent to which one self-selected incident is informative about the overall evaluation of one object (such as one's favourite football club). In other words, we believe that CIT researchers have overlooked a substantial validity issue: do the positive and negative aspects covered by the incidents really predict an overall evaluation? The specific purpose of this paper is to examine the issue in a football supporter context. This examination, we believe, would offer contributions not only to how football supporters come to appreciate one particular club; it also has the potential to address how people arrive at this or that overall evaluation in general—and what researchers should think about when they make attempts to capture causal factors in their theories and methods.

Theoretical Framework

The Overall Evaluation as an Attitude

Copious studies have dealt with the individual's overall evaluation of an object, and they are typically based on the premise that the evaluation of stimuli as good or bad is a basic and ubiquitous aspect of the way people respond to their environment (cf. Pratto and John, 1991). Many evaluation constructs, then, exist in marketing literature (e.g., brand attitude, perceived value, overall service quality and customer satisfaction). Here, our point of departure is one general evaluation construct: the overall attitude toward an object. Such attitudes are typically viewed as predictive of one's intentions vis-à-vis an object—and the intentions are assumed to affect behaviour. In marketing-related research, many different attitudinal objects are examined (e.g., an ad, a product, a brand and a store), yet here we are focusing on the overall attitude toward the football supporter's favourite football club. This attitude should be conceived of as a relative enduring evaluation along a bad-good continuum (cf. Eagly and Chaiken, 1993).

Critical Incidents as Determinants of the Overall Attitude

A critical incident is (by definition) one particular historic incident which—from the individual's point of view—was especially negative or positive in the individual's relationship with an object. Critical incidents thus represent *extreme* outcomes (Gremler, 2004), and one main (implicit) assumption behind the interest in critical incidents in service research is that they may induce change in the customer-supplier relationship (Edvardsson and Strandvik, 2000). More specifically, then, it is assumed that *one* incident may have change implications for a relationship. In addition to service research, and since the launch of the critical incident technique in a seminal article by Flanagan (1954), critical incidents have also attracted attention in health care research (Kemppainen, 2000), education research (Bycio and Allen, 2004) and management research (White and Locke, 1981). The notion of a critical incident is also conceptually related to the so-called major life event (cf. DeLongis et al., 1982; Kanner et al., 1981).

In general, it does seems clear that one single incident in one's life can indeed have a lasting effect and sometimes even branch people into totally new trajectories of life (Bandura, 1982). Here, however, our focus is more specific: we are interested in the potential for a critical incident to affect the overall attitude toward one's favourite football club. One main reason why critical incidents are likely to affect overall evaluations is predicated on the nature of the critical incident, which by definition is associated with very negative or very positive reactions. Such reactions are particularly likely to comprise emotions—both when they occur and when they are recalled later. Given this emotional content, we expect that incident-related emotions also colour overall evaluations in terms of a mechanism referred to as affect infusion (Forgas, 1995). In more specific terms, affect infusion can take place in terms of a heuristic of the type "if-this-particular-incident-made-me-feel-good-then-I-must-like-the-object-that-produced-the-incident"; that is, the emotional output of the incident is used as a shortcut to an overall evaluation of the object involved in creating the incident. Affect infusion may also manifest itself, however, when the incident activates memories with a similar valence as the incident, and such memories then provide a biased access to other material in memory on which the overall evaluation is based. In this case, memory biases encourage the evaluation to become valence congruent with the incident.

The affect-laden impact of critical incidents on overall evaluations is also consistent with the peak-end rule theory. This theory predicts that people's evaluations of an interaction episode are particularly likely to be influenced by the episode's peak and ending (Fredrickson, 2000). The peak in this case, "the most intense affective moment" (ibid., p 585), is indeed something which in a conceptual sense is closely related to a critical incident. Furthermore, the affective charge of incidents, and their link to memory, is also acknowledged in literature on so-called defining memories (DMs). DMs are memories with a particularly high level of affective intensity, and they are assumed to have an important impact on current and future preferences in a consumption context (Braun-LaTour et al., 2007). Here, we assume that the impact of DMs on preferences is mediated by overall evaluations.

Given this, we expect that a critical incident in a football supporter context is likely to have an impact on the overall attitude toward the favourite club, and we hypothesise the following associations:

H1: A negative critical incident is negatively associated with the overall attitude toward the favourite club

H2: A positive critical incident is positively associated with the overall attitude toward the favourite club

It can be noted that there may be room for more precise hypotheses at this point, with regard to the relative impact of positive versus negative events on the overall attitude, because many authors have stressed that negative events elicit more physiological, affective, cognitive and behavioural activity than positive events do (cf. Taylor, 1991). This assumption, and supporting empirical evidence, also appear in marketing contexts, in which it has been argued that one unit of negative performance on an attribute is likely to have a larger effect on an overall evaluation than a corresponding unit of positive performance (Mittal et al., 1998). The main rationale behind this response pattern (often labelled a negativity bias) is that negative events are threatening and call for action to a larger extent than positive events do (Taylor, 1991). Or, as Pratto and John (1991) argue, pleasure is simply less urgent than pain. With this in mind, then, it is tempting to hypothesise that a negative critical incident has a relatively stronger impact than a positive critical incident on the overall evaluation of the favourite football club. However, we will not do so, and we elaborate on the reason in the subsequent section.

Time and Memory: Moderating Variables

Even though several theories predict that a critical incident is likely to have an impact on an overall evaluation, it should again be noticed that a critical incident can be conceived of as a sample from a population of incidents—a population which may comprise many critical incidents (and many incidents with less extreme valence). It therefore seems likely that the individual incident's impact on the overall evaluation is moderated by characteristics of the population of incidents from which it is "drawn". Intuitively, it seems as if a large incident population, in which the individual incident is less salient and accessible, would attenuate the impact of one single incident. To explore this aspect, we focus on one specific variable which we believe may attenuate the impact: the time that has passed since the incident occurred.

One possible main hypothesis is that a critical incident would be subject to a reduced impact on the overall evaluation as time from the occurrence of the incident increases. More specifically, it is likely that the customer's mental categories assigned to deal with an object are filled with additional incidents as time passes and therefore the net result is that one single incident becomes less salient over time and thereby also less potent in a causal sense with regard to the overall evaluation. The assumption of a decaying impact over time, however, should be seen in the light of Odekerken-Schröder et al. (2000, p. 109) who conjecture that "critical incidents are top of mind even in the long run". Yet empirical research on the issue is scarce and thus it calls for an explicit empirical examination.

Further complexity is introduced if we take into account that positive and negative incidents may have an asymmetric impact on an overall evaluation (i.e., according to the notion of a negativity bias, the negative impact may have a relatively stronger impact than the positive incident). We do believe that negative events are likely to have a greater impact than positive events *at the moment when they occur.* When time passes, however, negative events become less accessible in memory than positive events (Taylor, 1991). A related aspect of this (Charles et al., 2003) is that one gets older when time passes, and age is negatively correlated with the frequency of experiencing negative emotions and positively associated with regulation of emotions (i.e., maintaining positive affect and reducing negative affect). Moreover, according to the rosy retrospection hypothesis, there is a tendency to recall an event as more positive compared to the evaluation of the same event when it occurred (Mitchell et al., 1997; Sutton, 1992).

We thus expect that the negative charge of a negative incident from the past decreases over time, while the positive charge of a positive incident increases over time. Given that the level of extremity of the charge affects the accessibility of the incident, and thereby also its causal potency vis-à-vis an overall evaluation, we expect that positive and negative events are subject to different impact on overall evaluations as time from the incident passes. To assess this in the context of football supporters, we hypothesise the following:

H3: As time passes from the occurrence of a negative critical incident, it will reduce this incident's negative impact on the overall attitude toward the favourite club

H4: As time passes from the occurrence of a positive critical incident, it will increase this incident's positive impact on the overall attitude toward the favourite club

It can be noted that if H3 and H4 are confirmed, it suggests that an explicit account of *when* a reported critical incident occurred would be useful in a CIT context; otherwise the researcher would run the risk of both overestimating and underestimating the impact of incidents from the past on overall evaluations made in the present. Yet such time data have rarely been collected with CIT (Edvardsson and Strandvik, 2000). We turn now to an assessment of these hypotheses.

Research Method

Data Collection and Participants

A web-based questionnaire was used to collect data regarding the hypotheses. We co-operated with one leading website for football supporters in Sweden, and visitors to this site were invited to take part in the study. As an incentive, the visitors were informed that they would participate in a lottery in which 10 FIFA 07 TV games served as prizes. Our instructions informed the participants that the questionnaire's target group was supporters of one of the 14 football clubs playing in the highest division in Sweden ("Allsvenskan") during the 2006 season. In the beginning of the questionnaire, the supporter was asked which of these 14 clubs s/he was supporting ("your favourite club"), and s/he was instructed to complete the questionnaire with this particular club in mind. Wann et al. (1996) used a similar design. The questionnaire was distributed just after the completion of the 2006 season.

In total, 1047 visitors completed the questionnaire, and we should view them as a convenience sample. The age of the respondents ranged from 12 to 64 ($M = 26$, $SD = 8.73$), and only 26 of the 1047 respondents were female. To assess the representativeness of this sample, we computed the zero-order correlation between (a) the average number of home game visitors for each of the 14 teams during the 2006 season, available from an official secondary source, and (b) the number of supporters for each of the 14 teams in our sample. The resulting correlation ($r = .91, p <.01, N = 14$) suggests that our sample at least mirrored the proportions of the number of team supporters in the population.

Moreover, to be a "supporter" should be seen as variable rather than a category, because supporters' involvement in a favourite team is subject to variation in intensity; some are casual attendees (sometimes referred to as "tourists" by hard core fans) and some are seriously devoted fanatics who attend every game. Some descriptive items in the questionnaire allow us to say something about the sample in this respect. First, we used a club involvement scale ranging from 1 (do not agree at all) to 7 (agree completely), comprising four individual items: "The first thing I read in the newspaper the day after my favourite club's game is the report of the game", "If it is not possible to follow my favourite club's games, I really miss something", "When I cannot read about my favourite club the day after a game, I really miss something" and "To follow my favourite club is one of the most important things for me". For this scale, Cronbach's alpha was .73, so we used the average response to the four items as a club involvement indicator. The mean involvement in the sample was 6.14 (*SD*

= 0.95) and this sample mean was significantly higher than the scale midpoint (i.e., 4; $t = 72.59$, $p < .01$). Second, we used a loyalty item ("I am a loyal supporter to my favourite club") scored along a dimension ranging from 1 (do not agree at all) to 7 (agree completely) to measure self-perceived club loyalty. This loyalty variable had a sample mean of 6.62 ($SD = 0.85$) and the sample mean was significantly higher than the scale midpoint ($t = 99.48$, $p < .01$). It can be contended, then, given the 7-point scale, that our sample comprised relatively highly involved and loyal supporters.

Measures

The *attitude toward the favourite club* was measured with four adjective pairs scored on a 7-point scale (uninteresting-interesting, bad-good, negative-positive, worthless-valuable). Cronbach's alpha was .88, thus suggesting an acceptable level of reliability in terms of internal consistency, and we used the unweighted mean of the responses to the four items as a measure of the attitude toward the favourite club. MacKenzie and Lutz (1989), Mitchell and Olson (1981) and Mitchell (1986) have used similar items to gauge attitudes in marketing-related research. In our sample, this attitude variable was negatively skewed (it took on values ranging from 3 to 7 and $M = 6.73$); the majority of the supporters thus had a very positive rather than a very negative attitude toward the club. The outcome mirrors the well-documented skewness of customer satisfaction (cf. Fornell, 1992), another global evaluation variable, and it is what we expect in a situation in which there are many choices for the supporter (given many possible clubs to support, a supporter is expected to support a club which s/he likes very much). To assess the nomological validity of this attitude measure, and given that attitudes are supposed to affect intentions, we also included a set of single-item intention measures in the questionnaire. They were framed in terms of intentions to perform behaviours (attend home games, attend away games, buy club souvenirs and watch the club's game on TV) in the coming season (i.e., 2007). Similar intention items for sport spectators appear in Trail et al. (2005). Each intention item had a response format ranging from 1 (not likely at all) to 7 (very likely). Then, we computed the zero-order correlations between the attitude measure and each intention variable, and the resulting positive correlations indicated that the attitude measure behaved as expected according to theory (attend home games: $r = .21$, $p < .01$; attend away games: $r = .18$, $p < .01$; buy club souvenirs: $r = .25$, $p < .01$; and watch the club's games on TV: $r = 0.19$, $p < .01$).

With respect to *critical incidents*, we collected data on both positive and negative incidents for each respondent. For positive incidents, we asked the respondent to provide an account of one particular situation from the past when it had felt particularly good to be a supporter of the favourite club. The respondent was explicitly instructed to consider the total period for which s/he had been supporting the favourite club. An open-ended response format was provided for this question. Then, in addition, the respondent was asked how positive this situation had felt; these responses were collected on a scale ranging from 1 (somewhat positive) to 7 (extremely positive). The same approach was used to collect data on negative incidents, but in this case the evaluation variable ranged from 1 (somewhat negative) to 7 (extremely negative). It should be noted that the typical CIT study does not capture information about the degree to which one specific critical incident is positive or negative (Edvardsson and Strandvik, 2000). Incidentally, not even untypical CIT studies, with the explicit purpose of comparing the CIT approach with other approaches to arrive at a set of causal antecedents of an overall evaluation, have captured such data (cf. Odekerken-Schröder et al., 2000; Stauss and Hentschel, 1992). This type of data, however, is necessary when one is interested in associations between variables (in our case: the association between the valenced charge of the incident and the overall evaluation). Some researchers, such as Swan and Rao (1975), however, have collected magnitude information on rating scales for each incident. Another example is Chung and Hoffman (1998), yet they did so only for negative incidents, but it is a rare practice to collect data also on an overall evaluation variable.

Moreover, with regard to the *time* variable, and for both positive and negative incidents, we asked the respondent to recall when the reported incident had occurred. We used an open-ended response format to capture the year of the selected incident, and we created a time variable for the subsequent analysis by subtracting the reported year from the year in which the study took place (i.e., 2006). The resulting time variable thus captures the number of years that have passed since the reported incident occurred. In the typical CIT study, however, such data are not captured (Edvardsson and Strandvik, 2000). Chung and Hoffman (1998) is an exception, but they did not use these data in their analysis.

The notion of a critical incident (i.e., a causally potent variable with regard to an overall evaluation of an object) should be seen in contrast to the relatively more prevalent approach to examine antecedents to the overall evaluation in terms of aggregated performance perceptions of the object's attributes. To come to terms with how important critical incidents really are, then, it would be enlightening to assess their impact in a context in which the prevalent approach is a point of reference. To obtain such a reference point, we included measures of some *aggregated performance perceptions* regarding specific club attributes likely to affect a supporter's overall attitude toward the favourite team. We asked the respondents to assess the performance of the club during the 2006 season in terms of (1) having played beautiful football (i.e., "jogo bonito"), (2) its official homepage, (3) the club's ambition to develop, (4) the players' star status and (5) the supporters' behaviour during games. These performance perceptions are aggregated in the sense that the questionnaire items required the respondent to summarise all impression (which may include several critical incidents but also more mundane incidents) regarding each attribute for the full 2006 season. For each of these items, we provided a scale ranging from 1 (poor performance) to 7 (high performance).

Analysis and Results

Initial Remarks

Although the specific content of the critical incidents is not a part of our hypotheses, it can be noted that the majority of the reported incidents dealt with team performance outcomes. Examples of positive critical incidents of this type are "when we eliminated Inter from Champions League", "when we won the UEFA Cup" and "when we qualified for Champions League by beating AEK Athens with 1-0". As for negative incidents, examples are "when we lost the FC Thun game" and "when we did not win the league in '98". The high frequency of such incidents is consistent with a finding in other studies: the outcomes of games are important when sport fans evaluate the quality of sporting event experiences (Kelley and Turley, 2001) and when fans provide reasons for following one particular team (Wann et al., 1996). Yet other types were also represented, such as incidents reflecting the supporter's own activities as a player (e.g., "when I played in one of the club's junior teams and won one particular cup") and the supporter's activities as a supporter (e.g.,"when I went to Belgrade to support my team in the victory against Partizan"). Clearly, a qualitative analysis of the incidents may reveal several discrete categories, which would be helpful in understanding supporters' attachment to one particular club, but this type of analysis is thus not the focus of the present study.

It should also be observed that our respondents were requested to focus on their favourite club and that there were 14 such clubs in the study. Even though the questions were identical for all respondents, the respondents thus answered the questions with different clubs in mind. This introduces heterogeneity in the data material, which reduces the sensitivity of statistical tests (Calder et al., 1981), so we adopted a relatively liberal significance level for the tests of the hypotheses (10 percent).

Moreover, the above mentioned skewness in the attitude toward the favourite club may create problems in OLS regression analysis (i.e., the main means we used to test the hypotheses). Since one common recommendation to deal with a negatively skewed variable is a square root transformation (cf. Hair et al., 1992), we did this before testing the hypotheses. However, it turned out that it produced the same results as a non-transformed dependent variable, so to keep the results as close as possible to the original data we present the outcomes of the tests for the non-transformed dependent variable below.

Assessing the Hypotheses

In the first step of the analysis, and to assess H1 and H2, we performed a regression with the two critical incident valence variables as independent variables and the overall attitude toward the favourite club as the dependent variable (Model 1). This analysis revealed that the combined influence of the two critical incident variables on the attitude was indeed modest yet significant ($R^2 = .02$, $F = 10.66$, $p < .01$). Both variables had the expected impact on the attitude; the positive incident was positively associated with the overall club attitude ($\beta = 0.10$, $p < .01$), and the negative incident was negatively associated with the overall club attitude ($\beta = -.13$, $p < .01$). H1 and H2 were thus supported by Model 1.

As for our point of reference for the assessment of the impact of the critical incidents, the aggregated performance perceptions as rival determinants of the overall attitude, we next assessed a model with the five aggregated performance variables by using them as independent variables in a regression in which the overall attitude was the dependent variable (Model 2a). This analysis resulted in a substantial improvement of the explained variance ($R^2 = .14$, $F = 34.09$, $p < .01$) in relation to Model 1. And each of the individual performance perception variables had a significant and positive impact on the overall attitude. In the next step, we re-examined the same model, but this time the two incident variables were included as independent variables, too (Model 2b). Model 2b produced a slight improvement of the explained variance ($R^2 = .15$, $F = 24.35$, $p < .01$), each performance perception variable remained significant and, in addition, the two incident variables were significant: $\beta = 0.05$ ($p = .09$) for the positive incident variable and $\beta = -0.10$ ($p < .01$) for the negative incident variable. It can be contended, then, that H1 and H2 were supported also in a context in which the incident variables had to compete with variables mirroring different assumptions regarding how individuals arrive at one particular overall evaluation.

With regard to H3, stating that the time (recall that we measured this in terms of years) that passes from the occurrence of a negative critical incident reduces this incident's negative impact on the overall attitude toward the favourite club, we again performed a regression analysis on the attitude toward the club. In this case, the independent variables were (1) the negative critical incident variable, (2) the time variable and (3) the interaction between (1) and (2). This is our Model 3a. A significant interaction would indicate that the time variable moderates the impact of the critical incident variable on the overall attitude (Sharma et al., 1981). We standardised (1)-(3) before this analysis to avoid multicollinearity problems (Dunlap and Kemery, 1997). The analysis revealed that (1) the negative incident variable was significant and negative ($\beta = -0.08, p = .01$), (2) the time variable was non-significant ($\beta = 0.04, p = .19$), and that (3) the interaction term was significant at the 10 percent level ($\beta = 0.06, p = .09$). Hypothesis 3 was thus supported: as the number of years since the incident increased, the impact of the incident on the attitude was reduced. Again, however, the explained variance was modest ($R^2 = .01, F = 3.67, p = .012$). To illustrate the effect of the time variable more clearly, we used the median of the time variable (the time that had passed since the negative incident occurred) to split the sample into two groups (short vs. long time since the occurrence of the negative incident), and we performed the same bivariate regression for each of the two groups (the valence of the negative incident variable was the independent variable and the attitude toward the club was the dependent variable). This showed that the impact of the negative incident variable was negative and significant in the short duration group ($\beta = -0.21, p < .01$), but non-significant in the long duration group ($\beta = 0.05$, NS).

Turning to H4, we used a regression on the overall club attitude in which (1) the positive critical incident variable, (2) the time variable and (3) the interaction between (1) and (2) were (standardised) independent variables (Model 4a). This analysis ($R^2 = .01, F = 3.58, p = .014$) showed that (1) the positive incident variable was significant and positive ($\beta = 0.09, p < .01$), (2) the time variable was significant ($\beta = -0.07, p = .06$) and that (3) the interaction term was non-significant ($\beta = 0.05, p = .18$). Hypothesis 4 was thus not supported; we contend that the positive incident variable's impact on the attitude did not increase over time. The same type of median-split analysis as for H3 revealed a positive impact of the positive incident valence variable on the attitude toward the club for the short duration group ($\beta = 0.11$, $p = .03$), but no significant impact for the long duration group ($\beta = 0.05$, NS).

Finally, as an additional step to examine H3 and H4, it can be noted that the supporter's age is another time variable with the potential of affecting other variables. First, as the supporter grows older, we expect a larger number of collected critical incidents. And as this population of incidents increases in size, it is possible that one individual incident becomes less salient and also less causally potent with regard to the overall evaluation. Second, growing older increases the possibility that one particular critical incident (selected on the request of the researcher) occurred in the relatively more distant past. This second aspect is indeed visible in our data, because there was a positive association between (a) the supporter's age and the positive incident time variable ($r = .52$, $p < .01$) and between (b) the supporter's age and the negative incident time variable ($r = .34$, $p < .01$). One the one hand, then, the aging of the supporter may reduce the relative impact of any particular critical incident, regardless of its valence, given that it becomes embedded in a growing pool of other incidents. On the other hand, however, given an asymmetrical impact of negative and positive incidents over time (as hypothesised in H3 and H4), and if older supporters select relatively more time-distant incidents, the asymmetric impact may become more pronounced for those who are older. To assess this, we re-estimated Model 3a by including also the supporter's age (Model 3b). However, this did not change the pattern in Model 3a; the supporters' age had a non-significant contribution ($p = .31$). Similarly, when the supporter's age was added to Model 4a, it did not change the pattern of the other variables' coefficients and it had a non-significant impact ($p = .95$). In addition, it can be noted that supporter age was unrelated to our team involvement variable ($r = -.01$, $p = .76$), so in our sample it seems as if supporter age per se is not a carrier of substantial information about the supporter's relationship with the favourite club.

Discussion

Summary of Main Results

Our analysis revealed that both negative and positive incidents in the life of football supporters had an impact on the overall evaluation of the favourite club. At the same time, however, the overall explained variance was modest. And substantially more variance was explained by aggregated performance perceptions at the attribute level. Given that the life of the football fan consists of accumulating many incidents over time, and many highly positive and negative incidents, it may thus be just too much to expect that one single incident should be highly informative. Nevertheless, this part of our results – the low level of explained variance by the critical incidents – is in stark contrast to one of the few existing attempts to compare the CIT approach and a performance-of-attributes approach, by Stauss and Hentschel (1992), who concluded that "the information produced by CIT is of higher value for the quality manager than attribute-type data". We also found that the impact of negative critical incidents was moderated by the number of years that had passed since the negative incident occurred, while the impact of positive critical incidents was unaffected by the time that had passed since their occurrence. This result should be seen in the light of Odekerken-Schröder et al. (2000) who have claimed that "critical incidents are top of mind even in the long run". In our case, this claim is warranted only with regard to positive critical incidents.

Implications

One main argument in favour of a CIT approach to identifying causal categories of incidents is that they offer concrete information with a high level of diagnosticity. From a management point of view, it can also be noted that the CIT has advantages from an internal communication point of view; it ought to be fairly easy for managers who strive for organisational change, given CIT results, to communicate how the resulting classifications are derived from the incidents collected from respondents. This should be seen in contrast to the performance-of-attributes approach, which requires some level of knowledge in statistics if one is to fully understand why one particular attribute is a determinant of an overall evaluation. Yet our results suggest that the critical incidents are less likely to contribute to overall evaluations than the aggregated performance perceptions. Therefore, one may question the use of CIT if this is the only means to arrive at factors that have an impact on overall evaluations.

Moreover, the final output from a typical CIT is a limited set of causal categories for positive critical incidents and negative critical incidents (something which thus requires that the researcher classifies the collected incidents in qualitative categories). And the content of this classification, it is argued by CIT researchers, can be used by managers for decisions regarding what to do with an offer. In general, the manager would want actions that maximise the occurrence of positive incidents and minimises the occurrence of negative incidents. However, given the notion of a "negativity bias", that is, negative events have larger effects than positive events, it may be tempting for managers to attach more significance to negative outcomes. Incidentally, this is precisely what some marketing scholars suggest. Mittal et al. (1998, p. 45), for example, claim that "it is more important to eliminate negative performance first and then focus on increasing performance in the positive direction". The same implication appears in Sommerfeld and Paulssen (2007). It may also have guided some CIT-based research in the sense that some studies comprise only negative critical incidents (cf. Chung and Hoffman, 1998). Yet this implication must be subject to qualifications, we believe, given our results. More specifically, given that time passes, our results indicate that the negative impact of negative incidents is attenuated. In a sense, then, it is possible that the "management" of negative incidents can be transferred to the customer – as time goes by, the negativity would be reduced by memory mechanisms. It should be observed that our finding related to the attenuation of negative incidents over time would also imply some caution in collecting aggregated performance perceptions from one particular point in time (i.e., cross-sectional data) without controlling for time effects, because negative attribute performance may decay over time, too. Only very few marketing authors, however, have acknowledged that attribute weights may shift over time in their impact on overall evaluations (Mittal et al., 1999).

In addition, the notion of "managing an offer" in a football club context becomes interesting from a critical incident point of view, because the content of the incidents collected in this study suggests that the majority of them (recall that a dominant category of incidents had to do with team performance outcomes) are difficult to manipulate for managers. In other words, if it was known how to always score significant goals, and how to always win matches and leagues and cups, the whole game of football would be very different. In our view, however, this uncontrollable aspect of the incidents does not necessarily reduce the potential for managerial implications from a critical incident approach; after all, and as a Socratian echo, good management is also about knowing the boundaries for what can be managed. Maybe the uncontrollable aspect of team performance also mirrors one significant reason why it is interesting and addictive to be a football supporter in the first place: it adds drama and suspense to life, which in many other ways may be unbearably predictable.

Limitations and Suggestions for Further Research

Some measurement aspects may reduce the potential contributions of this study. First, the time that had passed since the reported critical incidents was captured with a somewhat primitive notion of time (i.e., years). This framing of in terms of years resulted in loss of information for respondents who reported incidents from the same year as this study was conducted (15 percent for positive critical incidents and 23 percent for negative critical incidents). Second, our use of single-item measures for the valence of the incidents and for the time variables for the two incidents (and both these two aspects deals with recall), combined with our cross-sectional approach, does not allow for an estimation of reliability of these measures. And if the reliability was low, it would have attenuated the correlations. Previous results suggest that people remember emotions from the past fairly accurately (Levine and Safer, 2002), but that pleasant events are more accurately *dated* than negative events (Thompson, 1985). From a reliability point of view, then, the time variable for negative incidents may be more problematic than the other variables.

Moreover, it is evident that there was variation in terms of the time-space boundaries of the incidents in this study; some respondents referred to one very narrow event (e.g. "when Nebosja Novakovic scored 1-0 against Barcelona"), while others reported a broader event (such as winning one particular match). This indicates that a critical incident has fuzzy boundaries and that it may comprise a continuum ranging from one brief moment to activities evolving over a period (cf. Mitchell et al., 1997). And in the light of the improvements in the explained overall attitude variance when we added the performance perceptions (which by definition have a broader scope than an incident), it is possible that incidents with a less restrictive time-space character would be more important in a causal sense. In the only sport spectator application of the CIT we have found, Greenwell et al. (2007), for example, the incident-generating questions to the respondents were so broad, "What do you like best about attending (team's) games?" and "What do you like the least about attending (team's) games?", that they can be seen as not really probing for specific incidents – yet they may have stronger causal implications than the orthodox incident. Future research needs to pay attention to this particular aspect, and it also affects the way in which researchers should formulate questions about critical incidents when they collect data.

Another limitation is related to our analysis of the contribution of the critical incidents to the overall evaluation of the club: we asked the respondents to provide us with *one* positive and *one* negative incident. This approach, we believe, is in tune with the typical CIT study in which *one* incident is assumed to capture important information. Another approach, however, which is less restrictive, is used in research on major life events. In such studies, the researcher lists a set of negative and positive events, and the respondent is asked to assess the *frequency* of each such event in his or her life. Then, the researcher uses the frequencies as independent variables in assessments of outcomes such as overall satisfaction (cf. Russ and McNeilly, 1994 for a marketing application; in their study, however, the respondents were sales representatives and not customers). The same frequency-based analysis is also used in research on hassles and uplifts in life and their impact on health outcomes (Lazarus, 1984). Sommerfeld and Paulssen (2007) is a rare example of a frequency-based CIT application in a customer setting, in the sense that they used a design in which neither the number of positive incidents nor the number of negative incidents was restricted. These researchers also asked the customers about customer satisfaction on a global level, and they found a positive association between the number of positive incidents and satisfaction – and a negative association between the number of negative incidents and satisfaction (yet they did not include what we refer to in this paper as aggregated performance perceptions).

Still another approach, again from research on events in daily life, is to list a set of events that are likely to have a significant impact on people's life and to ask respondents to assess the extent to which each of these events has a positive or negative impact on the respondent's life (Sarason et al., 1978). In such approaches, it is thus implicitly assumed that the *accumulation* of incidents or events over time has an effect on overall evaluations. Before the final word is said about critical incidents and overall evaluations, then, we believe that such accumulation approaches merit further attention. Yet to date we have not seen any such applications in CIT-research on customers, services and overall evaluations.

Finally, it is worth underlining that we collected both a positive and a negative critical incident (in that order) from each respondent, and we did so within the same questionnaire. This may have affected the responses in ways which are difficult to assess in the absence of a more controlled setting. That is to say, the recall and elaboration of the first incident may have coloured the task of recalling and elaborating on the second incident. Research on contrast effects in sequences of events suggests that people prefer sequences that are improving in valence to those that are declining (Novemsky and Ratner, 2003), so in our case it is possible that the respondents may have underreported the negativity of the negative critical events.

References

Bandura, A. (1982). "The Psychology of Chance Encounters and Life Paths." *American Psychologist*, 37(7), 747-755.

Bitner, M. J., B. H. Booms and M. S. Tetreault (1990). "The Service Encounter: Diagnosing Favorable and Unfavorable Incidents." *Journal of Marketing*, 54(1), 71-84.

Braun-LaTour, K. A., M. S. LaTour. and G. M. Zinkham (2007). "Using Childhood Memories to Gain Insight into Brand Meaning." *Journal of Marketing*, 71(2), 45-60.

Bycio, P. and J. S. Allen (2004). "A critical incident approach to outcomes assessment." *Journal of Education for Business*, 80(2), 86-92.

Calder, B. J., L. W. Phillips and A. M. Tybout (1981). "Designing research for application." *Journal of Consumer Research*, 8(2), 197-207.

Charles, S. T., M. Mather and L. L. Carstensen (2003). "Aging and the Emotional Memory: The forgettable nature of negative images for older adults." *Journal of Experimental Psychology: General*, 132(2), 310-324.

Chung, B. and K. D. Hoffman (1998). "Critical incidents: Service failures that matter most." *Cornell Hotel and Restaurant Administration Quarterly*, 39(3), 66-71.

DeLongis, A., J. C. Coyne, G. Dakof, S. Folkman and R. S. Lazarus(1982). "Relationship of daily hassles, uplifts, and major life events to health status." *Health Psychology*, 1(2), 119-136.

Dunlap, W. P. and E. R. Kemery (1997). "Failing to detect moderating effects: Is multicollinearity the problem?" *Psychological Bulletin*, 102(3), 418-420.

Eagly, A. H. and S. Chaiken (1993). *The Psychology of Attitudes*. New York: Harcourt Brace Jovanovich.

Edvardsson, B. and T. Strandvik (2000). "Is a critical incident really critical for a customer relationship?" *Managing Service Quality*, 10(2), 82-91.

Edvardsson, B. and I. Roos (2001). "Critical incident techniques: Towards a framework for analyzing the criticality of critical incidents." *International Journal of Service Industry Management*, 12(3), 251-268.

Ferreira, M. and K. L. Armstrong (2004). "An exploratory examination of attributes influencing students' decisions to attend college sport events." *Sport Marketing Quarterly*, 13(4), 194-208.

Flanagan, J. (1954). "The critical incident technique." *Psychological Bulletin*, 51(4), 327-358.

Forgas, J. P. (1995). "Mood and Judgment: The Affect Infusion Model (AIM)." *Psychological Bulletin*, 117(1), 39-66.

Fornell, C. (1992). "A National Satisfaction Barometer: The Swedish Experience." *Journal of Marketing*, 56(1), 6-21.

Fredrickson, B. L. (2000). "Extracting meaning from past affective experiences: The importance of peaks, ends, and specific emotions." *Cognition and Emotion*, 14(4), 577-606.

Gilbert, D. C. and L. Morris (1995). "The usefulness of critical incident technique analysis in isolating travel satisfactions." *International Journal of Contemporary Hospitability Management*, 7(4), 5-7.

Greenwell, T. C., J. Lee and D. Naeger (2007). "Using the critical incident technique to understand critical aspects of the minor league spectator's experience." *Sport Marketing Quarterly*, 16(4), 190-198.

Gremler, D. D. (2004). "The Critical Incident Technique in Service Research." *Journal of Service Research*, 7(1), 65-89.

Hair, J. F., R. R. Anderson, R. L. Tatham and W. C. Black (1992). *Multivariate Data Analysis*. New York: Macmillan Publishing Company.

Holt, D. B. (1995). "How consumers consume: A typology of consumption practices." *Journal of Consumer Research*, 22(1), 1-16.

Johnson, M. D. (2001). "The evolution and future of national satisfaction index models." *Journal of Economic Psychology*, 22(2), 217-245.

Kanner, A. D. (1981). "Comparison of two modes of stress management: Daily hassles and uplifts versus major life events." *Journal of Behavioral Medicine*, 4(1), 1-39.

Kelley, S. W. and L. W. Turley (2001). "Consumer perceptions of service quality attributes at sporting events." *Journal of Business Research*, 54(2), 161-166.

Kemppainen, J. K. (2000). "The critical incident technique and nursing care quality research." *Journal of Advanced Nursing*, 32(5), 1264-1271.

Lazarus, R. S. (1984). "Puzzles in the Study of Daily Hassles." *Journal of Behavioral Medicine*, 7(4), 375-389.

Levine, L. J. and M. A. Safer (2002). "Sources of bias in memory for emotions." *Current Directions in Psychological Science*, 11(5), 169-173.

MacKenzie, S. B. and R. J. Lutz (1989). "An Empirical Examination of the Structural Antecedents of Attitude Toward the Ad in an Advertising Pretesting Context." *Journal of Marketing*, 53(2), 48-65.

Madrigal, R. (1995). "Cognitive and affective determinants of fan satisfaction with sporting event attendance." *Journal of Leisure Research*, 27(3), 205-227.

Meuter, M. L. (2000). "Self-Service Technologies: Understanding Customer Satisfaction with Technology-Based Service Encounters." *Journal of Marketing*, 64(3), 50-64.

Mitchell, A. A. (1986). "The Effect of Verbal and Visual Components of Advertisements on Brand Attitudes and Attitude Toward the Advertisement." *Journal of Consumer Research*, 13(1), 12-24.

Mitchell, A. A. and J. C. Olson (1981). "Are Product Attribute Beliefs the Only Mediator of Advertising Effects on Brand Attitude?" *Journal of Marketing Research*, 18(3), 318-332.

Mitchell, T., L. Thomson, E. Peterson and R. Cronk (1997). "Temporal adjustments in the evaluation of events: The "rosy view"." *Journal of Experimental Social Psychology*, 33(4), 421-448.

Mittal, V. W. T. Ross and P. M. Baldesare (1998). "The Asymmetric Impact of Negative and Positive Attribute-Level Performance on Overall Satisfaction and Repurchase Intentions." *Journal of Marketing*, 62(1), 33-47.

Mittal, V., P. Kumar and M. Tsiros (1999). "Attribute-Level Performance, Satisfaction, and Behavioral Intentions over Time: A Consumption-System Approach." *Journal of Marketing*, 63(2), 88-101.

Novemsky, N. and R. K. Ratner (2003). "The time course and impact of consumers' errorneous beliefs about hedonic contrast effects." *Journal of Consumer Research*, 29(4), 507-516.

Odekerken-Schröder, G., M. van Birgelen, J. Lemmink, K. de Ruyter and M. Wetzels (2000). "Moments of sorrow and joy: An empirical assessment of the complementary value of critical incidents in understanding customer service evaluations." *European Journal of Marketing*, 34(1-2), 107-125.

Pratto, F. and O. P. John (1991). "Automatic vigilance: The attention-grabbing power of negative social information." *Journal of Personality and Social Psychology*, 61(3), 380-391.

Richardson, B. (2004). "New consumers and football fandom: The role of social habitus in consumer behaviour." *Irish Journal of Management*, 25(1), 88-100.

Russ, F. A. and K. M. McNeilly (1994). "Critical Sales Events and Salesforce Attitudes." *Marketing Letters*, 5(3), 235-244.

Sarason, I. G., J. H. Johnson and J. M. Siegel (1978). "Assessing the Impact of Life Changes: Development of the Life Experiences Survey." *Journal of Consulting and Clinical Psychology*, 46(5), 932-946.

Sharma, S., R. M. Durand and O. Gur-Arie (1981). "Identification and Analysis of Moderator Variables." *Journal of Marketing Research*, 18(3), 291-300.

Sommerfeld, A. and M. Paulssen (2007). "Which critical incidents are really critical for consumer relationships?" *Paper presented at the 36th EMAC Conference, Reykjavik, Iceland, 23-25 May.*

Stauss, B. and B. Hentschel (1992). "Attribute-based versus incident-based measurement of service quality: Results of an empirical study in the German car industry." In *Quality Management in Services*. P. Kunst and J. Lemmink eds. Assen/Maastricht: Van Gorcum, 59-78.

Stauss, B. and B. Weinlich (1997). "Process-oriented measurement of service quality: Applying the sequential incident technique." *European Journal of Marketing*, 31(1), 33-55.

Sutton, R. I. (1992). "Feelings about a Disneyland visit." *Journal of Management Inquiry*, 1(4), 278-287.

Swan, J. E. and C. P. Rao (1975). "The Critical Incident Technique: A Flexible Method for the Identification of Salient Product Attributes." *Journal of the Academy of Marketing Science*, 3(3), 296-308.

Tapp, A. (2004). "The loyalty of football fans - we'll support you evermore?" *Journal of Database Marketing & Customer Strategy Management*, 11(3), 203-215.

Taylor, S. E. (1991). "Asymmetrical Effects of Positive and Negative Events: The Mobilization-Minimization Hypothesis." *Psychological Bulletin*, 110(1), 67-85.

Thompson, C. P. (1985). "Memory for unique personal events: Effects of pleasantness." *Motivation and Emotion*, 9(3), 277-289.

Trail, G. T., D. F. Anderson and J. S. Fink (2005). "Consumer satisfaction and identity theory: A model of sport spectator conative loyalty." *Sport Marketing Quarterly*, 14(2), 98-111.

Wakefield, K. L. and H. J. Sloan (1995). "The effects of team loyalty and selected stadium factors on spectator attendance." *Journal of Sport Management*, 9(2), 153-172.

Wakefield, K. L. and J. G. Blodgett (1996). "The effect of the servicescape on the customers' behavioral intentions in leisure service settings." *The Journal of Services Marketing*, 10(6), 45-54.

Wann, D. L., K. B. Tucker and M. P. Schrader (1996). "An exploratory examination of the factors influencing the origination, continuation, and cessation of identification with sport teams." *Perceptual and Motor Skills*, 82, 995-1001.

White, F. M. and E. A. Locke (1981). "Perceived determinants of high and low productivity in three occupational groups: A critical incident study." *Journal of Management Studies*, 18(4), 375-387.

CHAPTER FOURTEEN

COMPETITIVE BALANCE AND DEMAND FOR FOOTBALL: THE INFLUENCE OF A LIABILITY OF NEWNESS IN THE SPANISH FOOTBALL LEAGUE

JOSÉ LEJARRAGA AND GUILLERMO VILLA[1]

Within the broad research line assessing demand for sports, many studies consider both uncertainty of outcome and competitive balance as key drivers of attendance (for an extensive review, see Borland and MacDonald, 2003). These studies examine the proposition by Neale (1964) that the attractiveness of a league increases with its uncertainty of outcome. The proposition contrasts with the casual observation of attractive professional football leagues, where attendance is high and yet the public perceives a disparity in performance between traditional well-established teams and those recently promoted from a lower division. Newcomers are perceived as having a smaller chance of surviving relegation at the end of the season and this discrepancy between new and experienced teams reveals an unbalanced level of competition. This perception complies with the widespread opinion among organisational

[1] Lejarraga: Department of Business Administration, Universidad Carlos III de Madrid, Madrid 126, 28903 Getafe, Spain. Villa: Fundación Observatorio Económico del Deporte, Laboral - Ciudad de la Cultura, Luis Moya Blanco 261, 33203 Gijón, Spain. The second author wishes to thank the Spanish Government SEJ2004-00672 research project for the provision of financial support. Useful feedback was received from presentations of earlier versions of this chapter at the EconPsyFootball06, Mannheim, Germany, and at the XXXI Simposio de Análisis Económico, Oviedo, Spain. The authors would like to thank Jaume García, Tomás Lejarraga, James Nelson, Maud Pindard, Plácido Rodríguez, David Sargeant, the editors and an anonymous reviewer for useful comments on earlier drafts of the paper. The usual disclaimer applies.

scholars that new organisations have a liability of newness, implying a higher risk of failure for newer than for experienced organisations (Stinchombe, 1965; Freeman et al., 1983).

The present study suggests that, as in most organisational settings, professional sports leagues featuring an open-membership scheme display a liability of newness and that the presence of this phenomenon influences the attractiveness of the competition by reducing match attendance. The central idea stemming from this proposition is that the degree to which new and experienced teams differ in their respective chances of relegation can help diagnose a league's level of competition. These propositions are examined using data from the Spanish *Liga de Fútbol Profesional* (LFP) for the seasons 1992-93 to 2003-04. These data are particularly interesting, because the LFP has received little attention in the sports economics literature, despite being among the most attractive competitions in the world (García and Rodríguez, 2002). In order to examine the league's attractiveness, we focus on the audience attending the stadiums, as opposed to the TV audience. Fans attending the matches may be more sensitive to the league's charm than TV spectators, because attending the stadium requires more commitment than watching a match on TV.

Our results confirm that match attendance in the Spanish league is challenged by the presence of a liability of newness observed in the data. The results observed imply that the league's profits could be improved by enhancing the level of competitive balance. Furthermore, the special interest provided by an open-membership scheme, where the possibility of relegation is presumed to increase the curiosity of the audience, is undermined by the age-dependent patterns of mortality, which make the competition more predictable. These and other implications are discussed in the study.

This chapter is organised as follows. The next section is a brief review of the literature, followed by a conceptual model and the hypotheses of our study. Then, we present the data, the research methods and we model mortality probabilities, in order to test the proposed research hypotheses. In the last section, using mortality probability estimates, we develop a novel measure of competitive balance, which is tested as a predictor of match attendance.

Competitive Balance and Liability of Newness

The overall uncertainty of outcome in a league can be captured by its degree of competitive balance, which reflects the distribution of playing strength among the competing teams. Competitive balance theory suggests that, in a league where the level of competitive balance is high, the chances of winning the competition or being relegated are presumably equally distributed among all teams, making the outcome of the competition highly uncertain. In a league where competitive balance is low, a handful of leading teams tend to consistently dominate the competition.

Analysts, administrators and fans perceive that the football audience enjoys competitions where the uncertainty of outcome is high and that prefers balanced leagues to unbalanced ones (Will, 1999). According to a survey of British football fans, 96 percent of supporters thought that Arsenal had a realistic chance of winning the 2004-05 English Premier League, while the ten worst teams (Birmingham, Blackburn, Charlton, Crystal Palace, Fulham, Norwich, Portsmouth, Southampton, Tottenham and West Brom) were given zero chance of topping the competition (Michie and Oughton, 2004). This survey revealed that 82 percent of fans wanted a new system of redistributing resources more equally among all the teams in the English Premier League at that time. The hypothesis driving these arguments is that, *ceteris paribus*, sports leagues displaying higher levels of competition will be more attractive than those in which a few teams enjoy monopolistic power (Neale, 1964).

Although empirical support linking uncertainty of outcome in sporting competitions and attendance has been weak, the evidence found in season-level studies is much stronger than the one reported in match-level or long-run studies (Borland and MacDonald, 2003). Several studies on demand for football provide evidence of a positive relationship between measures of outcome uncertainty and attendance at the season-level (Jennet, 1984; Peel and Thomas, 1992, 1996; Dobson and Goddard, 1992; Szymanski, 2001; Forrest and Simmons, 2002; García and Rodríguez, 2002). Despite this evidence, the most attractive football leagues in the world may not enjoy balanced competitions (Frick and Prinz, 2004; García et al., 2005). This departure from perfect competitive balance in highly attractive leagues may be related to the perceived notion that teams recently promoted from the lower division have a hard time keeping their top category status during the seasons following promotion, implying the presence of a liability of newness.

Proponents of the liability of newness hypothesis have directed the attention of organisation scholars to the age-dependent decline in organisational death, identifying comparatively higher death rates for newer than for older organisations, as a general rule (Stinchombe, 1965; Carroll and Delacroix, 1982). The argument underlying this pattern is that new organisations are unable to compete effectively against older and, thus, well-established ones (Stinchombe, 1965; Freeman *et al.*, 1983). Numerous studies have addressed the liability of newness proposition in different industries, including manufacturing, financial, services, newspapers, healthcare and entertainment (Hannan and Freeman, 1977, 1989; Carroll 1983). This pattern, however, has not been examined in the organisational setting of professional sports teams.

The adoption of an open membership scheme in the European professional football leagues provides an interesting setting for examining organisational failure, as opposed to most American leagues, where a closed scheme does not allow for the renewal of teams at the end of each season through the promotion-relegation system. This is in addition to the fact that teams in open leagues are faced with the possibility of losing their status, which contributes to a fiercer competition (Frick and Prinz, 2004). Next, we explain how we model the phenomenon of interest and formally state the research hypotheses.

Research Model and Hypotheses

In an open-membership league, team sporting performance, reflected by the ranking at the end of the season, determines which teams survive relegation and which ones do not.[2] The central idea of our study is that the effect of being a new team or of having little experience in the top division has a direct effect on performance. We explore the effect of newness and tenure on mortality through the mediation of performance, because the effect of interest is indirect. Figure 1 depicts the conceptual model.

Our interest resides in the effects of newness and tenure (X) on mortality (Y). We test the indirect effects of these variables through the mediation of performance (M) following Baron and Kenny's (1986) steps to asses mediation, where all three paths (a, b and c) shown in Figure 1 are tested. In this model, we consider a team to be new if during the season prior to the observed one it was not playing in the First Division. The tenure of a team is reflected by the number of seasons played in the First Division competition since the team's first appearance in the league. Finally, we assume that a team perishes when it is relegated from the First Division at the end of a season.

---

[2] It is also possible to lose the category by defaulting payments on players, failing to achieve minimum infrastructure requirements of stadiums or incurring disciplinary sanctions, among other legal concerns.

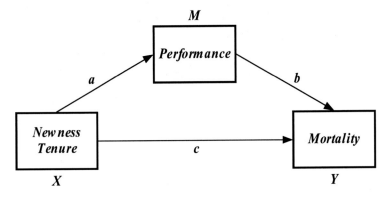

Figure 1: Effect of newness and tenure on mortality through the mediation of performance.

The liability of newness phenomenon states that, in the context of a professional football league, when a team is promoted to the top category, the risk of being relegated is highest at the end of the initial season and decreases as the team acquires experience through the seasons. Since it takes time and effort to adapt to the higher level of play and competition, new teams may initially display a lower sporting performance and may incur reduced survival probabilities. As opposed to more experienced teams, new teams are likely to have several organisational and budget constraints that are reflected in lower sporting success. The high income and the ability to raise money of experienced teams are essential for attracting top players and renowned coaches, as well as additional resources that may help the team to become stronger than newcomers (Frick and Prinz, 2004). Consistent with Frick and Prinz's (2004) proposition that recently promoted teams are in disadvantage with respect to experienced ones, we suggest a relation between the condition of being a new team and sporting performance. These arguments lead to the formulation of the first two hypotheses:

H1: New teams in the First Division have a lower performance than experienced teams.

H2: New teams in the First Division have a higher probability of being relegated to the Second Division than their experienced counterparts.

Proponents of the liability of newness hypothesis also hold that organisational death rates are age-dependent (Stinchombe, 1965; Freeman *et al.*, 1983). Experienced teams with a prolonged tenure in the First Division are used to the high level of competition, while inexperienced teams undergo an adaptation process where they learn about the new type and level of play. Successive participation in the First Division provides teams with a cumulative learning experience. This enables experienced teams to allocate their resources more efficiently than recently promoted teams (Frick and Simmons, forthcoming). Thus, teams spending many years in the First Division are likely to accumulate a greater wealth and develop a greater ability to attract financial resources than teams with little or no tenure in the top category. This difference in the ability to attract funds undermines new teams when competing with well-established ones. The experience accumulated over the years of tenure has a diminishing marginal effect on organisational performance, meaning that a team reaches a point where an additional year of tenure does not necessarily improve its performance. We propose the following hypotheses concerning tenure:

H3: The teams' length of tenure in the First Division has a positive and marginally decreasing impact on their performance.

H4: The teams' length of tenure in the First Division has a negative and marginally decreasing effect on their probability of being relegated to the Second Division.

The literature on sports economics reports several measures capturing a league's degree of competitive balance within a season. These measures assess the level of concentration in performance among the teams involved in the competition. Measures based on the dispersion of wins (Scully, 1989), the Lorenz curve (Quirk and Fort, 1992), the Gini coefficient (Schmidt and Berri, 2001), the level of entropy (Horowitz, 1997) and the Herfindahl index (Depken, 1999) are found among other competitive balance indicators (for a broad review, see Borland and MacDonald, 2003; Michie and Oughton, 2004).

Because the disparity in relegation probabilities among teams is related to the inequality of playing strength observed in a league, we propose the construction of a competitive balance measure based on dispersion of relegation chances. Following the arguments of the competitive balance literature, we expect the dispersion in relegation probabilities to have a negative impact on the attractiveness of the league. Hence, we formulate the following hypothesis:

H5: The dispersion in the probabilities of relegation reflects the league's level of competitive balance and negatively affects the attractiveness of the competition as measured by attendance.

Research Methodology and Design

The analytical section of the paper comprises two parts: a first analysis concerned with the presence of a liability of newness in the LFP, where hypotheses H1 through H4 are tested, and a second analysis, where a new competitive balance measure is constructed and tested in an attendance equation, addressing H5. Next, a description of the data and variables used in both analyses is presented. After that, the methodology applied to test the proposed research hypotheses is introduced.

Data

Data were drawn from the Spanish *Liga de Fútbol Profesional* (LFP). The sample covers the twelve year period between 1992-93 and 2003-04 seasons, and contains 244 team-season observations of all the teams competing in the First Division of the LFP. From these data, we observe newcomers in the league, as well as teams relegated to the Second Division at the end of each season, and also information regarding total goals scored and received by each team. Based on this information, we compute some of the variables included in the analysis. Data on attendance, season tickets sold, prices of match tickets[3] and teams' budgets were also provided by the LFP. Population estimates for each team's region were gathered from the Spanish National Statistics Institute (INE).

The first part of the analysis—where we test the effect of newness and tenure on demotion chances through the mediation of performance— includes the variables described below. Descriptive statistics and correlations appear in Table 1 and 2.

Mortality: This is the dependent variable and is modelled as a dummy that takes value one when a team is relegated to the Second Division and zero otherwise.

Performance: Sporting performance is the mediator variable of the model and is measured in terms of the goal difference of teams at the end of a season. Although this variable highly correlates with other commonly used performance measures, such as total points ($r = 0.80$, $p < 0.001$), goal

---

[3] Data on average prices of match tickets are only available for 1992-93 to 2000-01 seasons.

Table 1: Descriptive statistics.

$N = 244$	Mean	SD	Min	Max
Newness	0.15	0.36	0.00	1.00
Tenure	52.56	26.02	1.00	85.00
Performance	0.00	20.04	-64.00	54.00
Mortality	0.16	0.37	0.00	1.00
Quality	35527.08	38094.42	4345.10	243333.81
Direct	0.41	0.49	0.00	1.00

Table 2: Descriptive correlations.

$N = 244$	Newness	Tenure	Performance	Mortality	Quality	Direct
Newness	1.00					
Tenure	-0.40***	1.00				
Performance	-0.26***	0.29***	1.00			
Mortality	0.23***	-0.28***	-0.57***	1.00		
Quality	-0.20**	0.30***	0.50***	-0.19**	1.00	
Direct	0.03	0.20**	0.00	-0.02	0.34***	1.00

** Significant at the 1% level, *** significant at the 0.1% level.

difference is more informative, especially in the sample period where relegation occurs through a play-off system. As opposed to the number of points scored, this variable avoids the problems derived from changes in the scoring system made in the 1996-97 season[4] and from changes in the total number of teams participating in the league during the 1995-96 and 1996-97 seasons, when 22 teams played in the First Division competition instead of 20.[5] At the same time, we want to grasp not only the playing strength of teams, but also their playing quality, which we assume is a key characteristic that makes fans become attracted to watch certain

---

[4] Starting in that season, each win accounts for three points instead of two.

[5] In the summer 1995, Sevilla and Celta failed to comply with certain legal requirements imposed by the LFP and were consequently relegated to the Second Division. However, in terms of performance, Albacete and Valladolid had earned the relegation that same season but were invited to remain in the top category to cover the two spots left by Sevilla and Celta. After a legal battle between LFP authorities and the two teams involved in the quarrel, Sevilla and Celta were admitted back to the First Division tournament. As a result, 22 teams participated in the league in the 1995-96 and 1996-1997 season. We have considered Albacete and Valladolid as relegated teams in the 1994-95 season. These teams were not considered new in the following season, as they finally took part in the First Division tournament.

teams. Goal difference is informative in two ways: first, it is a proxy of team success during the season and, second, it describes how offensive or attack-oriented a team is, as a large goal difference implies a large amount of goals scored relative to goals received. Finally, this variable does not completely determine the ranking of teams, allowing us to observe the effects of other variables of interest.

Newness: To measure whether a team is new in the competition, we use a dummy variable taking value one if a team was playing in the Second Division in the previous season and zero otherwise.

Tenure: To capture a team's tenure, we count the number of seasons it has played in the First Division up to the observed season. We also compute the square of this variable ($Tenure^2$), in order to assess the hypothesised curvilinear effect of experience in the First Division.

Quality: The *ex ante* quality of a team is approximated by its budget (in thousand euros) at the beginning of each season. This figure is deflated by the Spanish consumer price index for each year.

Direct: A dummy variable is introduced to account for the change in the relegation system. Before the 1999-00 season, among the four worst performing teams, the lowest two were directly relegated to the Second Division, while the top two qualified to a play off against Second Division teams. In the 1999-00 season, the play-off system was abandoned and, from then on, the three worst performing teams were directly relegated at each season's end.[6]

The second part of the analysis, where we propose an innovative competitive balance measure and test it in an attendance equation, includes additional variables. Descriptive statistics and correlations appear in Table 3 and 4.

Attendance: This is the dependent variable in the demand equation and is constructed as the average seasonal attendance for each team. The units of this variable reflect thousands of spectators.

Price: The average price for each team and season is considered. Prices, in euros, appear in real terms, adjusted according to the Spanish consumer price index.

Market: This variable reflects the population, in thousands of inhabitants, within the team's region. When two or more teams are located in the same region, the population assigned to each team is weighted by the number of season tickets sold.

---

[6] In the 1996-97 season, four teams were directly relegated to the Second Division and only one team entered the play-off.

Table 3: Descriptive statistics.

N = 184	Mean	SD	Min	Max
Attendance	22404.64	16764.56	5345.00	91981.00
Price	20.58	5.38	6.66	44.23
Market	1123.47	1020.90	90.91	4821.12
Performance	0.00	20.91	-64.00	54.00
Balance	0.99	0.00	0.98	0.99

Table 4: Descriptive correlations.

N = 184	Attendance	Price	Market	Performance	Balance
Attendance	1.00				
Price	-0.15*	1.00			
Market	0.93***	-0.16*	1.00		
Performance	0.64***	-0.16*	0.62***	1.00	
Balance	0.06	0.05	0.00	0.00	1.00

* Significant at the 5% level, *** significant at the 0.1% level.

Balance: Two independent measures of competitive balance are considered and compared: the relative entropy of goals scored, similar to Horowitz's (1997) measure, and the new measure proposed in this article, which is described later.

Methodology

Testing the Liability of Newness Proposition

Previous to the regression analyses, we perform a simple bivariate exploratory examination to shed light on the differences between new and experienced teams. The difference in the average performance of new and experienced teams is tested, as well as the association between the condition of being a new team and being relegated.

The central idea in our model is that the effects of newness and experience on mortality are mediated by the performance of teams. A variable is considered a mediator if it accounts for the relation between the predictor and the criterion. To test the relations of interest, we follow the three steps below (Baron and Kenny, 1986):

$$\text{Step 1: } M = X\alpha 1 + Z\beta 1 + \varepsilon 1 \tag{1}$$

$$\text{Step 2: } Y = X\alpha 2 + Z\beta 2 + \varepsilon 2 \tag{2}$$

$$\text{Step 3: } Y = X\alpha3 + Z\beta3 + M\gamma3 + \varepsilon3 \qquad (3)$$

Where X is the matrix of variables of interest (*Newness* and *Tenure*); Z is the matrix of controls (*Quality* and *Direct*), which also includes a column of ones; M represents the mediator (*Performance*); Y the outcome (*Mortality*); α, β and γ are vectors of parameters and ε is a random shock.

Mediation can only be established if the following three conditions hold: (1) the variables of interest have to affect the mediator in step 1; (2) the variables of interest have to affect the outcome in step 2; and (3) the mediator must affect the outcome in step 3. Also, the effect of the variables of interest in step 3 has to be smaller than that in step 2. If the variables of interest present no effect in step 3, then perfect mediation is established. Coefficients in step 1 are estimated by simple OLS, while coefficients in steps 2 and 3 are estimated by a logit procedure. Following this approach, we assume the mediator as endogenous. Therefore, the model in step 3 is only identified if ε_1 and ε_3 are uncorrelated.

According to Baron and Kenny (1986), the steps above should be stated in terms of zero or nonzero coefficients and not only in terms of statistical significance, because small coefficients can be trivially significant with very large sample sizes. This kind of effect is not expected to occur in our medium-sized sample. Additionally, the conclusions from mediation are only valid if causal assumptions are true. In our case, reverse causal effects can be easily ruled out theoretically. Finally, the set of controls considered avoids the omitted variables problem, i.e. there is a variable causing both the mediator and the outcome.

Constructing a New Measure of Competitive Balance

We estimate *ex post* relegation probabilities using a simple logit model which includes performance and the change in the relegation system dummy as predictors of relegation. Once these probabilities are estimated, we construct an inverse dispersion index capturing how far apart the teams are in terms of their relegation likelihood. We name this index *RPID* (Relegation Probabilities Inverse Dispersion). For each season, the index is calculated as follows:

$$RPID_j = \frac{I_j}{\sum_{i=1}^{I}(P_{ij} - 0.5)^2} \qquad (4)$$

Where I_j is the total number of teams competing in season j and P_{ij} are the estimated relegation probabilities of team i in that season.

Observed relegation probabilities estimates range from values close to zero to values close to one. Our measure of competitive balance is intended to equally penalise extremely high or low relegation chances. Therefore, dispersion in relegation likelihood is measured with respect to the maximum uncertainty probability. Our measure is averaged, as the number of teams taking part in the competition has slightly changed throughout the time, and then inverted, in order to reflect positive competitive balance levels. Hence, the *RPID* index increases as the competition becomes more balanced.

Testing the *RPID* Index as a Predictor of Attendance

A typical demand equation is estimated, where we use the *RPID* index as a predictor of attendance. The dependent variable in this equation is *Attendance* (in logs). As predictors, we include the price of tickets (*Price*), a proxy for the market size (*Market*), a measure of performance during the league (*Performance*) and two independent measures of competitive balance (*Balance*). We contrast the effect of the new variable with a commonly accepted measure of competitive balance, relative entropy (Horowitz, 1997), and observe whether they substantially correlate and behave according to the theory. The demand model is estimated by GLS and includes team random effects.

Results

The analysis points towards the presence of a liability of newness in our sample. The average goal difference for newcomers in the league is -12.67, while for teams with some experience it is 2.19. This difference in means is significant ($p < 0.001$). Also, the *ex post* probability of descending to the Second Division, given that a team is new in the league, is 0.36, while for a team that is not new it is only 0.12. Furthermore, a χ^2 test indicates that *Newness* and *Mortality* are significantly associated ($p < 0.001$).

The results of our analyses, shown in Tables 5 and 6, support the proposed hypotheses. Note that all the continuous variables included in the models have been previously standardised to ease a convenient interpretation of the results. Hypothesis H1, regarding the lower performance of new teams, is supported in model 1 step 1, where *Newness* reports a negative significant coefficient. Support for H2 is found in step 2 of the same model, where *Newness* significantly affects *Mortality*. This effect is mediated by *Performance*, because *Newness* no longer affects

Table 5: Testing the liability of newness hypotheses: Baron and Kenny's (1986) three-step mediation models.

$N = 244$	Dependent variable		
	Performance	*Mortality*	*Mortality*
		Model 1	
Explanatory variables	Step 1	Step 2	Step 3
Newness	-0.44	0.83	-0.40
	(0.16)**	(0.43)$^+$	(0.77)
Tenure			
Tenure^2			
Performance			-5.79
			(1.06)***
Quality	0.53	-2.02	0.50
	(0.06)***	(0.76)**	(0.96)
Direct	-0.36	0.58	0.57
	(0.12)**	(0.45)	(0.73)
Constant	0.21	-2.64	-5.53
	(0.07)**	(0.44)***	(1.06)***
R^2	0.30	0.12	0.62
Correlation between residuals (steps 1 and 3)		-0.01	

$^+$ Significant at the 10% level, ** significant at the 1% level, *** significant at the 0.1% level. Standard errors in parentheses

Mortality after controlling for this variable. Hypotheses H3 and H4 also find support. As proposed by H3, the experience acquired by a team has a positive and significant influence on its performance and, beyond some point, additional experience does not improve performance. This is captured by the positive coefficient of *Tenure* and the negative one of *Tenure^2* in models 2 and 3 step 1. These are both significant. In step 2 of the same models, we also observe that the two variables have a significant effect on *Mortality*. Considering that, once we control for *Performance*, there is no longer a significant effect, we conclude that *Performance* fully mediates the effect proposed in H4. In the full model, the effect of *Newness* vanishes, because the condition of being new is already captured by *Tenure*. Additionally, all the regressions estimated in step 3 are identified, as the residuals of the equations adjusted in steps 1 and 3 show no significant correlation.

Table 5 cont.: Testing the liability of newness hypotheses: Baron and Kenny's (1986) three-step mediation models.

$N = 244$	Dependent variable		
	Performance	*Mortality*	*Mortality*
		Model 2	
Explanatory variables	Step 1	Step 2	Step 3
Newness			
Tenure	0.90	-1.91	-1.26
	(0.26)**	(0.77)*	(1.15)
Tenure^2	-0.75	1.53	0.90
	(0.26)**	(0.81)$^+$	(1.18)
Performance			-5.55
			(0.99)***
Quality	0.50	-1.72	1.01
	(0.06)***	(0.74)*	(0.89)
Direct	-0.34	0.58	0.57
	(0.12)**	(0.45)	(0.73)
Constant	0.14	-2.50	-5.40
	(0.07)$^+$	(0.43)***	(1.00)***
R-squared	0.33	0.15	0.63
Correlation between residuals (steps 1 and 3)		-0.00	

$^+$ Significant at the 10% level, * significant at the 5% level, ** significant at the 1% level, *** significant at the 0.1% level. Standard errors in parentheses

In the second part of the analysis, we predict *ex post* probabilities of being relegated to the Second Division for each team. These estimates serve as the input data to construct the *RPID* index, which captures, according to our arguments, the degree of competitive balance of the league. Our index displays similar behaviour to the relative entropy of goals scored and both measures are significantly correlated in this sample ($r = 0.51$, $p < 0.001$). Thus, these variables quantify the same construct, but reflect different aspects of the competitive level. Furthermore, when included in a classic attendance equation, both measures of competitive balance have a positive significant effect on attendance. The remaining variables are in accordance with expectations and report significant coefficients. The price of tickets negatively impacts attendance, whereas the market size and the teams' performance have a positive effect.

Table 5 cont.: Testing the liability of newness hypotheses: Baron and Kenny's (1986) three-step mediation models.

$N = 244$	Dependent variable		
	Performance	*Mortality*	*Mortality*
		Model 3	
Explanatory variables	Step 1	Step 2	Step 3
Newness	-0.22	0.34	-1.39
	(0.17)	(0.48)	(0.93)
Tenure	0.80	-1.79	-1.98
	(0.27)**	(0.79)*	(1.25)
Tenure^2	-0.68	1.45	1.44
	(0.26)*	(0.82)$^+$	(1.23)
Performance			-6.33
			(1.26)***
Quality	0.49	-1.62	0.86
	(0.06)***	(0.74)*	(1.00)
Direct	-0.32	0.53	0.80
	(0.12)**	(0.46)	(0.78)
Constant	0.17	-2.50	-5.98
	(0.07)*	(0.43)***	(1.23)***
R-squared	0.33	0.15	0.64
Correlation between residuals (steps 1 and 3)		-0.01	

$^+$ Significant at the 10% level, * significant at the 5% level, ** significant at the 1% level, *** significant at the 0.1% level. Standard errors in parentheses

Hence, hypothesis H5 is supported, because the probabilities of relegation have proved informative to diagnose the competitive situation of the LFP and also the dispersion in the chances of relegation is shown to influence the league's attractiveness.

Discussion and Concluding Comments

Consistent with Frick and Prinz (2004) and other studies of organisational failure (Carroll and Delacroix, 1982; Freeman et al., 1983), we find a liability of newness in the LFP. The evidence presented shows that the LFP's attractiveness, as measured by attendance, declines as the competition becomes more unbalanced. The age-dependent decline in mortality of football teams reflects a common pattern found in most

Table 6: Demand models.

$N = 184$	Dependent variable *Attendance* (in logs)	
Explanatory variables	Model 4	Model 5
Price	-0.09	-0.09
	(0.04)**	(0.04)*
Market	0.62	0.63
	(0.08)***	(0.08)***
Performance	0.08	0.07
	(0.04)*	(0.04)*
Balance (relative entropy)	0.14	
	(0.02)***	
Balance (RPID)		0.08
		(0.03)**
Constant	-0.24	-0.27
	(0.08)**	(0.08)**
R-squared	0.72	0.71
Breusch-Pagan test for random effects	145.73***	125.51***

* Significant at the 5% level, ** significant at the 1% level, *** significant at the 0.1% level. Standard errors in parentheses

organisational settings (Freeman et al., 1983). This study adds to the literature on organisational failure, providing empirical support to the liability of newness hypothesis present in a population comprising professional football teams.

Organisational scholars are divided among two opposing views regarding organisational failure. On the one hand, some scholars support that the liability of newness responds to a natural selection process (Hannan and Freeman, 1977; Freeman et al., 1983). On the other hand, scholars claim that an adaptation process takes place through learning and accumulation of skills over time and that organisations in early stages of this process have higher chances of failure (Cyert and March, 1963; Nelson and Winter, 1982).

Hannan and Freeman (1989) propose that the variation in performance declines with time and argue that the process of selection operates within a population eliminating those organisations with low reliability or accountability. Our results show that the experience of teams improves their chances to avoid failure. It is possible that, for two teams with the same goal difference, an experienced team will perform uniformly and with a lower variability, making use of the goals scored more efficiently and obtaining more points.

Differently, and in accordance to the learning effect, our results can also be interpreted under the adaptation viewpoint. Football teams may become more effective with age in two different ways. First, at the organisational level, it is likely that teams learn to raise money and to administrate it in a better way. They may also learn to hire better players and to develop improved incentive schemes for both players and coaches. Secondly, teams may learn how to compete with stronger teams and adapt to the new playing style of the top category, which is assumed to be different from that in lower divisions, i.e. it is faster, harder and overall more competitive.

Another idea stemming from the analysis is that the liability of newness found in the LFP suggests that attractive leagues may not have a balanced competition. This complies with the results found in the few studies on demand for the Spanish football (García and Rodríguez, 2002; García et al., 2005; Villa, 2006). The attractiveness of the Spanish league, although affected by the competitive balance, must be affected by other important factors, such as the presence of high quality football stars or long-lived rivalries among traditional teams, which attract viewers despite the intensity of the competitive level. The search for other key drivers of a league's attractiveness presents a promising research agenda for scholars devoted to demand modelling.

Arguments of the competitive balance theory were supported by the demand model, where the attractiveness of the competition declines during the less competitive seasons. An important implication is that balancing the competition would increase the league's attractiveness and could also provide a better allocation of resources among teams member of the LFP. If promoted teams were to remain in the First Division for a considerable number of seasons, these usually smaller teams would capture a substantial portion of the profits in the top category, leading to a better distribution of the league's resources. This implies that teams from all over the country may increment their wealth and the overall level of play of the Spanish league would increase.

This study reveals that even one of the most popular professional football leagues has room for improvements. Leagues' authorities could implement salary caps, loans for new teams or any other practice to balance the competition. Although the results presented here should be interpreted with caution and may not be generalised to other sports leagues, the notion that new and experienced teams tend to perform differently may hold in other sports leagues.

Possible extensions and improvements include extending the number of seasons considered and sampling other leagues, which could also serve as a comparison. Verifying whether experienced teams perform uniformly and reliably, as opposed to new teams, would also extend this study's arguments. Also, checking for a liability of smallness, as proposed by Freeman *et al.* (1983), can illuminate the results obtained in this study. Finally, comparing our measure of competitive balance with other established ones would improve its validity.

References

Baron, R. and D. Kenny (1986). "The Moderator-Mediator Variable Distinction in Social Psychological Research: Conceptual, Strategic, and Statistical Considerations." *Journal of Personality and Social Psychology*, 51(6), 1173-1182.

Borland, J. and R. MacDonald (2003). "Demand for Sport." *Oxford Review of Economic Policy*, 19(4), 478-502.

Carroll, G. (1983). "A Stochastic Model of Organizational Mortality: Review and Reanalysis'." *Social Science Research*, 12(4), 303-329.

Carroll, G. and J. Delacroix (1982). "Organizational Mortality in the Newspaper Industries of Argentina and Ireland: An Ecological Approach." *Administrative Science Quarterly*, 27(2),169-198.

Cyert, R. and J. March (1963). *A Behavioral Theory of the Firm.* Cambridge: Blackwell.

Depken, C. (1999). "Free-Agency and the Competitiveness of Major League Baseball." *Review of Industrial Organization*, 14(3), 205-217.

Dobson, S. and J. Goddard (1992). "The Demand for Standing and Seated Viewing Accomodation in the English Football League." *Applied Economics*, 24(10), 1155-1163.

Forrest, D. and R. Simmons (2002). "Outcome Uncertainty and Attendance Demand in Sport: The Case of English Soccer." *The Statistician*, 51(2), 229-241.

Freeman, J., G. R. Carroll and M. T. Hannan (1983). "The Liability of Newness: Age Dependence in Organizational Death Rates." *American Sociological Review*, 48(5), 692-710.

Frick, B. and J. Prinz (2004). "Revenue-Sharing Arrangements and the Survival of Promoted Teams: Empirical Evidence from the Major European Soccer Leagues." In *International Sport Economics Comparisons*. R. Fort and J. Fizel eds. Westport, CT: Praeger Publishers, 141-156.

Frick, B. and R. Simmons (forthcoming). "The Impact of Managerial Quality On Organizational Performance: Evidence from German Soccer." *Managerial and Decision Economics.*

García, J. and P. Rodríguez (2002). "The Determinants of Football Match Attendance Revisited: Empirical Evidence from the Spanish Football League." *Journal of Sports Economics*, 3(1), 18-38.

García, J. et al. (2005). "És el balanç competitiu la solució òptima per a les lligues professionals?" *Revista Econòmica de Catalunya*, 51, 70-81.

Hannan, M. and J. Freeman (1977). "The Population Ecology of Organizations." *American Journal of Sociology*, 82(5), 929-964.

Hannan, M. and J. Freeman (1989). *Organizational Ecology.* Cambridge: Harvard University Press.

Horowitz, I. (1997). "The Increasing Competitive Balance in Major League Baseball." *Review of Industrial Organization*, 12(3), 373-387.

Jennet, N. (1984). "Attendances, Uncertainty of Outcome and Policy in Scottish League Football." *Scottish Journal of Political Economy*, 31(2), 176-198.

Michie, J. and C. Oughton (2004). "Competitive Balance in Football: Trends and Effects." *The Sports Nexus.*

Neale, W. (1964). "The Peculiar Economics of Professional Sports." *Quarterly Journal of Economics*, 78(1), 1-14.

Nelson, R. and S. Winter (1982). *An Evolutionary Theory of Economic Change.* Cambridge: Harvard University Press.

Peel, D. and D. Thomas (1992). "The Demand for Football: Some Evidence on Outcome Uncertainty." *Empirical Economics*, 17(2), 323-331.

Peel, D. and D. Thomas (1996). "Attendance Demand: An Investigation of Repeat Fixtures." *Applied Economics Letters*, 3(6), 391-394.

Quirk, J. and R. Fort (1992). *Pay Dirt. The Business of Professional Team Sports.* Princeton: Princeton University Press.

Schmidt, M. and D. Berri (2001). "Competitive Balance and Attendance: The Case of Major League Baseball." *Journal of Sports Economics*, 2(2), 145-167.

Scully, G. (1989). *The Business of Major League Baseball.* Chicago: University of Chicago Press.

Stinchombe, A. (1965). "Social Structure and Organizations." In *Handbook of Organizations.* J. March ed. Chicago: Rand McNally, 142-193.

Szymanski, S. (2001). "Income Inequality, Competitive Balance and the Attractiveness of Team Sports: Some Evidence and a Natural

Experiment from English Soccer." *The Economic Journal*, 111(469), 69-84.

Villa, G. (2006). "Estimación de una ecuación de asistencia de pago para la Liga de Fútbol Profesional." *Boletín de la Sociedad de Estadística e Investigación Operativa*, 22(1), 39-44.

Will, D. (1999). "The Federation's Viewpoint on the New Transfer Rules." In *Competition Policy in Professional Sports: Europe after the Bosman Case*. S. Kesenne and C. Jeanrenaud eds. Antwerp: Standard Editions, 7-14.

CHAPTER FIFTEEN

EXPERT PREDICTIONS OF FOOTBALL: A SURVEY OF THE LITERATURE AND AN EMPIRICAL INQUIRY INTO TIPSTERS' AND ODDS-SETTERS' ABILITY TO PREDICT THE WORLD CUP

PATRIC ANDERSSON[1]

Perhaps the most unexpected outcome in the FIFA World Cup in Germany 2006 was the draw between Trinidad and Tobago and Sweden. At the time of the match, the teams held the positions of 49th and the 15th, respectively, at the FIFA world ranking list. Before the kick-off, numerous Swedish pundits as well as other kinds of, well-known or self-appointed, football experts had spent hours in analysing and commenting on potential outcomes. Their analyses predicted solidly that there would be a comfortable win for the Swedish team. In their view, there was no doubt that Trinidad and Tobago would be beaten by several goals, because Sweden was after all the better (ranked) team. The consensus among the football experts shaped the expectations of the Swedish population and, most probably, also influenced their bets. Obviously, the draw came as a big surprise and shattered many Swedish fans' belief that their beloved national team was invincible. Besides criticising the coaches for the poor performance of the Swedish team, football experts demanded immediate

[1] Andersson: Centre for Media and Economic Psychology, Stockholm School of Economics, Box 6501, S-113 83 Stockholm, Sweden, Tel.: +46 (0)8 736 9576, Email: Patric.andersson@hhs.se. The author is indebted to Mattias Ekman, Håkan Nilsson, Tim Rakow and Carsten Schmidt for valuable and helpful comments on earlier drafts of this chapter. Thanks also to Per Fylking, Kristoffer Strandqvist and Jan Tullberg for inspiring conversations. Financial support from Handelsbankens Forskningsstiftelser is gratefully acknowledged.

changes of tactics and players. In the aftermath of the match, the media also raised concern about the forecasting ability of football experts and asked how they could predict so poorly.

One might argue that the question of how well football experts make predictions has little scientific relevance. It should be of interest for the general public, because they may use expert judgements as guidelines when placing bets on football results. In this respect, these predictions fill a similar function as stock recommendations. Just like private investors want to learn about the adequacy of financial professionals' stock-picking skills, punters want to know whether the predictions of football experts can be trusted.

Studying the judgemental ability of football experts is scientifically relevant. Given the vast amount of data on expert predictions that are generally available, it is possible to empirically test hypotheses, which often are derived from findings in experiments with student participants, and develop theoretical propositions concerning performance, behaviour and reasoning. Such issues may not only have importance for economists and psychologists, but also for scientists sharing a particular interest in the study of expertise. This field is interdisciplinary and seeks to understand the phenomenon of expertise by exploring its performance, origin and underlying mechanisms (Ericsson et al., 2006).

The goal of the present chapter is to provide insights into the forecasting ability of football experts in football (soccer). In particular, it aims to survey the relevant literature from economics and psychology as well as reporting on a new inquiry into the ability of professional tipsters and odds-setters to predict the outcomes of World Cup matches. The inquiry is based on a unique set of data that vouches for fresh empirical evidence. In general, the chapter addresses the question: How good are football experts in predicting football?

The remainder of the chapter is organised into five sections. In the following section, the scientific study of expert judgement is briefly described and research investigating the forecasting performance of football experts is reviewed. The three next sections consider the empirical inquiry. Specifically, section 2 gives a methodological account for how the data were collected, whereas sections 3 and 4 report on the empirical results. The final section synthesises and discusses evidence from prior research and the results of the inquiry.

The Scientific Study of Expert Judgement and Prior Research on Predictions by Football Experts

The Scientific Study of Expert Judgement

An obvious and commonly used angle for studying expertise is to simply evaluate the quality of the judgements formed by experts. Typically, an expert is defined as an individual possessing exceptionally high levels of skills or knowledge in a specific domain. Over the years, scientists of various disciplines have conducted multiple studies of assessments, decisions, forecasts and predictions of experts, or—as they may be also referred to as—professionals, in a range of fields such as business, chess, finance, meteorology, medicine, psychiatry and sports (for overviews, see Bolger and Wright, 1992a; Camerer and Johnson, 1991; Koehler et al., 2002).

Basically, those studies have been based on two approaches: (1) analyses of archival data on expert judgements from real life and (2) the use of laboratory experiments, where experts are confronted with a series of cases and asked to assess them. An advantage with the second approach is the possibility to control for various factors (e.g., amount of information) and to measure behavioural variables (e.g., degree of confidence); parameters that are seldom captured by archival data. A disadvantage with experiments is that the selected tasks may be poor representations of the real world due to artificial information, inadequate feedback and lack of other naturalistically occurring elements (see e.g., Bolger and Wright, 1992b). Despite methodological differences, the two approaches seem to give consistent findings regarding the quality of expert judgements.

A large body of research, which is based on either archival data or experiments, paints a somewhat gloomy picture of the ability of experts to make accurate assessments and decisions (for overviews, see Yates and Tschirhart, 2006; Ayton, 1992; Camerer and Johnson, 1991). In particular, it has been widely documented that judgements of experts are rarely superior than those of trained novices; a paradoxical finding as there is a great deal of evidence suggesting that experts have not only more extensive knowledge but also more advanced mental processes than naïve individuals (Camerer and Johnson, 1991; Shanteau, 1992b). This paradox is often explained by the tendency of experts to use information in an inefficient manner (Camerer and Johnson, 1991). In addition, numerous studies show that simple statistical models generate predictions that are far more accurate than those made by experts (cf.Dawes et al., 1989; Dana and Thomas, 2006).

Shanteau (1992a) has claimed that the performance of experts must be viewed in light of the characteristics of the areas in which experts are working. When examining research on expert judgement, he concluded that experts tended to perform well in areas characterised by static stimuli and decisions about static targets (e.g., weather forecasting and livestock assessment), while they fared poorly in areas associated with changeable stimuli and decisions about human behaviour (e.g., clinical psychology and stock forecasting). Similarly, the degree of task predictability has been shown to be crucial for the ability of humans to make accurate forecasts (cf. Stewart et al., 1997). Specifically, it is possible for experts to excel when the task has high predictive value. For example, meteorologists tend to be most accurate when their forecasts concern the horizon of a single day and, consequently, their accuracy tends to diminish once the time period is widened (Sherden, 1998).

Furthermore, numerous studies suggest that experts generally exaggerate the correctness of their probability judgements, meaning that they are overconfident and have poor insights into the constraints of their expertise (e.g., Allwood and Granhag, 1999; Bolger and Wright, 1992b). For example, Törngren and Montgomery (2003) found that stock-brokers tended to substantially overestimate the accuracy of their stock-price predictions. Recently, Koehler et al. (2002) documented that experts in business and sports were inclined to systematically over- and underestimate their probability forecasts and that such tendencies was dependent on the size of probabilities. Although the tendency of overconfidence appears to be universal, there exist a few areas where experts have been found to be calibrated and, thus, aware of the limits of their knowledge. Noteworthy examples of such areas are weather forecasting (Murphy and Winkler, 1984) and bridge (Keren, 1987).

There seems to be relatively little research on the predictive ability of sports experts (Plessner and Haar, 2006). For example, it has been shown that (1) expert gamblers are able to pick winning horses at better-than-chance levels (Ladouceuret al., 1998); (2) editors predict American football less well than a simple model and the betting market (Boulier and Stekler, 2003); and (3) rankings are reliable predictors of the outcome in basketball, tennis and American football (Boulier and Stekler, 1999; 2003).

In sum, scientific evidence suggests that expert judgment in numerous areas is often somewhat inadequate, but might not be outperformed by novices. Experts also appear to have difficulties in predicting areas related to human behaviour and tend to exaggerate the accuracy of their predictions. The remainder of this section will show whether this dismal picture of expert judgment is also valid for football experts.

Prior Research on Predictions by Football Experts

The term "football experts" refers to a variety of people who have extensive knowledge of the game of football. In many cases, their knowledge has been acquired through playing or coaching football on a professional level. Alternatively, they have watched and covered countless games of football. Broadly speaking, football experts face two main tasks: (1) foreseeing future outcomes and (2) commenting on the actions of current and past matches. Obviously, these tasks require different types of competence; a circumstance that might be unknown for most experts and laypeople. In general, there exist three groups of football experts that are devoted to the first task: Tipsters, odds-setters and pundits. Some scientific evidence of how well those groups perform is briefly discussed below.

Performance of Tipsters

Tipsters are engaged by newspapers to issue match forecasts and betting advice. Research indicates that the quality of such judgements is modest.[2] Using a sample of 1694 English league games, Forrest and Simmons (2000) examined the performance and behaviour of three British newspaper tipsters. The tipsters were found to predict correctly about 42% of the games, whereas the strategy of always assuming home win resulted in 47.5% correct forecasts.[3] However, the authors regarded such a comparison as somewhat unfair to the tipsters, because their employers (i.e., newspapers) would have hardly hired them if they constantly predicted home win; implying that tipsters are expected to foresee varying outcomes. Therefore, Forrest and Simmons (2000) also used a random strategy and found that the tipsters performed better than its accuracy of

---

[2] An explanation could be that tipsters might try to recommend "good bets" rather than making accurate predictions. In other words, a tipster may know that Newcastle beating Arsenal is not the most likely outcome, but recommend betting on it if the odds on Newcastle winning are shorter than he believes they should be. I thank Tim Rakow for suggesting this explanation.
[3] In 2003 three students of mine evaluated 1976 forecasts of Swedish newspaper tipsters. Mean performance was circa 41% corrects and the tipsters were outperformed by always picking home win, which gave 45% correctly predicted matches.

36.4% correct forecasts.[4] Moreover, Forrest and Simmons (2000) found that British tipsters were inclined to ineffectively use public information. However, they concluded that the forecasts of the tipsters were equally accurate as those generated by a regression model utilising public information; a conclusion that is inconsistent with other research (cf. Dawes et al., 1989; Dana and Thomas, 2006).

Performance of Odds-Setters

Odds-setters, or as they are also referred to as book-makers, are employed by betting firms to quote odds. The odds for a certain outcome of a match depend on the perceived probability of this particular outcome as well as the margin to cover costs and profits (Pope and Peel, 1989). Assuming that this margin is more or less fixed, the task of odds-setters could be limited to assess and evaluate the probabilities of future outcomes of matches. As employees, they have incentives to perform well.

Basically, the task of odds-setters is to issue (implicit) probabilistic forecasts of sports events. On the basis of a sample of roughly 10,000 English league matches, Forrest, Goddard and Simmons (2005) transformed odds to implicit probabilities and then evaluated these measures using the standard methodology for assessing probabilistic forecasts (i.e., Brier Scores, see Yates, 1990). The scores of five odds-setters were pitted against those of a benchmark statistical forecasting model, which considered publicly available information relevant to match outcome. On the whole, the odds-setters and the model had similar levels of accuracy; a result that disagrees with the aforementioned research showing that experts often make worse judgements than those generated by statistical models.

Several studies have investigated the economic significance of the forecasting ability of odds-setters. Conducted by economists, these studies have examined whether the betting market on football is efficient in the sense that the quotes reflect the available information (cf. Dobson and Goddard, 2001; Vaughan William, 1999). It has been found that odds-setters fail to adequately incorporate all public information in their predictions (Goddard and Asimakopoulos, 2004; Forrest et al., 2005) and that the market is associated with some inefficiencies, whereby bets on certain outcomes have better expected values than other bets (Pope and Peel, 1989; Cain et al. 2000; Dobson and Goddard, 2001). One of these inefficiencies is the favourite-longshot bias, which basically refers to the tendency to underestimate (overestimate) the chances for favourites

---

[4] The accuracy of this strategy was calculated by $h^2 + d^2 + a^2$, where h, d and a denoted the actual frequencies of home win, draw and away win in the sample.

(underdogs). There is mixed evidence of whether this bias exists in betting markets oriented to (English) football leagues (Deschamps and Gergaud, 2007). In addition, such markets appear to be efficient, because it is difficult to find trading strategies that "can overcome the margins and tax deductions built into the bookmaker's prices" (Dobson and Goddard, 2001, p. 417). Even sophisticated strategies that, for example, exploit differences in odds between bookmakers have shown to be associated with negative returns (Deschamps and Gergaud, 2007).

Performance of Pundits

The third group of football experts is called pundits and refers to those highly knowledgeable individuals who make forecasts on a non-professional basis. Empirical evidence suggests that the judgmental ability of pundits has varying degrees of reliability. On the one hand, together with two colleagues I examined whether football experts were better at predicting the outcome of the first round of the World Cup 2002 than people with limited knowledge (Andersson et al., 2005). By the means of questionnaire, responses from 52 pundits (sports journalists, fans and coaches of the Swedish premier league), 166 Swedish students and 33 American students were collected.[5] All participants predicted better than chance. Despite having significantly more knowledge (and better information), the pundits failed to make better forecasts than the students and were outperformed by a simple rule following world rankings. On average, the pundits managed to correctly predict 56.3% of the teams going to the second round, whereas the naïve participants had 62.5% and the rule gave 75.0%. Andersson et al. (2005) argued that those observations depended on a combination of inefficient use of information by the pundits (see earlier discussion) and the reliance of simple but well-adapted heuristics by the students (cf. Gigerenzer et al., 1999).

On the other hand, Pachur and Biele (2007) sampled expert and laypeople predictions of the outcome of the matches in the first round of the Euro 2004. The aim was not to explicitly evaluate the forecasting ability of football experts but rather to test whether partial ignorance could be beneficial (i.e., the use of the recognition heuristic). On average, the 20

---

[5] A funny episode occurred while the responses were sampled. One of the participating experts submitted an angry letter where he stressed that accurate predictions of football demanded much time and, therefore, the estimated time to answer the questionnaire as stated in the instructions (15 – 20 minutes) was completely erroneous. He spent about 1.5 hours to analyse possible outcomes and make forecasts, whereas the average pundit took less than 20 minutes. Despite his thoroughness, he was outperformed by the naïve participants.

participating sports journalists were able to accurately predict 76.6% of the (non-draw) matches, whereas the 121 laypersons had only 64.5% corrects. Thus, the pundits were significantly better than the non-experts; an observation that runs counter to the finding of the aforementioned study.[6]

This inconsistency seems to be due to either differences in tasks or environments. While the participants of Andersson et al. (2005) simply ticked the 16 teams expected to advance, the participants of Pachur and Biele (2007) had to predict the winning team of every match in the first round. One could argue that the latter task was more difficult and provided a tougher test for expertise, because it required the skills to make multiple comparisons of the strengths of the teams. Comparing the strengths of football teams is complicated by the empirical fact that transitivity among teams is rare (cf. Wagenaar, 1988). In other words, there is no guarantee that team C will lose against team A just because team A has recently beaten team B which in turn has won against team C. Another reason for the inconsistency could be that predicting Euro 2004 was easier than World Cup 2002.

Besides forecasting performance, Andersson et al. (2005) investigated confidence. Most pundits overestimated the quality of their forecasts. On average, they expected that the accuracy would be 68.8%, while their actual performance was 56.3%. Other measures (e.g., confidence scales) also suggested that they put unrealistically great amount of faith in their predictions. Thus, pundits tend to be overconfident; a tendency they share with experts in many other areas.

To sum up, empirical research on football experts points out that forecasting abilities vary between the different types of football experts. Whereas tipsters seem to be poor at predicting the outcome of football league matches, odds-setters are able to produce accurate probabilistic forecasts of the very same matches. As regards the third group of football experts—the so-called pundits, there is mixed evidence concerning their ability to predict the outcome of international tournaments. It seems, however, safe to assume that they are inclined to overestimate their performance. As expected, research on football experts has come up with findings that often harmonise with those of scientists who have studied expert judgement in other areas.

The rest of this chapter is devoted to presenting additional but previously unpublished evidence on the forecasting ability of football

---

[6] When revising my manuscript, I learned about two unpublished investigations on football forecasting (Rakow & Harvey, 1997; Wood & Rakow, 2005). On the whole, their results agreed with those of published studies and showed the advantage of ranking models over punditry.

experts. Specifically, I will report on an empirical inquiry into the ability of tipsters and odds-setters to forecast the World Cup in football. The next section describes the data that constitute the bases of this inquiry.

Empirical Material on Expert Forecasts of World Cups

Collecting Data on Tipster Forecasts of World Cup Matches

Initially, the ambition was to collect FIFA World Cup (WC) forecasts from multiple tipsters using library archives, a procedure taken from Forrest and Simmons (2000). Due to constraints in library access, it was not possible to check newspapers outside Sweden. Searches of library archives indicated that since 1990 there had been only one major Swedish newspaper that has systematically published tipster forecasts for the World Cup finals tournament. Specifically, *Aftonbladet*, which is a daily and nationwide paper, carried columns where a tipster predicted the outcome of nearly all matches in the five recent World Cups. Outcome refers to the score when the ordinary 90 minutes (including injury time) had been played. Thus, each match had three possible outcomes: (1) a win for the team that was listed first according to the fixtures set by FIFA, (2) a win for the team that was officially listed second and (3) a draw. For the sake of simplicity, the former two possibilities will henceforth be called first team win and second team win.

To simplify the data collection, which mainly concerned the time-consuming activity of reading microfilms, I analysed the tipster forecasts from Aftonbladet. In all, the collected data involved 281 predictions made by five different tipsters (all males in the age of 30 – 50 years). Each tipster was responsible for forecasting a single World Cup-tournament. In particular, tipster A predicted WC 1990 (32 of out 52 matches), tipster B foresaw WC 1994 (51 of out 52), tipster C assessed WC 1998 (all 64), tipster D prognosticated WC 2002 (61 out of 64) and tipster E considered WC 2006 (all 64). Nine of the predictions for WC 1990 were so-called two-way forecasts, meaning that the tipster felt uncertain and chose to cover himself with two predicted outcomes (e.g., first team win and draw) in a match. Such kinds of hedges were omitted, leaving 272 tipster forecasts to analyse.

Collecting Odds for the Matches in the World Cups

I also sampled odds from the betting firm *Svenska Spel*, which is owned by the Swedish Government and has the monopoly of running the wagering and gambling market in Sweden. In contrast to British bookmakers, this firm quotes its odds as decimals, meaning that it describes the size of the net payoff (including the stake and the profit) that will be paid out in case of a realised bet. For example, *Svenska Spel* gave the odds that Trinidad and Tobago would draw against Sweden in the World Cup 2006 to be 3.25. Thus, a wager of €100 would have yielded a net payoff of €325 or a profit of €225, as the game actually ended in a draw. In sum, I collected odds for 288 of the 296 matches that have been played in the last five World Cups. The betting firm did not release odds for eight matches of the World Cup 1990. In particular, the sampled odds concerned the tournaments of 1990 (44 matches), 1994 (52), 1998 (64), 2002 (64) and 2006 (64). For each match, odds for three types of outcome (when the ordinary 90 minutes had been played) were available: first team win, second team win and draw.

Across the five tournaments, the odds for first team win, draw and second team win were, on average, 2.37, 3.01 and 3.59 (SDs = 1.57, 0.54 and 1.91) and were significantly different from each other (t (287) = -6.55, -6.56 and -5.68, p < 0.001). Thus, the odds-setters tended to give lower odds for the outcome that the first listed team would win. This tendency may be explained by the fact that this team was often better ranked than the second listed team, see below. The relationship between the odds for first team win and second team win was almost perfectly negative (r_s = -0.98, p < 0.001). The odds for draw were found to correlate negatively with the odds for first team win but positively with the odds for second team win (r_s = -0.44 and 0.31, p < 0.001).

Data on True Match Outcomes, World Rankings and Performance in Past World Cups

Via the web pages of FIFA (www.fifa.com), I obtained information about the official fixtures, true match outcomes and World rankings (at the beginning of each WC tournament). As the collected tipster forecasts and the sampled odds concerned full-time scores, the 26 matches, which went to extra time and, in some cases, also penalty shoot-out, were deemed to end in draw. Across those tournaments, mean ranks regarding the first and second listed teams were 17.8 and 22.0 (SDs = 14.8 and 14.2), a difference that was significant (t (243) = -3.1, p < 0.01).[7]

From the site of the Swedish Football Association (www.svenskfotball.se), I acquired data on the so-called marathon table of Word Cups. This table

---

[7] Factors that determine whether an international team will be listed first in a World Cup-match are, among other things, world rankings, randomisation, geographical considerations, performance in qualification games (FIFA, 2006).

shows how international teams are ranked with respect to the accumulated performance in every tournament that has been played. (Brazil and Germany are in the top.) Using the true match outcomes, I was able to establish what the marathon table looked at the time when each of the five previous World Cups started.

Ability of Tipsters to Predict Matches in World Cups

Forecasting Performance of the Tipsters

Performance was measured as the proportion of correctly predicted matches. As can be seen from Table 1, the performance of the five tipsters varied. Across the five World Cups, they managed to successfully predict 50.7% of matches; a proportion exceeding that of the tipsters in Forrest and Simmons (2000). A random strategy, which was calculated according to the methodology of those authors, gave 34.7% correct forecasts. Analyses showed that the tipster accuracy fluctuated over different stages of the World Cups (e.g., the first stage of the group play, second round and quarter finals), but the differences were not significant.

To evaluate whether the performance of the tipsters could be considered to be adequate, different benchmarks of accuracy were generated by four simple strategies. One of the strategies was extremely straightforward, whereas each of the others considered one single piece of public information (= one reason). In order, the strategies will be referred to as (1) the primitive rule, (2) the rule of past achievements, (3) the rule of rankings and (4) the rule of odds. The assumption of the primitive rule was that the team listed first in a match would win, which is the most naïve approach to foresee football results. The rule of past achievements made predictions on the basis of the so-called marathon table of World Cups and assumed that teams with higher positions in that table would beat teams with lower positions. The rule of rankings used recent records of the teams' strengths and, accordingly, followed the FIFA rankings (prior the start of the respective tournament). The logic of this strategy was that better ranked teams would beat those with worse ranks. Finally, the rule of odds considered the collected quotes from the Swedish betting firm and predicted that the outcome (i.e., first team win, draw or second team win) having the lowest odds would actually occur. In contrast to the other strategies, the rule of odds was able to forecast three different outcomes. For each strategy, the proportion of correct forecasts was calculated.

Table 1: Forecasting performance of the tipsters and benchmarks for each World Cup.

	1990	1994	1998	2002	2006	Overall
Number of forecasts	32	51	64	61	64	272
Percent of correct forecasts by tipsters	40.6	45.1	50.0	52.5	59.4	50.7
Percent of correct forecasts using the primitive rule	50.0	51.0	42.2	42.6	48.4	46.3
Percent of correct forecasts using the rule of past achievements	53.1	54.9	43.8	44.3	46.9	47.8
Percent of correct forecasts using the rule of odds	46.9	51.0	50.0	49.2	71.9	54.8
Percent of correct forecasts using the rule of FIFA rankings	n.a.	56.9	46.9	49.2	46.9	49.6

As shown by Table 1, the tipsters performed as well or better than the four strategies in three out of the five World Cups. As regards the 1990 and 1994 World Cups, their performance was, however, worse than the proportions of those strategies. Across the tournaments, they were only outperformed by the rule of odds, which correctly predicted 54.8% of the matches. Given that odds are assumed to reflect vast amounts of publicly available information (and to some extent also the pool of public behaviour), this rule might be argued to reflect the upper limit of the feasible accuracy.

Another way of evaluating the forecasting performance of the tipsters is to look at its economic significance. Suppose bets were made in accordance to the forecasts of the best tipster. Then the obvious question would arise: How profitable would such a betting policy be? Thanks to the collected odds, it was possible to (ex post) determine the yields on placing bets on the forecasts of the tipsters as well as those generated by the benchmarks. Across the five World Cups, a betting policy that strictly followed the tipster forecasts would have resulted in a loss of 32.0% of the stakes. As comparisons, the primitive rule, the rule of past achievements and the rule of odds would have given a yield of +39.1%, +34.4% and a loss of 27.2%, respectively. A reason for why the former strategies resulted in profits was that they sometimes predicted outcomes with higher odds than the tipsters. Over the four World Cups that it could be applied, the rule that considered world rankings would have theoretically generated a profit of 44.9%, whereas the corresponding figure for the tipsters would have been -30.8%. Thus, from the perspective of (uninformed) bettors, the tipster forecasts were not successful. It must, however, be noted that the betting firm from which the odds were acquired did not permit bets on a single match, but rather required bets on a combination of at least three matches. Consequently, the calculated losses and profits from betting policies were merely hypothetical.

Forecasting Behaviour of the Tipsters

Moreover, the forecasting behaviour of the tipsters was examined. Across the five tournaments, they predicted that 54.8% (25.7%) of the matches would end in wins for the first (second) listed teams.[8] For the individual tournament, the percentage of prediction of this particular outcome ranged from 41.0% to 65.6% (15.6% - 36.1%). In reality, the frequency of first team wins (second team wins) was 0.46 (0.27) and was rather stable over the respective World Cups. As a comparison, the proportion of home wins (away wins) in the data set of Forrest and Simmons (2000) was 0.48 (0.24). It is somewhat remarkable that the genuine home advantage (i.e., own stadium) leads to almost the same outcome as FIFA's method for deciding which team to list first.

As shown by Table 2, measures of association indicated that tipster forecasts were weakly related to true outcome; a finding consistent with the observed level of accuracy. Table 2 also reports analyses of the relationship between tipster forecasts and those of three benchmark strategies. These analyses aimed to investigate whether the tipsters relied on information about past achievements, world rankings and odds. Or, more precisely, to what extent their forecasts were aligned with those generated by one-reason strategies. Based on the size of the measures of association, it seems that the tipsters, consciously or unconsciously, considered odds and rankings to be more important than past achievements. In four World Cups, the rule of odds had the best fit with the tipster forecasts. Success in earlier World Cups appeared to be a less important factor. Given the moderate levels of measures of association in Table 2, there was indirect evidence that the tipsters did not base their forecasts solely on odds, rankings and marathon tables, but may also have considered other types of information. In light of the weak relationships

---

[8] The discrepancy between the proportions of wins for first team and second team gives the frequency of draws.

Table 2: Relationships between tipster forecasts, true outcome and benchmark strategies as evaluated by measures of association (Cramer's V).

Association between tipster forecasts and ...	1990	1994	1998	2002	2006	Overall
true outcome	0.21	0.22	0.28*	0.30*	0.42***	0.28***
the rule of past achievements	0.29	0.45***	0.34***	0.62***	0.43***	0.35***
the rule of rankings		0.64***	0.43***	0.56***	0.43***	0.49***
the rule of odds	0.70***	0.68***	0.77***	0.48***	0.56***	0.51***

* Significant at the 5% level, *** significant at the 0.1% level.

between true outcome and the rules of odds, rankings and past achievements (V = 0.28, 0.28 and 0.19, p <0.001), the tendency of the tipsters to look at additional cues appears to be reasonable. Nonetheless, those cues seem to have had dubious predictive values, because they did not improve the forecasting performance.

Summary and Conclusions

On the whole, the results reported in this section seem to suggest that tipsters are better at predicting the outcome of matches in the World Cups than of (English) league matches. Besides a greater accuracy, their forecasts were often more accurate than those generated by constantly assuming first team win and other simple strategies. One might, therefore, speculate that the league matches are associated with lower degrees of predictiveness than those of the World Cups.[9] Considering that about half of the forecasts were correct, tipster performance must still be regarded to be modest. Individuals who bet money on those forecasts would make considerable losses. In this regard, the tipsters resemble business journalists that issue stock recommendations, which are often unprofitable

---

[9] A reason could be that composition leagues like Serie A in Italy and the Premiership in England are the result of year-on-year relegation and promotion and confer financial advantages upon their teams. Presumably, those leagues have 20 of the 25 best teams in the country at any one time and most likely all of the best 10. Because qualification to the World Cup is regional and split into groups within region, there should be greater spread in the rankings of teams. The World Cup might contain 24 of the best 50 teams in the world and may not even have all of the best 10 by the time the tournament starts. Under such circumstances, ranking rules (or anything that uses such information implicitly or explicitly) will do better where there is a greater spread of ranks. I wish to thank Tim Rakow for pointing out those points to me.

(e.g., Kerl and Walter, 2007). Next section aims at analysing the ability of odds-setters to predict the World Cup.

Ability of Odds-Setters to Predict Matches in World Cups

Forecasting Performance of Odds-Setters

Similar to Forrest et al. (2005), the collected odds were converted to implicit probabilities. In the first step, the odds for first team win (f), draw (d) and second team win (s) were transformed according to $p(f) = 1/f$, $p(d) = 1/d$ and $p(s) = 1/s$, respectively. The sum of the transformed quotes regarding the outcome of a match exceeds inevitably one, as the odds also involve a margin to cover costs and profits for the betting firm (cf. Forrest et al., 2005). In the specific case, this sum equalled about 1.24; implying that the take-out-rate is 0.19 given that the bookmaker holds equal liabilities of the three possible outcomes (cf. Forrest et al., 2005). Implicit probabilities for first team win, draw and second team win, which summed to one, were obtained by the following calculations: $P(F) = p(f) / [p(f) + p(d) + p(s)]$, $P(D) = p(d) / [p(f) + p(d) + p(s)]$ and $P(S) = p(s) / [p(f) + p(d) + p(s)]$.

At first sight, the odds-setters seemed to be very good at assessing the chances for different outcomes.[10] Across the five World Cups, mean implicit probabilities for first team win, draw and second team win were 0.43, 0.27 and 0.29 (SDs = 0.16, 0.05 and 0.16). In reality, about 45% (26%) of the matches were won by the first (second) listed team and the percentage of draw was 29%. Thus, the discrepancies between subjective probability and actual frequency were, on average, extremely small; suggesting nearly perfect forecasting abilities. However, simply looking at such discrepancies is a weak approach for evaluating predictive abilities.

A more reliable approach is to calculate Brier scores, which are essentially squared forecasting errors. Such measures are commonly used to evaluate the performance of probabilistic forecasts (Yates, 1990) and have also been employed in earlier studies of odd-setters (e.g., Forrest et al., 2005). In the present study, Brier scores representing the three possible outcomes were calculated for every match. As regards first team win, a Brier score was defined as $[F_{i,j} - P(F)_{i,j}]^2$ where $F_{i,j}$ took the value 1 if the match between the teams i and j ended in a victory for the first listed team and the value 0 otherwise. The measures for draw and second team win were determined in a similar fashion. Averaging Brier scores over a series

---

[10] Apparently, the betting firm has employed several experts who make probability assessments and quote odds (cf. Jonsson, 2006).

of matches resulted in a measurement of forecasting performance that ranged between 0 and 1. The closer the measurement was to the lower limit, the more accurate were the forecasts of the odds-setters.

Table 3 shows that the Brier scores for the forecasting performance of the odds-setters varied with respect to the three different outcomes and the individual tournaments. Across the tournaments, the average scores concerning first team win and draw were similar, whereas those measures were significant different from the mean scores of second team win (t (287) = 3.49 and 2.07, p < 0.05). Parametric tests also indicated that the Brier scores did not vary significantly between the five tournaments.

The Brier scores in Table 3 could be viewed in light of those of the statistical model for rational odds-setting developed by Forrest et al. (2005). Although this model applies to matches in the English leagues, its forecasting performance might be used as benchmarks for the odds-setters of the present study. Forrest et al. (2005) reported that the Brier scores of this model ranged from 0.19 and 0.23. As a comparison, the mean scores of the odds-setters in the present study were between 0.12 and 0.24; indicating that they were at least equally good as the model.

A common procedure in research on probabilistic forecasting (Yates, 1990; Tetlock, 2005) is to decompose the mean Brier Score into three factors or indices: variability (VI), calibration (CI) and discrimination (DI).[11] Variability reflects the degree of ecological predictability that is associated with the forecasting task. It is based on the true frequency, or the base rate, of the predicted event. In general, the more often an event happens, the easier it is to predict. Theoretically, this factor varies from 0 and 0.25, where the lower limit indicates that the event is very easy to predict and the upper limit suggests unpredictiveness (cf. Tetlock, 2005). Calibration concerns to what extent the forecaster is able to state subjective probabilities for events that agree with their true frequencies. Ideally, this factor should be close to zero meaning that the forecaster is perfectly calibrated. As described above, it is rarely the case that the

---

[11] Mathematically, the decomposition could be expressed as follows (Yates, 1990):
Mean Brier Score = Variability Index + Calibration Index - Discrimination Index =

$$b(1-b)+\frac{1}{N}\sum_{t=1}^{T}n_t(p_t-b_t)^2 - \frac{1}{N}\sum_{t=1}^{T}n_t(b_t-b)^2$$

(1)

where b = the proportion of times a particular outcome occurs over all events (i.e., the base rate); b_t = the base rate for a specific probability category (e.g., 0.10 – 0.20); N = the total number of predicted events; T = the number of probability categories; p_t = the prediction of the tth probability category.

Table 3: Mean (SD) Brier scores for forecasting performance of the odds-setters.

| | World Cup tournaments | | | | | |
	1990	1994	1998	2002	2006	Overall
Number of matches	44	52	64	64	64	288
First team win	0.24	0.24	0.19	0.22	0.18	0.21
	(0.16)	(0.18)	(0.11)	(0.16)	(0.13)	(0.15)
Draw	0.23	0.17	0.21	0.20	0.19	0.20
	(0.23)	(0.20)	(0.22)	(0.20)	(0.16)	(0.20)
Second team win	0.17	0.18	0.16	0.19	0.12	0.16
	(0.21)	(0.18)	(0.21)	(0.18)	(0.16)	(0.19)

calibration of experts is perfect. Discrimination concerns the ability of the forecaster to assign different probabilities to different predictions, so that the proportions of correct forecasts between the probability categories differ from each other. A high value of discrimination suggests that this ability is good. In theory, its upper limit is determined by variability (Tetlock, 2005).

Following the common procedure (Yates, 1990; Tetlock, 2005), the Brier Scores of Table 3 were broken down into the aforementioned factors. Specifically, calculations were made for each of the three types of outcomes and across the five World Cups. The degree of variability was shown to be relatively poor ($0.20 < VI\ 0.25$), showing that the task of correctly predicting first team win, draw and second team win was rather complicated. The indices of calibration and discrimination suggested that the odds-setters were almost perfectly calibrated ($0.003 < CI < 0.008$), but poor at distinguishing between (implicit) probabilities of when first team win, draw and second team win would happen and those of when such events would not occur ($0.01 < DI < 0.04$).

Are Odds-Setters Overconfident and Victims of Favourite-Longshot Bias?

The calibration index gives somewhat limited insights into the ability of making probabilistic forecasts, as it only indicates to what extent the forecaster is, on average, calibrated across a series of predictions. It does not show whether the forecaster tends to interchangeably over- and underestimate the actual probabilities depending on the size of the likelihood (cf. Koehler et al., 2002). Such tendencies could be detected by

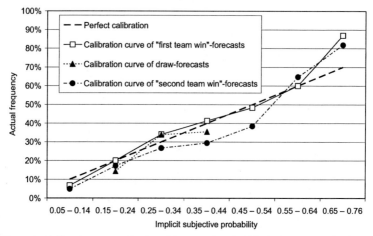

Figure 1: Calibration curves for the odds-setters' probabilistic forecasts of the three outcomes.

calibration curves, which examine the proportion of correct forecasts for each probability category. Similarly, calibration curves could also establish the existence of economic inefficiencies.

Figure 1 shows that the calibration curves concerning the forecasts of the three outcomes had varying agreement with the diagonal representing perfect calibration. These curves were calculated across the five World Cups. The curve of "first team win"-forecasts followed the diagonal rather closely except for the highest category (i.e., 0.65 – 0.76), where the true frequency exceeded the subjective probability; an indication of underconfidence. This tendency was also valid for the curve of "second team win"-forecasts, when the probability was greater than 0.55. Below this level of probability, the odds-setters tended to be overconfident meaning that they overestimated the chances for second team win. In particular, this overestimation seemed to be substantial for the probabilities ranging from 0.35 to 0.54. As regards the curve of draw forecasts, it did not deviate that much from perfect calibration. On the whole, the odds-setters seem to be slightly better calibrated than the experts investigated by Koehler et al. (2002).

Figure 1 also indicates the presence of favourite-longshot bias in regard to predictions of first team win and second team win. As previously mentioned, the odds-setters were deemed to be underconfident for outcomes that had the highest objective likelihood. In contrast, they tended to slightly overestimate the chances for outcomes that were objectively unlikely to happen. Accordingly, the observed propensity of under- and overconfidence relates to the favourite-longshot bias and harmonises with prior research on bookmakers (Cain et al., 2000; Deschamps and Gergaud, 2007).

It should be noted that the seven probability categories of Figure 1 involved different number of forecasts within each possible outcome. Table 4 indicated that about 75% of the first team win-forecasts were associated with probabilities of between 0.25 and 0.64. In contrast, about 69% of the second team win-forecasts had probabilities below 0.34. Interestingly, the range of draw forecasts was limited to three categories, whereby an overwhelming majority fell between 0.25 – 0.34.[12]

Economic Consequences of Observed Tendencies to Miscalibration

Figure 1 suggests some tendencies towards miscalibration, implying that the sampled odds were associated with (ex post) inefficiencies. To evaluate the economic significance of these tendencies, I calculated the expected value of placing, ex post, bets on each of the three different outcomes. (Transaction costs were not taken into account.) For each match and outcome, the dividend of a hypothetical bet of 100 units was determined using the following procedure. When a bet was realised, the odds for this bet were multiplied by 100 units and the stake of the 100 units was then subtracted from this product. When the bet was not realised, the loss was estimated to be 100 units. Averaging the dividends of the bets on first team win resulted in the expected value, or the mean return, of the strategy of consistently betting on this particular outcome. Similarly, the expected values concerning the respective strategies of making a wager on draw and second team win were established.

On the whole, the expected values of those betting strategies were significantly negative. See Table 4. For example, a punter, who had consistently put money on victory for the first (second) listed team in all of the World Cup matches, would have lost about 18.3% (34%) of his stake. In line with earlier empirical research on odds-setters (e.g., Pope and Peel, 1989), different probability categories were associated with different expected values. For instance, constantly placing bets on first team win when the implicit probabilities ranged 0.35 – 0.44 would have given a

---

[12] As suggested by Tim Rakow (email correspondence, May 14, 2008), the observed calibration curves might be dependent on the assumption that the profit margin of the betting firm is a proportionate to the odds.

Table 4: Number of observations and return on hypothetical betting across different probability categories and outcomes.

Probability category[a]	Number of observations			Mean return on hypothetical betting		
	First team win	Draw	Second team win	First team win	Draw	Second team win
0.05 – 0.14	15		41	-54,3%		-71,7%[*]
0.15 – 0.24	35	77	99	-19,3%	-48,2%[*]	-28,1%
0.25 – 0.34	44	180	60	-7,5%	-3,9%	-23,8%
0.35 – 0.44	46	31	34	-17,3%	-19,4%	-41,9%[*]
0.45 – 0.54	60		26	-22,8%[*]		-37,5%[*]
0.55 – 0.64	65		17	-20,1%[*]		-12,6%
0.65 – 0.76[b]	23		11	0,5%		-3,2%
Total	288	288	288	-18,3%[*]	-17,4%[*]	-34,0%[*]

[a] In order, the seven probability categories corresponded roughly to the following intervals of odds: 13.00 – 5.65, 5.50 – 3.30, 3.25 – 2.35, 2.80 – 1.80, 1.80 – 1.50, 1.45 – 1.25 and 1.20 – 1.05.

[b] This category includes a forecast with the implicit probability of 0.76 (odds = 1.05), which was played between Brazil and China in the World Cup 2002.

* Mean return significantly below zero at the 5% level.

mean return of -17.3%, while betting on the same outcome at the lowest odds would generated, on average, a trivial profit of 0.5% of the stake; an observation that agrees with the observed tendency of underconfidence in Figure 1. This tendency also harmonises with the observation that the expected value of bets on second team win was rather less negative for implicit probabilities above 0.55. Recall that the odds-setters tended to be overconfident when the probabilities ranged from 0.35 to 0.54. This behavioural pattern is also shown in Table 4, where the returns of these categories were solidly negative. To sum up, the inefficiencies resulting from the aforementioned tendencies of miscalibration seemed to be of little economic significance for the betting firm; a conclusion that agrees with earlier research (cf. Dobson and Goddard, 2001). Thus, bettors appeared to have limited opportunities to capitalise on those tendencies.

Summary and Conclusions

The aim of this section was to analyse how well odds-setters predict the World Cup in football. In sum, the observed performance agreed with prior research, which is described above. Odds-setters seemed to predict matches in the World Cup with similar degree of accuracy as league matches. Their probabilistic forecasts of World Cup matches tended to be fairly realistic, although for certain ranges of probabilities, they shown tendencies of under- and overconfidence; an indication that they were victims of the favourite-longshot bias. These tendencies lacked economic significance.

General Discussion and Conclusions

This chapter has given a mixed picture of the forecasting capability of football experts. On the one hand, there is evidence that they perform rather well. Generally, odds-setters tend to accurately assess the possibilities for certain outcomes of football matches, implying that they are well-calibrated. As earlier said, such behaviour is seldom observed among experts in other areas. On the other hand, there exist research findings suggesting that football experts are, in fact, poor at predicting football. In general, tipsters seem to be unable to reach a level of accuracy exceeding 55 percent correct forecasts. Their forecasts are often equally accurate as those generated by simple rules. When predicting league matches, tipsters are outperformed by the naïve strategy of picking first team win. However, this strategy seems not applicable to the World Cup. As regards the predictive ability of pundits, there is mixed evidence. While one study reported solidly that pundits were equally good as non-experts, another study indicated that this type of experts performed better than laypeople; an inconsistency that might be resolved by future research.

One might argue that the difference in forecasting performance of odds-setters and tipsters is due to differences in the use of decision aids.[13] It is likely that betting firms have developed statistical models that can assist odds-setters when producing probabilistic forecasts of possible outcomes. Such models are able to effectively weigh together all publicly available information (cf. Forrest et al., 2005). In contrast, tipsters possibly lack decision aids meaning that they are forced to process information and make assessments using their heads. A vast amount of research points out that predictions following formal and objective rules will always be superior than those that are based on subjective judgements (cf. Dawes et al., 1989; Dana and Thomas, 2006). Consequently, it is not surprising that odds-setters are more accurate than tipsters (and, probably also, pundits).

Furthermore, the poor forecasting performance of football experts could be viewed in light of task characteristics. Ultimately, the outcome of

---

[13] I would like to thank Håkan Nilsson for bringing my attention to this circumstance.

a football match is a matter of actions (and inactions) of the players on the pitch; implying that the prediction of football is, basically, a task of judging future behaviour of individuals playing together and against each other in front of enthusiastic and supportive crowds. Like other areas associated with human behaviour (cf. Shanteau, 1992a), football experts could be assumed to have difficulties in giving correct forecasts. Support for this assumption comes from scientific attempts to build econometric models for the prediction of football results. Despite a high degree of sophistication and reliance of rich amounts of information, these models are modestly accurate (cf. Dobson and Goddard 2001; Goddard, 2005).

In conclusion, when evaluating how well football experts predict, considerations must not only be taken to their abilities but also to the environment that is the subject for their analyses and inferences (cf. Simon, 1990). Bearing this in mind, one might argue that the forecasting performance of football experts is not too bad. Nonetheless, one cannot safely rule out that their forecasts are sometimes equally accurate as those made by simple models and naïve individuals.

References

Allwood, C. M. and P. A. Granhag (1999). "Feelings of confidence and the realism of confidence in everyday life." In *Judgment and decision making: Neo-Brunswikian and process-tracing approaches*. P. Juslin and H. Montgomery eds. Mahwah, New Jersey: Lawrence Erlbaum Associates, 123-146.

Andersson, P., M. Ekman and J. Edman (2005). "Predicting the World Cup 2002 in Soccer: Performance and confidence of experts and non-experts." *International Journal of Forecasting*, 21(3), 565-576.

Ayton, P. (1992). "On the competence and incompetence of experts." In *Expertise and decision support*. F. Bolger and G. Wright eds. New York: Plenum Press, 77-105.

Bolger, F. and G. Wright (1992a). *Expertise and decision support*. New York: Plenum Press.

Bolger, F. and G. Wright (1992b). "Reliability and validity in expert judgment." In *Expertise and decision support*. F. Bolger and G. Wright eds. New York: Plenum Press, 47-76.

Boulier, B. L. and H. O. Stekler (1999). "Are sports seedings good predictors? An evaluation." *International Journal of Forecasting*, 15(1), 83-91.

Boulier, B. L. and H. O. Stekler (2003). "Predicting the outcomes of National Football League games." *International Journal of Forecasting*, 19(2), 257-270.

Cain, M., D. Law and D. Peel, 2000 "The favorite-longshot bias and market efficiency in UK and football betting." *Scottish Journal of Political Economy*, 47(1), 25-36.

Camerer, C. F. and E. J. Johnson (1991). "The process-performance paradox in expert judgment: How can experts know so much and predict so badly?" In K. A. Ericsson and J. Smith eds. *Toward a general theory of expertise: Prospects and limits.* New York: Cambridge Press, 195-217.

Dana, J. and R. Thomas (2006). "In defense of clinical judgment... and mechanical prediction." *Journal of Behavioral Decision Making*, 19(5), 413-428.

Dawes, R. M., D. Faust and P. E. Meehl (1989) . "Clinical versus actuarial judgment." *Science*, 243(4899), 1668-1674.

Deschamps, B. and O. Gergaud (2007). "Efficiency in betting markets: Evidence from English football." *The Journal of Prediction Markets*, 1(1), 1-13.

Dobson, S. and J. Goddard (2001). *The economics of football.* Cambridge, UK: Cambridge University Press.

Ericsson, K. A., N. Charnes, P. J. Feltovich and R. R. Hoffman (Eds.) (2006). *The Cambridge handbook of expertise and expert performance.* Cambridge, UK: Cambridge University Press.

Forrest, D., J. Goddard and R. Simmons (2005). "Odds-setters as forecasters: The case of English football." *International Journal of Forecasting*, 21(3), 551-564.

Forrest, D. and R. Simmons (2000). "Forecasting sport: the behaviour and performance of football tipsters." *International Journal of Forecasting*, 16(3), 317-331.

Gigerenzer, G., P. M. Todd and the ABC Group (1999) . *Simple heuristics that make us smart.* New York: Oxford University Press.

Goddard, J. (2005). "Regression models for forecasting goals and match results in association football." *International Journal of Forecasting*, 21(2), 331-340.

Goddard, J. and I. Asimakopoulos (2004). "Forecasting football results and the efficiency of fixed-odds betting." *Journal of Forecasting*, 23(1), 51-66.

Jonsson, G. (2006, May 30). "De sätter oddsen inför VM [They set the odds of the World Cup]". *Dagens Industri*, p. 30.

Keren, G. (1987). "Facing uncertainty in the game of bridge - a calibration study." *Organizational Behavior and Human Decision Processes*, 39(1), 98-114.

Kerl, A. G. and A. Walter (2007). "Market responses to buy recommendations issued by personal finance magazines: Effects of information, price-pressure, and company characteristics." *Review of Finance*, 11(1), 117-141.

Koehler, D. J., L.A. Brenner and D. Griffin (2002). "The calibration of expert judgment: Heuristics and biases beyond the laboratory." In *Heuristics and biases: The psychology of intuitive judgment*. T. Gilovich D. Griffin and D. Kahneman eds. New York: Cambridge University Press, 686-715.

Ladouceur, R., I. Giroux, C. Jacques (1998). "Winning on the horses: How much strategy and knowledge are needed?" *The Journal of Psychology*, 132(2), 133-142.

Murphy, A. H. and R. L. Winkler (1984). "Probability forecast in meteorology." *Journal of the American Statistical Association*, 79(3), 489-500.

Pachur, T. and G. Biele (2007). "Forecasting from ignorance: The use and usefulness of recognition in lay predictions of sports events." *Acta Psychologica*, 125(1), 99-116.

Plessner, H. and T. Haar (2006). "Sports performance judgments from a social cognitive perspective." *Psychology of Sport and Exercise*, 7(6), 555-575.

Pope, P. E. and D. A. Peel (1989). "Information, prices and efficiency in a fixed-odds betting market." *Economica*, 56(223), 323-341.

Rakow, T. and N. Harvey. (1997). "It's a funny old game: Accuracy, confidence and overconfidence in the forecasting of football results." University College London: Unpublished research report.

Shanteau, J. (1992a). "Competence in experts: The role of task characteristics." *Organizational Behavior and Human Decision Processes*, 53(2), 252-266.

Shanteau, J. (1992b). "How much information does an expert use? Is it relevant?" *Acta Psychologica*, 81(1), 75-86.

Sherden, W. A. (1998). *The fortune sellers: The big business of buying and selling predictions*. New York: Wiley.

Simon, H. A. (1990). "Invariants of human behavior." *Annual Review of Psychology*, 41(1), 1-19.

Stewart, T., P. J. Roebber and L. F. Bosart, (1997) . "The importance of the task in analyzing expert judgment." *Organizational Behavior and Human Decision Processes*, 69(3), 205-219.

Tetlock, P. (2005). *Expert political judgment: How good is it? How can we know?* New Jersey: Princeton University Press.

Törngren, G. and H. Montgomery (2003). "Worse than chance? Performance and confidence among professionals and lay-people in the stock market." *The Journal of Behavioral Finance*, 5(3), 146-153.

Vaughan Williams, L. (1999). "Information efficiency in betting markets: A survey." *Bulletin of Economic Research*, 51(1), 1-30.

Wagenaar, W. A. (1988). *Paradoxes of gambling behavior.* Hove: Lawrence Erlbaum Associates.

Wood, D. and T. Rakow. (2005). "Forecasting Premiership football matches: A mugs game?" University of Essex: Unpublished research report.

Yates, J. F. (1990). *Judgment and decision making.* Englewood Cliffs, NJ: Prentice Hall.

Yates, J. F. and M. D. Tschirhart (2006). "Decision-making expertise." In *The Cambridge Handbook of Expertise and Expert Performance.* K. A. Ericsson, N. Charness, P. J. Feltovich and R. Hoffman eds. New York: Cambridge University Press, 421-438.

CHAPTER SIXTEEN

HOW ACCURATELY DO MARKETS PREDICT THE OUTCOME OF AN EVENT? THE EURO 2000 FOOTBALL EXPERIMENT

CARSTEN SCHMIDT AND AXEL WERWATZ[1]

This chapter deals with the predictive performance of markets drawn on the outcome of uncertain events: the outcome of football matches. Recently, scientist and companies have attempted to predict quality and duration of complex industrial projects (Ortner, 2000) or future sales of investment goods (Chen and Plott, 1998; Plott, 2000), on the basis of experimental asset markets. These kind of markets are operated as a futures exchange, where subjects buy and sell money-backed contracts drawn on the outcome of uncertain events. As opposed to a prognosis based on an individual expert's advice, such a market is able to aggregate the information of a large number of participants.

The market as a combination device has been studied in the information aggregation literature, demonstrating that markets are able to aggregate information fast and efficient (Forsythe and Lundholm, 1990;

---

[1] Schmidt: Sonderforschungsbereich 504, Mannheim University, L 13, 15, 68131 Mannheim, Germany, Email: cschmidt@sfb504.uni-mannheim.de. Werwatz: Technical University Berlin, Email: axel.werwatz@tu-berlin.de. The financial support of the German Science Foundation (Grants nos. SFB 373, A1 and C5) and the International Institute of Infonomics/Heerlen at the Maastricht University is gratefully acknowledged. We thank Jan Hansen and Rudolf Müller for discussion and their support in conducting the experiment. We thank Patric Andersson, Kimmo Eriksson and Magnus Johannesson for detailed comments and advice. We greatefully acknowledge insightful conversations on this subject with Werner Güth, Manfred Königstein, Loreto Llorente, Christian Schade, Peter Schmidt, Martin Strobel and Harald Uhlig and comments from audiences at Barcelona, Berlin, Heerlen and Wulkow. This chapter is an edited reprint of Chapter 5 of Schmidt's (2003) dissertation.

Plott and Sunder, 1988). Political stock market experiments in the U.S. were able to generate more precise election result forecasts than traditional polls (Forsythe et al., 1999), and these market forecasts proved to be slightly more accurate than polls, also in a European context (Berlemann and Schmidt, 2001). The idea to interpret prices of contracts in terms of an assessment of the event's probability goes back to Hanson (1995).

In this chapter, the predictive accuracy of experimental asset markets is investigated in the context of an Internet-based experiment dealing with football matches. To be more precise, we are going to evaluate the predictions of 21 real money markets, drawn on the winning team of a specific football match during the Euro 2000. To evaluate the experimental results, we took a benchmark model, the rolling dice, and empirical expert data, a professional bookmaker's odds, as a basis for comparison.

Contracts drawn on the outcome of sports events have a historic background in commercial stock markets. In the seventies, at a time, when the German stock market played a minor role, an active non-stock market trading of Olympic gold medals, football World Cup titles and election results of political parties was observed.[2] At that time private bets were backed with actual deals. When transactions were conducted during regular trading sessions the exchange supervision was called to act. Yet, brokers are not the only target group fascinated with trading sports contracts. In the experimental economics community there were at least two market based experiments for football events prior to our analysis. Experimental economists at CREED/Amsterdam conducted a market for the World Cup in 1994. For the World Cup 1998 we ran a small market at Humboldt University where participants from 10 different countries traded contracts drawn on football teams via the Internet. Several prediction markets without monetary involvement were also conducted for major football events. In the realm of finance, a prediction market was set up for the World Cup 1998 to test the influence of market makers on large-scale stock markets (Bochow et al., 2002). The authors are aware of a least three commercial prediction markets that were conducted during the Euro 2000.[3] To our knowledge our experiment was the only market for the Euro 2000 which involved real money investment.

---

[2] See the article "Vor der Bundestagswahl. Der neue Handelsblatt-Wahl-Dax. Kohl oder Schröder: Auf wen wetten die Börsianer?" in the March 27, 1998 issue of "Handelsblatt".

[3] The public TV station ZDF together with the online broker Consors organised a market in Germany; The online catalog Yahoo and the game organiser Neopoly also conducted a market for this event with participants from Germany, England

In markets where traders do not invest their own funds, regularly, traders with extraordinary performance win prices, usually high-quality consumer goods, while all the other traders do not receive monetary rewards. This implies that traders are not subject to monetary losses. On the one hand, this kind of game attracts a large number of participants. On the other hand, traders often cancel participation when their portfolios face severe losses. Several researchers used data of market based games to find out whether the posted prices correlate with the events observed. In some cases they found the forecasts generated by fantasy market data more reliable than expert opinions. Servan-Schreiber et al. (2004) report play money markets to perform with respect to predictions not different from real money markets when comparing predictions drawn on NFL football.

As we proceed, we are going to compare the bookmaker's odds with the market prognosis. Empirical data on sports betting odds is a data source for empirically testing of the market efficiency hypothesis in finance. Unlike company shares—who's true fundamentals are only disclosed in such rare events like bankruptcy—the fundamental values of bets are revealed after the result of the event is published. Racetrack betting markets odds are thought to be good estimates of win probabilities (Thaler and Ziemba, 1988) and some observers find point spread betting markets to deliver unbiased predictions of the event's outcome (Gandar et al., 1998). Nevertheless, in the empirical literature there are several statistical biases reported, most prominently the favourite-longshot bias in horse track racing (Thaler and Ziemba, 1988), which states that bettors overestimate the longshots' probability of winning. Most empirical studies that deal with economic evidence for the market efficiency hypothesis conclude, that betting strategies which take advantage of known biases might be successful, even when betting fees are taken into account (Vergin and Scriabin, 1978; Gandar et al., 1988; Dixon and Coles, 1997), yet these market inefficiencies tend to dissipate over time (Gray and Gray, 1997). Unfortunately, we were not able to test for statistical biases due to the limited scope of the available market data. In the spirit of an economic testing of the market efficiency hypothesis, we explore the question whether subjects are able to earn profits by using the bookmaker's odds to participate in the market and the other way around. Given the stochastic nature of the game the data generated by the experiment allows for a speculative outlook only.

The purpose of this chapter is to compare the market-generated prices to a benchmark model and to professional bet quotas, on the basis of

---

and France; Another market was conducted by Phillips corporation in the Netherlands.

statistical hypothesis testing. We identify the variables that are responsible for the quality of the markets' predictive success. Our data supports the hypothesis, that the market yields significantly more accurate results than the random predictor and that it is more accurate than professional bet quotas in the sense of mean square error. Moreover, the more certain the market predicts the outcome of an event, the more accurate is the prediction. This effect can not be observed for the bookmaker's odds. In addition, we find the markets to assign relatively higher certainty on the favourites' winning and less certainty on the longshots' prospects when compared to the bookmaker.

In the following section we give an overview on the organisation of the football event, as well as on the setup of market and bookmaker. Section 3 presents a description of the experimental setup. Section 4 briefly describes the data and Section 5 reviews the results. Open research questions for further exploration and concluding remarks are given in section 6.

Overview

The Football Event

The Euro 2000 was held from June 10th to July 2nd in the Netherlands and Belgium. 16 European national football teams qualified for this tournament. On the whole, 31 matches were scheduled, with 24 matches for the group stage and seven matches for the knockout stage. The tournament is organised in two parts. During the group stage four groups are drawn each including four teams. In each group the teams play round robin. For each match the winning team receives three points, while both competing teams receive one point for a draw. Teams are ranked according to their total number of points. In case that more than one team is winning the same number of points, the goal difference is used as a tie breaker. Out of each group the two top teams enter the knockout stage. Starting with the knockout stage, the outcome of a match has to be decided. When no decision is made after 90 minutes of regular playing time, the competitors need to play extra time. In the 30 minutes of extra playing time, the first goal recorded—also called the *golden goal*—decides the match. When no decision is reached in extra time, the match is decided on penalties.

One may suspect the three possible outcomes of a match in the European Championships are not equally likely. Two reasons, the home

Table 1. Historical frequencies *first listed team win, draw* and *second listed team win*, Euro 1980, 1984, 1988, 1992 and 1996.

Euro	Result		1980-1996
Group stage	*First listed team win*	1	.44
(n=72)	*draw*	0	.31
	Second listed team win	2	.25
Knockout stage	*Decision after 90 min*	1 & 2	.50
(n=18)	*no decision after 90 min.*	0	.50

Source: http://www.fussballarchiv.de.

advantage and a low likelihood of draws, are regularly mentioned. Unlike sports leagues, there is (about) no home advantage for the competing teams in such a type of tournament. All teams, except the team of the organising country, play on foreign ground. To answer the question whether a draw occurs in one out of three matches, we evaluated the results of all European Championship matches from 1980 until 1996.[4] The analysis revealed that in the group stage 30.6% of all matches led to a draw. Out of all matches in the knockout stage 50.0% were decided after regular time. Table 1 summarises these historic results.

The empirical data support the hypothesis that the likelihood of a draw is not different from 1/3.[5] Moreover, the ordering of the listing in the World Cup does not appear to be random (Andersson, Chapter 15). In this chapter we use the official UEFA fixtures of first and second listed team for presentation. Since the likelihood of the *first listed team win* is higher when looking at the historical data in Table 1, the usage of the random predictor as a benchmark model can be viewed as inappropriate when relying on the order of the listing. Our error measure makes use of the highest assigned probability and the realisation of the outcome and thus does not depend on the order of the fixtures.

---

[4] The football tournament is conducted every four years and follows the rules laid down since 1980. From 1980 to 1992 eight teams participated in the tournament with the group stage consisting of two groups with four teams, respectively. Since 1996 the number of teams was increased to 16.

[5] As one referee argued the introduction of the 3 point rule might have changed teams' incentives and thus the frequency of draws. Actually, Garicano and Palacios-Huerta (2005) find a decrease from 29.7 to 25.5 percent after the introduction of the 3 point rule in Spanish premier league competitions.

The Bookmaker

The structure of football betting is quite simple. The three possible outcomes of a match are *first listed team win, draw* and *second listed team win*. These outcomes are assigned to values 1, 0 and 2, respectively. The bookmaker offers a fixed quote for every outcome of the match. A quote of 2.5 for a win on the first listed team implies that for a one Euro bet the bettor receives 2.50 Euro in case of win and zero in the other cases. During knockout stage the rule is changed and the bet is redefined as "winning in regular playing time". Therefore, matches that are decided after regular time are assigned 0, similar to a *draw*.

For the evaluation of the experimental data in the later sections, we use data of the fixed-odds sports betting system "ODDSET" run by the German state-owned lottery. Bettors can participate via Internet and at any location in Germany, where state owned lotteries are accepted. The participation is restricted to German residents. In the lottery bettors choose combinations of bets. Combinations can be selected from up to 90 bets, typically the football matches from Tuesday to Monday.[6] The objective of a bet is a combined prediction of 3 to 10 bets. For example, if the bettor predicts all matches (out of three) correctly, the pay-off amounts to the multiplication of the three quotes times the investments, in case of failure the bettor receives nothing. Participants can invest in bets of 2.50, 5, 10, 15, 20, 25, or 50 Euro.[7] The investment is restricted to 300 Euro per week and the maximum pay-off is limited to 50,000 Euro.

Apart from the decision on how to set the quotes considering the probability of an event's outcome, the bookmaker's objective is to set the quote in a way that the bettor's investments distribute evenly on all three outcomes. In this case the bookmaker takes no risk. The bookmaker's implicit prognosis, computed from the quotes, may therefore be biased by a demand effect.

The Market

The design of the market experiment was similar to that of the Iowa Electronic Markets (Forsythe et al., 1992; Berg et al., 1997) that host markets on the outcome of political and economic events. In order to participate the trader had to invest real money. The maximum investment

---

[6] There are other kinds of bets offered, like point spreads, and bets on other sports events in non-football season. Due to the objective of the chapter we concentrate on football matches, especially on those conducted during the Euro 2000.

[7] We use an exchange rate of 2 DM for 1 Euro for ease of processing; the actual exchange rate is 1.95583 DM.

of an individual trader was restricted to 50 Euro.[8] With the investment the experimenter provided a trading account on the electronic marketplace. On the marketplace participants were given the option to take part in several individual markets. Each market was organised as follows. On the primary market subjects bought and sold zero-risk unit-portfolios from and to the bank. A unit-portfolio included one of each different contract on the market. The bank guaranteed to buy and sell this unit-portfolio at a constant price during the entire experiment. On the secondary market the subjects were asked to buy and sell individual contracts. As market institution a continuous double auction with queues was introduced to implement transactions between the participants. As opposed to markets with an initial public offering (IPO), which use a fixed amount of contracts, the institution of the unit-portfolio allows for a dynamic emission of contracts during the experiment. Finally, the zero sum property of the market mechanism guaranteed that the organiser did not make any profits or losses.

The experiment was accessible via the Internet and started five days prior to the football tournament. On the whole, it was conducted for 28 days during which time it was accessible around the clock. Participants were recruited from two portal sites, one located in Germany and one in the Netherlands. In Germany the market was made public by the name ribaldo7.de and by the name of voetbalmarkt.nl in the Netherlands. The Dutch organiser only permitted members of the University of Maastricht to participate. To participate at the German portal site subjects were required to have a German bank account.

Altogether, 238 subjects participated in the Euro 2000 market - 188 from Germany and 49 from the Netherlands. The subjects were mostly employees (50%) and students (27%). The average age was 30 years with a standard deviation of 9.6. Not surprisingly, only 10% of the participants were female.

The subjects' commitment was remarkably high. The total investment was 8,933 Euro with an average of 37.53 Euro (SD=18.25). The 238 traders conducted 2,950 trades, on average more than 24 trades per participant. Standard web sites, like search engines and catalogues, on average receive well below 10 page impressions per visit (PI/Visit).[9] The

---

[8] German participants received an additional five Euro on top of their investment, the total value of the portfolio of a German trader amounted to a range of six to 55 Euro.

[9] Page impression is a measure used in web site marketing to quantify the number of requested web pages. As opposed to the measure "hits", where the number of transmitted files is aggregated, a request of a web page, also containing several

Euro 2000 market made participants and visitors generate a remarkable average of 15 PI/Visit.

Experimental Setup

The experiment consisted of a set of markets, which the participants were asked to choose from. Each time a trader logged on to the experiment, he was right away connected to the championship market. This market was open for the entire time of the experiment, which implies that subjects could trade during the matches. The market consisted of 16 contracts representing the teams that qualified for the Euro 2000. The pay-off rule of this market was a very simple one, winner-take-all design. The contract of the Euro 2000 champion yielded a pay-off of 1,000 Centicent[10] all other 15 contracts yielded a zero pay-off.

In addition, participants were asked to participate in markets for individual matches.[11] These markets were organised similar to odds-setters' bets. For matches during the group stage a market consisted of three different contracts: *first listed team win*, *draw* and *second listed team win*. For the seven matches of the knockout stage, the number of contract types was reduced to two. In both settings, the group and the knockout stage, the winning contract yielded a pay-off of 100 Centicent and whereas the other contracts, two in the group stage, and one in the knockout stage, yielded a zero pay-off. The markets were open between three and five days prior to the matches and closed at the beginning of the corresponding match. In such a setup all information available to the traders should be included in the closing price of a contract. The day after the match all contracts were liquidated and the money was made available to the traders via the online accounts. This way, subjects regained liquidity to invest in upcoming markets. The championship market was open all the time,

---

files, is counted only once. A visit is a series of one or more page impressions, served to one user, which ends after a 30 minutes or more break between successive page impressions for that user.

[10] The Centicent was used as denomination during the experiment. 100 Centicent convert into one Euro cent.

[11] We offered four group markets that are not evaluated in this chapter. For the sake of completeness we briefly describe the organisation of these markets. Every group market contained for each of the four teams a different contract. The contracts of the two teams that participated in the knockout stage paid off 50 Centicent each, the other two zero. The markets were liquidated right after the results of the groups were available.

whereas all other markets were open for a limited time only. At the utmost, traders could participate in nine parallel markets.

The chapter empirically tests the efficient market hypothesis (Hayek, 1937, Fama, 1970) which claims that financial markets are efficient in the sense that there is no persistent opportunity for abnormal returns based on the observation of past prices or taking into account all public and private information. As soon as new information becomes publicly available it is immediately absorbed and incorporated into market prices. The following hypotheses are evaluated in the study: (1) the markets should predict the outcome of matches more precise than a rolling dice, (2) the markets' quotes should be meaningful: the more certain the market the more often the prediction of the market should be right and (3) the markets should generate more accurate probabilities than the bookmaker's odds. There are several reasons for the third hypothesis. First, the market is a zero sum game where investments are redistributed between and paid back to the participants. The bookmaker needs to charge a premium for his service which might bias the attractiveness of different categories of bets. Second, the markets do not have a demand effect due to a home team bias on the state of the participants. In our experiment German and Dutch participants were active on the same market, while the German bookmaker allows for German bettors only. Finally, the bookmaker has to set fixed quotes a couple of days prior to the match. The markets have the opportunity to incorporate new and current information until they close right before kick-off.

Data

Altogether, 31 matches were played during Euro 2000. For 21 of these matches we ran match markets.[12] The prices of the contracts in these markets just before kick-off can be used to generate predictions of the match's outcome. The converting of contract prices into predictions is straightforward: with the market's predicted outcome being the one with the highest contract price. The contract prices just before kick-off (i.e., the closing prices, with the individual match markets closing right before the beginning of the respective match) should incorporate all relevant information available to the market participants at this time. Indeed, if the match markets efficiently aggregate information, there should not be any other observable variable for the improvement of the prediction.

---

[12] Due to technical difficulties we were not able to conduct match markets for the first 10 matches of the Euro 2000.

A second set of predictions can be derived from the contract prices of the competing teams in the championship market. Just before the start of the match we take as the championship market's predicted winner the team with the higher contract price. Obviously, this prediction rule will never predict a draw, except in the unlikely event that both teams have identical contract prices. Finally, from the ODDSET Internet site (http://www.oddset.de) we obtained bookmaker quotes for 31 matches. At the bookmaker the bet with the lowest quote is expected to be the most likely outcome, while on the market, the contract with the highest price is most likely to pay-off.

Results

Is the Market as Reliable as a Random Predictor?

The goal of this section is to study an experimental market's capability to predict uncertain events. A natural reference point for the market's performance is a random mechanism that generates uninformed, unsystematic predictions, like the flipping of a coin. Indeed, some observers of football argued that the outcome of games is entirely random.[13] Therefore, we formally test the null hypothesis that the market delivers uninformed, random predictions.

Distribution of the Test Statistics under the Null Hypothesis

Let X_n be the number of correct predictions in n trials. To perform the test, we need to derive the distribution of X_n under the null hypothesis. At this point, we introduce notation that describes the games' outcomes as well as their predictions and probabilities. For reasons of simplicity, we ignore the fact that some of the Euro 2000 games had three possible outcomes in this paragraph (the matches in the group stage) while others had only two (the games in the knockout stage).

Let us suppose that each game has three possible outcomes: *first listed team win* (1), *draw* (0), and *second listed team win* (2), and define the random variable G_i accordingly, where i is used to index the games. Let q_{ij} be the true, objective probability that game i has outcome j. For instance, q_{70} indicates the probability that game 7 ends with a draw (outcome 0). Hence,

---

[13] See, for instance, the article titled "Sammer, Kohler, Nemax & Co. Some similarities between the stock market and football are striking - Is it all random?" in the April 17, 2000 issue of "Der Tagesspiegel".

$$G_i = \begin{cases} 0 \text{ with probability } q_{i0} \\ 1 \text{ with probability } q_{i1} \\ 2 \text{ with probability } q_{i2}. \end{cases}$$

Let R_i be the prediction of a random predictor of game i's outcome. For the time being, we will assume that the random predictor forecasts the outcome of each game independently and identically according to the following probabilistic rule:

$$R_i = \begin{cases} 0 \text{ with probability } 1/3 \\ 1 \text{ with probability } 1/3 \\ 2 \text{ with probability } 1/3. \end{cases}$$

Note the probability that the random predictor correctly predicts the outcome of game i as $P(R_i = G_i)$. It is obvious to show (see Schmidt, 2003) that $P(R_i = G_i)$ is $1/3$ for each game, even if the objective probabilities q_{ij} vary across matches. Consequently, the probability, that the random predictor will deliver x correct predictions in n trials is given by the binomial distribution with the parameters n and $1/3$. That is,

$$P(X_n = x) = \binom{n}{x}\left(\frac{1}{3}\right)^x\left(\frac{2}{3}\right)^{(n-x)}$$

Conducting the Test

From the distribution of the test statistics under the null hypothesis we are able to obtain the critical values for the desired significance level. Considering that of the 21 matches seven had two possible outcomes while fourteen had three possible outcomes, we obtain the exact distribution of the test statistics as a sum of two binomial distributions. Specifically, we obtain $X_n = Y_{14} + Z_7$ with $Y_{14} \sim Bin(n = 14, 1/3)$ and $Z_7 \sim Bin(n = 7, 1/2)$.

Using a significance level of $\alpha = 0.05$ the critical value for a one-sided test in the positive direction is $x_{cr} = 13$, as $P(X_n > 13) = 0.037 < 0.05$ under the null. It turns out, that match markets predicted the outcome of the game correctly in 15 out of 21 cases. Since 15 exceeds the critical value 13, we can reject the null hypothesis that the market is an uninformed, random predictor.

Distribution of the Test Statistics under the Alternative Hypothesis

The alternative hypothesis implicit in the one-sided test is that the predicting of the outcome of matches, by market prices is better than using a coin. But even if predictions derived from market prices are indeed superior, they need not to be correct all the time. Stated differently, the number of correct predictions, X_n, remains a random variable until all games have been played.

In the previous section, we were able to derive the exact distribution of X_n *under the null* hypothesis by showing that X_n is the sum of two binomially distributed random variables. However, deriving the precise form of the distribution of X_n under the alternative hypothesis is impossible since predictions are no longer Bernoulli trials (independent, with a constant probability of correctly predicting the outcome of a game). Rather, market participants observe the teams' performances during the course of the tournament, with market prices, and hence market probabilities, are conditional on the outcomes and events of previous matches.

Still, carrying out a right-sided test, i.e. rejecting the null hypothesis if (too) many games are correctly predicted, can be formally justified. This can be done by showing that if the market's assessment of the probabilities of a game's outcome, as revealed by the market prices, is equal to the true, objective probability then the expected number of correct predictions is higher for the market than for the random predictor.

Let M_i be the market's prediction of the outcome of game i and p_{ij} the market's assessment of the probability that game i has outcome j. We define

$$M_i = k \quad if \quad p_{ik} = \max{}_j p_{ij}$$

Suppose that the market's probabilities are equal to the objective probabilities, i.e. $p_{ij} = q_{ij}$ for all i and j. In this case, the probability that the market will correctly predict the outcome of game i is given by:

$$P(M_i = G_i) = P(\text{"outcome with highest prob. will occur"}) = \max{}_j q_{ij} = q^*_i$$

Let's define the random variable Y_i^m that measures the market's predictive success of game i as follows

$$Y_i^m = \begin{cases} 1 & if\ M_i = G_i \\ 0 & otherwise \end{cases}$$

Obviously, $E[Y_i^m] = P(Y_i^m = 1) = q^*_i$. The number of correct predictions in n trials by the market, X_m^n, has expected value

$$E[X_i^m] = \sum_{i=1}^{n} E[Y_i^m] = \sum_{i=1}^{n} q_i^*$$

Recall that under the null hypothesis (random predictor) and under the current assumptions (n games with three outcomes each) the number of correct predictions X_n is binomially distributed with mean $E[Xn|H_0] = n \times 1/3 = \sum_{i=1}^{n} 1/3$ which is smaller than (1) since $q^*_i \geq 1/3$.

Does the Market Beat the Odds?

In this subsection we are going to examine the question whether market prices are more accurate predictors than the quotes, posted by Germany's nationwide bookmaker, ODDSET.

Total Number of Correct Predictions

For the 21 matches, for which market predictions were available, we find that the bookmaker's quotes yield (about) the same number of correct predictions. There was only one instance in which the market's prediction differed from the bookmaker's: the first-round match Portugal vs. Germany, which the market predicted correctly when taking the higher trading volume with Portugal as a tie breaker. Moreover, there were two matches for whom the bookmaker quoted equal odds for the events *first listed team win* and *second listed team win*, therefore not yielding a definite prediction of the game's outcome. This leaves us with a total number of fourteen correct predictions derived from the bookmaker's odds, compared to the 15 correct predictions of the market experiment (see Table 2).

Mean Squared Prediction Loss

In the previous sections we focused on the qualitative predictions derived from prices and odds and did not take full advantage of the quantitative information inherent in their actual magnitude. After all, we can assume that market participants are much more confident that a team will win if its contract price is 99 rather than say, 51, while the qualitative prediction is identical. If the team turns indeed out to win, then a prediction based on a price of 99 should be regarded superior to a qualitatively equally correct prediction based on a price of 51. On the other hand, if the team loses, then the prediction based on 99 is to be regarded inferior to the qualitatively equally incorrect prediction based on 51.

The squared prediction loss is a criterion that takes these quantitative errors into account. In the case of matches with only two outcomes its definition is straightforward.

$$MSPL_2 = \frac{1}{n}\sum_{i=1}^{n}\left[I(G_i = M_i) - P_i^*\right]^2$$

Table 2. Implicit probabilities calculated from markets' closing prices and bookmaker's odds.

Group: Match	R^c	Match market			Champions.		ODDSET		
		1	0	2	1	2	1	0	2
D:Czech Rep-France	2	.12	.16	.72	.09	.91	.28	.28	.44
D:Denmark-Netherlands	2	.02	.04	.94	.01	.99	.20	.25	.55
A:Romania-Portugal	2	.19	.04	.77	.15	.85	.34	.28	.38
A:England-Germany	1	.33	.25	.42	.45	.55	.35	.30	.35
C:Slovenia-Spain	2	.17	.09	.74	.24	.76	.17	.24	.59
C:Norway-Yugoslavia	2	.50	.17	.33	.68	.32	.36	.28	.36
B:Turkey-Belgium	1	.21	.18	.61	.17	.83	.25	.29	.46
B:Italy-Sweden	1	.66	.16	.18	.98	.02	.48	.30	.46
A:England-Romania	2	.51	.22	.27	.68	.32	.50	.29	.21
A:Portugal-Germany	1	.45^a	.10	.45	.82	.18	.32	.27	.41
C:Yugoslavia-Spain	2	.39	.15	.46	.39	.61	.32	.30	.38
C:Slovenia-Norway	0	.25	.16	.59	.52	.48	.22	.28	.50
D:Denmark-Czech Rep	2	.00^b	.00^b	1.0	.50	.50	.27	.29	.44
D:France-Netherlands	2	.48	.00^b	.52	.54	.46	.33	.29	.38
1/4:Turkey-Portugal	2	.21	n.a.	.79	.15	.85	.28	.28	.44
1/4:Italy-Romania	1	.72	n.a.	.28	.62	.38	.50	.28	.22
1/4:Yugoslavia-Netherl.	2	.17	n.a.	.83	.11	.89	.25	.28	.47
1/4:Spain-France	2	.20	n.a.	.80	.22	.78	.28	.28	.44
1/2:France-Portugal	1	.69	n.a.	.31	.58	.42	.46	.29	.25
1/2:Italy-Netherlands	1	.49	n.a.	.51	.30	.70	.27	.28	.45
Final:France-Italy	1	.61	n.a.	.39	.64	.36	.43	.29	.28
Mean		.35	.13	.56	.42	.58	.32	.28	.40

^{a} Higher trading volume.
^{b} No trades in this contract.
^{c} Actual result: *First listed team win* (1), *draw* (0) or *second listed team win* (2).

That is, for game i the squared prediction loss can take on values from 0 (game is correctly predicted ($I(G_i = M_i) = 1$ with probability $P_i^* = 1$) to 1 (game is incorrectly predicted ($I(G_i = M_i) = 0$) with probability $P_i^* = 1$). Thus, a prediction based on a price of 99 is assigned a relatively small loss of $(1-.99)^2 = 0.01$ when compared to a prediction based on a price of 51 which is given $(1-.51)^2 = 0.2401$.

For games with three possible outcomes, we computed the squared prediction error as follows.

$$MSPL_3 = \frac{1}{n}\sum_{i=1}^{n}\left(I(G_i = M_i)\left[\frac{3}{4}\left(1 - P_i^*\right)\right]^2 + (1 - I(G_i = M_i))\left[\frac{3}{2}P_i^* + \frac{3}{4}\left(\frac{1}{3} - P_i^*\right)\right]^2\right)$$

We find that the match markets have the smallest mean squared prediction loss ($MSPL_m = 0.155$), when compared to the championship market ($MSPL_C = 0.215$) and the bookmaker ODDSET ($MSPL_O = 0.272$).

What Makes the Market Predict Accurately?

Further, we are concerned with the variables that make the market predict accurately. The following logistic regression investigates the dependence of the market's predictive success on variables, measuring market activity and market certainty. The dependent variable presents the correct prediction of an event's outcome.

$$Y_{m,i} = I(M_i = G_i) = \begin{cases} 1 & \text{if } M_i = G_i \\ 0 & \text{otherwise} \end{cases}$$

The explanatory variables include market certainty, calculated by $P^*_{m,i} = \max_j P_m(G_i = j)$ and a set of variables that are commonly used in the information aggregation literature. Berg et al. (1997) state, that the following variables influence the quality of the prediction: (1) number of contract types traded in a market (complexity of the market), (2) pre-election market volumes, and (3) differences in weighted market bid and ask queues on election eve. Berlemann and Schmidt (2001) find evidence for German data, that the absolute error rate of market prices, defined by the absolute difference between price of unit-portfolio at the bank and on the market, influences the market's prediction. In addition, we also tested whether number of traders, total volume and price volatility can account for the quality of the prediction.

It turned out, that only the market certainty $P^*_{m,i}$ has a significant effect. The effect is positive, therefore we conclude that the more confident the market, the more accurate the predictive performance. When we include further variables in the regression, including the absolute error rate of market prices and price volatility measured by the standard error of the price time series, we observe that the effect takes the expected direction, though the corresponding coefficients are not significant. For the following variables we observed a non-intuitive sign of the coefficient: market volume and number of contract types. The results of the logit regression are summarised in Table 3.

Finally, looking at the data of the bookmaker, we asked whether the certainty in the event's outcome is a significant factor. Therefore, we reran the logit regression for the highest probability of the ODDSET prediction $P^*_{m,i} = \max_j P_m(G_i = j)$. We observed that the effect of certainty noticed at the bookmaker is not significant.

Table 3.Logit fit of the determinants of predictive success

	Match markets[a]	Championship market[a]	ODDSET[a]
constant	-6.32	-8.38	-0.16
	(3.25)*	(4.18)*	(4.12)
$P^*_{m,i}$	11.97	13.34	1.52
	(5.64)*	(6.31)*	(8.92
n	21	20	19
Pseudo R^2	0.31	0.33	0.00

* Significant at the 5% level. Standard errors in parentheses.
[a] Dependent variable: $Y_{m,I}$: 1—if contract with highest implicit probability predicted the outcome correctly, 0—otherwise.

Discussion and Conclusions

In this chapter the predictive results of an experimental asset market drawn on a sports event were presented. The evaluation of the experiment's results was done by comparing to a benchmark model, the rolling dice, and the implicit prognosis of bookmaker's odds. The predictions were compared on the basis of statistical hypothesis testing.

The Euro 2000—won by France—consisted of few surprises. Given the outcome of the tournament, it turned out, that the market predicts more accurately than the random predictor. The qualitative predictions of the bookmaker's odds are not different from the market's prediction, yet the market was more accurate in terms of a quantitative mean square error. Moreover, the more certain the market predicts the outcome of an event, the more accurate is the prediction. A similar effect could not be observed with regards to the bookmaker's odds.

In the previous sections it turned out that the implicit probabilities generated from market prices differ from the bookmaker's probabilities. In the next step we ask how this observation can be used for the engagement in the different institutions. Overall, the market assigns relatively higher win probabilities to the favourites, whereas the bookmaker assigns relatively higher probabilities to the longshots. Therefore, a strategy to engage in the favourites is relatively higher rewarded at the bookmaker, and a strategy to engage in the longshots relatively pays-off at the market game.

Bets on a draw can be considered as "longshots", since in no case the markets and the bookmaker assigned the highest implicit probability in a single match. Since the markets provided binary contracts in the knockout stage and omitted the "draw" we are left with 14 observations in the group stage, only. Still, a clear pattern can be observed: assigned probabilities of the bookmaker are in the .20-.25 range and they are in every single match higher than in the market (see Table 2). Thus a strategy to engage in the draws is relatively higher rewarded at the market.--17

The data provides first evidence that the prediction markets on football outcomes assign relatively higher certainty on the favourites' winning and less certainty on the longshots' prospects when compared to the bookmaker. Further research should aim for a larger data sample, e.g. the complete season of a football league. This would provide the opportunity to test whether a (reversed) favourite-longshot bias can be observed with the market's prediction.

References

Berg, J., R. Forsythe, F. Nelson and T. Rietz (forthcoming). "Results from a Dozen Years of Election Futures Markets Research." *Handbook of Experimental Economics Results*, Elsevier.

Berg, J., R. Forsythe and T. Rietz (1997). "What Makes Markets Predict Well? Evidence from the Iowa Electronic Markets." In W. Albers, W. Güth, P. Hammerstein, B. Moldovanu and E. van Damme (eds). *Essays in Honor of Reinhard Selten*. Springer-Verlag, Berlin, pp. 444–463.

Berlemann, M. and C. Schmidt (2001). *Predictive Accuracy of Political Stock Markets – Empirical Evidence from a European Perspective*. Discussion paper, Sonderforschungsbereich 373, Humboldt-Universität zu Berlin.

Bochow, J., P. Raupach. and M .Wahrenburg (2002). "What do Market Makers achieve? Evidence from a large scale experimental stock market." In F. Bolle and M. Lehmann-Waffenschmidt (eds.). *Surveys in Experimental Economics - Bargaining, Cooperation and Election Stock Markets*, Springer.

Chen, K.-Y. and C. Plott (1998). *Prediction markets and information aggregation mechanism: Experiments and application*, Technical report, California Institute of Technology.

Dixon, M. and S. Coles (1997). "Modelling Association Football Scores and Inefficiencies in the Football Betting Market." *Applied Statistics* 46: 265–280.

Fama, E. F. (1970). "Efficient capital markets: A review of theory and empirical work." *The Journal of Finance*, 25(2): 383–417.

Forsythe, R. and R. Lundholm (1990). "Information aggregation in an experimental asset market." *Econometrica* 58(2): 309–347.

Forsythe, R., Nelson, F., Neumann, G. andWright, J. (1992). "Anatomy of an Experimental Political Stock Market." *American Economic Review* 82: 1142–1161.

Forsythe, R., T. Rietz. and T. Ross (1999). "Wishes, Expectations and Actions: A Survey on Price Formation in Election Stock Markets." *Journal of Economic Behavior and Organization* 39: 83–110.

Gandar, J., W. Dare, C. Brown and R. Zuber (1998). "Informed traders and price variations in the betting market for professional basketball games." *Journal of Finance* 53(1): 385–401.

Gandar, J., R. Zuber, T. O'Brien and B. Russo (1988). "Testing Rationality in the Point Spread Betting Market." *Journal of Finance* 43(4): 995–1008.

Garicano, L. and I. Palacios-Huerta (2005). *Sabotage in Tournaments: Making the Beautiful Game a Bit Less Beautiful.* CEPR Discussionpaper No. 5231.

Gray, P. and S. Gray (1997). "Testing Market Efficiency: Evidence from the NFL Sports Betting Market." *Journal of Finance* 52(4): 1725–1737.

Hanson, R. (1995). "Could Gambling Save Science? Encouraging an Honest Consensus." *Social Epistemology* 9(1): 3–33.

Hayek, F. (1937). "Economics and Knowledge." *Economica,* NS 4: 33-54.

Ortner, G. (2000). "Aktienmärkte als industrielles Vorhersagemodell." *Zeitschrift für Betriebswirtschaft,* ZfB-Ergänzungsheft 1/2000: 115–125.

Pennock, D., S. Lawrence, F. Nielsen and C. Giles (2001). "Extracting Collective Probabilistic Forecasts from Web Games." *Proceedings of the Seventh ACM SIGKDD International Conference on Knowledge Discovery and Data Mining* (KDD-2001).

Plott, C. (2000). "Markets as Information Gathering Tools." *Southern Economic Journal* 67: 2–15.

Plott, C. and S. Sunder (1988). "Rational expectations and the aggregation of diverse information in laboratory securities markets" *Econometrica* 56(5): 1085–1118.

Schmidt, C. (2003) *Predictive accuracy of experimental asset markets.* Shaker, Aachen.

Servan-Schreiber, E., J. Wolfers, D. M. Pennock and B. Galebach (2004). "Prediction Markets: Does Money Matter?" *Electronic Markets* 14(3): 243–251.

Thaler, R. and W. Ziemba (1988). "Parimutuel Betting Markets: Racetracs and Lotteries." *Journal of Economic Perspectives* 2(2): 161–174.

Vergin, R. and M. Scriabin (1978). "Winning Strategies for Wagering on National Football League Games." *Management Science* 24(8): 806–818

Chapter Seventeen

Accuracy, Certainty and Surprise - A Prediction Market on the Outcome of the 2002 FIFA World Cup

Carsten Schmidt, Martin Strobel and Henning Oskar Volkland[1]

The suspicion is that for all the caginess of the odd-setters, this year's Brazil are 1998's Germany—a team in terminal decline (Steve Davies, *Racing Post,* May 28, 2002).

If you can ever write off the Germans, it is this sorry bunch (Steve Davies, *Racing Post,* May 28, 2002).

No hiding place for Guus as Korea attempt to avoid home humiliation (Steve Davies, *Racing Post,* May 28, 2002).

[1] Schmidt: Sonderforschungsbereich 504, Mannheim University, L 13, 15, 68131 Mannheim, Germany, email: cschmidt@sfb504.uni-mannheim.de. Strobel: Department of Economics, Faculty of Economics and Business Administration, Maastricht University, P.O. Box 616, 6200 MD Maastricht, The Netherlands, email: m.strobel@algec.unimaas.nl. Volkland: Goldman Sachs & Co., Messeturm, 60308 Frankfurt am Main, Germany, email: oskar.volkland@gs.com. We would like to thank Patric Andersson and Pete Dawson for numerous comments and advice. This chapter is based on a master thesis Volkland has written under the supervision of Strobel. Schmidt revised, reorganised, added additional questionnaire data and shortened the manuscript to provide coherence with the previous chapter and to avoid redundancy. Stata do files of the statistical evaluation and the cdf plots can be made available upon request. Schmidt organised the experiment at the Max-Planck-Institute of Economics, Jena and gratefully acknowledges the financial support from the Max-Planck-Society and the Deutsche Forschungsgemeinschaft (SFB 504). Strobel gratefully acknowledges support from the Dutch Science Foundation (NWO) through the Vernieuwingsimpuls program.

In this chapter, we present our empirical investigation of the forecasting accuracy of a prediction market experiment drawn on the outcome of the World Cup 2002. We analyse the predictive accuracy of 64 markets and compare to bookmakers' quotes and chance as benchmarks. We revisit the evaluation of Schmidt and Werwatz (Chapter 16) and compare our results directly to their findings. In addition, we propose a new method for testing predictive accuracy by means of a non-parametric test for the similarity of probability distributions and we evaluate the incorporation of information in market prices by comparing pre-match and half-time price data.

We find a reversed favourite-longshot bias when analysing market prices before the start of the match and this bias does not disappear with the inflow of new information until half-time. Unlike the market based predictions bookmakers appear to be perfectly calibrated. Since there were substantial deviations in outcome between the 2000 European Championship and our data, we offer possible explanations for the much worse performance of the 2002 World Cup prediction market. Consistent with Schmidt and Werwatz (Chapter 16) prediction markets do assign relatively higher probabilities to the favourite when compared to the odds-setters. Together with a long streak of surprising outcomes this fact appears most likely to be responsible for the predictive inaccuracy.

The chapter empirically tests the efficient market hypothesis. The term was introduced into the economics literature by Hayek. He argued that investors communicate and coordinate their decisions through market prices (Hayek, 1937). The efficient market hypothesis in its most common form claims that financial markets are efficient in the sense that there is no persistent opportunity for abnormal returns based on the observation of past prices or taking into account all public and private information (Fama, 1970). As soon as new information becomes publicly available it is immediately absorbed and incorporated into market prices.

In particular we test the following hypotheses: (1) the markets should predict the outcomes of matches more precisely than chance, (2) the markets should generate more accurate implicit probabilities than the bookmakers' odds and (3) the markets' quotes should be meaningful in a sense that the more certain the market the more often the prediction of the market should be right.

The remainder of this chapter is organised as follows. Section 2 describes the experimental design and data. Section 3 briefly revisits and compares to Schmidt and Werwatz (Chapter 16). Section 4 introduces the new distribution-based test that provides for an alternative test of hypothesis 3. Section 5 looks at explanations for the poor prediction ability of the markets and Section 6 concludes.

The Experiment

The Football Event

The FIFA World Cup 2002 was held in South Korea and Japan. Thirty-two participating teams had qualified for the tournament through a system of regional competitions. The tournament was organised in two stages of 48 (group stage) and 16 (knockout stage) matches, respectively. In the group stage the teams played round robin in eight groups of four to qualify for the knockout stage. The winning team of a match in the group stage received three points; the losing team received zero points. In case of a draw after 90 minutes each team received one point. At the end of the first stage teams were ranked according to the total number of points won from the three group matches. In each group the teams ranked first and second advanced to the knockout stage. In the case that two or more teams obtained the same number of points the direct comparison, i.e. the result of the match against each other, was used as a tie-breaker.[2] Starting with the knockout stage, a game that was not decided after regular time was continued for a maximum additional time of thirty minutes. The first goal to be scored within this extra time, the so-called 'golden goal', decided the game. If a game was still not decided after the additional time, the match outcome would be determined by a penalty shootout. The winner of a game in the knockout stage would progress to the next round.

Experimental Setup

The market experiment used the same rules and software platform as Schmidt and Werwatz (Chapter 16) and was accessible from May 23rd, eight days before the start of the tournament. It remained available until July 2nd, two days after the finals. The first trading day was May 27th, four days before the opening match. Altogether 134 traders participated in the football markets, 72 (54%) were German. The other traders used the English speaking portal. The initial deposits in traders' accounts ranged from a minimum of 10 Euro to a maximum of 50 Euro.

---

[2] Further subordinate tie-breakers are the difference between the numbers of goals scored and received, with the advantage to the team with the higher positive difference, the total number of goals scored in the group stage, the FIFA country coefficient, and, finally, tossing a coin.

The number of participants is lower compared to the 2000 European Championship finals but the number of match markets was three times higher. The total commitment in monetary terms was € 3,893 with an average investment of € 29.05. Again, it is a zero sum game—thus no commission is charged and all investments will be redistributed and paid back to the participants. Both the total number of trades (19,839) and the average number of trades per participant (148) are five times greater than the corresponding figure for the 2000 European Championship market.

There were two categories of markets that traders could choose to trade in: the championship market and the 64 individual match markets. In the championship market securities issued on each of the 32 participating team were traded. The pay-offs had a winner-takes-all structure: only the contracts of the winning team, the "champion", paid-off at the end of the tournament, all other contracts expired worthless. The championship market was the only market that remained open for the entire time of the experiment. In the match markets contract design was similar to that of sports bets. During the group stage match market contracts were contingent on one of the three possible outcomes of a match: *first listed team win* (1), *draw* (0) and *second listed team win* (2). In the knockout stage the number of different contracts traded in each market was reduced to two as the contract corresponding to a draw was dropped. The winning contract in a match market, i.e. the contract contingent on the true outcome of a match, yielded a fixed pay-off. All other contracts expired worthless. On the day after a match the liquidation value of their contracts was forwarded to traders through their online accounts. This ensured that traders regained liquidity to reinvest in upcoming markets. The match markets were operated for a limited time prior to a match and closed with the end of this match. Participants could therefore continue to trade in match markets while matches were broadcast live on television. This was not possible in the 2000 European Championship match markets when individual markets were closed at the beginning of their respective game (Schmidt and Werwatz, Chapter 16).

Data

We use professional bookmakers' fixed odds as a further benchmark for evaluating the predictive accuracy of the market forecasts. For games in the group stage bets can be placed on any of the three outcomes at quotes set by the bookmaker. In the knockout stage the outcome *draw*, or 0, is assigned to games that are not decided after regular time.

We have collected two complete sets of betting odds offered by internet betting agencies. ODDSET data has also been used previously to evaluate the performance of the 2000 European Championship market (Schmidt and Werwatz, Chapter 16). Since ODDSET—which is run by the German state-owned lottery—only allows for German residents to engage in betting, we decided to add the English agency Eurobet to control for potential differences in country specific odds-setting. An obvious difference is due to the differences in competition: the German quasi-monopolist has a take-out rate of about 25% whereas the English betting agency charges roughly 10%.

We have taken the prices from the match markets prior to the start of the game in order to extract the markets' pre-game predictions. According to the theoretical framework described in the introduction prices in the markets should at all times aggregate all relevant information and expectations about the performance of competing teams. Therefore, the relative prices in a market should reflect opinion about the likelihood that the market assigns to the individual outcomes of a game. Moreover, we collected match markets' prices at half-time. This allows us to test whether new information—based on each team's performance during the first 45 minutes of play—is incorporated in prices and thus implicit probabilities converge to the outcome. In addition, we have collected pre-match prices of the championship market.

The contract with the highest price was selected as the market's predicted winner, i.e. the contract linked to the outcome deemed most likely by the market. We have taken the bets with the lowest quote to be the bookmakers' forecast of a game's outcome. In addition to the qualitative forecasts that the prediction markets and the bookmakers made about the winner of a game, we have also calculated the implicit probabilities assigned to each possible outcome from the market prices and betting odds, respectively.

There were six match markets in the group stage with incomplete trading, in the sense that one or two contracts were not traded at all. For example, in the market for the game Paraguay vs. South Africa there was no trade activity in the contracts *draw* and *second listed team win*, respectively. This was most likely due to a low interest in the match as implied by the low number of trades—8 trades compared to an average number of 38 trades (SD 29)—and the low trade volume—9 Eurocent compared to an overall average trade volume of 39 Eurocent (SD 37)—in the corresponding market. We are aware that assigning not traded contracts the probability 0 might give a flawed view of the market's assessment of the likelihood of the outcomes of the games. Therefore, we also did the empirical analysis by leaving out these matches. Because we did not find significant differences in the results between including and leaving out incomplete matches, the empirical analysis reported in this chapter is based on all 64 matches. This also enables us to directly compare our results with those of Schmidt and Werwatz (Chapter 16).

We observed the same prices for win and lose in the championship market in two matches. To generate a prediction of the outcome we resolve one tie in the championship market (South Korea vs. USA) by assigning the prediction to the contract with the higher pre-match trading volume. Prior to the small final contracts of the contestants South Korea and Turkey were already worthless in the championship market. We use the higher price of both teams' contracts on midnight prior to the first played of both half-finals to resolve this tie and get Turkey win as prediction.

Besides the three matches with equal odds by ODDSET and the one match with equal odds by Eurobet there has been only one disagreement between the bookmakers (Belgium vs. Russia) on the assignment of the highest win probability (the lowest odd). Therefore, we use in case of equal odds the prediction of the other bookmaker to resolve the tie when predicting the winner. Again, when leaving out matches with equal probabilities from the analysis the results do not change. In addition, we will use in the following section error measures that do not depend on the predicted outcome of the game.

Evaluation of the Predictive (In)Accuracy

Is the Market as Reliable as a Random Predictor?

In the following analysis we will revisit the three hypotheses of Schmidt and Werwatz (Chapter 16) and compare their findings with the results from our data. The first hypothesis makes use of a random predictor, a rolling dice, as a benchmark for the capability of the experimental markets to predict the outcome of uncertain events. We have obtained empirical data on the outcomes of matches in 13 past World Cups from www.fifa.com. The documentation is incomplete for the earlier tournaments in the sense that there is no reference to the first listed team in the official FIFA fixtures. We find 29.5% drawn matches in the group stage and the remaining 70.5% distributed over the two other outcomes. Andersson (Chapter 15) finds the teams listed first to be systematically higher ranked and to win more often compared to the teams listed second. Thus the two outcomes are not equally likely. In order to defend the applicability of the benchmark random dice model, we will use a thought model that randomly assigns the team of record, i.e. the team from which perspectives win or lose is defined. In fact, our following evaluation does not depend on the order of the fixtures. Hence, H_0 states the markets deliver uninformed, random predictions.

Let X_n be the number of correct predictions in n trials. We need to derive the distribution of X_n under the null hypothesis. Since 48 markets were based on three outcomes and 16 markets on two outcomes, $X_n = Y_{48} + Z_{16}$ is the sum of two binomial distributions with $Y_{48} \sim Bin(48,1/3)$ and $Z_{16} \sim Bin(16,1/2)$. We can reject H_0 in favour of H_1 with a one-sided test at a 5% significance level if we have 31 or more correct predictions.

The match markets correctly predicted the outcome of a match in 34 out of 64 cases. The championship market generated 32 correct predictions. The match markets at half-time (HT) performed best with 35 correct predictions. We can reject the null hypothesis that the match market and the championship market is an uninformed, random predictor on a conventional significance level.

Does the Market Beat the Odds?

Compared to the data of the 2000 European Championship markets, the 2002 World Cup markets' and the bookmakers' predictive performance were rather poor. Again, the prediction of the outcome—which is the event having the highest price in the markets and the one possessing the lowest odds with the bookmakers—is not different across markets and bookmakers. ODDSET and Eurobet correctly predicted 31 and 30 out of 64 matches, respectively. It should however be noted that in the knockout stage odd-setters have a disadvantage since they allow for three different outcomes. The distribution of X_n under the null hypothesis now reads $X_{64} \sim Bin(64,1/3)$ and H_0 can be rejected at a significance level of 5% having 29 or more correct predictions. Thus both odds-setters' predictions are significantly different from the predictions of a random dice. Table 1 provides frequencies of correct predictions for the group stage, the knockout stage and all matches.

Next we make use of the extra information inherent in the magnitude of the markets' predictions in order to evaluate whether the markets were able to generate superior forecasts when compared to the bookmakers as a benchmark. The first measure we employ is the mean squared prediction loss.

$$MSPL_2 = \frac{1}{n} \sum_{i=1}^{n} \left[Y_i - P_i^* \right]^2$$

Table 1. Relative frequency of correct predictions.

	Group stage	Knockout stage[a]	Total
Match market	.50*	.63	.53*
Match market HT	.54**	.56	.54*
Championship market	.46*	.63	.50*
ODDSET	.48*	.50	.48*
Eurobet	.46*	.50	.47*
N	48	16	64

* Significantly different from chance at the 5% level, ** significantly different from chance at the 1% level.
[a] Match markets allowed in the knockout stage for betting on *first listed team win* and *second listed team win* only.

For each game i the squared prediction error can take on values from 0, if a game is correctly predicted (Y_i=1) with probability P_i^*=1, to 1, if a game is incorrectly predicted (Y_i=0) with probability P_i^*=1. The set of predictions that yields the lowest MSPL is hence considered superior. The above formula gives the definition of the MSPL with 2 outcomes—Schmidt and Werwatz (Chapter 16) provide the definition of the MSPL with three outcomes.

The MSPL is higher in the championship market and the match market when compared to the bookmakers' predictions. The implicit predictions generated from ODDSET's quotes yielded the lowest MSPL of 0.249 with Eurobet relatively close at 0.256. The championship market had the highest error of 0.339 and the match market had an error of 0.300. Only after the first half of games was the match market able to somewhat narrow the gap with the bookmakers; the half-time mean squared prediction loss of the match markets is 0.268.

These results are in contrast to the 2000 European Championship data reported by Schmidt and Werwatz (Chapter 16). In their study the match market was found to be superior to the championship market and to the bookmaker ODDSET in terms of MSPL. The bookmakers' predictive accuracy has been rather constant over the tournaments with a slight improvement for ODDSET from 0.272 in 2000 to 0.249 in 2002.

As a second measure of forecast accuracy we employed the mean logarithmic score (MLS), which has been applied in other studies on prediction markets by, for example, Pennock et al. (2001) and Debnath et al. (2003).

$$MLS = \frac{1}{n}\sum_{i=1}^{n}\log P_i^R$$

Table 2. Mean squared prediction loss (MSPL), mean logarithmic score (MLS) and Brier score (BS).

	MSPL	MLS	BS
Match Market	0.300	-1.068	.629
Match Market half-time	0.268	-0.974	.574
Championship Market	0.339	n.a.	n.a.
ODDSET	0.249	-1.001	.588
Eurobet	0.256	-1.006	.593
N	64	64	64

Although both are measures of forecast accuracy, the MSPL and the MLS start from two different focal points. MLS is based on the probability assigned to the ex-post realisation P^R of match i rather than on the ex-ante prediction delivered by the highest probability. Therefore, it does not measure the (in)accuracy of a prediction about the anticipated winners, like MSPL, but rather the (in)accuracy of a prediction about the actual winners.

The MLS is defined with 0 being the maximum and negative infinity the minimum. Higher scores (scores closer to zero) are considered superior. The lower the score's value turns out to be the higher is the surprise of the market or bookmaker about the outcome. The results of our MLS calculation are reported in Table 2. For a comparison we also calculated the corresponding MLS values for the 2000 European Championship: -0.624 for the match markets and -0.980 for ODDSET respectively.[3]

The market's MLS in 2002 is lower than the MLS for the two bookmakers if we consider all matches. This finding is reversed when compared to the 2000 European Championship data. Again, ODDSET's predictive performance with respect to MLS has been rather constant across tournaments. Thus, both measures, the MSPL and the MLS, consistently provide evidence for predictive inaccuracy of the 2002 World Cup finals prediction market.

---

[3] We cannot provide a MLS for the championship markets, since the information obtainable from its prices allows for a statement about the anticipated winner only and not for a complete probability distribution over all three possible outcomes. To be more precise, the relative prices of two teams' contracts in the championship market do yield a probability assigned to the anticipated winner—the team with the higher contract price—but they do not yield a probability assigned to the outcome draw unless the two contracts were traded at the exact same price. There is no such case in the 2002 World Cup market data. Therefore, we leave out this type of markets from the MLS analysis.

In addition, we also computed the Brier score, which is the standard methodology for assessing probabilistic forecasts (see Yates, 1990).

$$BS = \frac{1}{n}\sum_{i=1}^{n}\sum_{s=1}^{S}(P_{si} - Y_{si})^2$$

For each possible outcome of the game S (*first listed team win, draw* and *second listed team win*) a squared error of its realisation Y_{si} (1 if outcome occurred, 0 otherwise) and its assigned probability P_{si} is aggregated. This parameter is averaged across matches *i*. Forrest et al. (2005) and Andersson (Chapter 15) report the Brier score for *win, draw* and *lose* separately. For a comparison with the Brier scores reported in Table 2 one has to aggregate their Brier score values over the three events.

The magnitude of the brier score is consistent with the results of the MSPL and the MLS. The prediction market before the start of the match performed worst (.629) and improved until half-time (.574). The bookmakers' Brier scores (.588 and .593, respectively) are lower compared to the market before the match. Again, the bookmakers are in a disadvantage by allowing for three outcomes in the 16 matches of the knockout stage compared to the two outcomes of the prediction market.

Determinants of Predictive (In)Accuracy

The next stage of the analysis is to identify variables that influence the accuracy of the market predictions. Assuming some forecasting power in the market predictions we should find that the more certain the market was the more often its predictions were correct. To this end, we follow Schmidt and Werwatz (Chapter 16) in using a logistic regression to quantify the effect of certainty on forecast accuracy for the championship market and the bookmakers. The results are reported in Table 3. It turns out that certainty—measured as the magnitude P_i^* of the contract with the highest probability—has a significant effect on the two bookmakers' predictions. This is not the case with pre-match predictions of the market; only at half-time the degree of certainty has a significant effect. Once again, these findings from the 2002 World Cup prediction market are not in line with the results of the 2000 European Championship market.

A Distribution-Based Test for Predictive (In)Accuracy

In this section we use a novel approach for testing the accuracy of market-generated predictions which tries to integrate the prediction of the

Table 3. Logit fit of the determinants of predictive success.

	Match market[a]	Match market HT[a]	Champion- ship market[a]	ODDSET[a]	Eurobet[a]
Constant	-1.167	-2.483	-2.589	-3.900	-3.558
	(1.290)	(1.181)*	(1.529)	(1.477)**	(1.344)**
$P^*_{m,i}$	1.887	3.916	3.161	7.688	6.678
	(1.851)	(1.704)*	(1.831)	(2.914)**	(2.559)**
N	64	64	64	64	64
Psydo R^2	0.01	0.07	0.04	0.09	0.09

* Significant at the 5% level, ** significant at the 1% level. Standard errors in parentheses.
[a] Deependent variable: $Y_{m,I}$: 1—if contract with highest implicit probability predicted the outcome correctly, 0—otherwise.

outcome and the certainty of the prediction. The test can be seen as an extension of Pennock et al. (2001) who sorted market predictions according to their prediction probability into different buckets. With each of the buckets they ran a binomial test with the average prediction probability as base probability.

Instead of grouping into buckets we order all different contracts—win, draw and lose—according to their assigned probability and give the value 1 to the winning contracts and 0 otherwise. The collection of all different contracts with their assigned values of 0 or 1 reflects a pseudo probability density function (pdf) of the distribution of the paying-off contracts. If we move along the probability spectrum from 0 to 1 and add up the assigned binary values of the contracts we get a trace of the cumulative frequency of the 64 contracts that actually paid-off. In other words, the cumulative frequency of success mimics the cumulative distribution function (cdf) of the distribution of the 64 paying-off contracts among the total number of different contracts. This pseudo cdf is a step function that makes 64 jumps of constant height of 1/64, each at a point within the probability spectrum that corresponds to one of the 64 paying-off contracts. In what follows, we will refer to this pdf and cdf as the actual distribution of success, since it mirrors the way the tournament has evolved ex-post. If predictions were accurate, then from the segment of the probability spectrum around .10 about one in ten contracts should have won, two out of ten contracts around .20, and so on. We call this the actual cdf.

A second distribution will be called the theoretical distribution, since it mirrors the way that the prediction markets and the bookmakers have theoretically (ex-ante) anticipated the tournament to evolve. We assign to each different contract the value of its market- or odds-setter determined probability. Naturally, the resulting cdf has many more jumps than the actual cdf, each of unequal height. A jump occurs at each value from the probability spectrum of the three (two) different outcomes of the 64 events. The height of this jump is determined by the value of the probability assigned to the particular contract. Predictive accuracy is positively related to similarity in shape and, hence, the closeness of the actual and the theoretical cdf.

We introduce a third distribution in order to reconsider some results from earlier sections that used the random predictor as a benchmark for predictive accuracy. It assumes that there is absolutely no predictive power in markets' and bookmakers' implicit probabilities. We call it the agnostic distribution, since it assigns the same probability to all different contracts. The height of the jumps of the agnostic cdf is constant at the value 1/N, with N being the total number of different contracts. Since the markets allow for two different contracts in the knockout stage and the bookmakers for three we get N=176 for the markets' cdf and N=192 for the bookmakers' cdf. Again, each jump occurs at the market or bookmaker assigned probability.

We observe that the distribution of the probabilities the markets assigned to events ranges from 0 to 1—when not considering the 6 matches with incomplete contracts the range is 0.01 to 0.97—whereas the distribution of the bookmakers' implicit probabilities is less extreme. Eurobet issued quotes with an implicit probability from 0.04 to 0.82 whilst ODDSET seems to publish the most conservative quotes with values ranging from 0.08 to 0.73 (compare x-axis, Figure 1).

The convex shape of the markets' theoretical cdf displayed in Figure 1 in both upper panels provides evidence for a too high concentration of implicit probabilities at the very high and very low end of the probability spectrum. Furthermore, this high degree of certainty in the markets' assigned probabilities implies a relatively flat increase of the cdf over the middle range of probability. This appears to be because extreme positions tend to drive out conservative mid-range bets. As a consequence, the degree of certainty in the markets influences the degree of convexity of the theoretical cdf.

In other words the market participants systematically over-estimated very likely outcomes and under-estimated very unlikely outcomes. This observation provides evidence for the presence of a reversed favourite-longshot bias in markets' prices, stating that bettors overestimate the favourites' probability of winning and underestimate the longshots' probability of winning. The reversed favourite-longshot biased can be

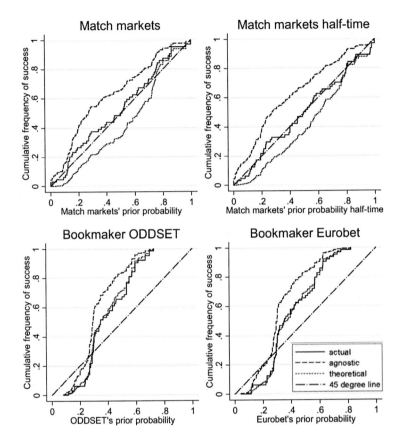

Figure 1. Actual-, theoretical- and agnostic cdf of the distribution of successes. Predictive accuracy is positively related to similarity in shape and closeness of the theoretical and the actual cdf.

observed for the markets at half-time as well meaning that the inflow of new information does not drive out the bias. This bias cannot be observed for the bookmakers' quotes.

In the next step we formally test the closeness and similarity of shape of the three different distributions. If the realisation of the football tournament is not different from a rolling dice we should not find a

Table 4. Kolmogorov-Smirnov test of the similarity of the cumulative distribution.

Hypothesis	Match market[a]	Match market HT[a]	ODDSET[a]	Eurobet[a]
1 theoretical vs. agnostic	0.341***	0.341***	0.177**	0.193***
2 actual vs. agnostic	0.210***	0.256***	0.224***	0.198***
3 theoretical vs. actual	0.296***	0.205***	0.068	0.089
N	176	176	192	192

** Significant at the 1% level, *** significant at the 0.1% level.
[a] Kolmogorov-Smirnov test statistic D

significant difference between the agnostic and the actual cumulative distribution. If the markets and bookmakers predict well, we should not find significant differences between the theoretical and the actual cumulative distribution. If the markets and bookmakers do not take any information into account we should not find significant differences between the theoretical and the agnostic distribution. We formulate the following hypotheses:

H1: *The market's/bookmakers' prediction is not systematically different than would be predicted by a random predictor (theoretical vs. agnostic).*

H2: *The actual realisation is not systematically different than would be predicted by a random predictor (actual vs. agnostic).*

H3: *The market's/bookmakers' prediction is not systematically different from the actual realisation (theoretical vs. actual).*

We use a Kolmogorov-Smirnov equality-of-distributions test.[4] The results of the hypothesis tests are provided in Table 4. We can reject the first hypothesis for all sources and find that the market prediction and the bookmakers' quotes do differ from a random predictor. We can reject the second hypothesis and find that the actual realisation of the tournament's outcomes is different from rolling a dice. Finally, we are unable to reject

---

[4] We are aware of the fact that the three (two) contracts of a match are not iid and significance levels might be inflated. An alternative way to proceed is to consider one of the three outcomes only. Since the FIFA fixtures of *first listed team win* and *second listed team win* are not random it is not possible to provide a unique agnostic cdf. We have tested hypothesis 3 for all three possible outcomes separately. We find the D statistic of the K-S test in the match market (at half-time) for *first listed team win* 0.297** (0.156), *draw* 0.271* (0.229) and *second listed team win* 0.219[+] (0.266*). There are no significant differences when comparing the distribution of the cdf of actual outcome to bookmakers' predictions.

the third hypothesis for the two bookmakers, thus we are not able to find significant differences between bookmakers' predictions and actual realisation. This is not the case with the markets, which observe significant differences between the distribution of the prediction and actual realization. The two lower panels of Figure 1 visualise the test results: bookmakers' actual and theoretical cdf appear to be quite similar across the full range of the probability spectrum. The bookmakers seem to be perfectly calibrated, whereas the markets are biased when considering very low and very large probabilities. In general, the rather close correspondence between the test results from our new method with the findings of the previous sections mutually confirms our results.

Two Explanations for the Predictive (In)Accuracy

Prior beliefs

The rather poor predictive accuracy appears to be evidence against the functioning of the markets as an information aggregation mechanism that is able to accurately predict the outcomes of uncertain events. However, previous studies on laboratory experiments and prediction markets have, in the majority of cases, presented highly convincing results in favour of the information aggregation potential of the markets (Plott and Sunder, 1988, Sunder, 1995, Hanson, 1998; Gruca et al., 2003). Besides, a substantial fraction of traders in the 2002 markets had already participated in the 2000 European Championship experiment. This casts further doubt on the idea of a structural problem of the markets' design.

A remaining hypothesis is that the 2002 World Cup markets were able to accumulate and to process the information held by the participants, but that traders were just collectively wrong too often. Gruca et al. (2003) have used a prediction market in a laboratory experiment in order to examine the relationship between the aggregation of trader information and the accuracy of a forecast of new product success. The authors find a high degree of effectiveness in aggregating information but a relatively bad forecast accuracy. They could not verify a strong relationship between the degree of aggregation and forecasting accuracy and therefore promote a careful distinction between these two outwardly similar concepts.

In order to determine whether traders were collectively wrong we will evaluate the a priori expectations of traders. A questionnaire was presented to the subjects when they logged in for the very first time. Since we decided to ask for prior beliefs before the first match only, we are left

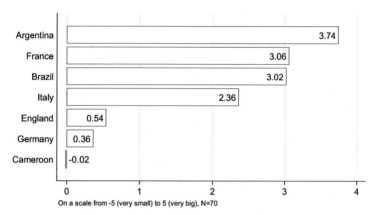

Figure 2. "What is the likelihood a team will win the championships?" Selected teams from the self-reported subject questionnaire filled out at the first login and prior to the start of the tournament.

with responses from 70 out of 134 traders. We asked them to rate the probability a team will be the overall champion from -5 (very small) to 5 (very big). Figure 2 displays selected teams.

It turns out that not many of the traders' prior beliefs were confirmed by subsequent match outcomes. The traders in our experiment appear to have had difficulties in judging the prospects of seemingly strong teams. The most prominent example of a "surprise team" was the defending champion France, who failed to score in their three group matches and who consequently did not qualify for the knockout stage. The probability of a victory for France in the opening match against Senegal was set at 75% by the match market before kick-off. For the record, France took its assigned 9% chance and lost this game. One might ask whether the traders reacted upon the observed performance of a team over the course of the tournament and adjusted their expectations accordingly.

However, a second look at the probability assigned to a victory of the obviously weak French in the two subsequent group matches does not imply such expectation-revising behaviour: it was 77% in the match against Uruguay (final outcome 0:0, 14%), and 73% in the match against Denmark (final outcome 0:2, 12%). The market remained uncritically certain that the French would still qualify from the group.

There is, however, another aspect that supports the idea of a collectively wrong perception about the matches and their likely outcomes

Table 5. Odds for the 2002 World Cup winner published three days in advance of the start of the tournament.

	Bet365	Bet Direct	Coral	William Hill	Ladbrokes
France	7-2	3	4	3	3
Argentina	5	9-2	9-2	9-2	9-2
Italy	9-2	5	5	5	5
Brazil	11-2	6	6	11-2	6
England	14	14	10	9	9
Germany	14	12	14	16	20
Cameroon	33	40	40	25	33

Source: *Racing Post* World Cup 2002 Preview Pull-out. May 28, 2002.

that does not contradict our assumption of a well functioning information aggregation mechanism. In more than 90% of the games the predictions of the match markets as well as bookmakers hinted at the exact same outcome. Recall that the bookmakers in our sample represent experts from two different countries. Since the numbers of correctly predicted outcomes are also more or less stable across prediction markets and bookmakers we might say that traders and experts did all share essentially the same a priori information and both equally surprised by the final outcomes.

On May 28th, 2002, three days before the start of the tournament, the British sports betting journal Racing Post published a pull-out with all tournament related bets offered by British betting agencies. Total betting turnover was said to dwarf any other sporting event with an estimated £200m staked in the UK, twice the 2000 European Championship total.[5] Given this enormous financial outlay we believe that UK betting agencies qualified as experts on the upcoming event. Table 5 shows a selection of the quotes of the tournament's extended set of favourites published in the pull-out in order to sketch the a priori consensus opinion of most experts. There is no disagreement between bookmakers and only slight disagreement between market participants and bookmakers. For example market traders identified Argentina as the tournament favourite and bookmakers the then-defending champion France. Nevertheless, neither France nor Argentina did well in the 2002 World Cup. To this end we are convinced that there was a big surprise element about the actual outcomes among bookmakers and traders.

---

[5] In *Racing Post* World Cup 2002 Preview Pull-out. May 28, 2002.

Table 6. Correlations of the degree of certainty measured as probability of the favourite across market's and bookmakers' predictions.

Probability of win by the favourite P^*_i Correlations (lower part)	Match market	Match market half-time	Champ-ionship market	ODDSET	Eurobet
Mean (SD)	.67 (.13)	.67 (.16)	.82 (.15)	.50. (.10)	.52 (.12)
Median	.71	.67	.86	.51	.49
N	64	64	64	64	64
Match market	1				
Match market half-time	.67	1			
Championship market	.50	.32	1		
ODDSET	.53	.33	.66	1	
Eurobet	.43	.25	.62	.95	1

Biased quantitative predictions, preferences for the favourite and commissions

The next part of the investigation is to establish the markets' relatively poor accuracy with respect to the bookmakers' quotes on a quantitative level. The bookmakers do not appear to have been able to aggregate more or "better" information given their equally low numbers of correctly predicted outcomes. The markets and the bookmakers predicted the same outcomes in more than 90% of the matches. As a consequence, their respective number of incorrect predictions is also approximately the same. Nevertheless, the markets' MSPL is considerably higher than bookmakers' prediction error. Recall that the MSPL rewards and punishes a high degree of certainty in case of a correct prediction and in case of a false prediction, respectively. With the many incorrect predictions at hand, a more conservative approach is likely to have been rewarded. Therefore, we believe that the prediction markets on football are more certain by assigning higher probabilities to their anticipated winners. This effect should be strongest in the championship market that has produced the highest MSPL over the whole tournament (see Table 3). However, it should be intuitively clear that the average certainty is the highest in the championship market, since its win-lose prediction guarantees a minimum probability of .5 to an anticipated winner. The bookmakers on the other hand have been less certain about their favourites and avoided assigning extremely high (or low) probabilities to any single outcome.

Table 7. Number of games and MSPL forecast error by correctly and incorrectly predicted games, European Championship 2000 experiment for comparison.

		World Cup 2002		European Championship 2000[a]	
	Prediction	N	MSPL	N	MSPL
Match market	Correct (Incorrect)	34 (30)	.07 (.55)	15 (6)	.08 (.39)
Match market HT	Correct (Incorrect)	35 (29)	.06 (.51)	-	-
Championship market	Correct (Incorrect)	32 (32)	.04 (.64)	14 (7)	.08 (.43)
ODDSET	Correct (Incorrect)	31 (33)	.13 (.36)	13 (8)	.18 (.37)
Eurobet	Correct (Incorrect)	30 (34)	.12 (.38)	-	-

[a]Source: Schmidt and Werwatz (Chapter 16).

Table 6 provides some insight into the differences in predictions and certainty from a comparison of the favourites' probabilities across prediction markets and bookmakers. The two bookmakers exhibit roughly the same degree of certainty and a high correlation. The pre-match and half-time predictions from the match market are also quite close to each other, although their correlation is less than that of the bookmakers. As expected, the certainty about its predictions was highest in the championship market.

The implication of the high degree of certainty in the markets can be observed from the comparison of the prediction error produced in correctly and incorrectly predicted games (see Table 7). Whenever the markets' predictions were correct they yielded an extremely low forecast error (0.07, 0.06 and 0.04 per correct game), much lower than ODDSET and Eurobet (0.13 and 0.12 per correct game). Whenever the predictions were incorrect, however, the opposite is true: the markets produced a per-game forecast error that was much higher than the corresponding odds-setter's error (0.55, 0.51 and 0.64 vs. 0.36 and 0.38). This pattern is roughly the same as in the 2000 European Championship experiment. The high degree of certainty that was the greatest strength of the markets in the less surprising 2000 situation has become their greatest weakness in the highly surprising 2002 tournament.

We now consider a possible explanation for the weak calibration of the predictions' generated from the 2002 World Cup market. The literature has attributed biases in predictions to be due to a preference for the favourite and differences in commission (Williams and Panton, 1998). The so called reversed favourite-longshot bias has been observed in the baseball fixed odds betting market (Woodland and Woodland, 1994, 2003), which is characterised by comparatively low commissions. Smith et al. (2006) find a reduced favourite longshot bias in exchange based betting when they compared to fixed odds in horse racing. Preferences for favourites on the demand side have been reported by Levitt (2004) who finds bettors to have a higher demand for wagers on the favourites in American football fixed-spread betting.

The high degree of certainty by market participants with respect to their favourites goes hand in hand with a low degree of certainty for longshots (see Figure 1). Together with the differences in commissions— the markets did not charge any commission whereas ODDSET's and Eurobet's take is substantial—the observed reversed favourite-longshot bias with the markets is in line with the predictions of Williams and Panton (1998).

Conclusions

In this chapter we have evaluated the predictive performance of experimental asset markets that were conducted during the 2002 World Cup. Contracts in the markets were contingent on the outcomes of football matches. According to the theory of efficient markets and rational expectations, contract prices from the markets should be the best available forecast for the outcome of a match since they reflect the consensus opinion of all traders about the match. Previous work in the field, in particular the study of Schmidt and Werwatz (Chapter 16) based on the 2000 European Championship, found a predictive performance of markets that was superior to forecasts from odds-setters.

In this chapter we find market performance and bookmaker performance to be significantly different from a random predictor. In contrast to the findings from the preceding 2000 European Championship experiment, the market's predictions were less accurate than the predictions from two expert bookmakers. In addition, the certainty of the market's prediction was not significant in explaining the predictive success of the markets. In fact, no explanatory factor could be identified that was significant in explaining predictive accuracy by the markets. We argue that the nature of the underlying sports event is a key element in explaining the deviations in outcome between the two studies. The aggregation of all relevant a priori information about a sports event may well be a feasible task for markets of our type, but that does not imply that the resulting forecast is necessarily of superior accuracy. The 'human' factor remains too high in the football game and does at times lead to surprising outcomes as was quite apparent in the 2002 World Cup. Consistently with Schmidt and Werwatz (Chapter 16) we found the implicit probabilities derived from market prices to be more certain about the outcome than the probabilities derived from bookmakers' odds. This certainty was met by the many surprising outcomes and has resulted in the poor predictive performance by the markets. The bookmakers on the other hand took much less extreme stakes and were not hit as hard by the surprising outcomes. Betting behaviour and the degree of certainty of the implicit probabilities generated from market prices and bookmakers' odds were remarkably alike across experiments, and we therefore favour surprise as the chief explanation for the difference in findings.

The favourite-longshot bias, stating that bettors overestimate the longshots' probability of winning, is well recorded in the racetrack literature. It has recently been investigated in another Iowa Electronic Market type experiment (Berg and Rietz, 2002). The authors find in their study that there exists a reverse favourite-longshot bias that is attributable to overconfidence among traders. As a consequence, contracts with relatively bad win prospects are priced significantly too low and vice versa. The price data from the 2002 World Cup markets is consistent with this finding.

We further developed and implemented a new approach to test for the accuracy of market-generated predictions. Specifically we used a Kolmogorov-Smirnov test for a comparison of the empirical distribution function of match outcomes with the distribution of all prediction market and bookmaker predictions. It turned out that the distribution of the market predictions was significantly different from the distribution of the tournament's actual outcome. This is not the case with both bookmakers who are perfectly calibrated in the 2002 World Cup. Nonetheless, the market predictions (and the bookmakers' predictions) were significantly different from a random predictor. We consider these results to provide further support for our previous explanations.

Further research should aim for more participation in the markets that will generate more data for more sophisticated analyses. In particular, the new opportunity to keep trading during matches has generated limited additional data in the 2002 World Cup experiment. Thus, we could not have made any meaningful analysis of how prices react to events during a game. Gil and Levitt (2008) use intrade data from the 2002 World Cup and study contracts while the game is played. They find mixed evidence for market efficiency in this market: prices react to goals, yet prices continue to trend higher for 10 to 15 minutes after the goal. We were able to show that in the context of the 2002 World Cup prediction market prices react with respect to predictive accuracy to new information inflow until half-time. Yet, this new information at half-time is not able to drive out the reverse favourite-longshot bias observed with market prices in the 2002 World Cup prediction market.

Predicting the outcome of football matches is a highly uncertain task. An empirical argument was put forward by Wagenaar (1988), who argued that transitivity with respect to the match outcome among teams in World Cup games is rare. For the 2002 World Cup competition Group D might serve as an illustrative example where the transitivity of outcomes is violated: USA won over Portugal, Portugal over Poland, yet Poland succeeded over the USA. One underlying reason why chance plays such a big role in football outcomes might be the game's low scoring property. It remains an open issue for further empirical investigations whether the degree of surprise in the 2002 World Cup is the norm for World Cup and European Championship matches or an outlier.

References

Andersson, P. (2008). "Expert Predictions of Football: A Survey of the Literature and an Empirical Inquiry into Tipsters' and Odds-Setters' Ability to Predict the World Cup." In *Myths and facts about football: The economics and psychology of the world's greatest sport.* P. Andersson, P. Ayton and C. Schmidt. eds. Cambridge: Cambridge Scholars Press.

Berg, J. and T. Rietz (2002). *Longshots, Overconfidence and Efficiency on the Iowa Electronic Market.* Working paper, University of Iowa.

Debnath, S., D. Pennock, S. Lawrence, E. Glover, and C. Giles (2003). "Characterizing Efficiency and Information Incorporation in Sports Betting Markets." In *Proceedings of the Fourth Annual ACM Conference on Electronic Commerce* (EC'03).

Fama, E. F. (1970). "Efficient Capital Markets: A Review of Theory and Empirical Work." *The Journal of Finance*, 25(2):383–417.

Forrest, D., J. Goddard and R. Simmons (2005). "Odds-Setters as Forecasters: The Case of English Football." *International Journal of Forecasting*, 21(3), 551-564.

Gil, R. and S. D. Levitt (2008). "Testing the Efficiency of Markets in the 2002 World Cup." *The Journal of Prediction Markets*, 1 (3): 255-270.

Gruca, T., J. Berg, and M. Cipriano (2003). *Limits to Information Aggregation in Electronic Prediction Markets.* Working paper, University of Iowa.

Hanson, R. (1998) "Consensus by Identifying Extremists." *Theory and Decision*, 44(3):293-301.

Hayek, F. (1937). "Economics and Knowledge." *Economica,* NS 4, 33-54, 1937.

Levitt, S. D. (2004). "Why are Gambling Markets Organised so Differently from Financial Markets?" *The Economic Journal*, 114: 223-246.

Pennock, D., S. Lawrence, C. Giles, and F. Nielsen (2001). "Extracting Collective Probabilistic Forecasts from Web Games." In *Proceedings of the Seventh ACM SIGKDD International Conference on Knowledge Discovery and Data Mining* (KDD-2001).

Plott, C. and S. Sunder. (1998). "Rational Expectations and the Aggregation of Diverse Information in Laboratory Security Markets." *Econometrica*, 56(5):1085-1118.

Schmidt, C. and A. Werwatz. (2008). "How Accurately Do Markets Predict the Outcome of an Event? The Euro 2000 Football Experiment." In *Myths and facts about football: The economics and psychology of the world's greatest sport.* P. Andersson, P. Ayton and C. Schmidt. eds. Cambridge: Cambridge Scholars Press.

Smith, M. A., W. D. Paton and L. V. Williams (2006). "Market Efficiency in Person-to-Person Betting." *Economica* 73, 673–689.

Sunder, S. (1995). "Experimental Asset Markets: A Survey." In J. Kagel and A. Roth, editors, *The Handbook of Experimental Economics*, Princeton University Press, 415-500.

Wagenaar, W. A. (1988). *Paradoxes of Gambling Behavior.* Hove: Lawrence Erlbaum Associates.

Woodland, L. M and Woodland, B. M. (1994). "Market Efficiency and the Favourite-Longshot Bias: The Baseball Betting Market." *Journal of Finance*, 49: 269-279.

Woodland, L. M and Woodland, B. M. (2003). "The Reverse Favourite-Longshot Bias and Market Efficiency in Major League Baseball: An Update." *Bulletin of Economic Research*, 55(2): 113-123.

Williams, L. V. and D. Panton (1998). "Why are Some Favourite-Longshot Biases Positive and Others Negative?" *Applied Economics*, 30: 1505-1510.

Yates, J .F. (1990). *Judgment and Decision Making.* Englewood Cliffs, NJ: Prentice Hall.

CHAPTER EIGHTEEN

TEAM PERFORMANCE AND INDIVIDUAL CAREER DURATION: EVIDENCE FROM THE GERMAN BUNDESLIGA

BERND FRICK, GUNNAR PIETZNER AND JOACHIM PRINZ[1]

Player careers in professional team sports are, on average, of a rather short duration, i.e. few players manage to survive in the respective top division for more than just two or three seasons. In most cases, players have to retire quite early either due to an injury or because they are unable to reach the required level of skill and fitness (as in the case of "newcomers") or they are unable to maintain their performance levels (as in the case of "veteran players"). Moreover, contrary to the situation in the "hermetic" Major Leagues in the United States, where incumbent players are threatened by upcoming youngsters only, the relegation system that is being used across all Western European team sports leagues[2] has an additional threat to the teams' athletes: Being on the roster of one of the poorly performing teams may mean that a talented and successful player has to leave the league without a reasonable chance to return.

[1] Frick: Corresponding author, Department of Management, University of Paderborn, Warburger Strasse 100, 33098 Paderborn, Germany. E-mail: bernd.frick@notes.upb.de Pietzner: Ramboll Management, Kieler Strasse 301, 22525 Hamburg, Germany. E-mail: gunnar.pietzner@ramboll-management.com, Prinz: Department of Management, University of Paderborn, Warburger Strasse 100, 33098 Paderborn, Germany. E-mail: joachim.prinz@wiwi.uni-paderborn.de, Pietzner: Ramboll Management, Kieler Strasse 301, 22525 Hamburg, Germany. E-mail: gunnar.pietzner@ramboll-management.com
[2] For an economic analysis of the promotion and relegation system in the English football league see Noll (2002).

The aim of our study is, therefore, twofold: First, we want to identify the individual characteristics that influence the duration of player careers and, second, we try to isolate the impact of team performance on individual career length by particularly looking at the relative importance of the relegation system. Therefore, we analyse the duration of player careers in the top division of professional football in Germany, the "1st Bundesliga". Since playing in a first division team is far more lucrative in terms of salaries and endorsement contracts than playing in a second division club—or even further down in the league hierarchy (see Frick 2007)—we restrict our analysis to player careers in the first division of professional football in Germany.

Our paper is structured as follows: Section 2 offers a review of the available literature and section 3 provides a brief description of the structure of the promotion and relegation system in professional football in Germany. Section 4 describes the data set, section 5 introduces the estimation methods used and section 6 presents our empirical findings. We conclude with a summary and some implications for further research (section 7).

Literature Review

A number of studies have looked at the factors influencing career length in professional team sports. Using a random sample of players entering the National Football League between 1971 and 1980 (n=260 quarterbacks, running backs and wide receivers), Atkinson and Tschirhardt (1986) report an average career length of 4.5 years. Among the statistically significant individual characteristics affecting a player's career length are his race, academic achievements, position and physical fitness: Black players have—other things equal—shorter careers than white players, quarterbacks survive longer in the NFL than either running backs or wide receivers, players with a bachelor's degree are less likely to be cut from the league than those without academic credentials and players with serious lower-body injuries have to retire earlier. Moreover, players under contract with more successful teams (i.e. those with a higher winning percentage) are likely to remain in the league for longer periods of time.

Hoang and Rascher (1999) analyse the careers of all players selected in the first two rounds of the 1980-1986 NBA draft (n=275) and calculate an average duration of 5.9 years. They find that individual performance has the expected impact on the duration of player careers: While the number of games played per season and the number of points per minute reduce the risk of being cut from the league, the number of injuries and a high draft number increase the exit probability. Controlling not only for individual performance, but also for team characteristics (arena capacity, winning percentage) they also find strong evidence of higher exit rates for black players: White players have a 36 percent lower hazard rate than black players which translates into an expected career length of 7.5 years for the former and 5.5 years for the latter group.

Replicating the latter study with data from the 1989-1999 seasons (n=1,113 different players; 4,476 player-year-observations), Groothuis and Hill (2004) report an average career length of 5.7 years. They also find that individual performance increases career length. In particular, the number of games played in a season, the number of assists per minute, blocks per minute and points per minute all increase the probability of remaining in the NBA for another season. Moreover, players with higher draft numbers have shorter careers even after controlling for individual performance. Perhaps surprisingly, exit discrimination of black players is found not to exist any longer. The latter finding is explained by the fact that the fans' preferences for winning have recently superseded their racial preferences.[3]

Spurr and Barber (1994) analyse the career prospects of baseball players entering two different minor leagues in the US (the "A" League and the "Rookie" League) in the period 1975-1988. Controlling for player age they find that the more a pitcher's performance diverged from the mean in either direction, the less time was required to make a decision about that player's future: Those who did best were promoted soonest and those who did worst were first to be terminated. In the estimations, earned run average and strikeouts per inning turned out as the best predictors of a player's promotion/termination probability.

Using data from Japanese professional baseball during the period 1977-1990 (n=595 batters with 2,900 player-year observations and 395 pitchers with 1,719 player-year observations), Ohkusa (2001) calculates an average career length of 7 years. He finds that, first, a higher income reduces the quit probability for both groups and that, second, the individual productivity (the slugging rate for batters and the hit rate for pitchers) also significantly reduces the probability of being cut from the league.

---

[3] Since the percentage of non-German players in the Bundesliga has increased considerably over the last 40 years - recently, more than half of the active players were born abroad - we will control, inter alia, for player nationality in our estimations (see below).

Finally, Goddard and Wilson (2004) find that in English football in the seasons 1986-2002 average career duration was about six years. The sample they use consists of some 25,000 player-year-observations from all four divisions. It appears that before as well as after the "Bosman-ruling" a player's age, his position on the field, the number of previous clubs and the number of appearances all have an impact on the exit hazard: Other things equal, older players are more likely to be cut from the league, defenders, midfielders and particularly forwards survive for shorter periods of time than goalkeepers (the reference category) and a higher number of employers increases the risk of being cut from the league. Moreover, the higher the number of career appearances and the number of appearances in the recent employment spell, the more likely a player is to survive in his current division. We emphasise here that contrary to our measure of career duration (section 4), Goddard and Wilson (2004) continue to observe players who are transferred from a first division team to a second, third, or fourth division club.

Organisation of the Relegation System

In the summer of 1963 the Bundesliga started its inaugural season with 16 teams that had been admitted out of 46 applicants. Eleven years later a second division (with a Northern and a Southern league) was introduced. The latter two leagues merged before the season 1981/82 to form the 2nd Bundesliga. Following the reunification of East and West Germany, the 1st Bundesliga in 1991/92 was expanded to twenty teams to integrate the two top teams from the former 1st division in East Germany. In the same year the 2nd Bundesliga was once again divided in a Northern and a Southern division with 12 teams each to integrate six more top teams from the former GDR. While the 1st Bundesliga reduced its size again after only one season by relegating four teams and promoting only two, the 2nd Bundesliga played a second season with 24 teams, but this time in one division, i.e. each team had to play 46 games instead of 22 in the season before (for an overview see Frick 2006).

Thus, although the organisational structure of professional football in Germany has been modified several times during the last forty years, the number of promoted and relegated teams has remained fairly constant: While in the first decade (1963/64-1973/74) the two worst performing teams were relegated at the end of the season, that number was increased to three in the following seven years (1974/75-1980/81). Between 1981/82 and 1990/91 the team ranked 16th in 1st Bundesliga had to play against the

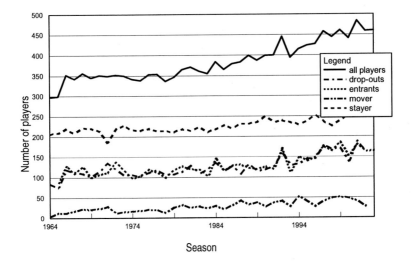

Figure 1: Labour Market Dynamics in the Bundesliga (1963/64-2002/03).

team ranked 3rd in 2nd Bundesliga to determine the final member of the 1st Bundesliga for the season to come. Since 1992/93, it is again the three worst performing teams in the 1st Bundesliga that are relegated to the second division and replaced by the three best performing clubs from 2nd Bundesliga.[4]

Albeit rather limited in size, the labour market we study has been growing rapidly during the last four decades. Competing in the national championship, one of the European cup competitions and the national cup competition can easily result in up to 50 matches per season. Moreover, many of the top players are also active for their home country's national team, which can easily result in an additional 10-12 matches per

---

[4] Due to this promotion and relegation system, 48 different clubs have spent at least one season in the top tier of German football over the first 40 seasons (1963/64-2002/03). Some clubs (1. FC Nuernberg, VfL Bochum, Bayer Uerdingen and Hannover 96) have been promoted five times in the period under investigation, while a number of other teams (Fortuna Duesseldorf, FC St. Pauli Hamburg, Kickers Offenbach, Karlsruher SC and Hertha BSC Berlin) have gained admission to the top tier of German professional football four times each. Teams such as Blau-Weiss 90 Berlin, Tasmania Berlin, Preussen Muenster, SSV Ulm, VfB Leipzig have been relegated after their first season and never showed up again in the Bundesliga.

year (in 2006, for example, the German national team played 18 matches).
Thus, particularly the top teams had to increase their squads in order to be
able to offer their players the opportunity to recover from competition as
well as from injuries, resulting in larger roster sizes. Not surprisingly,
therefore, the number of players appearing in at least one match per season
has increased considerably (from 300 to about 450; see 1) over the last
forty years (for recent summaries of labour markets in professional team
sports see Rosen and Sanderson (2001) and Kahn (2000). Moreover, Frick
(2007) provides an overview of the labour market for football players in
Europe). This growth is, first, due to the increase in the number of teams
admitted to the league (from 16 in 1963/64 to 18 in recent years) and due
to the increasing number of players that can be substituted during a match
(from zero in 1963/64 to three since 1995/96). Second, and perhaps more
important, it is due to the expansion of the playing schedules particularly
of the top teams.

Assuming that only few players of the relegated clubs are hired by the
better performing teams, about one sixth of the players leave the league
involuntarily each season as their teams are relegated. Since these
players—as well as those exiting voluntarily to sign a more lucrative
contract abroad and those leaving involuntarily as their contracts have
not been renewed—are replaced by those under contract with the
promoted teams and those signing their first contract with one of the
established clubs, the annual turnover rate amounts to some 30% (see
Figure 1).[5]

Data

Our empirical investigation is not based on the annual cross-sections
described above, but on an unbalanced panel including all players
employed by any one of the 48 teams in any of the 40 Bundesliga seasons
1963/64-2002/03. It has been compiled from a compendium published by
the German Football League (Bender 2003) and various special issues of a
highly respected football magazine ("Kicker"). While the number of
different players is 4,116, the number of different spells amounts to 5,354
(see Table 1). This implies that quite a number of players exit the league at
some point in time and then return after one or more seasons. The
departing players either leave the league voluntarily by signing with a

---

[5] Since the number of exiting and arriving players is more or less identical, the two
respective lines in Figure 1 can hardly be distinguished.

Table 1: The Size of the Player Population (1963/64-2002/03).

Number of different players	4,116	
Number of different spells	5,354	
Number of exits[a]	3,662	4,900
Incomplete spells	454	
Number of player-year-observations	15,299	

[a] The first number is for individuals, the second for spells.

team abroad (in Italy, Spain, England or France, for example) or involuntarily either because they retire (mainly because they are not offered a new contract at acceptable terms) or because their team is relegated. In this sense, less than 20% of all departures are voluntary.

Consequently, some players cannot be observed temporarily and are thus removed from the risk pool for the duration of their absence. In order to account for these temporary exits we distinguish between "spell duration", a term that is used to describe a period that is not interrupted by a temporary exit and a subsequent re-entry and "career duration", a term that refers to the total number of years a player has been active in the Bundesliga. More than one third of all players "disappear" again after their first season and only one career out of twelve lasts for 10 years and more (see Figure 2). The observation that very short spells are more frequent than very short careers (46% vs. 34%) is due to the fact that recently promoted teams have a high probability of being relegated again after just one season (Frick and Prinz 2004).

Thus, players who are under contract with one of the promoted teams are more likely than others to disappear again after their first season. Since a number of teams have been oscillating between first and second division for years, many players manage to play first division more than once, but very often for rather short periods of time. Moreover, a number of teams have been playing in the Bundesliga for one or two seasons only before they disappeared again in the 2nd Bundesliga or even further down in the league hierarchy.

Thus, overall career duration (our dependent variable in the estimations presented below) is considerably higher than average spell length (4 years vs. 3.4 years; see also Table 2).[6] Recall that career duration is defined as the total number of years an individual has been playing in the Bundesliga, ignoring exits and re-entries. Spell duration, on the other hand, only counts the years without any interruption.

---

[6] For an empirical analysis of the duration of the individual spells see Frick et al. (2007).

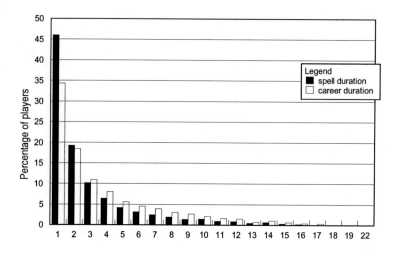

Number of seasons

Figure 2: Distribution of Spell and Career Duration.

Moreover, it appears from Table 2 that players are on average 26 years old and that they have spent 2.7 years with one and the same employer (not necessarily in the first division only; players might have been active for their current team before that team was promoted). The average number of goals scored per season is 2.5, the average number of yellow cards is 1.7 and players are used for 20 matches per season (note that the values displayed in Table 2 are for player-year-observations and not for individuals or spells).[7]

Methods

Using an individual data set that contains information on every single player who appeared in at least one match in the Bundesliga since it was

---

[7] The term "player-year-observation" has the following meaning: Paul Caligiuri, for example, appeared in the Bundesliga only one season (for FC St. Pauli Hamburg in 1995/96) while Jürgen Klinsmann had seven seasons (five with VfB Stuttgart (between 1984/85-1988/89) and two with Bayern Munich (1995/96-1996/97)). We have, therefore, one player-year-observation for the former and seven for the latter athlete.

Table 2: Summary Statistics.

Variable	Mean	SD	Min.	Max.
Career length (dep. variable)	3.96	3.32	1	22
Exogenous Variables				
Player age	26.52	4.07	17	44
Tenure	2.67	2.32	1	19
Games played per season	19.93	10.94	1	38
Goals per season	2.48	3.83	0	400
Red cards per season	0.09	0.31	0	3
Yellow cards per season	1.75	2.33	0	16
Final league position	9.67	5.18	1	20
Exogenous dummy variables				
Goalkeeper	0.09	-	0	1
Defender	0.32	-	0	1
Midfielder	0.31	-	0	1
Forward	0.28	-	0	1
German	0.82	-	0	1
Eastern Europe	0.05	-	0	1
Western Europe	0.05	-	0	1
North America	0.00	-	0	1
South America	0.03	-	0	1
Asia	0.01	-	0	1
Africa	0.03	-	0	1
Australia	0.01	-	0	1
League size 16	0.04	-	0	1
League size 18	0.93	-	0	1
League size 20	0.03	-	0	1
N of foreigners <=3	0.21	-	0	1
N of foreigners unrestricted	0.11	-	0	1

established in the summer of 1963, we estimate failure time models that explain the length of what can be termed a rather risky career. In an attempt to analyse the impact player characteristics, changes in the institutional environment and—in particular—team performance might have on an individual player's career length (reflecting the clubs' decision either to retain or to cut players) we estimate a number of Cox-models that differ in the sets of explanatory variables used (see Models 1-4 in Table 3 below).

Statistical analysis of survival data in general and career length in particular is difficult insofar as there is no satisfactory way of handling right-censored data, i.e. the individuals for which the event of being cut from the league is not observed within the time period of the study (t_4 in Figure 3). This problem, however, is less dramatic as more than 90% of the players in our data set have retired. At the same time we also observe players whose spells are left-censored (again less than 10% of all observations). These are the individuals who might have started their careers before the Bundesliga was established in 1963/64 (t_5 in Figure 3). Unfortunately, we are unable to distinguish between players who started their careers in 1963/64 and those who had already been active in one of the "Oberliga", i.e. those who had already been playing as (semi-)professionals before. However, estimating our model with and without the players with right- and/or left-censored spells leaves the findings virtually unchanged. This is not surprising, since the overwhelming majority of the players begin and end their careers during the period of observation.

We estimate a number of Cox's (1972) semi-parametric proportional hazard models, a well recognised and commonly used statistical technique for analysing survival data. It is the most general regression model developed to investigate survival data, because it does not impose any assumption concerning the nature or the shape of the underlying survival distribution. The model assumes that the underlying hazard rate (rather than the survival time) is a function of the independent variables. The Cox model does not limit the pattern of the hazard rate like parametric models with a Weibull, exponential or log-logistic distribution and it further solves the problem of censored observations (Kiefer 1988).

In the Cox model the conditional hazard function, given the vector z of covariate values at time t or the corresponding time interval, is assumed to be of the following form:

$$\lambda(t \mid z) = \lambda_0(t)\exp(\beta z),$$

(1)

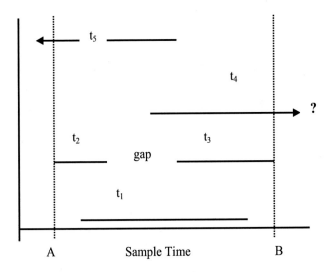

A: Start of observation period (season 1963/64)
B: End of observation period (season 2002/03)
t_1: Completed spell
t_2, t_3: Intermediate exit with subsequent re-entry
t_4: Right-censored spell (no information on players after 2002/03)
t_5: Left-censored spell (no information on players before 1963/64)

Figure 3: Spells and Censoring.

where β is the vector of regression coefficients and λ_0 (t) denotes the baseline hazard function. The baseline hazard function corresponds to the probability for the respective player of leaving the league either voluntarily or involuntarily (or generally reaching an event) when all the explanatory variables are zero. The baseline hazard function is analogous to the intercept in ordinary regressions (since $\exp^0 = 1$). One additional feature of the model is that the exogenous variables can be time-constant (such as nationality), but also—and more important—time-varying (such as performance or age). The regression coefficients $\hat{\beta}$ (the covariates of interest) give the proportional change that can be expected in the hazard, related to changes in the independent variables.

Findings

Our estimations are straightforward and few—if any—of our variables warrant further explanation. In our estimations we include measures of player age and experience in the current club, games played and goals scored per season, number of yellow and red cards per season, position dummies and dummies representing the region of origin of a player (see Table 2 above). Moreover, we control for individual career interruptions by including a number of variables measuring either the occurrence of an interruption, the number of interruptions as well as the eventual duration of the interruption(s).

Since our period of investigation is rather long, covering four decades, we also control for changes in the institutional environment by taking into account changes in league size and in the number of foreign-born players allowed on the team. Of particular importance are two other blocks of variables:

- Team performance is measured not only by league position at the end of the season, but also by whether a team is relegated at the end of the season. Given the rather modest changes in the organisation of the Bundesliga (see section 3 above) we expect a nearly constant influence of team performance on individual career duration.

- Above and beyond the on-field performance we also control for unobservable differences in managerial quality by adding team dummies to our estimations. For the sake of brevity we do not report the respective coefficients, but they are available upon request.

Table 3 includes the results of our estimations.[8] Each of the four models displays a considerably better fit than the null model. This implies that the accumulated effect of the different sets of covariates on the probability of leaving the Bundesliga is statistically significant at all conventional levels. The four estimations differ only with regard to the measures on individual career interruptions included. Model (1) has no measure of individual career interruption(s), while models (2) and (3) in addition either use an interruption dummy or the number of interruptions a player has experienced during his career in the Bundesliga. Finally, model (4) includes the aggregated number of years an individual has spent outside before returning to the Bundesliga. As expected, the four

---

[8] The results of the four corresponding log-logistic models are virtually identical. They are available from the authors upon request.

estimations produce quite similar results. In the models presented above the hazard ratio for, say, age and games played per season, is interpreted as the proportional change in hazard when age or the number of matches played is increased by one unit (here: +9 to + 25% versus -6%). We start the discussion of our findings with the coefficients of the variables characterising the individual players.

Not surprisingly, most of the available performance statistics have a positive, yet decreasing impact on the duration of individual careers (apart from number of games played and number of goals scored per season the majority of the squared terms proved to be statistically significant): While age has a statistically positive influence on the probability of being eliminated from the Bundesliga (i.e. the hazard ratio has a value of larger than one), tenure with the current team, the number of games played and the number of goals scored per season all have a statistically negative influence (i.e. the hazard ratio in the three cases takes a value of less than one). Depending on the specification, an additional year of age increases the drop-out probability considerably (between 9% (Model 3) and 26% (Model 4)). Scoring one more goal per season reduces a player's probability of being cut from the league by 6-7%. Of course, goals are not only scored by forwards, but also by defenders and midfielders (some of the latter are quite "offensive"). Moreover, some goalkeepers take virtually every penalty kick for their team and are, therefore, also scoring goals. However, interacting the number of goals scored with the position dummies leaves the basic findings virtually unaffected. Similarly, playing one more match per season also reduces the exit hazard by 6%, indicating the relative risk that arises from not playing. Moreover, sanctions in the form of yellow or red cards have no influence on the probability of being eliminated suggesting that "aggressiveness" has no statistically discernible influence on the duration of player careers.

As expected, the coefficients of all position dummies are statistically significant indicating that defenders, midfielders and forwards have significantly shorter careers than goalkeepers (the reference category). Perhaps surprisingly, defenders survive considerably longer than midfielders and especially forwards. Depending on the concrete specification of the model, forwards survive between 2.1 and 2.5 years, midfielders between 2.6 and 3.0 years and defenders between 2.8 and 3.2 years.[9]

---

[9] These result are at least in part due to the fact that the performance of a forward is relatively easy to measure, i.e. "number of goals scored" is an obvious metric while "number of tackles won" as the main performance measure for defenders is certainly more difficult to quantify.

Table 3: Cox Models.[10]

Independent variables	Model (1)[a]	Model (2)[a]	Model (3)[a]	Model (4)[a]
Player age	1.247	1.107	1.091	1.261
	(6.89)***	(3.26)***	(2.77)***	(7.17)***
Player age^2	0.998	1.000	1.000	0.998
	(3.72)***	(0.02)	(0.52)	(4.09)***
Tenure	0.966	0.833	0.823	0.981
	(1.76)*	(9.00)***	(9.62)***	(0.90)
Tenure^2	1.003	1.011	1.012	1.003
	(2.12)**	(6.46)***	(6.99)***	(1.53)
Games played per	0.940	0.942	0.942	0.940
season	(8.25)**	(7.94)***	(8.06)***	(8.21)***
Goals per season	0.935	0.934	0.934	0.936
	(4.52)***	(4.70)***	(4.67)***	(4.48)***
Yellow cards per	0.983	0.987	0.987	0.982
season	(1.90)*	(1.48)	(1.39)	(1.94)*
Red Cards per	0.952	0.948	0.947	0.953
season	(0.90)	(0.97)	(0.98)	(0.88)
Individual career dynamics				
Interruption (yes=1)	-	0.432	-	-
	-	(26.93)***	-	-
Number of interruptions	-	-	0.530	-
	-	-	(27.10)***	-
Duration of interruptions	-	-	-	1.027
	-	-	-	(2.86)***
Player position (reference position: goalkeeper)				
Defender	1.437	1.303	1.251	1.439
	(7.12)***	(5.16)***	(4.45)***	(7.11)***
Midfielder	1.519	1.374	1.309	1.521
	(7.98)***	(6.07)***	(5.24)***	(7.95)***
Forward	1.856	1.670	1.605	1.853
	(11.72)***	(9.81)***	(9.23)***	(11.60)***
Region of origin (reference category: Germany)				
Eastern Europe	1.226	1.121	1.115	1.242
	(3.55)***	(2.08)**	(1.98)**	(3.77)***

Continued on next page.

---

[10] Including the squared term of number of games played and number of goals scored leaves the remaining coefficients completely unaffected. The results are available from the authors upon request.

Table 3 cont: Cox Models.

Western Europe	1.247	1.131	1.126	1.260
	(4.25)***	(2.48)**	(2.39)**	(4.43)***
North America	1.510	1.484	1.435	1.536
	(1.39)	(1.45)	(1.31)	(1.47)
South America	1.255	1.176	1.163	1.266
	(2.81)***	(2.14)**	(1.95)*	(2.91)***
Asia	0.954	0.817	0.815	0.971
	(0.35)	(1.51)	(1.52)	(0.23)
Africa	1.158	1.061	1.050	1.173
	(2.17)**	(0.85)	(0.69)	(2.37)**
Australia	0.905	0.846	0.823	0.914
	(0.46)	(0.83)	(0.97)	(0.42)
Institutional characteristics				
League size = 16 clubs	0.824	0.740	0.748	0.831
(1=yes)	(2.80)***	(4.43)***	(4.26)***	(2.68)***
League size = 20 clubs	0.871	0.908	0.908	0.866
(1=yes)	(1.66)*	(1.19)	(1.22)	(1.73)*
N of foreigners <=3	0.705	0.728	0.737	0.704
(1=yes)	(6.93)***	(6.33)***	(6.13)***	(6.97)***
N of foreigners Unrest.	0.717	0.724	0.728	0.713
(1=yes)	(8.25)***	(8.09)***	(7.93)***	(8.37)***
Team performance				
Club relegated	2.279	2.419	2.448	2.279
(0=no; 1=yes)	(19.79)***	(21.65)***	(22.10)***	(19.79)***
Final league position	1.035	1.033	1.034	1.035
	(8.47)***	(8.34)***	(8.39)***	(8.43)***
Team dummies	Included			
Observations	15,299	15,299	15,299	15,299
LL null model	-27,445.3	-27,445.3	-27,445.3	-27,445.3
LL full model	-25,782.6	-25,590.9	-25,580.1	-25,780.7
Pseudo R^2	6.1	6.8	6.8	6.1
Wald Chi^2	5,847.5	6,617.4	6,596.2	5,911.4

* Significant at the 5% level, ** significant at the 1% level, *** significant at the 0.1% level. T-values in parentheses.
[a] Dependent variable: probability of being eliminated from the Bundesliga.
Model (1): No measure of individual career interruption; Model (2): Interruption dummy included; Model (3): Number of interruptions a player has experienced during his career; Model (4): Aggregated number of years an individual has spent outside before returning to the Bundesliga.

Career interruptions that may occur, for example, due to injury or due to "degradation" to the junior team clearly have an important impact on the aggregate duration of player careers. Controlling for other (potential) determinants of career length, each interruption tends to reduce the duration by about 50% or two years. This result is completely unaffected by the concrete specification of the interruption variable (dummy vs. number of interruptions).

We now turn to the coefficients of the "region of origin" dummies to see, whether players from specific areas of the world are discriminated against with regard to the duration of their individual careers: The positive and statistically significant coefficients for Eastern and Western Europeans as well as South Americans indicate that players from these regions face a higher risk of being eliminated from the Bundesliga. This, however, is certainly not necessarily indicative of discrimination in the sense that either managers or fans prefer players of German origin. Rather, especially players from Western Europe and South America leave the Bundesliga voluntarily because they sign more lucrative contracts with teams in Spain, Italy, England and France. This explanation, however, does not apply in the case of players from Africa, Asia and Eastern Europe, who may indeed suffer from discrimination. Kalter (1999), for example, has demonstrated that the number of replica shirts sold is significantly influenced by the players' origin: While shirts with the names of players from Eastern Europe do not sell well, those with the names of South American players are bestsellers. Thus, the results reported by Atkinson and Tschirhart (1986) for the NFL as well as by Hoang and Rascher (1999) for the NBA receive little support with regard to foreign players in the Bundesliga. Moreover, since particularly players from Western Europe and South America receive a considerable pay premium (see Frick 2008), discrimination on the basis of nationality is apparently not a problem in the Bundesliga.

Most revealing are the coefficients of the variables indicating changes in the institutional environment. When looking at the impact of the Bosman-ruling and the ensuing further liberalisation of the player market on individual career duration, we find that the respective hazard ratios are always smaller than one and statistically significant in every model for three of the four variables, indicating that a "liberalised" player market does not reduce, but rather increase the career durations of Bundesliga players. Given the influx of "cheap labour" especially from Eastern Europe, Africa and Asia this is a surprising finding.[11] A possible

---

[11] Of course, salaries have not declined in recent years, but have reached record-levels almost year after year during the 1990s. It is very likely, however, that this

explanation for this observation might be that the additional labour supply deters shirking behaviour within the incumbent workforce. This is consistent with findings reported by Feess et al. (2004) who—using an unbalanced panel of some 1,800 player-year-observations—find that shirking is quite prevalent in German soccer: Players whose contracts are about to expire (i.e. those who are in the last year of their contracts) perform significantly better than those who have just signed a new contract or are still farther away from renegotiations.

We now turn our attention to the impact of team characteristics on the duration of individual player careers. It first turns out that the poorer the performance of the team (in terms of league position at the end of the season), the higher the individual player's risk of termination (an increase in the final position by one rank increases the probability of being cut by almost 3%). This implies that being under contract with the team winning the championship instead of the team finishing 15th (i.e. just avoiding relegation) reduces the hazard rate by almost half. Moreover, the coefficient of the relegation dummy is also highly significant in all specifications, suggesting that a particularly poor team performance reduces the career duration of the affected players by more than 30%.[12] Summarising, it appears that the performance of the team for which

---

increase would have been even larger without the liberalisation of the player market. Consistent with this argument, Frick (2008) finds that even after controlling for previous and current performance, players from Africa and North America earn significantly less than comparable players from either Western Europe or South America. This, in turn, indicates that the labour supply of a particular group of players affects their relative income position. Moreover, as the number of players from these regions increases, the salaries of other players will be affected, too.

[12] Finally, the team dummies themselves indicate that even after controlling for the performance of the team it does make a difference for the athletes for which club they are playing in terms of the duration of their careers: In many cases players who were active for a team that was relegated at the end of the season are not able to sign with another first division club and are, therefore, likely to disappear in the 2nd or even 3rd division (such as Fortuna Koeln, SSV Ulm, Preussen Muenster and VfB Leipzig). On the other hand, there are a number of notable exceptions, i.e. teams whose players have a high chance of being re-hired by other first division teams in the case of relegation. Among them are clubs like Eintracht Braunschweig, Waldhof Mannheim, KFC Uerdingen, Kickers Offenbach and Rot-Weiss Essen (it may well be that these clubs have a particularly well developed youth training and scouting system, producing players who can succeed almost everywhere). Many of these players managed to stay in the league even in case their former team got relegated. Moreover, even among the established teams there are considerable differences in average career length of the individual players:

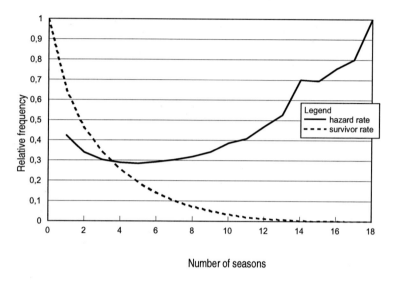

Figure 4: Survivor Rate and Hazard Rate of Professional Football Players in the Bundesliga (1963/64-2002/03).

a player is active is nearly as important for his career length as the athlete's individual performance.

Additional measures of team performance, such as the number of tickets sold per season, capacity utilisation of the stadium or qualification for a European cup competition, proved to be insignificant in all specifications.[13]

Figure 4 displays the survivor as well as the hazard rate of players in the German Bundesliga. It appears, that the hazard rate declines until the fifth season and then increases nearly monotonically, resulting in a u-shaped pattern. The survivor rate, in turn, declines monotonically, thereby exhibiting the expected pattern that has already been documented by, inter alia, Atkinson and Tschirhart (1986) for the NFL and by Hoang and Rascher (1999) for the NBA.

Being under contract with VfL Wolfsburg exposes the players to a rather high risk of being cut at the end of the season while players active for Energie Cottbus, Hannover 96, VfL Bochum, Werder Bremen and Bayer Leverkusen survive for a particularly long time in the Bundesliga.

[13] The results are, of course, available from the authors upon request.

Summary and Implications

The present paper identifies the individual as well as the team characteristics that affect the duration of player careers in the German Bundesliga. Player age, position, tenure with the current team, number of games played and number of goals scored per season all affect the length of player careers in the expected direction. Equally important, however, is the performance of the club for which a player is active: The closer a team finishes to the bottom of the league, the higher is the probability that its individual players disappear from the league.

While the findings presented above are conclusive, the potential of our data set is by no means exhausted yet. For the 1990s, we have additional information on player salaries, contract duration and more detailed performance statistics (such as international caps[14]). Moreover, we have complete information on transfer fees[15] that have been paid since 1981/82 by the Bundesliga teams. Although that information is available only for a sub-period it will enable us to control for additional (potential) determinants of career duration in a risky environment. Moreover, it is certainly advisable to repeat the estimates for sub-periods, such as 1963-1970; 1971-1980; 1981-1990 and 1991-2000 in order to check for the stability of the point estimates over time. Finally, we will certainly try to estimate a competing risk model that takes into consideration the different reasons for leaving the Bundesliga (voluntary vs. involuntary exit, for an application see, inter alia, Dolton and van der Klaauw 1999).

Moreover, the finding that teams may discriminate against players from Eastern Europe should be subject to further research. The most pertinent question in this context is whether teams pay a penalty for their management's or their supporters' taste for discrimination (for empirical evidence on this point see, for example, Szymanski 2000).

In principle the data allows testing Rottenberg's (1956) invariance hypothesis as well as Daly and Moore's (1981) transactions cost approach. In case the invariance hypothesis holds we should observe that player mobility is unaffected by changes in the legal environment, such as the "Bosman-ruling" of the European Court of Justice in December 1995. If, however, transactions costs are reduced by restricting player mobility, then "excess mobility" detrimental to the value of the league may be the consequence of such a "liberal" regime.

---

[14] This term denotes a player's appearances in his home country's national team.

[15] By that we mean the amount of money that is being paid to a team that „sells" one of his players to another club before that player's contract has expired.

References

Atkinson, S. and J. Tschirhart (1986). "Flexible Modelling of Time to Failure in Risky Careers." *Review of Economics and Statistics*, 68(4), 558-566.

Bender, T. (2003). *Bundesliga-Lexikon*. Leipzig: Sportverlag Europa.

Cox, D. R. (1972). "Regression Models and Life-Tables (with Discussion)." *Journal of the Royal Statistical Society Series B*, 34, 187-220.

Daly, G. and W. J. Moore (1981). "Externalities, Property Rights and the Allocation of Resources in Major League Baseball." *Economic Inquiry*, 19(1), 77-95.

Dolton, P. and D. van der Klaauw (1999). "The Turnover of Teachers: A Competing Risks Explanation." *Review of Economics and Statistics*, 81(3), 543-550.

Feess, E., Frick, B and Muehlheusser, G. (2004). "Legal Restrictions on Outside Trade Clauses - Theory and Evidence from German Soccer." *Discussion Paper 1180*. Bonn: Institut Zukunft der Arbeit.

Frick, B. (2006). "Football in Germany." In *Handbook on the Economics of Sport*. W. Andreff and S. Szymanski eds. Cheltenham: Edward Elgar, 486-496.

—. (2007). "The Soccer Players' Labour Market." *Scottish Journal of Political Economy*, 54(3), 422-446.

—. (2008). "Player Remuneration in Professional Football: Empirical Evidence from the German "Bundesliga"." *Unpublished manuscript*. Department of Management: University of Paderborn.

Frick, B. and J. Prinz (2004). "Revenue-Sharing Arrangements and the Survival of Promoted Teams: Empirical Evidence from the Major European Soccer Leagues." In *International Sports Economics Comparisons*. R. Fort and J. Fizel eds. Westport, CT: Praeger, 141-156.

Frick, B., Pietzner, G. and Prinz, J. (2007). "Career Duration in a Competitive Environment: The Labor Market for Soccer Players in Germany." *Eastern Economic Journal*, 33(3), 429-442.

Goddard, J. and J. O. S. Wilson (2004). "Free Agency and Employment Transitions in Professional Football." *Unpublished manuscript*. School of Management: University of St. Andrews.

Groothuis, P. A. and J. R. Hill (2004). "Exit Discrimination in the NBA: A Duration Analysis of Career Length." *Economic Inquiry*, 42(2), 341-349.

Hoang, H. and D. Rascher (1999). "The NBA, Exit Discrimination, and Career Earnings." *Industrial Relations*, 38(1), 69-91.

Kahn, L. (2000). "The Sports Business as a Labor Market Laboratory." *Journal of Economic Perspectives*, 14(3), 75-94.

Kalter, F. (1999). "Ethnische Kundenpräferenzen im professionellen Sport: Der Fall der Fußball-Bundesliga." *Zeitschrift für Soziologie*, 28(4), 219-234.

Kiefer, N. (1988). "Economic Duration Data and Hazard Functions." *Journal of Economic Literature*, 26(2), 646-679.

Noll, R. G. (2002). "The Economics of Promotion and Relegation in Sports Leagues. The Case of English Football." *Journal of Sports Economics*, 3(2), 169-203.

Ohkusa, Y. (2001). "An Empirical Examination of the Quit Behavior of Professional Baseball Players in Japan." *Journal of Sports Economics*, 2(1), 80-88.

Rosen, S. and A. Sanderson (2001). "Labour Markets in Professional Sports." *Economic Journal*, 111(469), 47-68.

Rottenberg, S. (1956). "The Baseball Player's Labor Market." *Journal of Political Economy*, 64(3), 242-258.

Spurr, S. J. and W. Barber (1994). "The Effect of Performance on a Worker's Career: Evidence from Minor League Baseball." *Industrial and Labor Relations Review*, 47(3), 692-708.

Szymanski, S. (2000). "A Market Test for Discrimination in the English Professional Soccer Leagues." *Journal of Political Economy*, 108(3), 590-603.

CHAPTER NINETEEN

RELATIVE INCOME POSITION, INEQUALITY AND PERFORMANCE: AN EMPIRICAL PANEL ANALYSIS

BRUNO S. FREY, SASCHA L. SCHMIDT AND BENNO TORGLER[1]

In recent years, the application of economic thinking to the sports' business has gained increasing attention. A sub-field of this research focuses on football, a worldwide sports' discipline, which has become increasingly commercialised over recent decades.[2] Unlike the economics of North American sports like baseball, basketball, or American football, which have been analysed since the 1950s, the economics of football is still in its infancy. However, even though increased commercialisation of football has led to more transparency and new data sources, data on football is scarce when compared to the information on North American sports activities. Indeed, as Dobson and Goddard (2001, p. xv) point out, despite football's

[1] Frey: Institute for Empirical Research in Economics, University of Zurich, Switzerland, Email: bsfrey@iew.unizh.ch: Torgler: School of Economics and Finance, Queensland University of Technology, Australia, Email: benno.torgler@qut.edu.au: Schmidt: European Business School, International University, Oestrich Winkel, Germany, Email: sascha.schmidt@ebs.de. The authors are also associated with CREMA—Center for Research in Economics, Management and the Arts, Switzerland. Benno Torgler and Bruno S. Frey are also associated with CESifo, Poschingerstrasse 5, D-81679 Munich, Germany.
[2] For instance, the FIFA World Cup has become a major spectacle and one of the world's largest sporting events, having been broadcast in 2002 in more than 200 countries and regions around the world, covering over 41,100 hours of programming and reaching an estimated 28.8 billion television viewers (see FIFA Media Information, November 21, 2002, http://fifaworldcup.yahoo.com).

prominent public profile, and despite the fact that its weekly or daily
audience (including television viewers) run into millions, academic
economists have devoted relatively little attention to professional soccer.

A promising line of research is to use sports' data to test existing
theories in other such areas like labour economics. In our case, we explore
the relationship between pay and performance. Lazear (2000, p. 1346)
points out that: "Much of the theory in personnel economics relates to
effects of monetary incentives on output, but the theory was untested
because appropriate data were unavailable". Contrary to previous studies,
we investigate the relevance of the relative income position rather than
only the absolute position. Leading economists, such as Adam Smith, Karl
Marx, Thorstein Veblen or James Duesenberry, have long expressed the
importance of the relative position and social concerns. Nevertheless,
standard economics pays little attention to the consequences of the relative
position. Accordingly, Senik (2004), providing an overview of the
literature, points out that "it is surprising that in spite of the large
theoretical literature on relative income and comparison effects [...]
empirical validation of this conjecture is still scarce" (p. 47).

Our broad data sample covers eight seasons of the German premier
football league (*Bundesliga*) between 1995/1996 and 2003/2004, and
includes a large number of players, a salary proxy and several performance
variables. The empirical data has low variable errors. Performance is
clearly observable and is free of discrepancies, compared to frequently
used performance variables, such as GDP. Furthermore, football games are
comparable to field experiments, due to the fact that a match takes place in
a controlled environment. All football players are faced with the same
rules and restrictions. Thus, when investigating the connection between
relative concern and performance, many factors can be controlled for.

The chapter starts with a short overview of the relevant literature and
develops our theoretical approach. Afterwards the empirical model and the
empirical results are presented. Finally, the implications for business use
are discussed and concluding remarks are offered.

Positional Concerns: An Overview

Positional concerns due to relative judgments are common. People
constantly compare themselves with their environment and care very much
about their relative position, which influences individual choices. Thus,
not only is the absolute level of an individual's situation important (e.g.
income), but also the relative position, and Frank (1999) emphasises that
research provides "compelling evidence that concern about relative

position is a deep-rooted and ineradicable element in human nature" (p. 145).

Marx (1849) stresses that we measure our desires and pleasures in relation to society. Similarly, Galbraith (1958) points out that consumer demands are largely influenced by society. Veblen (1899) emphasises the importance of one's relative position in society with his concepts of conspicuous leisure and consumption. Contrary to standard utility theory, Duesenberry's (1949) utility concept is characterised by systematically interdependent utilities. Thus, he explicitly incorporated relative preferences into consumer theory. Marshall (1961), the creator of the modern demand theory, "recognised the power and prevalence of the human desire for 'distinction'" (p. 12). Social sciences, such as social psychology, sociology or anthropology, have emphasised the relevance of relative preferences as fundamental to human motivation. The psychological theory of social comparison (see Festinger, 1954) and the sociological theory of relative deprivation (Stouffer, 1949) show that comparisons with others are an important aspect. Relative deprivation theory investigates interpersonal and inter-group relations and comparisons. It stresses that a lower perception of one's own (group) status or one's own welfare in relation to another person (group) can be the source of hostility towards the other individuals or groups. A person may feel frustrated when his/her situation (e.g. individual earnings) declines relative to the reference group. The person feels deprived. If improvement of the situation is slower than expected, the experience of frustration can even lead to aggression (for example, see Walker and Pettigrew, 1984).

Research on happiness (for example, Easterlin, 2001, Clark and Oswald, 1996, Frey, 2008, Frey and Stutzer, 2002, Luttmer, 2005, Ferrer-i-Carbonell, 2005) has stressed and found strong empirical support for the importance of the relative position. Laboratory experiments, using the ultimatum game, also indicate that subjects are concerned with their relative position (Frank and Sunstein, 2001, Kirchsteiger, 1994). Furthermore, as an alternative strategy, some researchers have used hypothetical questions regarding choice between alternative states or outcomes, where the choices allow for checking out relative positional concerns (for example, see Tversky and Griffin, 1991). Nevertheless, many economists are still sceptical about the importance of positional concerns, because empirical evidence about its behavioural relevance remains scarce.

Theoretical Considerations

Our first research question is based on the assumption that football players compare themselves with other players, especially their team-mates. Thus, their individual salary position relative to that of other team-mates may have an impact on performance and therefore warrants empirical investigation. Yet few such investigations have been undertaken. An individual's income is a key factor in comparisons. When people compare salaries, it is generally with people close to them (Layard, 2003). Positional concerns are extremely widespread in the workplace. Layard (2003) points out: "In organisations, calm can often be maintained only by keeping peoples' salaries secret" (p. 8). Elster (1991) reports that, in China, model workers spend their bonuses on a good meal for everybody to avoid harassment by their colleagues. A manager may keep bonuses low because he fears the reaction of the other workers and because he wants to avoid the envy of other executive officers. Frank and Sunstein (2001) report that surveys of employers and employees suggest that salaries depend on what employees think other people are paid. Furthermore, the perception of the relative position has a large effect on their morale.

Festinger (1954) emphasises that people do not generally compare themselves with the rest of the world, but with a much more specific group, typically with others they see as being similar to themselves or, in his words, "close to one's own ability" (p. 121). Thus, football players, like in other team sports, compare themselves with other football players, such as team-mates, due to having the same work profile. Similarly, soldiers in World War II seem to have made comparisons primarily with members of their own military group (Stouffer, 1949). Thus, it seems reasonable to assume that a football player's income position, relative to other team-mates' and league players' income position, has an impact on his own behaviour.

There are two countervailing theories about how income differences influence performance. One stream of literature stresses the negative consequences of envy (for example, see Schoeck, 1966). An envious person may "prefer that others have less, and he might even sacrifice a little of his own wealth to achieve that end" (Zeckhauser, 1991, p. 10), behaviour that has been found in experiments (for example, see Kirchsteiger, 1994). An envious person increases his utility by destroying some of the others' assets, even if such an action carries its own costs (*cutting off one's nose to spite one's face*). Thus a negative sum interaction is started. The performance of those with lower income may decrease due to frustration ("it *could* have been or it *should* have been me"). They feel it impossible to "keep up with the Joneses" – in the case of football, with the team superstars. As a consequence, performance drops. It is even possible that players express their resentment of the players with a higher salary by, for example, not passing the ball so frequently to reduce a superstar's performance.

Relative income effects may include negative aspects that go beyond envy per se. Players dislike being in a lower income position, because the relative position may signal that they and their future prospects are lowly evaluated by others. Such perceptions and signals harm their relationships with others, and affect their self-conception and performance.

A contrasting theory argues that large income differences lead to better performance, as they raise the incentive to achieve a similar status. A positional arms race is provoked through the process of rivalry (see Landers et al., 1996).

> H1: Our first hypothesis therefore leaves open whether positional income concerns in general have a positive or a negative impact on individual performance but suggests that relative income matters.

It seems a natural and interesting exercise to investigate to what extent not only the relative income position within a team affects individual performance, but also which mechanisms enforce positional concerns. The level of inequality within a team affects its climate. Strong differences may reduce the climate within the team and provide the ground for positional concern effects. Thus, we would expect that teams with a higher income inequality are more vulnerable to such positional concerns.

> H2: The second hypothesis suggests that a larger income difference within a team strengthens positional concerns. Thus, positional concern effects are more visible in teams with a stronger income inequality.

Our third research hypothesis concentrates on the impact of team effects. According to the literature, individual productivity – and thus player performance – varies in different settings as co-workers offer different levels of assistance (see Idson and Kahane, 2000). Therefore, teamwork, an important topic in labor economics, is desirable because it allows realisation of gains from complementarities in production and facilitates gains from specialisation in the form of accumulated task-specific human capital, which may be valuable to other team members (see Lazear, 1998). In addition, Hamilton et al. (2003) find that team composition has a strong impact on team productivity. However, empirical studies on this phenomenon are rare because of the difficulty of obtaining data (see Idson and Kahane, 2000).

Our data set, however, enables the investigation of the impact of team-mates on player performance. In line with Idson and Kahane (2000) and Torgler (2007), we measure this impact on individual i by calculating the average values for the team-mates (excluding the values for player i). Thus, we specifically investigate whether team-mates' average ages, exchanges and sending-offs in a game affect individual performance.

H3: The third hypothesis suggests that team-mates' profiles affect individual performance.

Empirical Model

Data

This paper uses a unique data set of professional football players in the German premier football league *Bundesliga*, which is one of the most important football leagues in the world. IMP, the official data provider of the *Bundesliga*, and several broadcasting networks, made the data available to us. This data includes football players' individual performances (e.g. goals, assists, ball contacts) and personal background data (e.g. age, nationality, position) over a period of eight seasons between 1995/1996 and 2003/2004.[3] During the eight seasons, 28 different clubs participated in the league due to annual promotion and relegation.

Dependent Variable: Performance
Player performance and player background data were collected by the firm *IMP* in Munich and several broadcasters. Not only do these data allow the development of several seasonal variables at the individual player level, but IMP also provides personal characteristics like age, nationality or position for all players who played during the different seasons. We use two key performance variables, namely goals, assists and ball contacts for every season played.

Independent Variable: Income
Because data on players' salaries are not publicly available in Germany, previous studies on the *Bundesliga* have used proxies derived from press reports (Forrest and Simmons, 2002; Huebl and Swieter, 2002; Lehmann and Weigand, 1999). Most studies are based on data collected by the *Kicker Sportmagazin*, the most prominent football magazine in Germany (see Eschweiler and Vieth, 2004; Forrest and Simmons, 2002; Huebl and Swieter, 2002; Lehmann and Weigand, 1999). Thus, in line with previous

---

[3] The data for ballcontacts is available after season 1998.

studies, we use the salary proxy provided by *Kicker Sportmagazin*, whose editorial staff assesses each *Bundesliga* player's market value prior to a new season using individual characteristics (position in team, previous season performance, transfer price) and team characteristics (ticket sale earnings, merchandising, sponsoring). Most important, these data have been collected in a consistent and systematic manner for several years.[4]

To check the extent to which the market value estimations used in our paper correctly reflect actual salaries, we investigate the correlation between players' effective reported salaries, as provided by another data source called *Transfermarkt.de,* and our salary proxies. The correlation between these two data sources is high ($r=0.754$).[5] Thus, measurement errors do not seem to be a major problem.

Empirical Model

To test our first two predictions, we propose the following baseline equation:

$$PERF_{it} = \beta_0 + \beta_1\, CTRL_{it} + \beta_2\, ABSAL_{i(t-1)} + \beta_3\, RELSAL_{i(t-1)} + TEAMD_i + TD_t + \mu_i + \varepsilon_{it} \tag{1}$$

where $PERF_{it}$ is the performance of player i at time t. $ABSAL_{i(t-1)}$ is the player's lagged absolute salary and $RELSAL_{i(t-1)}$ is the player's lagged relative salary, measured as the difference between team-mates' average salaries and players' individual salaries. The regression also contains several control variables $CTRL_{it}$ such as AGE, AGE SQUARED, players' position in the game (ATTACK, MIDFIELD, DEFENSE) and team dummy variables ($TEAMD_i$), as many players change their position in the field and in their team over time. Team dummy variables are included, as it can be argued that the results are driven by unobserved team characteristics that are correlated with income and performance. Team fixed effects allow us to control for such possible omitted variable biases. Similarly, the estimates include a set of time dummies (TD_t) to control for possible differences in the players' environment; μ_i is the individual effect

---

[4] These data are then used in a so-called manager game (*Kicker-Managerspiel*), in which individuals (aged 18+) can participate. Compared to the performance data, the salary variable has some missing values. However, imputing missing values on the basis of the other independent variables produces similar results.

[5] The publicly available data from *Transfermarkt.de* was only available for the season 2003/2004. Historical data was not available, as the Internet site only started to collect this information in 2005. Furthermore, *Transfermarkt.de* only covers a limited number of players in the German *Bundesliga*.

of player i, and ε_{it} denotes the error term. To test our third hypothesis in a better manner, we use the following extended equation:

$$PERF_{it} = \beta_0 + \beta_1 \, CTRL_{it} + \beta_2 \, ABSAL_{i(t-1)} + \beta_3 \, RELSAL_{i(t-1)} + \beta_4 \, TEAM_{it} + TEAMD_i + TD_t + \mu_i + \varepsilon_{it} \qquad (2)$$

$TEAM_{it}$ denotes a vector that contains the values for the team-mates of each player i at time t, calculated in such a manner as to remove each individual i value. For example, we first calculate the average age of the whole team, excluding the age of individual player i. We then follow the same procedure to construct the variables EXCHANGES and SENDING-OFFS.

We first apply three different methodologies (pooling regression, random effect model and fixed model) to all available performance measures. To identify which empirical method is most suitable, we performed two statistical tests: the Lagrangian Multiplier (LM) test (see Breusch and Pagan, 1980) of the random effect model and the Hausman specification test (Hausman, 1978) in order to compare the fixed effect and the random effect models. The LM test indicates that the null hypothesis of the individual effect μ_i being 0 is rejected in all cases at the 1% significance level. Thus, the results suggest that the cohort effect is not zero, which means that the pooling regression is not suitable. In all cases, the Hausman specification test rejects the null hypothesis that the individual-level effects are adequately modelled by a random effect model at the 1% significance level. Thus, individual effects are not uncorrelated with the independent variables supporting the use of individual fixed effect models. However, it should be noted that the results we obtain remain robust with all three methodologies.

Causality

To reduce possible causality problems, we use the players' values from the *previous* season (dependent variable = current season), which allows us to use salary as an independent variable. In *Table 2,* we also report 2SLS estimations along with several diagnostic tests.

Results

Descriptive Analysis

In the first step, we build different groups within the data set. The income distribution is shown in *Figure* 1 using the Lorenz curve. The

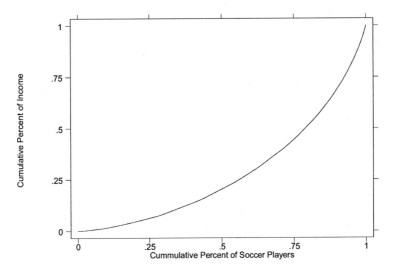

Figure 1: Income Inequality in the Bundesliga.

further the actual reported Lorenz curve bends away from the 45-degree line, the more unequal is the distribution of income. It shows to what extent a sports' discipline is a winner-take-all market (see Frank and Cook, 1995). The Gini coefficient or, in other words, the ratio of the area between a 45-degree line and the Lorenz curve to the area under the 45-degree line, is 0.403 in our case. Porter and Scully (1996) find similar values for American football (0.40) and higher values for basketball (0.51). Frick (1998) finds 0.47 for the 1996/1997 NBA season. In general, Fort (2003) reports that Gini coefficients in team sports can be as high as 0.50 and, in the economy at large, Gini coefficients are typically around 0.30. Higher inequality values are observable in individual sports such as golf. For example, Fort (2003) presents evidence from the men's 1999 Nissan Open and the women's 1999 Sunrise Hawaiian Open, showing values of 0.64 in men's golf and 0.62 in women's golf.

    In order to split the sample in our case, the mean team GINI coefficient over the investigated period was calculated. The teams ranked above average were placed in one group labelled "high income inequality" (GROUP A), and the remaining teams were placed in the other group (GROUP B).

Multivariate Analysis

Table 1 presents the first results using goals and assists as dependent variables, differentiating between teams with a higher income inequality and teams with lower income inequality (group A versus group B). *Table 2* presents the results focusing on ball contacts. Including ball contacts is insofar important as one could criticise that only a small fraction of players will score a significant amount of goals and will make a significant number of assists. Moreover, we present estimations with and without team-mates' factors (team-mates' age, exchanges and sending-offs). The results suggest that the relative income position is important in group A but not in group B. In all six regressions of group A, we observe that all the coefficients of RELATIVE VALUE are statistically significant with a negative sign. If a player's salary is below-average and this difference increases, his willingness to perform decreases and the negative effect of positional concerns are stronger. At the same time, a positive performance impact is observable for players with above-average salaries. The positive impact of an above-average salary change towards a greater difference in relation to the team-mates is also observable. The respective coefficients are highly statistically significant, controlling for the absolute level of the salary. Thus, players in teams with a higher income inequality are indeed more vulnerable to the consequences of income differences than players in teams with a lower income inequality. On the other hand, in most of the cases is the coefficient not statistically significant in group B. Thus, hypothesis 2 cannot be rejected. This finding is also consistent with the *first hypothesis* that the relative income level has an impact on performance, and the theories proposing that a disadvantage in the relative income position worsen performance.

We also test the joint hypothesis that the absolute and the relative income as a group have a coefficient that differs from zero. The results in both tables indicate a clear rejection of this hypothesis for group A but not group B. In addition, the results support hypothesis 3. Team effects are important. Based on an *F*-test for joint significance, we may conclude that team-mates play a significant role in the determination of individual performances. We also observe an increase in the *R*-squared. The strongest effect is observable for EXCHANGES. This result is surprising. More exchanges are correlated with higher individual performance because of an increase in the team-mates' average physical strength. Similarly, more exchanges may also indicate good second line-up players. There is also the tendency that sending-offs are negatively correlated with performance. This result is consistent with Torgler's (2004) finding for the World Cup

Table 1: Determinants of Performance.

	GROUP A: High Inequality			
	Dep. V.: Goals Fixed effect	Dep. V.: Goals Fixed effect with team-mates effects	Dep. V.: Assists Fixed effect	Dep. V.: Assists Fixed effect with team-mates effects
Independent variables	Coeff. t-value	Coeff. t-value	Coeff. t-value	Coeff. t-value
A) Salary				
RELATIVE VALUE$_{(t-1)}$	-0.314* -2.57	-0.312* -2.55	-0.435*** -3.82	-0.429*** -3.79
ABSOLUTE VALUE$_{(t-1)}$	-0.101 -0.73	-0.114 -0.82	-0.280* -2.17	-0.286* -2.23
SQ ABSOLUTE VALUE$_{(t-1)}$	-0.010^{+} -1.94	-0.009^{+} -1.67	-0.005 -1.10	-0.004 -0.83
B) Sociodemographics				
AGE	1.294*** 3.74	1.247*** 3.60	1.257*** 3.91	1.178*** 3.66
AGE SQ	-0.027*** -4.41	-0.026*** -4.23	-0.024*** -4.20	-0.023*** -3.93
Team-mates				
AGE		0.009 0.08		-0.067 -0.65
EXCHANGES		0.464** 2.61		0.527*** 3.20
SENDING-OFFS		-0.771 -0.83		-1.242 -1.45
Position	Yes	Yes	Yes	Yes
Team	Yes	Yes	Yes	Yes
Season	Yes	Yes	Yes	Yes
Players	Yes	Yes	Yes	Yes
Test for joint significance (rel. and absol. Inc.)	5.08**	4.75**	7.94***	7.69***
Test for joint significance (team-mates effects)		2.84*		4.76**
R-squared	0.117	0.124	0.102	0.115
Prob > F	0.000	0.000	0.000	0.000
Groups	583	583	583	583
Number of observations	1575	1575	1575	1575

Continued on next page.

Table 1 cont.: Determinants of Performance.

| Independent variables | GROUP B: Low Inequality | | | | | | | |
| | Dep. V.: Goals Fixed effect | | Dep. V.: Goals Fixed effect with team-mates effects | | Dep. V.: Assists Fixed effect | | Dep. V.: Assists Fixed effect with team-mates effects | |
	Coeff.	t-value	Coeff.	t-value	Coeff.	t-value	Coeff.	t-value
A) Salary								
RELATIVE VALUE$_{(t-1)}$	-0.340	-1.56	-0.201	-0.92	-0.281	-1.48	-0.241	-1.25
ABSOLUTE VALUE$_{(t-1)}$	-0.004	-0.02	0.262	0.94	-0.093	-0.38	0.000	0.00
SQ ABSOLUTE VALUE$_{(t-1)}$	-0.094**	-3.12	-0.114**	-3.84	-0.048$^+$	-1.83	-0.057*	-2.15
B) Socio-demographics								
AGE	1.373**	3.11	1.174**	2.71	1.482**	3.85	1.401**	3.64
AGE SQ	-0.028**	-3.53	-0.025**	-3.17	-0.029**	-4.29	-0.028**	-4.07
Team-mates								
AGE			-0.207$^+$	-1.70			-0.021	-0.19
EXCHANGES			0.796**	4.11			0.319$^+$	1.85
SENDING-OFFS			-3.613**	-3.36			-1.776$^+$	-1.86
Position	Yes		Yes		Yes		Yes	
Team	Yes		Yes		Yes		Yes	
Season	Yes		Yes		Yes		Yes	
Players	Yes		Yes		Yes		Yes	
Test for joint significance (rel. and absol. Inc.)	1.89		2.26		1.30		1.26	
Test for joint significance (team-mates effects)			10.02**				2.29*	
R-squared	0.127		0.168		0.102		0.112	
$Prob > F$	0.000		0.000		0.000		0.000	
Groups	624		624		624		624	
Number of observations	1258		1258		1258		1258	

$^+$ Significant at the 10% level, * significant at the 5% level, ** significant at the 1% level, *** significant at the 0.1% level.

tournament in Korea/Japan that expulsions have a strong negative impact on the probability of winning a game because losing a team-mate reduces team strength. Specifically, the team structure must be reorganised, which, because football skills are highly specialised, tend to reduce players' and team-mates' comparative advantages. Interestingly, we also observe that team-effects are stronger among those teams that have a lower income inequality.

Looking at the control variables, age tends to influence performance, having a concave performance profile—that is, rising with age but decreasing as physical condition deteriorates. Even though age may be linked to greater experience in the game, as players get older, their physical feats, like speed and athleticism, decline.

In Table 3 we pool both groups together and report 2SLS estimations together with several diagnostic tests and the first stage regression results. Table 3 indicates that, for the 2SLS, the coefficient of the variable RELATIVE INCOME is always statistically significant with a negative sign. Thus, these results also support our first hypothesis. We perform a Hausman specification test to see whether there is sufficient difference between the coefficients of the instrumental variables regression and those of the standard regression (see Hausman, 1978). The Prob>chi2 statistics indicate that we cannot reject the hypothesis that the standard regression is an inconsistent estimator for our equation, which supports the argument that there is no endogeneity problem with our estimates. Nevertheless, we use nationality, i.e. whether a player is a foreigner or not, as an instrument for the relative income position. Foreign players may be subject to more pressure to conform than domestic players, which affects the strength of the relative income effect. As an instrument for absolute income, we take the number of spectators at home in the past season. More spectators in the previous season are connected with higher revenue in the past, which should affect players' salary. The results show that the instruments are effective in explaining the relative and absolute salary. All factors are statistically significant at the 1% level. The F-tests for the instrument exclusion set in the first-stage regression are also statistically significant in all cases at the 1% level. In addition, *Table 2* reports a test for instrument relevance, using the Anderson canonical correlations LR for whether the equation is identified. The test shows that the null hypothesis can be rejected, indicating that the model is identified and that the instruments are relevant (see Hall et al., 1996). The 2SLS specifications also support the previous findings that team-mates are important.

Table 2: Ball Contacts.

Independent variables	GROUP A: High Inequality			
	Dep. V.: Ball Contacts		Dep. V.: Ball Contacts	
	Fixed effect		Fixed effect with team-mates effects	
	Coeff.	t-value	Coeff.	t-value
A) Salary				
RELATIVE VALUE$_{(t-1)}$	-56.792*	-2.17	-65.309*	-2.46
ABSOLUTE VALUE$_{(t-1)}$	10.217	0.36	-0.939	-0.03
SQ ABSOLUTE VALUE$_{(t-1)}$	-2.030*	-2.07	-1.820$^+$	-1.84
B) Socio-demogr.				
AGE	275.989**	2.92	258.939**	2.73
AGE SQ	-5.718***	-3.28	-5.405**	-3.09
Team-mates				
AGE			4.352	0.15
EXCHANGES			81.129$^+$	1.83
SENDING-OFFS			6.985	0.04
Position	Yes		Yes	
Team	Yes		Yes	
Season	Yes		Yes	
Players	Yes		Yes	
Test for joint significance (rel. and absolute income)	6.98**		7.11***	
Test for joint significance (team-mates effects)				
R-squared	0.133		0.138	
$Prob > F$	0.000		0.000	
Groups	412		412	
Number of observations	1026		1026	

Continued on next page.

Table 2 cont.: Ball Contacts.

	GROUP B: Low Inequality			
	Dep. V.: Ball Contacts		Dep. V.: Ball Contacts	
	Fixed effect		Fixed effect with team-mates effects	
Independent variables	Coeff.	t-value	Coeff.	t-value
A) Salary				
RELATIVE VALUE$_{(t-1)}$	-92.788$^+$	-1.68	-96.524$^+$	-1.75
ABSOLUTE VALUE$_{(t-1)}$	-35.429	-0.49	-25.205	-0.35
SQ ABSOLUTE VALUE$_{(t-1)}$	-6.719	-1.01	-9.108	-1.35
B) Socio-demogr.				
AGE	534.808***	4.13	527.743***	4.10
AGE SQ	-10.854***	-4.69	-10.698***	-4.64
Team-mates				
AGE			-42.931	-1.25
EXCHANGES			66.111	1.40
SENDING-OFFS			-638.519*	-2.45
Position	Yes		Yes	
Team	Yes		Yes	
Season	Yes		Yes	
Players	Yes		Yes	
Test for joint significance (rel. and absolute income)	1.88		2.29	
Test for joint significance (team-mates effects)	1.29		2.62$^+$	
R-squared	0.153		0.170	
$Prob > F$	0.000		0.000	
Groups	436		436	
Number of observations	843		843	

$^+$ Significant at the 10% level, * significant at the 5% level, ** significant at the 1% level, *** significant at the 0.1% level.

Table 3: 2SLS Estimations.

Independent var.	Dep. V.: Goals		Dep. V.: Assists		Dep. V.: Ballcontacts	
	2SLS		2SLS		2SLS	
	Coeff.	t-value	Coeff.	t-value	Coeff.	t-value
A) Salary						
RELATIVE VALUE$_{(t-1)}$	-0.924**	-2.73	-0.553$^+$	-1.93	-217.506*	-2.10
ABSOLUTE VALUE$_{(t-1)}$	0.062	0.22	-0.104	-0.44	69.647	0.79
SQ ABSOLUTE VALUE$_{(t-1)}$	-0.033	-1.17	-0.005	-0.2	-12.344*	-2.42
B) Socio-demographic						
AGE	0.005	0.01	0.201	0.67	-70.276	-0.98
AGE SQ	0	0.04	-0.003	-0.63	1.279	1.02
Team-mates						
AGE	-0.133	-1.49	-0.057	-0.76	-29.321	-0.94
EXCHANGES	0.672***	3.56	0.594***	3.71	131.460**	2.87
SENDING-OFFS	-1.172	-1.41	-1.595*	-2.26	-303.362$^+$	-1.80
Position	Yes		Yes		Yes	
Team	Yes		Yes		Yes	
Season	No		No		No	
Players	No		No		No	
F-Test Team-mates effects	17.49***		18.01***		10.99***	
First stage regression: relative income						
Foreigners	-0.183***	-3.88	-0.183**	-3.88	-0.260***	-4.77
Test of excluded instruments	25.80***		25.8***		13.37***	
First stage regression: absolute income						
Number of spectators at home (last season)	1.33e-06***	6.02	1.33e-06***	6.02	1.17e-06***	3.47
Test of excluded instruments	46.48***		46.48***		22.99***	
Anderson canon. corr. LR statistic	32.352***		32.352***		26.846***	

$^+$ Significant at the 10% level, * significant at the 5% level, ** significant at the 1% level, *** significant at the 0.1% level.

We have seen that the 2SLS estimation reports robust findings. In addition one can argue that if the mechanism were simply that "better players earn more", then we would expect to see the effect of positional concerns in *all* sub-sample. However, the effect is primarily present in teams with a higher level of income inequality. Furthermore, several recent studies have shown at the team that the causality runs from pay to performance and not the other way round (see, e.g., Dobson and Goddard, 1998, Davies et al., 1995, Hall et al., 2002). Hall et al. (2002), for example, also stress that n English football, players are hired on relatively short-term contracts, ranging from one to five years, and players' trading and mobility are key parts of the league. The mobility costs are also lower, due to the relative geographic proximity to each other. Moreover, young stars at the beginning of their career are more mobile, which is comparable to the stars of the league, where trade clauses are "virtually unheard of in English football" and

> leading teams regularly trade their top stars in search of a better line-up, whereas players frequently express their ambition to play for a variety of clubs in a variety of leagues during their career (p. 158).

These factors are also visible in the German *Bundesliga*. Our data indicates that the number of active seasons in the league per player varies between one and eight, with an average of 2.7 seasons per player. Overall, a change of team has been observed in 12.7% of the cases, a similar result that also Carmichael et al. (1999) report from the English league (12.3% of the players changed teams in the seasons 1993-1994).

Conclusions

The empirical results presented suggest that the *relative income position* has an impact on individual performance. If a player's salary is below-average and this difference increases, his willingness to perform decreases and the negative effect of positional concerns is stronger. At the same time, a positive performance impact is observable for players with above-average salaries. We also investigate what factors lead to more marked relative income effects. We find that such effects are stronger among teams with a higher level of income inequality.

Lastly, we investigate the impact of team effects. Although it can be argued that the importance of team effects in a team sport (or team environment like a project organisation) is obvious, studies that empirically quantify such effects are rare. However, our results indicate that team effects are observable. Specifically, they suggest that, *ceteris paribus*, a player on a team with more exchanges and less sending-offs performs considerably better than players not on such a team. We also find a non-linear age effect; that is, after the turning point, more experience is overshadowed by lower physical performance.

To what extent can these findings on football players' behaviour be transferred to business use? What can managers learn from them? First of all, the results are relevant for the design of incentive mechanisms. Positional concerns are important in areas where measurable performance is directly linked to salary. Pay-for-performance schemes address extrinsic motivation, and leave intrinsic motivation aside. According to Frey and Osterloh (2005), such schemes tend to reinforce selfish extrinsic motivation, crowding out intrinsic motivation. Managers need to consider the motivational aspects of the transparency of relative income positions in terms of corresponding benefits and downside risks. Negative effects of output-oriented financial incentives, such as pay-for-performance schemes, should be complemented with process-oriented non-financial incentives, such as rewards for the best team player, best rookie, or most innovative team member of the year. This takes the individual's need for social distinction into account, using a non-material extrinsic reward (see Frey 2005). In addition, the effects of team-mate exchanges observed in our analysis raise some interesting questions; for instance, whether the analogy to teams in a corporation can be drawn. Thus, among other issues, it would be interesting to investigate whether higher turnover in a working team enforces healthy competition among team members or dilutes individual performance by destroying team cohesiveness.

References

Breusch, T. and A. Pagan (1980). "The Lagrange multiplier test and its applications to model specification in econometrics." *Review of Economic Studies*, 47(1), 239-253.

Carmichael, F., D. Forrest and R. Simmons (1999). "The labour market in association football: Who gets transferred and for how much." *Bulletin of Economic Research*, 51(2), 75-180.

Clark, A. and A. Oswald (1996). "Satisfaction and comparison income." *Journal of Public Economics*, 61(3), 359-381.

Davies, B. et al. (1995). "The demand for rugby league: Evidence from causality tests." *Applied Economics*, 27(10), 1003-1007.

Dobson S. M. and J. A. Goddard (2001). The economics of football. Cambridge: Cambridge University Press.

Dobson, S. M. and J. A. Goddard (1998). "Performance and revenue in professional league football: Evidence from Granger causality tests." *Applied Economics*, 30(12), 1641-1651.

Duesenberry, J. S. (1949). *Income, saving and the theory of consumer behavior*. Harvard: Harvard University Press.

Easterlin, R. A. (2001). "Income and happiness: Towards a unified theory." *Economic Journal*, 111(473), 465-484.

Elster, J. (1991). "Envy in social life." In *Strategy and choice*. R. J. Zeckhauser ed. Cambridge, MA: MIT Press, 49-82.

Eschweiler, M. and M. Vieth (2004). "Preisdeterminanten bei Spielertransfers in der Fußball-Bundesliga." *Zeitschrift für Betriebswirtschaft*, 64(6), 671-692.

Ferrer-i-Carbonell, A. (2005). "Income and well-being: An empirical analysis of the comparison income effect." *Journal of Public Economics*, 89(5-6), 997-1019.

Festinger, L. (1954). "A theory of social comparison processes." *Human Relations*, 7(2), 117-140.

Forrest, D. and R. Simmons (2002). "Team salaries and playing success in sports: A comparative perspective." *Zeitschrift für Betriebswirtschaft*, 72(4), 221-237.

Fort, R. D. (2003). *Sports economics*. New Jersey: Prentice Hall.

Frank, R. H. (1999). *Luxury fever: Why money fails to satisfy in an era of excess*. New York: The Free Press.

Frank, R. H. and P. J. Cook (1995). *The winner-take-all society*. New York: Free Press.

Frank, R. H. and C. R. Sunstein (2001). "Cost-benefit analysis and relative position." *University of Chicago Law Review*, 68(2), 323-374.

Frey, B. S. (2008). *Happiness: A revolution in economics*. Cambridge, MA: MIT Press.

—. (2005). "Knight fever: Towards an economics of awards." *CREMA Working Paper 2005-12*. Center for Research in Economics, Management and the Arts: Basel.

Frey, B. S. and M. Osterloh (2005). "Yes, managers should be paid like bureaucrats." *Journal for Management Inquiry*, 14(1), 96-111.

Frey, B. S. and A. Stutzer (2002). *Happiness and Economics*. Princeton: Princeton University Press.

Frick, B. (1998). "Management abilities, player salaries, and team performance." *European Journal for Sport Management*, 5(3), 6-22.

Galbraith, J. K. (1958). *The affluent society*. Boston: Houghton-Mifflin.

Hall, A. R., G. D. Rudebusch and D. W. Wilcox (1996). "Judging instrument relevance in instrumental variable estimation." *International Economic Review*, 37(2), 283-298.

Hall, S., S. Szymanski and A. S. Zimbalist (2002). "Testing causality between team performance and payroll: The cases of Major League Baseball and English football." *Journal of Sports Economics*, 3(2), 149-168.

Hamilton, B. H., J. A. Nickerson and H. Owan (2003). "Team incentives and worker heterogeneity: An empirical analysis of the impact of teams on productivity and participation." *Journal of Political Economy*, 111(3), 465-498.

Hausman, J. A. (1978). "Specification tests in econometrics." *Econometrica*, 46(6), 1251-1271.

Huebl, L. and D. Swieter (2002). "Der Spielermarkt in der Fußball-Bundesliga." *Zeitschrift für Betriebswirtschaft*, 72(Special Issue 4), 105-123.

Idson, T. L. and L. H. Kahane (2000). "Team effects on compensation: An application to salary determinants in the National Hockey League." *Economic Inquiry*, 38(2), 345-357.

Kirchsteiger, G. (1994). "The role of envy in ultimatum games." *Journal of Economic Behavior and Organization*, 25(3), 373-389.

Landers, R. M., J. B. Rebitzer and L. Y. Taylor (1996). "Rat race redux: Adverse selection in the determination of work hours in law firms." *American Economic Review*, 86(3), 329-348.

Layard, R. (2003). "Income and happiness: Rethinking economic policy." *Lecture 2*. London: London School of Economics. (cep.lse.ac.uk/events/lectures/layard/RL040303.pdf).

Lazear, E. P. (1998). *Personnel economics for managers*. New York: Wiley.

—. (2000). "Performance pay and productivity." *American Economic Review*, 90(5), 1346-1361.

Lehmann, E. E. and J. Weigand (1999). "Determinanten der Entlohnung von Profifußballspielern - Eine empirische Analyse für die deutsche Bundesliga." *Betriebswirtschaftliche Forschung und Praxis*, 51(2), 124-135.

Luttmer, E. F. P. (2005). "Neighbors as negatives: Relative earnings and well-being." *Quarterly Journal of Economics*, 120(3), 963-1002.

Marshall, A. (1961). *Principles of economics*. London: Macmillan.

Marx, K. and F. Engel (1849). "Wage labour and capital." In *Selected Works Vol. 1*. Moscow: Progress Publishers.

Porter, P. K. and G. W. Scully (1996). "The distribution of earnings and the rules of the games." *Southern Economic Journal*, 63(1), 149-163.

Schoeck, H. (1966). *Envy: A theory of social behaviour*. Indianapolis: Liberty Fund.

Senik, C. (2004). "Revitalizing relativizing income." *Delta Working Paper 2004-17*. Paris.

Stouffer, S. A. (1949). *The American soldier*. Princeton: Princeton University Press.

Torgler, B. (2004). "The Economics of the FIFA football worldcup." *KYKLOS*, 57(2), 287-300.

—. (2007). "'La Grande Boucle': Determinants of success at the Tour de France." *Journal of Sports Economics*, 8(3), 317-331.

Tversky, A. and D. Griffin (1991). "Endowment and contrast in judgments of well-being." In *Strategy and Choice*. R. J. Zeckhauser ed. Cambridge, MA: MIT Press, 297-318.

Veblen, T. (1899). *The theory of the leisure class*. New York: MacMillan.

Walker, I. and T. F. Pettigrew (1984). "Relative deprivation theory: An overview and conceptual critique." *British Journal of Social Psychology*, 23(2), 301-310.

Zeckhauser, R. J. (1991). *Strategy and choice*. Cambridge: MIT Press.

CHAPTER TWENTY

DETERMINANTS OF SHARE PRICE VARIATIONS OF LISTED FOOTBALL CLUBS: EMPIRICAL EVIDENCE FROM ENGLISH FOOTBALL LEAGUES

JOSÉ ALLOUCHE AND SÉBASTIEN SOULEZ[1]

The purpose of this chapter is to investigate the strategic and organisational development of the particular entity of football clubs. The leading question is: How do sports performance, the management of players and coaches and economic events affect the stock-market valuation of listed football clubs? In particular, do football clubs that are quoted on the stock-exchange satisfy the conditions of operation of financial markets? What factors shape the perception of the stock-market concerning how listed football clubs operate? Is there a hierarchy between these factors?

To find some answers to those questions, we investigated the influence of the following factors in regard to the valuation of the stock-market: (1) sports performance, (2) decisions of buying and selling players and coaches, as well as (3) the role of economic and financial events. England was chosen for the present research, because this country has a structured stock-exchange for football clubs that has existed for more than 10 years, with 23 listed clubs. The time period of this research is limited to three seasons (from 1998/1999 to 2000/2001).

In this chapter, we first present the research context, the literature review and the main hypotheses. This is followed by a presentation of the

[1] Allouche: IAE of Paris, University of Paris I Pantheon Sorbonne, 21 rue Broca, 75005 Paris, France. Soulez: IUT of Colmar, University of Haute Alsace, 34 rue du Grillenbreit, 68000 Colmar, France. The authors wish to thank the editors, Peter Dawson and anonymous reviewers for helpful and valuable comments on earlier versions of the manuscript.

data set and the methodology of event studies. Then we outline the results of the study and we conclude by highlighting the challenges for quoted football clubs, as well as discussing ideas for future research.

Literature Review and Hypotheses

Football Clubs and Stock Exchange

In the academic domain, it is possible to classify research carried out in the sporting entities market into three main groups: research in the economic domain, research into strategic management and research into marketing. Firstly, economists have addressed diverse questions such as the determinants of transfer fees (Dobson and Gerrard, 1999; Dobson et al., 2000), the financing of sport (Benveniste and Arnold, 1988), the correlation between revenue and sporting achievements (Dobson and Goddard, 1998), models of forecasting (Dobson and Goddard, 2003), the replacement of a manager (Audas et al., 2002), as well as models of strategic decision-making with respect to the scoring or conceding of a goal (Palomino et al., 1999). Secondly, in management sciences, little academic research has been published concerning the sports market. Minquet (1998) studied sporting investment, notably management of Human Capital, image rights and communication policy. Thirdly, in marketing, some work has been published, in particular on sponsoring (Walliser and Nanopoulos, 2000). Finally, it should be noted that Deloitte publishes a study on the finances of the football sector in every year (for details, see e.g., www.footballfinance.co.uk).

The topic under consideration, stock price reactions of listed sporting clubs, has been studied by some authors (Brown and Hartzell, 2001; Dobson and Goddard, 2001; Ashton et al., 2003; Gerrard and Lossius, 2004; Stadtmann, 2004; Palomino et al., 2005). However, to our knowledge, there exists only one published study investigating how events of football clubs quoted on the Stock Exchange influence their share prices. Specifically, Renneboog and Vanbrabant (2000) employed the methodology of event studies to analyse how sports performances of quoted British football clubs affected the fluctuation of share prices of the clubs. Whilst this study is interesting and useful as it is unique in its methodology and in the way it poses questions, the vision of a football club as an organisation whose value is a set of decisions and productive human and financial events was dismissed. This chapter uses slightly different perspective and assumes that sporting events are the natural central activities of the listed football clubs. We have identified the following factors: (1) reactions of supporters, (2) profits from ticket sales, merchandising, broadcasting rights and sponsors, (3) the financial reports that are published at least twice a year, as well as (4) the constraints of human resources management (HRM) with respect to the players and coaches as part and parcel of their activity. Consequently, the central hypothesis has been formulated by considering the influence on the stock-market value of football clubs based on these three events: Sports performance, financial performance and performance in the management of specific human resources assets (i.e., the players and coaches).

Event Studies

The methodology used in this chapter is that of the event study. This methodology is much used in financial research (Halpern, 1983, Acharya, 1993, Brav, 2000). Studies of events have been carried out to measure the effects on stock prices of companies with regard to different announcing decisions: adoption of new organisational structures (Das et al., 1998; Houston and Johnson, 2000), company name change (Horsky and Swyngedouw, 1987), issuing of prises for '*affirmative action*' programmes (Wright et al., 1995) and illegal and socially irresponsible behaviour (Dranove and Olsen, 1994; Frooman, 1997). This list, which is not exhaustive, demonstrates to what extent event studies are part and parcel of methodologies commonly used by researchers in different management disciplines. Our study of factors influencing stock prices of football clubs is based on this tradition.

The model of event study is based on three major theoretical hypotheses (Brown and Warner, 1985): (1) the stock-markets are efficient, (2) the event was unanticipated and (3) there were no confounding effects during the event window. The stock price is supposed to reflect the real value of the company as it translates the actualised value of future *cash-flows*. It also includes all pertinent information necessary for actors in the stock-market in their arbitrating procedures (McWilliams and Siegel, 1997). However, the viability of events studies supposes, in addition to the hypotheses mentioned, four principal points (McWilliams and Siegel, 1997): the size of the sample (because the test statistics used are based on normality assumptions associated with large samples), the statistical tests (sensitive to outliers), the length of the event window and its justification (short event windows capture better the significant effect of an event) and the eventual confounding effects (it is a problem if there are many events during the same event window).

If these hypotheses are fully satisfied, it becomes possible to define the normal and abnormal return of a share. The normal return means the return which would have been observed if no events had happened during the period studied and the abnormal return means the difference between the real return observed and the normal return calculated by the means of a market model, whose classic form is:

$$R_{it} = \alpha_i + \beta_i . Rm_t + \varepsilon_{it} \qquad (1)$$

where R_{it} and Rm_t respectively are the return of the i share and the average market returns on the t period (t = 1, ..., 160). The β of the model is estimated by the mean of the daily closing prices on a 160-day period before the day preceding the event window.

The abnormal return gives the possibility of estimating the non-anticipated reaction of the stock-market (by the shares evolution) generated by an event (sporting, economic, financial or human resources event in this research). This abnormal return is then the difference between the observed share return on a period and the share return on that period if the event has not occurred. The abnormal return, for each share and on each period of the event window, is:

$$AR_{it} = OR_{it} - NR_{it}$$

$$\text{with} : NR_{it} = R_{it} = \alpha_i + \beta_i . Rm_t \qquad (2)$$

where AR_{it}, NR_{it} and OR_{it} respectively are the abnormal return, the normal return and the observed return of the i share on the t period. An event window has to be defined, in which the influence of an event on the share will be sought. Average abnormal returns (AARt) are then calculated and cumulated on the event window. One concludes that there exists an influence of an event on the share price of a firm when the observed return is different from the normal return during the retained event window.

Hypotheses

In this chapter, the following research question is addressed: What are the determinants of the stock-market returns of quoted football clubs with respect to sporting activities, management of human resources activities and economic and financial management of the club? To answer this question, we formulated a general hypothesis and three specific hypotheses.

General hypothesis: The stock prices of football clubs are influenced by information arriving on the stock-market, that is information about the collective events which dictate club activity in the sporting domain, in the economic and financial domains and in the Human Resource domain.

H1: Sporting results influence the stock-market value of these clubs: wins improve the stock prices and losses lower them. A hierarchy exists according to types of wins and defeats.

H2: The publication of economic and financial results influences the stock-market value of the club. Positive financial results improve stock prices whilst negative results make them fall. The bringing of supplementary assets linked to sponsoring and to the sale of broadcasting rights improves stock prices. Information concerning investment projects in sporting equipment or facilities (construction or renovation of stadiums) is seen as something positive by the stock-market.

H3: Footballers are specific types of human assets. They participate in an active labour market which contributes to the improvement or to the reductions of club finances when they are sold or bought. In modern accountancy, they are considered as cost items and not as valued capital in the accounts. When the recruitment of a new player is announced this is seen as being something negative by the stock-market in that his arrival is seen as a burden to club finances. Inversely, the sale of a player is perceived as being something positive by the stock-market in that the sale improves the finances of the club. It is consistent with the event studies on HR which demonstrate that announcements of permanent staff reductions are associated with significant increases of stock prices around the announcement date (see for example Abowd et al., 1990).

Data

Research Data

All events concerning 14 English football clubs quoted on London Stock Exchange or the AIM/Alternative Investment Market were collected for the seasons 1998/1999, 1999/2000 and 2000/2001. As shown by Table 1, between its introduction onto the stock-market and the end of the time-period under review in this investigation, Manchester United was the only club to have not had its share price fall.[2]

We collected data containing events likely to influence the stock prices of the aforementioned listed football clubs which was published in the

---

[2] This observation was always true before the purchase of the club by the American businessman M. Glazer and its subsequent removal from the stock-market.

Table 1: Share prices of the selected clubs (in pence).[3]

Clubs	Rate at introduction (date)	Highest rate (date)	Lowest rate (date)
Aston Villa	1,070.00 (07/05/1997)	1,070.00 (07/05/1997)	103.00 (12/07/2002)
Birmingham	54.37 (07/03/1997)	54.37 (07/03/1997)	11.00 (09/10/2002)
Charlton	61.00 (21/03/1997)	80.00 (26/05/1998)	14.00 (26/06/2002)
Chelsea	60.00 (01/04/1996)	170.00 (07/02/1997)	14.00 (28/03/2003)
Leeds United	18.70 (28/02/1994)	47.00 (17/01/1997)	2.38 (27/11/2003)
Leicester	102.50 (23/04/1997)	110.42 (08/07/1997)	6.75 (26/09/2002)
Manchester U	19.00 (10/06/1991)	412.50 (23/03/2000)	13.00 (17/07/1992)
Newcastle	140.00 (02/04/1997)	140.00 (02/04/1997)	19.50 (28/03/2002)
Preston	397.92 (29/09/1995)	591.91 (21/10/1996)	112.50 (29/01/2003)
Sheffield U	392.22 (30/01/1989)	662.33 (31/10/1989)	4.50 (08/04/2002)
Southampton	56.81 (30/04/1994)	145.87 (20/01/1997)	23.50 (16/12/2002)
Sunderland	733.50 (24/12/1996)	760.00 (11/02/1997)	47.50 (06/05/2003)
Tottenham H.	95.00 (13/10/1983)	138.00 (17/01/1997)	15.00 (02/11/1992)
West Bromwich	27,300.00 (03/01/1997)	27,300.00 (03/01/1997)	4,050.00 (13/06/2003)

period between June 1, 1998 and July 31, 2001. The data was categorised into three main blocks: (1) sporting events (matches), (2) economic events such as the publication of financial reports, the creation of or the extension of a stadium, a new sponsor, a partnership or a new partnership in the club and (3) human resource events like purchases or sales of players and appointment and dismissal of coaches. Altogether, we collected information on 2,540 events with respect to the 14 listed English football clubs. We identified 21 sporting events, three economic events and two human resource events which were analysed in this chapter.

The Methodology of the Research

To keep as closely as possible to the rules established by McWilliams and Siegel (1997), the database was modified to avoid confounding effects (amplification or contraction of abnormal/exceptional returns) linked to the capture of more than one event during the time a selected window was open. Therefore, any event arising in the five days before or after a selected event was removed from the database. The only sporting financial or human resource events retained for statistical treatment were,

---

[3] The shareholding Chelsea Village is no longer quoted since 28 July 2003, when the company Chelsea limited owned by the Russian businessman Roman Abramovich bought it. The shareholding Leicester City plc is no longer quoted since 21st October 2002 when the company was placed under judicial control.

Table 2: Event data.

Events	Number of initial events	Number of events selected
1. Sporting events	2313	681
2. Economic and financial events	94	63
3. Management of HR events	133	87
Total events observed	2540	831

2,313 specific sporting events (2,134 official matches /968 wins – 525 draws – 641 losses/ + 179 special sporting events /12 Trophy wins + 30 series of matches without a defeat + 13 series of matches without wins + 61 'important' qualifications in National cup competition or European Cup competition + 18 qualifications for taking part in a European Cup competion the following year).

94 economic and financial events (announcement of financial results, of the extension or the construction of a stadium, of a sponsoring contract, of a partnership or external participation in the club).

133 HR events (all the identified available events over the period of the study from 1st June 1998 to the 31st July 2001).

All data has been taken from the online site www.soccerbase.com (for sporting events and events linked to specific human asset management), archives of the daily The Guardian and the online site of the company specialised in financial announcements, UK-Wire Limited (for economic and financial events).

The stock prices came from two sources of data: Datastream and JCF Quant. Reliance on these two different databases allowed for the validation of the definition of necessary data (the rate at the close of trading each day) and ensured the quality and the pertinence of the data collected. The stock prices were collected for the three aforementioned seasons. As this study deals with both sporting and economic events, it was decided to lengthen the period of study by two months in order to take into account, useful data on transfers and economic events in the first and the last year. Stock prices were therefore noted between 1st June 1998 and 31st July 2001. As market indices, we chose the FTSE index All Share, which notably includes the index Leisure, Entertainment and Hotel of which listed football clubs are members, as well as the Bloomberg Football club index, which is the most representative index available in the football sector.

those which were not in competition with other events concerning the same club for a period of five days before or five days after the event observed. In total, 831 events were selected and used in order to test the hypothesis of an influence on stock prices, equalling a third of all events concerning the 14 English quoted clubs for the investigated period. It should be noted that for certain types of events, the size of the sample could be quite small. However, the very small samples, those smaller than 15 events, were not analysed.

Using the aforementioned formulas, average abnormal returns were
calculated for each type of events in a window comprising five days of
trading activities before and after the investigated event in order to be able
to observe eventual market anticipations. The event window was therefore,
at its largest, eleven days long. The event window is necessarily short in
view of the risk of interference between the events as the matches often
take place every three days. In a case such as this, the two events were
removed from the sample being analysed. The average abnormal returns
were cumulated in the window of the completed event (t = -5... 0... +5),
then over different sub-periods, according to the type of event being
analysed. Over a period (t1-t2) belonging to the event window, we could
thus evaluate a cumulative abnormal return/CAR(t1-t2) for the purpose of
estimating the global influence of the type of event over the period
considered (t1-t2). The statistical significance of these cumulative
abnormal returns was systematically tested. The analysis of these results
was, therefore, based on the direction of the influence of the event
(negative or positive), on the intensity of cumulative abnormal returns
(strong or weak) as well as the significance of associated statistical tests
(simple Student T tests).

Results

Sports Performance

Match Results: the Triptych Victory/Draw/Defeat
The detailed analysis of abnormal returns over the eleven day period,
window (-5-+5) with 0 for the day of the match, indicates in the three
kinds of outcomes (victory, draw and defeat), a polarisation of stock-
market reactions on the day following the match, with a gradual increase
over the subsequent week.

Hypothesis 1 was validated in its global vision, as shown by Table 3. A
victory led to a stock-market increase in value of the winning club of
around +0.47% of the abnormal return on the day following the match and
+0.72% between Day+2 and Day+5. A defeat lowered the value of the
club by around -0.72% of the abnormal return on the day following the
match and -0.41% between Day+2 and Day+5. A draw implied a weak
abnormal return of -0.21% uniquely on the day after a match.

Everything happens as if the effect of a victory is immediately transformed
into a positive anticipation of prospects for the club by the market actors.
This anticipation is sustained for a whole week. The importance of the

Table 3: Daily average abnormal returns after a match.

Window	Victory		Draw		Defeat	
of event	AR(t)	Student T	AR(t)	Student T	AR(t)	Student T
Day of the match	-0.07 %	-0.77	-0.10 %	-0.93	-0.09 %	-0.88
D_{day+1}	0.47 %	2.80**	-0.21 %	-1.09	-0.72 %	-4.26***
D_{day+2}	0.05 %	0.44	0.04 %	0.42	-0.19 %	-1.76*
D_{day+3}	0.21 %	1.77*	-0.07 %	-0.55	-0.07 %	-0.38
D_{day+4}	0.01 %	0.07	0.08 %	0.64	-0.08 %	-0.72
D_{day+5}	0.45 %	0.90	-0.05 %	-0.39	-0.07 %	-0.55

* Significant at the 5% level, ** significant at the 1% level, *** significant at the 0.1% level.

'next day' effect could be explained by the double intervention on the stock-market by investors (economic rationality) and of supporters (affective rationality). We can then speculate that the prolonged nature of the effect over the next four days is explained by actions of investors who regard the victory of the club in light of its competitors. In contrast, a defeat may be sanctioned by the stock-market in two stages. Firstly, the drop in the stock price is greater on the day following the defeat but less so over the next four days. This smoothing effect could be explained by the behaviour of supporters who maintain their support following negative results, thereby leaving investors as the main actors in the stock-market. Secondly, it seems that a draw has little effect on market actors.

In sum, we see that the stock-market reactions to the outcomes of the matches are not identical. Table 4 recapitulates the average abnormal returns for each type of match result selected in the database and for each type of club. The statistical analyses were carried out successively for the victories, the draws and defeats. Treatments were then conducted for whole set of the clubs quoted on the Stock Exchange—with the exception of *Manchester United*—for *Premier League* clubs and lastly for the clubs of Divisions 1 and 2.

The influence of a victory is significantly different for each type of club. There was little influence for D1 and D2 clubs (average abnormal return on the day following the match: +0.32%) and more influence for *Premier League* clubs (average abnormal return the next day of +0.53%). We found no difference whatsoever for *Manchester United* (negative average abnormal return but not statistically significant). The influence of one defeat was also significantly different according to the nature of the club concerned, but the gaps are reversed. A defeat was always

Table 4: Influence of generic sporting results—daily abnormal returns.

Events	Window of Events
Victories	[+1]
All clubs (N=206)	0.47% (t=2.80)***
All clubs except MU (N=180)	0.57% (t=3.03)**
Premier League (N=146)	0.53% (t=2.39)**
Premier League excluding MU (N=120)	0.70% (t=2.63)***
MU (N=26)	-0.21% (t= n.s.)
D1+D2 [a] (N=60)	0.32% (t=1.63)
Defeats	[+1]
All clubs (N=171)	-0.72% (t=4.26)***
All clubs excepting MU (N=167)	-0.74% (t=4.27)***
Premier League (N=117)	-0.63% (t=3.47)***
Premier League excepting MU (N=113)	-0.66% (t=3.49)***
D1+D2 (N=54)	-0.90% (t=2.50)**

** Significant at the 1% level, *** significant at the 0.1% level.
[a] Division 1 and Division 2 clubs, that is all clubs excluding Premier League.

insignificant for *Manchester United* (average abnormal return statistically insignificant), perturbing for *Premier League* clubs (average abnormal return on the following day: -0.63%) and very perturbing for D1 and D2 clubs (average abnormal return the following day: -0.90%).

These differences can probably be explained by the nature of the clubs concerned. *Manchester United* is a club which is well established on the stock-market. It offers a very attractive shareholding for investors with a continuity assured by many factors, including those outside the sphere of competitions. In other terms, this club has earned autonomy from the constraints of weekly matches. The solidity of its economic model and the stability of a history of strong sporting achievements leave investors unperturbed by single performances. Other *Premier League* clubs such as *Chelsea, Newcastle, Aston Villa and Tottenham,* have to face competitive sporting events' ups and downs with more adventurous economic models. A victory is an opening to qualification for a lucrative European Cup competition and a defeat is synonymous with a return to the treadmill of national competitions. Thus, the result of every match attracts the attention of the stock-market. Shares might be bought by supporters and investors in the case of a win, or might be sold in the case of a defeat, assuming that investors and supporters are rational and profit-maximising. For D1 and D2 clubs the situation is not symmetrical: a weak positive abnormal return for a victory and a strong negative abnormal return for a defeat. As such clubs have a very weak volume of shares being exchanged each day on the stock-market, we may assume most of the trade is carried out by supporters and club managers. We can then speculate that a victory allows supporters to justify the buying of shares and especially their being retained, whereas, a defeat produces an effect of panic which favours the selling of shares.

National Cup Victories and Defeats

In the universe of football competitions, National Cup-ties, FA Cup and League Cup have the particular status of competition with direct elimination. The economic and financial situation of clubs involved in cup matches is therefore reliant on the number of rounds reached by the team in the qualifying matches: more ticket sales, more TV broadcasting rights sold, more appeal to sponsors, etc. In order to measure the influence of results obtained in these competitions, the qualifications for the highest rounds and the premature eliminations during the first two rounds were selected as criteria for measurement.

As shown by Table 5, for all types of clubs, a Cup qualification gives rise to a positive average abnormal return. On the morning following a winning match for qualification, the average abnormal return for all clubs qualifying is +1.23% (p < 0.01).

For *Premier League* (minus *MU*) clubs, the growth of the stock price is limited to the day following the match. *Manchester United* distinguishes itself, as the abnormal return is directed towards an increase, but only weakly so and without any statistical soundness. Qualification has become 'routine' and is nothing new for the club. Its reputation is not modified by the result and its financial situation is in no way transformed by this qualification.

Elimination from a Cup-tie logically produced a negative and statistically significant average abnormal return for practically all types of club in the sample, confirming the Hypothesis 1. The effect is particularly clear on the day following a match: -0.32% for the whole set of the clubs and -0.58% for *Premier League* excluding *MU*. One can underline a slight effect which is statistically significant: the anticipation of elimination on the day of the match by the stock-market. Once the moment of disappointment has gone, on the day after the match leading to the premature elimination from National cup-ties, the cumulative abnormal returns became positive within three days (D_{day+2}/D_{day+4}): +0.80% for the set of *Premier League* minus *MU*. This takes place as if the market actors interpreted positively, after reflection and with dispassion, to the

Table 5: Influence of victories and defeats in national cup-ties—cumulative abnormal returns.

Events	Event Windows		
Qualification in National Cup comp.	[0,+1] [a]	[+1] [a]	[+2,+4] [a]
All clubs (N=41)	1.39% (t=2.04)*	1.23% (t=2.70)**	0.66% (t= n.s.)
Premier League excl. MU (N=29)	0.97% (t= n.s.)	0.75% (t=1.96)*	0.01% (t= n.s.)
Elimination in National Cup comp.	[0,+1)	[+1]	[+2,+4]
All clubs (N=37)	-0.28% (t=1.71)*	-0.32% (t=1.87)*	0.60% (t= n.s.)
Premier League excl. MU (N=22)	-0.49% (t=1.93)*	-0.58% (t=2.14)*	0.80% (t=1.43)

* Significant at the 5% level, ** significant at the 1% level.
[a] For example, the event window [+2,+4] is the period between D_{day+2} after the match and D_{day+4} after the match.

premature elimination. The elimination permits the conservation of players' health and consequently, preserves the eliminated team's chances in other more important competitions.

Qualifications and Eliminations in European Cup-Ties
    The European Cup-ties, *Champions League* and *UEFA Cup* have a mixed nature. *Champions League* has an initial phase in the form of a mini-championship and a second one in the form of direct elimination. *UEFA Cup* is just a series of knockout rounds. Table 6 describes how the stock prices of the listed English football clubs are affected by performance in the European Cup competitions.
    The results in Table 6 give partly support for Hypothesis 1. A win in a European Cup match generated a strong positive effect on the stock prices of the investigated clubs. On the day following a match, the average abnormal return was +0.93% for the set of *Premier League* clubs and +1.55% for the same clubs excluding *Manchester United* (p < 0.01).
    The qualification of clubs was interpreted positively by stock-market. On the day following a victory in a qualification match, the average abnormal return was +1.70% for *Premier League* clubs. There was a difference between *MU*—a club whose financial position seems to be

Table 6: Influence of victories and defeats in European Cup competition—cumulative abnormal returns.

Events	Event Windows		
Qualification for Europe	[-2,0] [a]	[+1] [a]	[+2,+5] [a]
Premier League (N=17)	-0.33% (t= n.s.)	0.76% (t=1.81)*	-2.01% (t=2.32)*
Qualification in European Cup comp.	[-2,0]	[+1]	[+2,+5]
Premier League (N=15)	2.41% (t=1,79)*	1.70% (t=2.06)*	1.12% (t=1.45)
European Cup comp. victories	[-2,0]	[+1]	[+2,+5]
Premier League (N=62)	-0.27% (t= n.s.)	0.93% (t=2.34)*	0.17% (t= n.s.)
Premier League excl. MU (N=39)	-0.47% (t= n.s.)	1.55% (t=2.59)**	0.37% (t= n.s.)
European Cup comp. defeats	[-2,0]	[+1]	[+2,+5]
Premier League (N=24)	-1.41%(t=2.29)*	-1.46%(t=3.81)***	-2.01%(t=2.84)**
Premier League excl. MU (N=19)	-1.62%(t=2.14)*	-1.81%(t=4.03)***	-2.16%(t=2.48)*

* Significant at the 5% level, ** significant at the 1% level, *** significant at the 0.1% level.
[a] For example, the event window [-2,0] is the period between D_{day-2} before the match and the day of the match.

largely unaffected by sporting results—and other *Premier League* clubs whose financial value appears, on the contrary, to depend on European competition results. Market actors anticipate a qualification after a match, from the second day before and up to the day of the match itself. For *Premier League* clubs, the cumulative abnormal return was +2.41%. This is a particularly high figure demonstrating that the importance of European competitions as a condition of financial performance for clubs.

Defeats in European matches significantly influence the share price of the investigated clubs. The average abnormal return calculated on the day following a match was -1.46% for the *Premier League* clubs and of -1.81% for the same clubs, excluding *Manchester United* (p < 0.001). These figures are significantly higher than those observed for defeats in domestic games. This shows the reaction of the stock-market when faced with deterioration of the financial situation for these clubs following this sort of defeat. This reaction, which is practically identical to that observed on the day following a European match victory, was proportionately higher: -1.46% for a defeat and +0.93% for a victory. The observation of average abnormal returns for nine days (2 before and 5 after) with a relative deterioration of -4.88%, following a defeat in a European match illustrates stock-market behaviour well. This reaction might stem from a combination of sports knowledge and economic rationality.

Three phases can be observed: (1) anticipation of the defeat (D_{day-2}/D_{day0}), CAR = -1.41%, (2) realisation of the defeat on the day following the match (D_{day+1}), CAR = -1.46% and (3) accentuation of stock-market wariness in the day following the match (D_{day+2}/D_{day+5}), CAR = -2.01%. In other words, the market seemed to have foreseen the defeat (suggesting knowledge of sports), then marked its wariness regarding the financial consequences of this defeat for club (indicating economic rationality).

A defeat by *Manchester United* in a European match was the only case of a sporting result which significantly influenced the share value. This demonstrates the major importance of European competitions for quoted clubs–including a club whose stock-market value seems to be independent of sporting results. Over the four days following a defeat, a negative reaction of the market was provoked with a *cumulative* abnormal return of -2.10% (p < 0.05).

In considering the above observations, we conclude that the qualification for a European competition must constitute, especially for a quoted club, an essential objective. The market reaction to this qualification is often a positive appreciation in its effect on the financial performance of the club. For the three studied seasons, 17 qualifications for European competitions were identified: five concerning *Manchester United* and twelve concerning other *Premier League* clubs in our sample. The results obtained partly confirm Hypothesis 1. On the day following the official qualification, (D_{day+1}), the cumulative abnormal return was positive up to +0.76% (p < 0.05). A reversal of the situation occurred over the following four days: the *cumulative* abnormal return (D_{day+2}/ D_{day+5}) became very negative at -2.01%. The initial positive appreciation probably gave way to pessimism on the part of investors on the day after a qualification as, in consequence, qualifying clubs plan to reinforce their sporting prowess to the detriment of salary costs.

Influence of the Development and Investment Cycle: Economic and Financial Performance

Disclosure of Financial Reports

Companies listed on the stock exchange publish financial report at least twice a year. Such reports might influence market value of companies. Within the framework of our study, 16 positive (profits) and 17 negative (losses) results published were classified without overlapping other events affecting investigated clubs for five days before and five after the publication of the reports.

As shown by Table 7, the publication of positive financial reports has no significant effect. The announcement was probably preceded by rumours concerning contents of the publication and the stock-market didn't react positively once the favourable financial results were presented.

The announcement of negative financial reports perturbed the stock-market to a greater extent than the publication of positive reports. All clubs presenting negative reports were significantly affected by a negative reaction by the stock-market: -4.11% for the period (D_{day-5}/D_{day+3}) (p < 0.01). Investors convey their mistrust towards clubs when faced with unfavourable financial reports. The intervening by investors over a long period of time in the cycle of events affected the life of a football club: no less than eight days of stock-market dealing, four days before and three days afterwards. The mistrust was stronger when the negative reports concerned the *Premier League* clubs rather than for clubs in the first and second divisions.

Other Economic Events

Many other economic events may affect the share price of a listed football club including the announcements of the extension or the construction of a stadium, of a sponsoring contract, of a partnership or external participation in the club.

The global turnover for a football club depends on ticket sales, TV broadcasting rights, sponsoring contracts and benefits earned when trophies are won. In England, ticket sales are considerable in view of the large number of spectators at matches. These sales depend entirely on the capacity of the stadium and the services offered. This is the reason why English clubs are often engaged in renovation work and even in constructing their own new stadiums. Investment into stadiums has a double effect on the stock-market: an increase in the property value of the club and, as is hoped, a future increase in ticket sales.

Table 7: Influence of economic and financial management—cumulative abnormal returns.

Events	Event Windows	
Positive Financial Reports	$[-1, +1]$ [a]	$[-5,+3]$ [a]
All clubs (N=16)	1.15% (t= n.s.)	-1.09% (t=n.s.)
Negative Financial Reports	$[-1,+1]$	$[-5,+3]$
All clubs (N=17)	-1.71% (t=1.44)	-4.11% (t=3.19) **
Economic Events	$[-1,+1]$	$[+2,+5]$
Premier League (N=30)	3.90% (t=2.65) **	-1.98% (t=1.86) *
Premier League without MU (N=22)	4.24% (t=2.15) *	-1.49% (t=1.19)

* Significant at the 5% level, ** significant at the 1% level.
[a] For example, the event window $[-5,+3]$ is the period between D_{day-5} before the report and D_{day+3} after the report.

The amount of capital allocated to financing football club activities has considerably increased over the past few years due to the following factors: the influence of European Cup competitions, the ensuing competition between clubs to obtain supplementary resources, the inflation of salaries and costs, as well as the burden of financing issues following the Bosman-ruling (e.g., transfers, salaries and bonus packages) and to its unavoidable consequences of higher bids designed to compel the signing of contracts of recruitment. Club action is particularly orientated towards the quest for sponsors such as sporting equipment manufacturers, but also companies wishing to use the club as a vehicle for their own communication and/or partners integrated into the social capital of the club.

As shown by Table 7, these three kinds of economic events lead to contrasted stock-market reactions. First of all, for three days concentrated around the announcement, (D_{day-1}/D_{day+1}), the stock-market evaluated the announcement favourably: the cumulative abnormal return reached +3.90% for the investigated *Premier League* clubs (with +4.24% for the *Premier League* excluding *Manchester United*). Secondly, for four days (D_{day+2}/D_{day+5}), the appreciation of the stock-market was inversed and became negative: the cumulative abnormal return reached -1.98% for the investigated *Premier League* clubs (with -1.49% for the *Premier League* with the exclusion of *Manchester United*). This inversion could be caused by two things: the taking of profit after a lively increase and/or internal politics such as rumours of internal dissension within the club as a consequence of the arrival of a new shareholder.

Table 8: Influence of human assets management—cumulative abnormal returns.

Events	Event Windows	
Selling of Players	[-3,+1] [a]	[0] [a]
All clubs (n=49)	0.64% (t=0.98)	0.56% (t=1.92)*
Signing-on of Players	[-3,+1]	[0]
All clubs (n=38)	-1.06% (t=2.34)**	-0.36% (t=1.81)*

* Significant at the 5% level, ** significant at the 1% level.
[a] For example, the event window [-3,+1] is the period between D_{day-3} before the selling and D_{day+1} after the selling.

Influence of Human Resource Management: The Valuation of Specific Human Assets

For investors, players under contract constitute a financial guarantee before constituting a sporting guarantee. Players are specific human resource assets for the club to the extent that they participate in an active labour market which contributes to the improvement or deterioration of club finances as players are sold or bought. They are considered – within the logistics of a modern accounting system– as costs and not as capital value in the accounts. It is in this spirit that the Hypothesis 3 was put forward.

The database contained information related to 49 sales of players for a price above £3,000,000. Sales and purchases took place away from all other events within a window of eleven days (five days before and five days after the official announcement).

The results confirm Hypothesis 3. As shown by Table 8, the sales of players were positively appreciated by the stock-market. The average abnormal return on the official day of the sale (D_{day0}) for all investigated clubs reached around +0.56% ($p < 0.05$). This relative appreciation was anticipated in the three days which preceded the official announcement of the sale. The selling of a player might be perceived as instant income (the product of a sale) and as a reduction in overheads (loss of a salary no longer to be paid) leading to improved club financial results. One might argue that the intervention of the stock-markets is practically exclusive of the intervention of supporters. In general supporters are emotionally attached to players wearing the club strip and it is unlikely that they will rejoice at the transfer of the player. Inversely, the buying of a player was negatively perceived by the stock-market. The average abnormal return on the day of the sale (D_{day0}) reached -0.36% for the whole of the quoted clubs ($p < 0.05$). This negative view extended, in fact, around the announcement and over 5 days (D_{day-3}/D_{day+1}), with a significant cumulative abnormal return of -1.06% for those clubs ($p < 0.01$). The explanation is, of course, symmetrical to the effects of the selling of a player. The purchase of a player might be perceived as an immediate expense (the global price of the transfer: buying out the original contract from the original club plus agents' and intermediaries' fees) and as an increase in charges (new elevated salary in the context of a rapid increase in players' salaries) leading to a reduction of the financial resources of the club.

In the two cases, sale and purchase, there was support for Hypothesis 3 and thereby gives further evidence for the general hypothesis driving our study. The football club is, in many ways and with reference to the results already analysed, a quasi-enterprise managed in a traditional accountancy and managerial framework of which the specific human resource asset is seen as a cost and not as an asset.

Discussion and Conclusion

In all, the multiple tests carried out give support for the general hypothesis and, at least partly, for Hypothesis 1–3. The sporting results influence the stock-market positively after a victory in a match, a qualification and the winning of a Cup competition and negatively after a defeat or an elimination. Club managerial decisions in terms of running and investment directly influence stock prices positively in the case of sponsoring, investment in sporting facilities and positive financial results and negatively after the announcement of unfavourable financial results. The management of human resources (e.g., recruitment and dismissal of players and coaches) also influences how the listed football club is perceived by the stock market.

In accordance with our hypotheses, a hierarchy between the factors influencing the stock price of quoted clubs was observed. In this way, it appears that the stock-markets attach a greater importance to the announcement of sponsoring contracts or financial participation in the club. It does therefore seem that economic and financial criteria prevail over sporting results and human resource management in a club. This result, however, needs to be qualified to the extent that, in reality, we can observe three models differentiated according to the type of club. Firstly, the stock price for *Manchester United* depends, almost exclusively, on economic and financial factors, with human resource and sporting events having less influence. The notable exception concerns defeats in the European Cup competitions, which are the only sporting result that may threaten the finances of the club. Secondly, the stock prices of the other listed *Premier League* clubs depends closely on three types of events: Economic and financial announcements are the most important ones, but the human resource and sporting events also play a large role, in particular in European Cup matches. Thirdly, D1 and D2 clubs follow a specific model. Their stock prices depend essentially on their sporting results in National league and in National Cup matches.

The quality of results obtained thus interprets the diversity of situations of clubs according to their status. One club stands out: *Manchester United*. Being so well established on the stock-market, the quality and the regularity of its sporting results and its management orientated towards a great variety of sources of financing, leads to its great stock-market stability and its significant autonomy in the consideration of its sporting results. The market actors intervene significantly on other *Premier League* clubs with strongly contrasted effects, whereas clubs from the first and second divisions suffer from relative indifference.

Beyond the results obtained and of their statistical significance, two limits subsist in the use of the methodology of studying events in relation to English football clubs. First, the market for shares in this sector could probably be considered by some as relatively inefficient in terms of the poor volume of shares changing hands and of the irregularity of these exchanges. Second, we know nothing of the differentiation of actors who intervene in this market, their scale of preference or their aims.

Concerning the results of this study, some limitations appear. Firstly, the majority of the sporting events happen on a week-end day, others during the week and we have not tested for the reaction of the investors whereas it is likely that they react differently to Saturday matches than matches played immediately prior to days when the stock-market is open. Secondly, our analysis does not consider the number of stock trades of listed football clubs and, namely, the possible influence of events on trade volumes. It could have been an interesting variable to interpret and discuss. Thirdly, the Dobson/Goddard method (Dobson and Goddard, 2001), which uses betting odds to control for expectations, is not used in this study because of limited access to the data for older years. Fourthly, this event study did not use a sophisticated risk correction, like the Fama/French three-factor model, but it appears to be unnecessary given the length of the event windows was about a few days and expected market returns within this period was near zero. Finally, Hypothesis 3, which claims that players are a cost factor rather than an asset from the stock-markets' point of view, could be criticised in that some players move on free transfers. They are indeed an asset and not a cost in this particular situation. This relationship may also depend on the age of the player.

An enlarged research project would lead to extending the analysis to all of the clubs quoted in Europe. Other suggestions for future research could investigate the fans vs. institutional investors reactions to the events studied in our chapter. For example, one might examine whether supporters are buy-and-hold investors or "irrational" investors who buy and sell according to the sporting results of their favourite team. It would also be interesting to empirically describe the typical shareholder structure of the football clubs. Are there large shareholders of Manchester United who do not trade? Is trading volume significantly lower for Manchester United? Finally, the reasons behind most European clubs' reluctance to go public should be investigated.

References

Abowd, J. M., G. T. Milkovich and J. M. Hannon (1990). "The effects of human resource management decisions on shareholder value." *Industrial and Labor Relations Review*, 43(3), 203-236.

Acharya, S. (1993). "Value of latent information: Alternative event study methods." *Journal of Finance*, 48(1), 363-385.

Ashton, J. K., B. Gerrard and R. Hudson (2003). "Economic impact of national sporting success: Evidence from the London Stock Exchange." *Applied Economic Letters*, 10(12), 783-785.

Audas, R., S. Dobson and J. Goddard (2002). "The impact of managerial change on team performance in professional sports." *Journal of Economics and Business*, 54(6), 633-642.

Benveniste, I. and T. Arnold (1988). "Funding and football: Same players, different games." *Accountancy*, 102(1141), 77-79.

Brav, A. (2000). "Inference in long-horizon event studies: A Bayesian approach with application to initial public offerings." *Journal of Finance*, 55(5), 1979-2016.

Brown, G. W. and J. C. Hartzell (2001). "Market reaction to public information: The atypical case of the Bolton Celtics." *Journal of Financial Economics*, 60(2-3), 333-370.

Brown, S. and J. Warner (1985). "Using daily stock returns: The case of event studies." *Journal of Financial Economics*, 14(1), 3-31.

Das, S., P. K. Sen and S. Sengupta (1998). "Impact of strategic alliances on firm valuation." *Academy of Management Journal*, 41(1), 27-41.

Dobson, S. and B. Gerrard (1999). "The determination of player transfer fees in English professional soccer." *Journal of Sport Management*, 13(4), 259-279.

Dobson, S., B. Gerrard and H. Simon (2000). "The determination of transfer fees in English nonleague football." *Applied Economics*, 32(9), 1145-1161.

Dobson, S. and J. Goddard (1998). "Performance and revenue in professional league football: Evidence from Granger causality tests." *Applied Economics*, 30(12), 1641-1653.

Dobson, S. and J. Goddard (2001). *The economics of football*. Cambridge: Cambridge University Press.

Dobson, S. and J. Goddard (2003). "Persistence in sequences of football match results: A Monte-Carlo analysis." *European Journal of Operational Research*, 148(2), 247-265.

Dranove, D. and C. Olsen (1994). "The economic side effects of dangerous drug announcements." *Journal of Law and Economics*, 37(2), 323-348.

Frooman, J. (1997). "Socially irresponsible and illegal behavior and shareholder wealth." *Business and Society*, 36(3), 221-249.

Gerrard, B. and E. Lossius (2004). "Playing the stock market: The relationship between news and equity prices in professional team sports." *Working Paper presented at the North American Society of Sport Management (NASSM) Conference*. Atlanta, GA.

Halpern, P. (1983). "Corporate acquisitions: A theory of special cases? A review of event studies applied to acquisitions." *Journal of Finance*, 38(2), 297-317.

Horsky, D. and P. Swyngedouw (1987). "Does it pay to change your company's name? A stock market perspective." *Marketing Science*, 6(4), 320-335.

Houston, M. B. and S. A. Johnson (2000). "Buyer-Supplier contracts versus joint ventures: Determinants and consequences of transaction structure." *Journal of Marketing Research*, 37(1), 1-15.

McWilliams, A. and D. Siegel (1997). "Event studies in management research: Theoretical and empirical issues." *Academy of Management Journal*, 40(3), 626-657.

Minquet, J. P. L. (1998). "Est-il rentable d'investir dans le sport en Europe?" *Accomex*, 21.

Palomino, F., L. D. R. Renneboog and C. Zhang (2005). "Stock price reactions to short-lived public information: The case of betting odds." *Finance Working Paper 81/2005*. European Corporate Governance Institute.

Palomino, F., L. Rigotti and A. Rustichini (1999). "Skill, strategy and passion: an empirical analysis of soccer." *Working Paper 129*. Tilburg University.

Renneboog, L. and P. Vanbrabant (2000). "Share price reactions to sporty performance of soccer clubs listed on the London stock exchange and the AIM Center for Economic Research." *Working Paper 2000-19*. Tilburg University.

Stadtmann, G. (2004). "An empirical examination of the news model: The case of Borussia Dortmund GmbH & Co. KgaA." *Zeitschrift für Betriebswirtschaft*, 74(2), 165-185.

Walliser, B. and P. Nanopoulos (2000). "Qui a gagné la Coupe du Monde 1998? Déterminants et importance de l'association durable des sponsors à l'événement." *Actes du Congrès de l'Association Française de Marketing*. Montréal.

Wright, P., S. P. Ferris, J. S. Hillier, M. Kroll (1995). "Competitiveness through management of diversity: Effects on stock price evaluation." *Academy of Management Journal*, 38(1), 272-287.

CHAPTER TWENTY-ONE

THE ONLY WAY IS UP? MATCH OUTCOME AND STOCK PRICE REACTIONS OF BORUSSIA DORTMUND GMBH & CO. KGAA

JAN-CHRISTOPH RÜLKE AND GEORG STADTMANN[1]

A central assumption of the news model as proposed by Frenkel (1981) is that agents collect every piece of publicly available information and incorporate this information set in their asset price expectation. This leads to a scenario where asset prices are efficient in a semi-strong form as defined by Fama (1970), i.e. asset prices reflect all publicly available information. As a consequence, changes in asset prices are the outcome of the appearance of new, non-expected information that was not considered in asset prices so far. Frequently, this information is labelled as a *signal* with respect to the fundamental value of an asset. When testing the news model, it would be ideal to have signals at hand that occur very frequent, are easy to quantify, occur solely when financial markets are closed, become publicly available to all agents at the same point in time, and have ex-ante observable expectations.

Regularly, signals such as earnings announcements are used to test the news model. A disadvantage of using earnings announcements is that such information occurs only infrequently, since such an analysis is based on quarterly reports. Furthermore, some agents have access to this information in advance which can lead to substantial problems due to insider trading. Additionally, information regarding quarterly reports is already expected to some extent and is therefore—at least partially—reflected in market prices. All characteristics mentioned above lead to a

[1] Rülke: WHU – Otto Beisheim School of Management, Burgplatz 2, 56179 Vallendar, Germany: Stadtmann: University of Southern Denmark, Department of Business and Economics, Campusvej 55, 5230 Odense M, Denmark.

scenario, where earnings announcements can not be regarded as pure signals so that the news content is not easy to quantify (Brown and Hartzell, 2001).

A stock market segment where signals come close to fulfilling the above mentioned criteria is the sports industry with publicly traded sports clubs, like football teams. Football teams participate in different competitions like the national championship, the national cup competition, as well as international competitions such as, on an European level, the Champions League, UEFA and UI-Cup. Therefore, financial agents receive information on the strength of a team regularly and frequently. Another feature is that matches normally take place on weekends or at night, so that the outcome of the games materialises when financial markets are closed. Additionally, the outcome of the games becomes public knowledge at the very same time and it can thus be excluded that financial agents act on inside information. A very important aspect is also the fact that betting odds are available for all matches. These betting odds can be used to extract market expectations and ex-ante winning/losing probabilities. Therefore, one can control for the ex-ante expected match outcome. Given these industry characteristics, it becomes clear that publicly traded sport clubs can be regarded as a very appropriate candidate for an application of the news model. Nevertheless, one may argue that the football industry may also have some disadvantages. Football fans are often regarded to act irrationally and one can not rule out that football fans also engage in stock market trading. However, some institutional investors hold major stakes in Borussia Dortmund GmbH & Co. KGaA which is the subject of this analysis. For example, in 2000 and 2001 the Deutsche Bank was holding a stake of more than 10 % and an international investment fund was holding a 5 % in the company (Borussia Dortmund, 2001, p. 9).[2] Largest single shareholder in 2002 was still the Ballspielverein Borussia 09 e.V. Dortmund which held a stake of more than 25 % (Borussia Dortmund, 2002, p. 30).[3] Furthermore, the Deutsche Bank was the main underwriter during the IPO process.

Apparently a large proportion of Borussia Dortmund's stockholders are institutional investors and do not hold the stock due to sentiments to the club itself. Therefore, the stock market development of Borussia Dortmund should highly reflecting news regarding changes in expected profits. This will also become clear in part 4.3 of this paper, when we analyse some important events that caused large fluctuations in stock

---

[2] Borussia Dortmund Annual Report July 2000 - June 2001.
[3] Borussia Dortmund Annual Report July 2001 - June 2002.

prices. In February 2008 Borussia is still listed on the Frankfurt Stock Exchange.

Brown and Hartzell (2001) provide the most comprehensive analysis of the impact of sporting results on share prices. Their focus is on the performance of the Boston Celtics in the NBA competition and subsequent stock price reactions. To control for the role of expectations they use betting market point spreads. As a result they find that match performance significantly affect share prices, trading volume and volatility. Furthermore, they find asymmetric price reactions to wins and losses and that playoffs have a larger impact on returns compared to regular season games. However, their analysis is limited to sport events only. In this paper, we will also check whether corporate governance related news influenced the stock price of Borussia Dortmund.

Until now, empirical evidence with respect to the link between sporting success and subsequent stock performance of publicly listed football companies is limited. Lehmann and Weigand (1998), Renneboog and Vanbrabant (2000), Dobson and Goddard (2001), as well as Palomino et al. (2005) analyse the performance of the British football clubs. Lehmann and Weigand (1998) analyse the corporate governance problematic of publicly listed sports clubs and come to the conclusion that the number of IPOs in the football industry will be limited. This hypothesis especially holds for the German market since only one club is listed at the stock exchange so far. Renneboog and Vanbrabant (2000) analyse the whether or not the share prices of soccer clubs listed on the London Stock Exchange are influenced by the soccer teams' weekly sporty performances. They find positive abnormal returns at the first trading day following a soccer victory while defeats or draws are yield negative abnormal returns. Dobson and Goddard (2001) support the previous results and extend the analysis by accounting for the expected outcome applying betting odds. Ashton et al. (2003) analyse the economic impact of national sport events on the stock market by applying the event study methodology. However, their focus is not on the impact of match outcome on clubs' stock market prices but on the impact of England's national football team results on the FTSE100 index. Results show that stock market return is indeed positive after wins and negative after losses. Edmans et al. (2007) provide a comprehensive study of the impact of national sport outcomes on the stock market return. They find a significant decline after soccer losses and loss effects after international cricket, rugby and basketball games. Dahlke and Rott (2001) who focus on Borussia Dortmund do not use econometric methods to examine the stock performance but concentrate on corporate governance related issues.

The purpose of this paper is to econometrically explore the link between match outcome and the stock price reaction of Borussia Dortmund during the seasons 2000/2001 to 2004/2005. Since Borussia Dortmund is the only German club that is listed on a stock market this paper is limited to stock price development of one single club. We focus on Borussia Dortmund since the sample period is characterised by substantial sport as wells as corporate governance related events.

The remainder of the paper is organised as follows. In Section 2, we focus on the football industry. We develop a theoretical framework that highlights the link between the sporting success and the economic success. Equipped with this theoretical framework, we derive the main hypotheses which are tested in the empirical part of this paper. In Section 3, we present the results of our empirical analysis. In particular, we focus on the role of the expectation formation process by using betting odds information to control for the ex-ante expected fundamentals. In Section 4, we apply the so called reversed news model to test the robustness of our findings. The last section concludes.

The Professional Football Industry

The Structure of the German and European Football Competitions

The top football division in Germany is the Bundesliga, which was founded in 1963. It currently consists of 18 teams which play each other for the German championship in home and away matches, alternating between their home and their opponent's stadiums. Thus, each team must play 34 Bundesliga matches per season. In addition to the Bundesliga matches, a competition is held each year for the DFB Cup. Under the current rules, 64 teams take part in the first round of the cup competition. In addition to all teams from the first and second Bundesliga, which are automatically included, clubs from the two regional leagues and amateur teams can qualify via qualification matches to participate in the main round of the DFB cup competition. The DFB Cup competition is played using a knockout system, i.e., only the winning side in a given match qualifies for the next round. The pairings are drawn by lot (Borussia Dortmund, 2000, pp. 21 – 22).[4]

Since the beginning of the 1999/2000 season, 32 European top teams have been participating in the Champions League (CL), a championship

---

[4] Borussia Dortmund Offering Circular October 28, 2000.

organised by the UEFA.[5] In addition to the competition's sporting dimension, the significant financial value of participation is of great importance to football clubs. Under the current rules, the first two teams in the Bundesliga automatically qualify to play in the CL. The third ranked team may also qualify for the CL via a qualifying round.[6] The competition initially begins with two rounds of matches where the teams in each group play each other. The best eight teams then qualify for the quarterfinals. Thereafter, the competition is continued under a knockout system with home and away matches. Since the season 2003/2004, the rules have changed: there is only one round and the best 16 teams qualify for a knockout system with home and away matches. The final is held at a neutral stadium.

Since the 1999/2000 season and the abolition of the European Cup Winners' Cup competition, the only competition on an European level other than the CL is the UEFA Cup. The competition is conducted using a knockout system with home and away matches. In the third round, eight teams that were knocked out following the first round of group matches in the CL are added to the UEFA Cup competition. The fourth to sixth placed teams from the Bundesliga qualify for the UEFA Cup, as well the DFB Cup winner.[7] Two other Bundesliga teams may qualify to participate in the competition via a further qualification round, the so-called UEFA Intertoto Cup ("UI-Cup").

Table 1 gives an overview of the sporting success of Borussia Dortmund for the time span under consideration (10/2000 – 09/2004). In the Bundesliga, Borussia Dortmund was quite successful with a third place at the end of the 2000/2001 season and winning the national championship

---

[5] The Union des Associations Europeennes de Football ("UEFA"), an association formed under the law of Switzerland, was founded in 1954. It is the umbrella organisation of the European football associations, and today has 51 members. In addition to the European Championship, which is held every four years, UEFA organises club championships such as the CL and the UEFA Cup each year.

[6] In the 2000/2001 and 2001/2002 season even the fourth placed team had the chance to qualify for the CL. Those teams that fail to qualify for the CL via qualification matches are automatically qualified for the UEFA Cup competition (see Kicker Sonderheft Finale 1999/2000, p. 3 and Kicker Sonderheft Finale 2000/2001, p. 3).

[7] If the winner of the DFB Cup competition is also qualified for the CL, the loser of the DFB Cup final is qualified for the UEFA Cup. The number of starting places per national football association depends upon the clubs' rating in the UEFA Five Year Evaluation, depending on the results of the respective national club teams during the preceding five years.

Table 1: Overview of the Different Competitions.

Season	Borussia Dortmund		German Cup Competition "DFB-Pokal"	Bayern München
	German Bundesliga	European Competitions		German Bundesliga
2000/2001	• 3rd rank at the end of season	• Not qualified, since Dortmund was only on 11th rank at the end of 1999/2000 season	• Out in 3rd round against Schalke 04 (11/29/2000)	• 1st rank at the end of season • Winning of the National Championship (5/19/2001)
2001/2002	• 1st rank at the end of season • Winning of the National Championship (5/4/2002)	• Winning of the qualification games to the CL against Donezk (8/7/2001 and 8/22/2001) • Out after 1st round in the CL • Switch to 3rd round of the UEFA Cup competition • Loosing of the UEFA Cup final against Feyenoord Rotterdam (5/8/2002)	• Out in 1st round against Wolfsburg Amateure (8/25/2001)	• 3rd rank at the end of season

2002/2003	• 3rd rank at the end of season	• 2nd rank in the first phase of CL, qualification to 2nd phase, • Out in CL after 3rd rank at the end of 2nd phase	• Out in 2nd round against SC Freiburg (5/11/2002)	• 1st rank at the end of season • Winning of the National Championship (5/24/2003)
2003/2004	• 6th rank at the end of season	• Loosing of CL qualification against Brügge (8/13/2003 and 8/27/2003) • Switch to UEFA Cup Out in 2nd round against FC Sochaux (11/27/2003)	• Out in 2nd round against Borussia Mönchengladbach (10/29/2003)	• 2nd rank at the end of season
2004/2005	• currently 11th rank, after four games played	• Out in 1st round of UEFA Intertoto Cup against RC Genk	• still in the competition (2nd round)	• currently 5th rank, after four games played
Summary	130 Matches: 64 Win, 38 Draw, 28 Lost	37 Matches: 17 Win, 8 Draw, 12 Lost	7 Matches:[a] 3 Win, 4 Lost	129 Matches: 77 Win, 28 Draw, 24 Lost

[a] The first two matches of the DFB Cup in the 2000/2001 season took place before Borussia Dortmund AG went public and are therefore not considered in this analysis.

at the end of the following season. Taking all observations for this competition together, one can analyse the influence of the outcome of 130 Bundesliga matches, 64 of them were won while 28 games were lost and 38 games ended in draws. Table 1 also highlights that Bayern München has to be regarded as the main competitor in the German Bundesliga.

The good performance in the national competition allowed Dortmund to qualify two times for the CL. Although they dropped out after the first round in the CL in 2001/2002, they took the chance to compete in the UEFA Cup competition subsequently and made it to the final. Therefore, we observe 37 signals of the international competitiveness of Borussia Dortmund.

While being highly successful in the two competitions mentioned before, Dortmund failed early in the DFB Cup competition against "underdogs" of the second or third league. Hence, we only have a limited number of observations for this competition.

The Link Between the Sporting Success, Revenues and Profits

There is a close link between the success in the national and international competitions and the revenues generated by a football club (see Lehmann and Weigand, 1997). This is true due to the following linkages:

- If a team is successful and has a good position in the overall national ranking, the club has the chance to qualify for an European competition like the CL, UEFA, or UI-Cup. With a qualification for a European competition, the club can generate additional funds from selling the broadcasting rights of this competition.
- Furthermore, successful teams also have a higher gate attendance leading to higher ticket and merchandising revenues. Gärtner and Pommerehne (1978), Lehmann and Weigand (1997) as well as Czarnitzki and Stadtmann (2002) analyse the link between sporting success and attendance figures for the German football industry. All studies find a significant positive link between success and revenues due to a higher gate attendance for the Bundesliga. Additionally, Peel and Thomas (1988) and Forrest et al. (2002) provide empirical evidence for this link analyzing the British soccer league. Baimbridge et al. (1996) focus on the relationship between gate attendances, live TV-broadcasting and find that, although live transmission reduces attendance, the net

Table 2: Consolidated profit and loss statement of Borussia Dortmund.

	2004/ 2005	2003/ 2004	2002/ 2003	2001/ 2002	2000/ 2001	1999/ 2000
Match Operations	17,505	20,300	17,898	19,619.6	14,972.4	17,959.2
Advertising	26,416	25,682	44,260	30,782.1	16,258.8	26,672.9
Radio, TV	14,884	19,333	49,919	45,975.7	19,339.1	35,020.5
Transfer Revenues	729	13,062	316	1,235.5	25,259.6	3,047.4
Merchandising	13,693	16,858	15,692	12,672.7	7,512.6	9,795.7
Renting	-	-	97	532.3	212.4	12.3
Other Revenues	2,048	2,833	931	2,161.1	1,290	136.3
Total Revenues	75,275	98,068	129,113	112,979.0	84,844.9	92,644.3
Other Operating Income	3,891	1,797	33,143	37,406.6	29,720.5	2,534.1
Group Net Income	-79,594	-67,730	3,257	755.4	-10,920.7	42.4

Source: Borussia Dortmund (Annual Report, various issues). The figures of the year 2001/2002 are not adjusted due to a change of the basis of consolidation compared to 2002/2003. Figures are in thousand Euro.

- financial consequences are positive for Premier League teams. Since the beginning of the 2003/2004 season Borussia Dortmund increased the stadium capacity to more than 80,000 spectators in Bundesliga matches (Borussia Dortmund 2002, p. 42) and experienced an average gate attendance of 79,647 spectators in that season.
- A successful team is able to generate higher advertising and sponsoring revenues, because most sponsoring agreements provide for graduated revenues based on the team's performance. Especially, a participation in European competitions can generate additional funds (Borussia Dortmund 2000, p. 29 and 2001, p. 15).

Table 2 focuses on the revenue structure of Borussia Dortmund. The figures of the profit and loss statement highlight the importance of those revenues that can be generated through selling broadcasting rights and advertising/sponsoring. Furthermore, this table also shows the immense decrease of revenues during the 2000/2001 season, when Dortmund did not qualify for an European competition. When controlling for those revenues stemming from transfer operations, revenues decreased by more than 30 % during fiscal year 2000/2001 compared to the fiscal year 1999/2000.[8] Despite the immense sporting success, overall profits can be

---

[8] The high amount of transfer revenues in the fiscal year 2000/2001 stem mainly from selling the transfer rights of player Evanilson to AC Parma. Nevertheless, Evanilson was in the team of Dortmund until 2005 due to a licensing agreement with AC Parma (see Borussia Dortmund, 2001, p. 16).

regarded as relatively low. The sum of the group net income over the time period 1999 – 2003 is negative (Table 2). This statement especially holds, because other operating income contributed significantly to the group net income. At the time of the writing this chapter (February 2008), Borussia Dortmund has not yet paid any dividends even after winning the German championship in 2002.

However, higher revenues should also increase the profitability of the club which should also lead to higher (expected) dividend payments. Szymanski and Smith (1997, p. 136) find in an empirical analysis of the English football industry that the function between profit and position in the league has a negative slope. This negative slope indicates that increased spending on players is—on average—not self financing through higher performance and higher revenues. Higher expected dividend payments will—according to the standard theory of finance—lead to higher stock prices. Hence, if all relations hold as supposed in our framework, the outcome of a game should influence stock prices. Hence, we test the following hypotheses:

> *H1: A won match should influence stock returns positively.*

> *H2: A lost match should influence stock returns negatively.*

> *H3: Due to the fact that Borussia Dortmund was one of the top teams in the Bundesliga in the time span under consideration, a match that ended in a draw has be to regarded as a negative information. As a consequence the stock market should react in most cases negatively after a match ended in a draw.*

As stressed above when analyzing the revenue structure of Borussia Dortmund, the high amounts of money that can be earned in the European competitions should be considered. Hence, the third hypothesis is:

> *H4: A won/lost game in a European competition will influence stock returns to a larger extent than a win/defeat in the national competition.*

The Empirical Analysis

Controlling for Expectations

The main idea of the news model is that only the difference between the realised fundamentals and the expected fundamentals, i.e. the unexpected component has to be regarded as the news component. Put differently, only the error should influence stock prices. Therefore, if a home win was already anticipated to a large extent (there always remains some kind of uncertainty), stock prices should not react that much. One method to control for the expected match outcome is to use betting odds information. The betting odds used in this analysis were kindly provided by gamebookers.com, an online bookmaker. Using the conventional abbreviation for a home win (1), a draw (0) and an away win (2), Table 3 highlights the background of the "news proxy" used in the following analysis.

For example, on May 19th, 2001, Dortmund played at home against 1. FC Köln. The quotes prior to the game were 1.35 for a home win of Dortmund, 4.25 for a draw and 6.90 for an away win of 1. FC Köln. This means a bettor who put 1 Euro on a draw received 4.25 Euro.[9] Comparing the different quotes for this match already highlights that Dortmund was regarded as the favorite in this match. Summing up the inverse of the quotes $(1/1.35 + 1/4.25 + 1/6.90 = 1.12)$, yields the mark-up of 1.12 of the betting company. The higher this mark-up, the higher the price for the bet is. By controlling for this mark-up, one can compute the probability implicit in the betting odds for a home win which amounts to 66 % $[1/(1.35*1.12)]$, for a draw which is equal to 21 % $[1/(4.25*1.12)]$ and the away win of 13 % $[1/(6.10*1.12)]$, respectively. These implicit probabilities show that Dortmund was indeed regarded as the favourite.

Having these probabilities at hand, it is possible to control for the expectations of the financial agents. Because the winning team receives 3 points and a draw will lead to 1 point, the expected number of points for Dortmund in the match against Köln is equal to 2.19 $(3*0.66 + 1*0.21)$. Since Dortmund drew in this match, the outcome has to be interpreted as a negative information and the expectation error amounts to -1.19 $(1 - 2.19)$. Only this expectation error has to be regarded as the new information which has to be priced in on Monday morning. Due to the fact that Dortmund underperformed in this match, stock prices should decrease. In a second example, the expected number of points in the away match where Dortmund plays in München is equal to 1 $(1*0.28+3*0.24)$.[10] Hence, the outcome of the match was in line with the prior expectations and should therefore, have no impact on stock prices. In Bundesliga

---

[9] We calculate the profits in terms of euro just for convenience although we are aware that the euro cash was initially introduced in 2002.

[10] The team which plays at home always has a home field advantage. See Schwartz and Barsky (1977) and Vergin and Sosik (1999). However, this does not mean, that the home team is always expected to win. As can be seen in Table 3, Hansa Rostock was regarded as the underdog when playing at home against Dortmund.

Table 3: Betting odds and implicit probabilities for match outcome.

Date / teams / result (actual points)	Betting odds (Implicit probabilities in %)			Actual - expected = unexpected points
	1 Home win	0 Draw	2 Away win	
05/19/2001, Dortmund vs.	1.35	4.25	6.90	$1.00 - 2.19 =$
1. FC Köln: 3:3 (1)	(66 %)	(21 %)	(13 %)	−1.19
08/18/2001 Hansa Rostock	3.60	3.30	1.87	$3.00 - 1.71 =$
vs. Dortmund 0:2 (3)	(25 %)	(27 %)	(48 %)	1.29
02/09/2002 Bayern München	1.85	3.25	3.72	$1.00 - 1.00 =$
vs. Dortmund 1:1 (1)	(48 %)	(28 %)	(24 %)	0

matches which ended in a draw on average 1.65 points where expected beforehand. Therefore, *on average* a match that ended in a draw has to be regarded as a negative signal for the stock market because the team only gained one point in these matches.

Description of the Data

In addition to the match outcome variables described in the previous paragraph, we also consider ad-hoc announcements of Borussia Dortmund as a signal which could influence stock prices. We considered whether a player renews his contract, a new player is hired, or a player is sold to another club. However, no coefficient turned out to be significantly different from zero. On the one hand, this result could be interpreted in a way that this information does not influence the fundamental value of the asset. On the other hand, since it is possible that these events were anticipated by the public, we can not rule out that the signal was already reflected in market prices when it became public knowledge. We checked for this by extending the coverage of the dummy variables, but did not find any effects. Hence, we dropped these variables from our final specification.

Daily stock data of closing prices as well as the development of the SDAX are taken from Datastream.[12] Figure 1 highlights the development

---

[12] We justified the choice of the SDAX since the market capitalisation as well as volatility is comparable to the firms in the SDAX. We refrain from comparing the stock price development of Borussia Dortmund with an international index as the time period between 2000 and 2004 was subject to high international volatility.

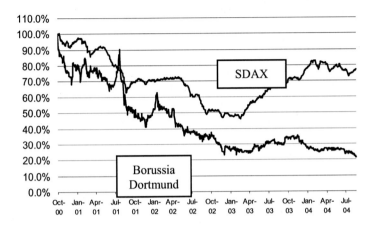

Figure 1: Performance of Borussia Dortmund AG compared to the Benchmark SDAX.

of the stock price of Borussia Dortmund after going public at the end of October 2000.[13] Since the IPO, market capitalisation decreased by more than 75 %. While the development of the stock price was in line with the overall stock market development until the end of 2002, the stock of Borussia Dortmund significantly under-performed afterwards.

Regression Results

We estimate the following Model 1

$$\Delta DORT_t = \beta_0 + \beta_1 \Delta SDAX_t + \varepsilon_t \qquad (1)$$

---

[13] Since the data on the daily trading volume was not available for the full observation period we do not include the trading volume in our empirical study.

[17] We tested for stationarity by using the Augmented Dickey Fuller Test. It turned out that the log of the time series of the share prices and the index series are not stationary. Hence, we tested whether the first difference of the logged time series are stationary, which turned out to be the case. The test results are available from the authors upon request.

where ΔDORT denotes the percentage change in stock prices and ΔSDAX the percentage change in the relevant stock market index.[17] Model 1 serves as a control specification. As a consequence, we are able to separate which part of the variance in the change in stock prices is explained by changes in overall market conditions and match outcome variables, respectively.

Estimates are presented in Table 4. Model 1a is estimated over the full range of trading days (1,019 observations). The estimated slope coefficient takes the value of β_1=0.40, meaning that a 1 % change of the SDAX only leads to an under-proportional change in the stock price (0.4 %). When we condition on the fact that a match took place on the day before, we are left with 174 observations (84 wins, 46 draws and 44 losses). Model 1b shows that the slope coefficient is not significantly different from zero anymore. This is a hint that company specific, match related variables may be more important compared to the overall market conditions on trading days following a match day.

The news model states that only the unexpected part of an information drives stock market prices. We already described in Section 3.1 our method to disentangle the expected from the unexpected part by using betting odd information. Before presenting the results of our empirical analysis, we would like to briefly explain our testing procedure which is in line with Dobson and Goddard (2001, p. 388):

In a first step, we include variables that measure the actual match outcome (numbers of points gained) in each competition (Bundesliga/EU matches). In a second step, we include an additional variable that measures the expected match outcome in each competition. In case that only the unexpected part of the match outcome has an impact on share prices, the coefficient on the actual performance should be the negative value of the coefficient on expected performance. If this condition is met, it is justified to combine the information of actual performance and expected performance in a single measure "unexpected performance".

In line with the procedure described above, we estimate model 2:

$$\Delta DORT_t = \beta_0 + \beta_1 \Delta SDAX_t + \beta_2 BUND\_actual + \beta_5 EU\_actual$$
$$+ \beta_8 DFB\_Win + \beta_9 DFB\_Loss + \varepsilon_t \qquad (2)$$

where BUND_actual is a variable measuring the number of points gained in the matches in the German Bundesliga competition and the EU variable measures the performance in European matches, respectively. Since the DFB Cup is played in a knock-out modus, we just control for won and lost games for this competition. Furthermore, one should keep in mind that we have only a very limited number of observations for the DFB Cup competition (7 matches). As a consequence, one should not stress the interpretation of the estimation results with respect to this competition too far.

The estimated coefficients measuring the effect of the number of points gained in a Bundesliga match as well as in a European match are positive and significantly different from zero. Hence, we can not reject the hypotheses H1 –H3. This provides evidence that a won (draw/lost) match influences stock returns positively (negatively) and, therefore, supports our argument above. In contrast to this, a comparison of the size of the Bund_actual coefficient and the EU_actual coefficient leads to the insight that both coefficients are not significantly different from each other. This finding is in sharp contrast to hypothesis H4.

With respect to the goodness-of-fit of the model, the adjusted R^2 takes a value of 0.16, which has to be regarded as exceptionally high for stock market studies. By comparison of the goodness-of-fit of Model 1b and 2, one gets the impression that sport related variables are of high importance to explain variations in stock prices—compared to overall market conditions.

Since we are interested in whether only the unexpected part of an information drives stock prices, we add two variables that control for the expected performance:

$$\Delta DORT_t = \beta_0 + \beta_1 \Delta SDAX_t + \beta_2 BUND\_actual + \beta_3 BUND\_expected$$
$$+ \beta_5 EU\_actual + \beta_6 EU\_expected \qquad (3)$$
$$+ \beta_8 DFB\_Win + \beta_9 DFB\_Loss + \varepsilon_t$$

The regression results are also presented in Table 4 (Model 3). The estimated BUND_actual coefficient takes a value of $\beta_2 = 0.01$ while the estimated BUND_expected coefficient takes a value of $\beta_3 = -0.00$. A formal test of the hypothesis that $\beta_2 = -\beta_3$ comes to the result that the null hypothesis can not be rejected on a 90 % confidence level. The same result applies to the estimated coefficients for the EU matches $\beta_5 = -\beta_6$. As a consequence, it is justified to combine the information of the actual match outcome and the expected match outcome in a single variable unexpected match outcome. Therefore, we perform this regression as Model 4:

$$\Delta DORT_t = \beta_0 + \beta_1 \Delta SDAX_t + \beta_4 BUND\_unexpected$$
$$+ \beta_7 EU\_unexpected + \beta_8 DFB\_Win + \beta_9 DFB\_Loss + \varepsilon_t \qquad (4)$$

The coefficients of interest β_4 and β_7 have the expected positive sign and are significantly different from zero. Compared to Model 3, Model 4 is a more parsimonious specification. All further robustness checks will depart from this benchmark.

Table 4: OLS-regressions of the determinants of percentage change in Borussia Dortmund's stock price.

		Model 1[a]	Model 1b[b]	Model 2[a]	Model 3[a]	Model 4[a]	Model 5[a]	Model 6[a]
β 0	Constant	-0.001	-0.010	-0.029	-0.024	-0.029	-0.010	-0.009
		(0.001)	(0.003)***	(0.005)***	(0.011)[+]	(0.005)***	(0.003)***	(0.003)***
β 1	SDAX	0.400	0.279	0.307	0.281	0.307	0.324	0.345
		(0.153)**	(0.349)	(0.341)	(0.335)	(0.341)	(0.340)	(0.337)
β 2	Bund_Actual	–	–	0.012	0.010	–	–	–
				(0.002)***	(0.002)***			
β 3	Bund_Expected	–	–	–	0.010	–	–	–
					(0.006)			
β 4	Bund_Unexpected	–	–	–	–	0.012	0.011	0.010
						(0.002)***	(0.002)***	(0.002)***
β 5	EU_Actual	–	–	0.011	0.017	–	–	–
				(0.004)**	(0.004)***			
β 6	EU_Expected	–	–	–	0.005	–	–	–
					(0.008)			
β 7	EU_Unexpected	–	–	–	–	0.011	–	–
						(0.004)***		
β 7a	UEFA_Unexpected	–	–	–	–	–	0.014	0.014
							(0.006)[+]	(0.006)[+]
β 7b	CL_Unexpected	–	–	–	–	–	0.020	0.020
							(0.007)**	(0.007)**
β 8	DFB_Win	–	–	0.030	0.025	0.030	0.010	0.010
				(0.009)***	(0.014)	(0.009)	(0.009)	(0.009)
β 9	DFB_Loss	–	–	-0.004	-0.009	-0.004	-0.023	-0.023
				(0.015)	(0.018)	(0.015)	(0.015)	(0.015)
β 10	Bayern_Unexpected	–	–	–	–	–	–	-0.004
								(0.002)

Obs.	1009	174	174	174	174	174	174
R^2	0.01	0.00	0.19	0.20	0.18	0.19	0.20
Adj. R^2	0.01	-0.00	0.16	0.17	0.16	0.16	0.16
Prob. F-Test	$F(1,1007)=0.02$	$F(1,172)=0.42$	$F(5,168)=0.00$	$F(7,166)=0.00$	$F(5,168)=0.00$	$F(6,167)=0.00$	$F(7,166)=0.00$

+ Significant at the 10% level, significant at the 1% level, significant at the 0.1%-level. Standard errors in parenthesis.
a Dependant variable: percentage change in Borussia Dortmund's stock price.

One may argue that the variable that measures the outcome of the European matches is a combination of games that are played in the CL and games that are played in the UEFA Cup competition. Hence, it may bring further insights to separate the outcomes of the two competitions (β_{7a} and β_{7b}). Therefore, regression equation of Model 5 reads as follows:

$$
\begin{aligned}
\Delta DORT_t = \ &\beta_0 + \beta_1 \Delta SDAX_t + \beta_4 BUND\_unexpected \\
&+ \beta_{7a} UEFA\_unexpected + \beta_{7b} CL\_unexpected \\
&+ \beta_8 DFB\_Win + \beta_9 DFB\_Loss + \varepsilon_t
\end{aligned}
\tag{5}
$$

The estimated coefficient for the CL variable is positive and somewhat larger than the coefficient estimated for UEFA Cup or Bundesliga matches (Model 5). This finding points towards that the CL can be regarded as a cash-cow for football clubs. However, in statistical terms, the difference between the BUND_unexpected and the CL_unexpected coefficient is still not significant. All other coefficients lie in the same range as in Model 4.[18]

Until now, we only considered the match outcome of Borussia Dortmund as an explanatory variable. Therefore, one may criticise that we have neglected an important competition factor: The overall ranking in, for example, the Bundesliga is not only influenced by the sporting success of Borussia Dortmund but also by the sporting success of its major competitors. As can be seen from the last column of Table 1, Bayern München has to be regarded as the main competitor for the national championship. Hence, we augment Model 5 by a variable that measures the unexpected match outcome of Bayern München. In order to be consistent with the previous analysis we calculate the unexpected number of points gained for Bayern München similar to Borussia Dortmund (Table 3). Therefore, we estimate Model 6:

$$
\begin{aligned}
\Delta DORT_t = \ &\beta_0 + \beta_1 \Delta SDAX_t + \beta_4 BUND\_unexpected \\
&+ \beta_{7a} UEFA\_unexpected + \beta_{7b} CL\_unexpected \\
&+ \beta_8 DFB\_Win + \beta_9 DFB\_Loss + \beta_{10} Bayern\_unexpected + \varepsilon_t
\end{aligned}
\tag{6}
$$

The coefficient β_{10} has the expected negative sign and is significantly different from zero on a 10 % level. This implies that a success of Bayern München influences the stock price of Borussia Dortmund negatively. Furthermore, a comparison of β_4 and β_{10} leads to the insight that the direct

---

[18] Some of the investigated matches were played on Saturdays and holidays, implying that the stock-market cannot react immediately on the news about the match outcome. We used the stock market reaction on the first trading day after the match took place as a measure for the stock price reaction.

effect of Borussia Dortmund is larger than the indirect effect of Bayern München.

The Reversed News Model

Comparison of the Approaches

Empirical studies which test the news model of asset price determination traditionally apply the following approach: In a first step, a theoretical model is derived that identifies the different news categories which are assumed to drive asset prices. In a second step, the influence of the different news categories on the asset price is quantified empirically. This is also the approach we applied so far: On the basis of the industry model we hypothesised that match outcome is a key value driver for Borussia Dortmund. Subsequently, we quantified the influence of match outcome on stock prices empirically.

An alternative approach is the so called reversed news model (see Ellison and Mullin, 2001). Key to this approach is that it is not estimated how new information influence stock prices. In contrast to the traditional approach, we identify at first large stock price reactions which can not be explained by overall stock market conditions. In a second step, we check whether we can identify company specific information that can explain the stock price reactions.

The reversed news model was already applied by Gerrard and Lossius (2004) for eleven English listed football teams. Gerrard and Lossius argue that the reversed news model is a proper method to circumvent some pitfalls of traditional event studies, such as the problem of choosing the appropriate length of the event window. Gerrard and Lossius (2004) identified about 100 days with abnormal stock price reactions during the time period July 1997 – June 2003. About half of these extreme stock price reactions can be related to match results and about 40 % to company specific financial news.

Empirical Analysis

To control for the overall stock market reaction, we regress the relative change of Borussia Dortmunds' stock price on a constant and the relative change of the SDAX (time span: season 2003/2004). We sort all absolute error terms according to their size. In Table 5 we present the 15 largest error terms. We tried to identify for each date company specific news that may have caused the unexplained reaction in stock prices. Table 5 highlights that

- the speculation about the issuing of a 100 mill. Euro bond,
- the non-qualification to the CL as well as
- the investment decision of a large blockholder (Norman Rentrop) influenced Borussia Dortmund's stock market prices. Therefore, we were able to proof by applying the reversed news model that not only match outcome but also corporate governance related information are important drivers of stock market price. Hence, we would like to give some more details to the different news that we identified by the reversed news model.

Three Important Events

Non-Qualification to the Champions League

One event which must be considered as a new information for all market participants was the non-qualification of Borussia Dortmund for the CL in the 2003/2004 season. In the night of 8/27/2003, Dortmund lost a dramatic penalty shootout against FC Brügge. As a consequence Dortmund was not allowed to play in the lucrative CL, but would play in the UEFA Cup competition. Since public interest for this competition is only minor, the financial attractiveness of the UEFA Cup competition is also lower when compared to the CL. On the subsequent trading day, stock prices dropped from 3.60 Euro to 3.30 Euro (-8.3 %). If one considers 19.5 mill. shares outstanding, market capitalisation was reduced by 19.5*0.30 = 5.85 mill. Euro.

How can one explain the size of decline in market capitalisation? Firstly, one has to consider that the information about the drop out did not hit the market unexpectedly. As betting odds indicated, the chance prior to the game to qualify for the main round of the CL amounted only to 50 %. Secondly, one has to know that a team which qualifies to the first main round of the CL gets about 15 mill. Euro TV-revenues, guaranteed by the UEFA.[19] This is the case, because TV-rights for the CL are centrally marketed by the UEFA. Since the odds were 50:50 prior to the game, about 7.5 mill. Euro were already priced in by the market. Thirdly, one has to consider that Dortmund would play at least one home game in the UEFA Cup competition which would also generate some income through gate attendance and TV-revenues. In sum, the market capitalisation should decrease by less than 7.5 mill. Euro. Since the actual reduction of market capitalisation was about 6 mill. Euro the capital market had apparently accounted for the above mentioned calculations and, hence, had fully

---

[19] Schnell, C. "Borussia Dortmund verliert auch an der Börse." Handelsblatt, August 29, 2003.

Table 5: Results of the Reversed News Model.

No.	Date	Price reaction[a]	Event[b]	Category[c]
1	12/22/2003	-9.56 %	100 mill. Euro bond	CG
2	10/16/2003	8.95 %	Norman Rentrop	CG
3	8/28/2003	-8.73 %	Non-qualification to CL	MO
4	12/30/2003	-7.42 %	Transparency discussion	CG
5	1/2/2004	6.82 %	Transparency discussion	CG
6	1/7/2004	-6.14 %	Transparency discussion	CG
7	6/3/2004	-5.48 %	n.a.	
8	5/6/2004	5.26 %	n.a.	
9	7/22/2003	-4.99 %	n.a.	
10	5/4/2004	-4.79 %	n.a.	
11	3/1/2004	-4.37 %	Bayern München – VfL Wolfsburg 2:0 Werder Bremen – Bor. Dortmund 2:0	MO
12	7/8/2003	-4.36 %	n.a.	
13	7/14/2003	4.22 %	n.a.	
14	3/17/2004	-4.19 %	n.a.	
15	12/15/2003	-4.08 %	Bayern München – VfB Stuttgart 1:0 Bor. M'gladbach – Bor. Dortmund 2:1	MO

[a] Price reaction of Borussia Dortmund stocks; not explained by overall market reaction.
[b] N.a.: no news identified.
[c] CG: Corporate Governance related news. MO: Match Outcome related news.

incorporated the non-qualification to the CL into the stock price. Therefore, this example is a strong hint for the efficient market hypothesis.

The Blockholder Norman Rentrop

On 10/16/2003 the public was informed about the fact that an individual investor (Normal Rentrop) bought a 14.4 % share of Borussia Dortmund from the Deutsche Bank. After this information hit the market, share prices increased from 3.37 € to 3.69 €. To explain this stock price reaction, two different kinds of arguments can be given. Firstly, one has to consider that the Deutsche Bank took over a 24.9 % block of Borussia Dortmund during or in the aftermath of the IPO which took place in October 2000. Since the Deutsche Bank sold a substantial amount of their position over the secondary market the Deutsche Bank put downward pressure on the stock price of Borussia Dortmund. This downward pressure was eliminated by selling the remaining blocks of shares to one single shareholder, namely Norman Rentrop. This line of argumentation was frequently found in the financial press and could serve as one explanation for the increase in the stock price of Borussia Dortmund on 10/16/2003.

A second line of argumentation is more corporate governance related: A single large blockholder who is interested in the company, may be able to put pressure on the management to follow the interest of shareholders and increase the shareholder value. This second argument could also serve as an explanation for the positive stock price reaction to the new information.

Our finding that large investors have an impact on share prices of publicly traded football clubs is in line with the finding of Gerrard and Lossius (2004). They show that the takeover bid of BSkyB in September 1998 caused an abnormal return of Manchester United share prices of about 30 %. Furthermore, takeover bids and rumors about takeover bids also had a major impact on the stock price of other publicly traded football teams such as Newcastle United or Southampton Leisure Holding.

The 100.000.000 Euro Bond

Another event which resulted in an extreme reaction of the stock price of Borussia Dortmund was a newspaper story published in the sports-magazine Kicker[20] and the daily newspaper Süddeutsche-Zeitung[21] on December 22, 2003. The story line was as follows: The non-qualification to the CL as well as the early knock-out in the subsequent UEFA Cup competition would reduce revenues dramatically and would also lead to a substantial loss at the end of the fiscal year as well as to a serious liquidity problem. Furthermore, it was reported that the management of Borussia Dortmund would plan to issue a 100 mill. Euro bond secured by future gate attendance revenues.

The management of Borussia Dortmund reacted immediately in a press conference and denied the stories published in the press. Zayer and Kunz (2003) provide a description of the field of responsibilities of a controller at Borussia Dortmund. However, the management confirmed the negotiations with respect to issuing a bond but also stated that the face

---

[20] Hennecke, T. "Borussia Dortmund bemüht sich um eine Riesen-Anleihe." Kicker, 104, December 22, 2003, p 17.

[21] Röckenhaus, F. "Horrorschulden und Bilanztricks: Borussia Dortmund vor dem Finanzcrash." Süddeutsche Zeitung online, December 22, 2003.

value will definitely be lower. Additionally, the management announced that it would lawsuit the journalists and publishing houses for misleading the public.

During the subsequent days, new information was published with respect to the liquidity and profitability status of Borussia Dortmund. From this discussion an "objective" observer must have gotten the impression that Borussia Dortmund is not the most transparent company. As can be seen from Table 5 as well as Figure 1 this discussion had a major influence on the stock price. Volatility was sky-rocking and a downward trend emerged.

Conclusion

We have applied the news model to the football industry to analyse, whether new information regarding the sporting success can explain subsequent changes in the stock price of Borussia Dortmund. The football industry proves a very appropriate candidate for applying this model due to specific characteristics: Signals are very frequent and easy to quantify, occur solely when the markets are closed, become publicly available to all agents at the very same time and have observable expectations due to the existence of betting odds.

According to the news model, only the unexpected part of information should influence stock prices. Hence, we use betting odds information to control for the ex-ante expected match outcome. Although, our analysis is limited to one football club only, we find evidence in favour of a close link between the sporting success and subsequent changes in the stock market. Therefore, the main hypotheses H1 – H3 derived from a theoretical model can not be rejected. Hypothesis H4, predicting that the outcome of European matches should have a higher impact on the stock price than the outcome of Bundesliga matches, is not supported. Although the estimated coefficient on CL matches is larger compared to the coefficients on Bundesliga or UEFA Cup matches this difference is not significant in statistical terms.

As a robustness check, we applied the reversed news model to identify those events that had a major impact on the stock price of Borussia Dortmund. We find that—besides the match outcome—several corporate governance related news also played an important role.[22] A comparison of

---

[22] See also Lehmann and Weigand (2002) for a discussion of corporate governance and professional football in Germany.

the traditional approach and the reversed news model gains the following insights:

- One advantage of the news model is that this method is an appropriate way to identify "forgotten" news categories which were not identified in the theoretical model. As a consequence, an omitted variable bias can be circumvented.
- One disadvantage of the reversed news model can be seen in the fact that this model is not able to detect news categories that have a significant, but only small impact on stock prices.

Therefore, a reversed news model should not be estimated in isolation. However, it seems to be an appropriate robustness check when testing the traditional news model. Beside this, our analysis is subject to some limitations which call for further research. Particularly, the impact of match outcomes on the trading volume seems to an interesting topic. However, we leave this to further research. Additionally, we should keep in mind that Borussia Dortmund is a unique case in so far as only one German club is listed so far at a stock exchange.

References

Ashton, J. K., B. Gerrard and R. Hudson, (2003). "Economic impact of national sporting success: Evidence from the London stock exchange." *Applied Economics Letters*, 10(12), 783-785.

Baimbridge, M., S. Cameron and P. Dawson (1996). "Satellite Television and the Demand for Football: A Whole New Ball Game?" *Scottish Journal of Political Economy*, 43(3), 317-333.

Brown, G. W. and J. C. Hartzell (2001). "Market reaction to public information: The atypical case of the Boston Celtics." *Journal of Financial Economics*, 60(2-3), 333-370.

Czarnitzki, D. and G. Stadtmann (2002). "Uncertainty of Outcome versus Reputation: Empirical Evidence for the German Premier-League Football." *Empirical Economics*, 27(1), 101-112.

Dahlke, M. and A. Rott (2001). "Fußballaktionäre in der Abseitsfalle? Erste Erfahrungen mit dem BVB-Papier." *Dortmunder Diskussionsbeiträge zur Wirtschaftspolitik 106, Januar 2001*.

Dobson, S. and J. Goddard (2001). *The Economics of Football*. Cambridge, UK: Cambridge University Press.

Edmans, A., D. García and O. Norli (2007).. "Sports Sentiments and Stock Returns." *The Journal of Finance*, 62(4), 1967-1998.

Ellison, S. F. and W. Mullin (2001). "Gradual Incorporation of Information: Pharmaceutical Stocks and the Evolution of President

Clinton's Health Care Reform." *Journal of Law and Economics*, 44(1), 89-129.

Fama, E. F. (1970). "Efficient Capital Markets: A Review of Theory and Empirical Work." *The Journal of Finance*, 25(2), 383-417.

Forrest, D., R. Simmons and P. Feehan (2002). "A Spatial Cross-Sectional Analysis of the Elasticity of Demand for Soccer." *Scottish Journal of Political Economy*, 49(3), 336-355.

Frenkel, J. A. (1981). "Flexible exchange rates, prices, and the role of "news": Lessons from the 1970s." *Journal of Political Economy*, 89(4), 665-705.

Gärtner, M. and W. W. Pommerehne (1978). "Der Fußballzuschauer - ein homo oeconomicus? Eine theoretische und empirische Analyse." *Jahrbuch für Sozialwissenschaften*, 29, 1089-1095.

Gerrard, B. and E. Lossius (2004). "Playing the Stock Market: The Relationship between News and Equity Prices in Professional Team Sports." *Working Paper presented at the North American Society of Sport Management (NASSM) Conference*. Atlanta, GA.

Lehmann, E. and J. Weigand (1997). "Money Makes the Ball Go Round: Fußball als ökonomisches Phänomen." *ifo Studien - Zeitschrift für empirische Wirtschaftsforschung*, 43(3), 381-409.

Lehmann, E. and J. Weigand (1998). "Wieviel Phantasie braucht die Fußballaktie?" *Zeitschrift für Betriebswirtschaft*, Ergänzungsheft 2/1998, 101-120.

Lehmann, E. and J. Weigand (2002). "Mitsprache und Kontrolle im professionellen Fußball: Überlegungen zu einer Corporate Governance." *Zeitschrift für Betriebswirtschaft*, Ergänzungsheft 4/2002, 43-61.

Palomino, F., L. Renneboog and C. Zhang (2005). "Stock Price Reactions to Short-Lived Public Information: The Case of Betting Odds." *European Corporate Governance Institute (ecgi) Finance Working Paper 81/2005*.

Peel, D. A. and D. A. Thomas (1988). "Outcome Uncertainty and the Demand for Football: An Analysis of Match Attendances in the English Football League." *Scottish Journal of Political Economy*, 35(3), 242-249.

Renneboog, L. and P. Vanbrabant (2000). "Share Price Reactions to Sporty Performance of Soccer Clubs Listed on the London Stock Exchange and the AIM." *Center for Economic Research Working Paper 2000-19*. Tilburg University.

Schwartz, B. and S. F. Barsky (1977). "The Home Advantage." *Social Forces*, 55(3), 641-661.

Szymanski, S. and R. Smith (1997). "The English Football Industry: Profit, performance and industrial structure." *International Review of Applied Economics*, 11(1), 135-153.

Vergin, R. C. and J. J. Sosik (1999). "No Place like Home: An Examination of the Home Field Advantage in Gambling Strategies in NFL Football." *Journal of Economics and Business*, 51(1), 21-31.

Zayer, E. and J. Kunz (2003). "Controlling ist Pionierarbeit - Ein Gespräch mit Detlef Thiemann, Leiter Controlling bei Borussia Dortmund." *Zeitschrift für Controlling & Management (ZfCM)*, 47(4), 228-230.

LIST OF CONTRIBUTORS

Allouche, José. IAE of Paris, University of Paris 1 Pantheon Sorbonne, France.

Andersson, Patric. Center for Media and Economic Psychology, Stockholm School of Economics, Sweden.

Ayton, Peter. Department of Psychology, City University, London, United Kingdom.

Azar, Ofer H. Department of Business Administration, Guilford Glazer School of Business and Management, Ben-Gurion University of the Negev, Israel.

Bar-Eli, Michael. Department of Business Administration, Guilford Glazer School of Business and Management, Ben-Gurion University of the Negev, Israel.

Bornstein, Gary. Department of Psychology, The Hebrew University, Jerusalem, Israel.

Braennberg, Anna. Department of Psychology, City University, London, United Kingdom.

Brand, Ralf. Department of Sport Science, University of Posdam, Germany.

Daum, Moriz M. Department of Psychology, Max Planck Institute for Human Cognitive and Brain Sciences, Leipzig, Germany.

Dawson, Peter. Department of Economics and International Development, University of Bath, United Kingdom.

Frey, Bruno S. Institute for Empirical Research in Economics, University of Zurich, Switzerland.

Frick, Bernd. Department of Management, University of Paderborn, Germany.

Goldschmidt, Chanan. Department of Psychology, The Hebrew University, Jerusalem, Israel.

Jevtushenko, Vyacheslav. Center for Consumer Marketing, Stockholm School of Economics, Sweden.

Kocher, Martin G. Department of Economics, University of Munich, Germany and University of Innsbruck, Austria.

Landsberg, Mathias. Center for Consumer Marketing, Stockholm School of Economics, Sweden.

Leininger, Wolfgang. Department of Economics, University of Dortmund, Germany.

Lejarraga, José. Department of Business Administration, Universidad Carlos III de Madrid, Spain.

Lenz, Marc V. Department of Economics. University of Cologne, Germany.

Ockenfels, Axel. Department of Economics, University of Cologne, Germany.

Page, Katie. Heythrop College, University of London , United Kingdom.

Page, Lionel. Westminster Business School, University of Westminster, London, United Kingdom.

Pietzner, Gunnar. Ramboll Management, Hamburg, Germany.

Plessner, Henning. Department of Psychology, University of Leipzig, Germany.

Prinz, Joachim. Department of Management, University of Paderborn, Paderborn, Germany.

Rauch, Jan. Department of Psychology, University of Zürich, Switzerland.

Rülke, Jan-Christoph. WHU – Otto Beisheim School of Management, Vallendar, Germany.

Schmidt, Carsten. Sonderforschungsbereich 504, Mannheim University, Germany.

Schmidt, Sascha L. European Business School, International University, Oestrich Winkel, Germany.

Simmons, Rob. The Management School, Lancaster University, United Kingdom.

Söderlund, Magnus. Center for Consumer Marketing, Stockholm School of Economics, Sweden.

Soulez, Sébastien. IUT of Colmar, University of Haute Alsace, Colmar, France.

Stadtmann, Georg. Department of Business and Economics, University of Southern Denmark, Odense, Denmark.

Strobel, Martin. Department of Economics, Faculty of Economics and Business Administration, Maastricht University, The Netherlands.

Sutter, Matthias. Department of Economics, University of Innsbruck, Austria and University of Gothenburg, Sweden.

Torgler, Benno. School of Economics and Finance, Queensland University of Technology, Australia.

Unkelbach, Christian. Institute of Psychology, University of Heidelberg, Germany.

Villa, Guillermo. Fundación Observatorio Económico del Deporte, Laboral - Ciudad de la Cultura, Gijón, Spain.

Volkland, Henning Oskar. Goldman Sachs & Co., Frankfurt am Main, Germany.

Werwatz, Axel. Department of Economics. Technical University Berlin, Germany.

Wilkening, Friedrich. Department of Psychology, University of Zürich, Switzerland.

Subject Index

FOOTBALL INDEX